D0859321

Bath
Planning

Guidelines ◆ Codes ◆ Standards

Kathleen Parrott Ph.D., CKE, Julia Beamish Ph.D., CKE,
JoAnn Emmel Ph.D. and Mary Jo Peterson, CKD, CBD, CAPS

Professional Resource Library

About The National Kitchen & Bath Association

As the only non-profit trade association dedicated exclusively to the kitchen and bath industry, the National Kitchen & Bath Association (NKBA) is the leading source of information and education for all professionals in the field.

NKBA's mission is to enhance member success and excellence by promoting professionalism and ethical business practices, and by providing leadership and direction for the kitchen and bath industry.

A non-profit trade association with more than 36,000 members in North America and overseas, it has provided valuable resources for industry professionals for more than 40 years. Its members are the finest professionals in the kitchen and bath industry.

NKBA has pioneered innovative industry research, developed effective business management tools, and set groundbreaking standards for safe, functional and comfortable design of kitchens and baths.

NKBA provides a unique, one-stop resource for professional reference materials, seminars and workshops, distance learning opportunities, marketing assistance, design competitions, consumer referrals, job and internship opportunities and opportunities for volunteer leadership activities.

Recognized as the kitchen and bath industry's education and information leader, NKBA provides development opportunities and continuing education for all levels of professionals. More than 100 courses, as well as a certification program with three internationally recognized levels, help kitchen and bath professionals raise the bar for excellence.

For students entering the industry, NKBA offers Supported and Endorsed Programs, which provide NKBA-approved curriculum at more than 47 learning institutions throughout North America.

NKBA helps members and other industry professionals stay on the cutting-edge of an ever-changing field through the Association's Kitchen/Bath Industry Show, one of the largest trade shows in the country.

NKBA offers membership in four different categories: Industry, Associate, Student and Honorary. Industry memberships are broken into eleven different industry segments. For more information, visit NKBA at www.nkba.org.

THANK YOU TO OUR SPONSORS

The National Kitchen & Bath Association recognizes with gratitude the following companies who generously helped to fund the creation of this industry resource.

PATRONS

www.americanwoodmark.com

www.kohler.com

BENEFACTORS

www.monogram.com

www.subzero.com

www.wolfappliance.com

CONTRIBUTOR

www.groheamerica.com

SUPPORTERS

www.nyloft.net

www.showhouse.moen.com

TOTO®

www.totousa.com

DONORS

Rev-A-Shelf

Viking Range Corp.

Whirlpool Corp.

This book is intended for professional use by residential kitchen and bath designers. The procedures and advice herein have been shown to be appropriate for the applications described; however, no warranty (expressed or implied) is intended or given. Moreover, the user of this book is cautioned to be familiar with and to adhere to all manufacturers' planning, installation and use/care instructions. In addition, the user is urged to become familiar with and adhere to all applicable local, state and federal building codes, licensing and legislation requirements governing the user's ability to perform all tasks associated with design and installation standards, and to collaborate with licensed practitioners who offer professional services in the technical areas of mechanical, electrical and load bearing design as required for regulatory approval, as well as health and safety regulations.

Information about this book and other association programs
and publications may be obtained from the
National Kitchen & Bath Association
687 Willow Grove Street, Hackettstown, New Jersey 07840
Phone (800) 843-6522
www.nkba.org

Copyright ©2006 by the National Kitchen & Bath Association.

ISBN 1-887127-57-7

First Edition 2006

Illustrations and Drawings: Jean Anguiano, Jessica Best,
Nicole Daniels, Jerry Germer and Bridget Miller

Top cover photo courtesy Bonnie Crawford – Seattle, WA
Bottom cover photo courtesy Holly Rickert – Ridgewood, NJ

Figure 8.25 printed with permission from Key Porter Books Ltd.
Copyright ©1997, 2004 by Anne Harding and Janice Biehn

Published on behalf of NKBA by Fry Communications, Irvine, CA

Peer Reviewers

Timothy Aden, CMKBD	Jim Krengel, CMKBD
Julia Beamish, Ph.D, CKE	Chris LaSpada, CPA
Leonard V. Casey	Elaine Lockard
Ellen Cheever, CMKBD, ASID	Phyllis Markussen, Ed.D, CKE, CBE
Hank Darlington	Chris J Murphy, CKD, CBD, CKBI
Dee David, CKD, CBD	David Newton, CMKBD
Peggy Deras, CKD, CID	Roberta Null, Ph.D
Kimball Derrick, CKD	Michael J Palkowitsch, CMKBD
Tim DiGuardi	Paul Pankow, CKBI
Kathleen Donohue, CMKBD	Jack Parks
Gretchen L. Edwards, CMKBD	Kathleen R. Parrott, Ph.D, CKE
JoAnn Emmel, Ph.D	Al Pattison,CMKBD
Jerry Germer	Les Petrie, CMKBD
Pietro A. Giorgi, Sr., CMKBD	Becky Sue Rajala, CKD
Tom Giorgi	Betty L. Ravnik, CKD, CBD
Jerome Hankins, CKD	Robert Schaefer
Spencer Hinkle, CKD	Klaudia Spivey, CMKBD
Max Isley, CMKBD	Kelly Stewart, CMKBD
Mark Karas, CMKBD	Tom Trzcinski, CMKBD
Martha Kerr, CMKBD	Stephanie Witt, CMKBD

INTRODUCTION

Our goal, our hope, is that this book will help you to be a better designer—more creative and more knowledgeable. This is not the type of book that you read cover to cover. It is a book to be used!

We hope that we find this book, and its companion one on kitchens, on a shelf near your drawing board, computer or table. We hope this book will be in your studio, office or showroom—wherever you are at your creative best. We envision a book that gets worn, with your comments written in the margin and "sticky notes" coming out in all directions.

To put the subject of bathroom planning into perspective, we first included information on historical and consumer trends, plus research on bath design and planning.

The majority of this book was then developed around the National Kitchen & Bath Association's Bathroom Planning Guidelines and associated Access Standards. With these as a core, we included the infrastructure, environmental, electrical, and mechanical considerations needed to apply the Planning Guidelines.

We added sections on gathering and assessing information about the client that is necessary to design a bathroom. In addition, we provided ideas for designing spaces related to bathrooms, such as closets, laundries, exercise areas and home spas. Finally, throughout the book, we wove in an emphasis on understanding client needs and on integrating knowledge of universal design.

We organized and presented this book as if we were talking to a new bathroom designer, just starting a career. At the same time, we offered information, ideas, suggestions and tips of use to the more experienced designer. We firmly believe we can all learn something new—as we certainly did in writing this book! We assumed our readers have little knowledge of, or background in, bathroom design. In addition, we cross referenced other books in the NKBA's Professional Resource Library series that contain additional information, such as on construction, mechanical systems, products and graphics standards.

Design is visual, and therefore, a book on design must be visual. We have included many drawings, diagrams and dimensioned plans to aid you in understanding the concepts presented. We have added photographs to show how the content is integrated into "real life" settings and to spark ideas of your own.

There are many worksheets and checklists to use in your work and with your clients. Feel free to use them as is or to adapt them to be useful to you.

We are excited that we have been able to provide these worksheets and checklists in an electronic form on the CD that comes with this book. The electronic format will enable you to use them on a computer or edit them for your business before printing.

CHAPTER 1: Bathroom History and Trends

Although the bathroom has changed throughout history, it has always reflected the prevailing cultural attitudes towards hygiene, cleanliness, privacy, relaxation, socializing, and even morality and religion. The development of our modern bath has also been dependent upon evolution in public infrastructure, technology, codes and other policies.

Today the bathroom is not only the center for personal hygiene, but also a place for relaxation and even recreation. Research continues to contribute important knowledge related to designing bathrooms for function and safety. Today's bathrooms are becoming larger, and make use of a variety of materials and designs to produce a unique and personalized room for a household.

The changing demographic makeup of North American households will continue to alter the way our bathrooms look and how they serve users, especially in light of the growing number of older people in our population.

This chapter examines the history of the bath, reviews important research in bathroom design, and provides an overview of key demographic and psychographic trends that are now affecting bathroom design.

The typical American bathroom as we know it today has a relatively short history. The early "bath room" or "bath house" was strictly for bathing. It was not until the mid 19th Century that one room in the home included all personal hygiene activities in one place. However, some of the activities and rituals currently enjoyed in our baths had their origins centuries ago.

Early Civilizations and the Bath

Although evidence indicates that ancient Egyptians and the residents of Crete had bathing facilities, the bath was taken to new levels by early Minoan and Roman civilizations who embraced it as a way to escape the stresses of everyday life. After soaking, bathers were covered with ointments and oils. Most people found the experience so soothing that they typically bathed daily in public bath houses.

3

Many times these early bath houses were highly decorated with paintings, statues and elaborate architectural details to add to the pleasure. In addition to both hot and cold tubs, filled from pipes or aqueducts, these ancient bath houses may have included steam chambers, showers, and rooms with dry heat. These efficient systems would not be matched for another 1500 years.

The public bath house was also the center of social activities and a form of recreation. For example, baths in the Roman City of Herculaneum included courts for playing ball and a gymnasium. Because of the bath house's significance in society, these cultures found no need for incorporating baths into private homes.

In addition to making bathing an enjoyable experience and a prominent part of their lives, the Greeks' and Romans' understanding and practice of good sanitation were extraordinary for the time. The Greek and Roman concept of the "bath" and their belief in the power of water has come full circle to the pools, hot tubs, mineral baths and spas we enjoy today.

Public baths were a part of other cultures as well. The "Turkish Bath," a steam bath that is followed by a shower and massage, developed when Roman bathing customs were combined with those of nomadic people such as the Byzantines. The early Japanese culture also embraced communal public baths.

Latrines

Just as baths were public facilities in early Roman and Greek civilizations, so were latrines. (Although, some early evidence of the home chamber pot was also recorded.) Roman water closets and latrines were actually flushed by water. Studies of ancient cultures have found underground conduits for removing waste as early as 2500 BC. In addition to a public water supply, achieved through aqueducts, the Roman Empire also established quite sophisticated sewer systems, which did not appear again until the 19th Century.

The Middle Ages

With the fall of the Roman Empire, the bath was no longer an important part of daily life and disappeared for centuries. Through the Middle Ages, the 5th to 15th Centuries, bathing was not a common activity and little attention was given to personal hygiene. Much of the decline was due to physicians who thought bathing was harmful to health, and clerics, in particular the Puritans, who thought nakedness and bathing to be indecent and sinful. The spread of diseases and the tightening of church doctrine eventually closed down communal baths in Europe.

Sanitation in general suffered during the Middle Ages. Few, if any, advances were made in devices to collect waste. Without a sewer system or other disposal methods, chamber pots were usually emptied out the windows and sometimes waste poured onto the streets below. Water for home use was drawn from the closest water supply, which could easily be contaminated by free-flowing waste. During the Middle Ages, there was an awareness of the link between sanitation and disease, but no real effort was made to improve the conditions.

17TH AND 18TH CENTURIES

The European immigrants brought similar beliefs about the indecency and harmful effects of bathing to America. During the 17th and much of the 18th Century in America, little attention was given to body care. Pioneers who desired to bathe did so infrequently because it was so difficult. They first needed to find a container large enough to bathe in, and then carry in water and heat it. These obstacles also meant that clothes were washed infrequently.

The Bathtub

Bathing for the middle class during this time usually involved a portable bathtub placed in the kitchen, typically the warmest room in the house. The fireplace used to cook the family meals also heated water for the bath. Eventually fireplaces were built with a water reservoir, making hot water more accessible. Once the bathtub was filled, it usually served the entire family, with the dirtiest family member going last. These tubs were also used for other purposes such as laundry.

Bathing in private was very limited at this time. Wealthy households, who generally used servants to carry water for the bath and dispose of it afterwards, had the luxury of locating bathtubs in the privacy of their bedroom. More elaborate bathtubs in the bedroom incorporated a hinged cover that could hold the wash basin and pitcher when the lid was down. A pitcher was filled with water and poured into the bowl as need.

For families who did not have the luxury of a bathtub in the home, or if someone wanted to freshen up between infrequent baths, the bowl was used for a sponge bath that could take place in the privacy of the bedroom. The idea of incorporating a bathtub of any type into the home evolved very slowly. Even in 17th and 18th Century Europe, these facilities were only present in homes of royalty and the very wealthy.

Hot Water

The task of supplying hot water to the bath became easier with new innovations, one of which was the cast iron stove. A water vat was located at the back of the stove. As the family baked and prepared meals, the stove heated water for baths and other uses.

Heaters were eventually attached to the portable tub so that hot water did not need to be carried. They were later attached to the permanently installed tub, and eventually the hot water came from a single source in the home, the water heating system most homes use today.

The Privy

Facilities for toileting have also changed over time. The 17th and 18th Century American homes made use of the privy (an English word derived from the Latin word "privates" meaning secret, not publicly known) or outhouse installed outside the house. Indoors, the chamber pot was used during bad weather or at night, and the waste was disposed of as quickly as possible. A small ceramic or metal pot, it could be stored under a bed, in a cabinet or in a stool often called a commode. Or it was stored in a piece of furniture like a chair called a "closestool" or night chair with the bottom enclosed to hide the pot. Other chamber pots were allowed to sit out in the room and these were usually highly decorated.

Sanitation

Colonial America also did not have the luxury of a public water supply or sewer system so the disposal of waste was as primitive as it had been for centuries. Outdoor privies were built over large pits. In some cases, the pit was deep enough to reach the water table which allowed waste to gradually dissolve and wash away, possibly into a stream or the well next door. Other families emptied their chamber pots into the back yard. When the accumulation became large enough, it needed to be hauled away. As in earlier times, for some lazier households in cities, the streets became the collection area.

Water Closet

The first modern water closets in America most likely came from England. The term "water closet" developed as water was used in the waste disposal process. Although there is evidence of some type of built-in water closet existing in the palaces of Crete, the first attempt at the modern water closet was by Sir John Harington, around 1596 in England, who designed the device for his home and also installed one in the home of his godmother, Queen Elizabeth I. The device did not live up to expectations, so the idea was disregarded as too undependable to duplicate. Although a patent was filed in 1617 for a newer version of the water closet, a more successful flushing water closet appeared in 1775.

As American cities became more congested, the issue of sanitation grew more acute. Yellow fever epidemics erupted in the U.S., particularly in New York, in the mid 18th Century, prompting physicians to declare publicly that unsanitary conditions were the root of the disease. They asked that taxes be levied to develop a sewer system to remedy the problem. Many larger U.S. cities began to look into developing safe water supplies and disposal systems.

As a result of this awareness, the 19th Century brought many changes in how people viewed personal hygiene, as well as changes in the infrastructure and technologies that made the home bathroom a reality for the masses. One important step towards improving personal hygiene was primarily due to the medical profession. The medical field now supported the idea of hydrotherapy and also publicized the importance of personal and public hygiene, especially as cities grew larger and more congested. Increased awareness of the germ theory in the 1880s, and the connection between disease, germs and personal hygiene, led to a preoccupation with personal cleanliness and sanitation.

Water and Sewer Systems

To deliver the necessary fresh water for personal hygiene in the home, a safe and reliable water supply needed to be developed. Prompted by a series of cholera epidemics, city officials took a closer look at public sanitation. As cholera was linked to drinking water, the officials now realized the entire population was at risk, not just those living in less sanitary neighborhoods. This realization had a dramatic impact on the establishment of sewer systems and the sanitation movement began.

THE AMERICAN BATHROOM TAKES SHAPE—19TH CENTURY AND BEYOND

The prison system was actually a pioneer in the provision of toilet facilities. However, the idea of a permanent water closet indoors was slow in coming to most homes. People were accustomed to using the outdoor privy. They were well aware of the odors produced there and did not want them inside the house. There was also the issue of where the water closet could be placed in the home. In addition, the development of the indoor toilet was dependent on the advances made in public water supply and sewer systems, which were slow in coming to many areas.

City sanitation began with moving the waste out of neighborhoods. The earliest indoor water closets were disguised as furniture, much like the chamber pot. They were located in a separate un-vented room or "closet" without running water, which was often located at the end of the hall, under the stairs, or on the stair landing. Water had to be carried to the water closet for any flushing. One variation of the water closet was the "earth closet," but it too required much work and added waste materials to the back yard.

EARTH CLOSET

The earth closet was like a water closet, but instead of washing waste away, dry soil was added after each use to absorb moisture and cover offensive odors. Periodically the contents were removed and the soil with the decomposing organic matter was used as compost. The earth closet, popular in the 1860s because of the undependable water supplies, was quite labor intensive. So it was not widely used unless the household had servants to haul soil in and out of the home.

Improvements in sanitation began as some cities incorporated drainage systems that carried waste through canals or pipes to the nearest river or stream. Although these systems cleaned up the neighborhoods to some extent, they basically just moved the problem from one place to another. Chicago built its first sewer system around 1856. Around 1880, municipalities began to pay more attention to city plumbing problems, and health departments in New York City, Washington, D.C., and Brooklyn, N.Y. established some of the first plumbing codes.

Sanitation problems increased as populations grew larger and more concentrated in metropolitan areas. City officials recommended that a standard of at least one water closet per family be in place before the end of the 19th Century. This goal was not met, however. An 1893

Bureau of Labor report stated that only 2.83 percent of the people in some parts of New York City and Chicago had bathroom facilities. Running water and disposal facilities were limited to the middle class and wealthy.

Improvements to the water supply continued at a slow pace. Modern plumbing, including fresh water supplies and effective sewer systems, did not become widely used until the late 19th Century. One improvement was replacing wooden pipes with lead pipes.

Indoor Plumbing

The bathroom did not become common in the average home until there was a reliable supply of running water. Before public water supplies, households used a faucet or hand pump that drew water from a cistern in the attic. Water was collected from the rain or pumped up from below. The introduction of running water made it both practical and economical to bring personal hygiene activities all into the same space. With the water supply in the attic, it made sense to locate the home's bathroom on the second floor, although many were also on the first floor next to the kitchen

THE LEGEND OF THOMAS CRAPPER

Perhaps the most familiar name associated with the modern toilet is Thomas Crapper. Crapper was born in England in 1836, and operated a successful plumbing business from 1861–1904. Although he had a number of plumbing related patents, there is no evidence that Thomas Crapper actually invented the toilet, as many people think. Just how Crapper became so closely associated with the device is not clear. One theory is that he bought the patent for the toilet and marketed it with his name. Then, World War I doughboys passing through England brought together Crapper's name and the toilet, thus establishing the slang name "the crapper."

With running water available, the next generation of water closets was a "washout" or "wash down" design that used a tremendous amount of water to flush waste away completely. The water closet that incorporated running water was the first application of indoor plumbing for the middle class. In 1895, a siphon action water closet was developed that used vacuum action to more efficiently flush away the waste with less water. This siphonic action is used by most modern toilets. The water closet or toilet, as we know it today, did not become a common household fixture in American homes until the early 20th Century.

Bathing

Bathing methods also changed with the availability of running water. A concern about hygiene prompted people to question how someone could become clean while sitting in a tub of water that became increasingly dirty as one bathed. Such concerns led to an interest in the vapor or steam bath, and the shower, as superior alternatives to the tub bath.

The shower became possible when a method was found to pump hot water up a pipe for the overhead spray. It was increasingly recommended as a preferred bathing method over the bathtub in both private homes and public baths of the working class. A simple shower used a hand pump to move water up a pipe over a portable or outdoor tub. Eventually, public water supplies included enough pressure to reach the shower head.

The modern concept of the shower evolved from military barracks and gyms commonly used by men. At the time, the idea of water drenching the bather from overhead was considered too vigorous for the "gentle sex." It was not uncommon to contact a physician before undertaking a shower.

Because of their invigorating water action, the first home showers were considered to have therapeutic value. The state-of-the-art shower at the time was a needle spray which had a series of sprays placed around the body for various needs. It included a kidney spray, a spinal spray, a bidet spray, etc., all with separate controls. A crude valve for mixing hot and cold water often left the bather either scalding or chilled.

Most likely the last fixture to be plumbed was the lavatory. The new fixture was designed much like the former wash basin and stand, emerging as a bowl-shaped basin on a pedestal base with a drain in the middle, turning a china bowl on a marble stand into a china bowl in a marble stand. The first faucet used a hand pump to draw water, and later a faucet with hot and cold water controls was attached. Soon the pedestal lavatories disappeared as cabinetry entered the bathroom, and sinks were installed into vanities that contained the much desired and needed built-in storage. This design became common by the 1950s.

Figure 1.1 White was the only choice for early bathrooms, which lacked space and storage. Rectangular bathtubs included controls and spout mounted vertically on the wall.

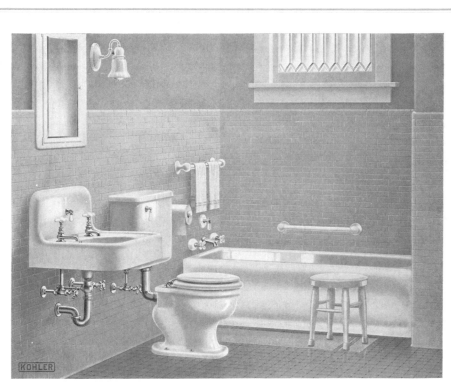

Bath Room FH

F-17-R 5 foot "Viceroy" Bath Tub with F-1785 supply and waste fixture.

F-332-UO 18x24 inch "Emmet" Lavatory fitted with F-2156 faucets, F-2175 ⅜ inch supply pipes, F-2271 lift waste with china *lever* handle, F-2220 1¼ inch "P" trap.

F-1349 Closet Combination.
F-1968 Built in Cabinet.
F-1998 18 inch Hand Rail.
F-2004 24 inch Towel Rack.
F-2031 Bath Room Stool.
F-2071 Toilet Paper Holder.

Size of room 6x8½ feet.

17

A Real Bathroom

The earliest bathrooms belonged to the wealthy who usually converted a spare bedroom into a bathroom. By the mid 19th Century, finer homes were built with a separate bathroom, large enough to accommodate servants. Although it was possible to have hot and cold running water by the late 1800s and early 1900s, it was still considered a luxury and only incorporated into the homes of the wealthy. The finest luxury bathrooms of the time often included a sitz bath, foot bath, bidet, pedestal lavatory, siphon jet water closet, enameled tub, and shower bath with receptor.

Older homes did not have an extra space that could be devoted to a complete bathroom. It was easy to add a small toilet or a lavatory, but including a bathtub required a significant amount of space. Bathrooms might be fitted into a bedroom or dressing room, but because they were considered a functional space, it was considered a waste to devote too much room to them. Small, functional bathrooms had fixtures crowded together for efficiency and were welcomed because servants were no longer around to carry the water and perform other duties.

During the late 19th and early 20th Centuries, people who did convert a room to a bathroom were not quite sure how it should appear, so the earliest bathrooms were unique in design and layout. Many styles emerged during this era including wood encased bathrooms, with a wooden toilet tank, seat and a wood-trimmed tub, that were massive and imposing. Some luxury rooms were heavily draped, elaborately wallpapered and carpeted. They included marble, glass and glazed tiles.

For the middle class, however, the stark, simple, hygienic bathroom with plaster walls and hardwood floors eventually became the standard. Early in the 20th Century, the compact sanitary bathroom with its white walls and fixtures became the model of the modern bathroom, and an American symbol. Pipes were left exposed, partly to show the shiny, sanitary fixtures, but also because many people still feared the dangers of trapped gas.

The bath was minimal in size and contained three standard fixtures—a toilet, a sink, and a bathtub/shower. As the popularity of the bathroom increased, more households found ways to convert space to accommodate a bathroom. As bathrooms became required by codes, floor plans for new homes replaced a closet or pantry with a bathroom.

To overcome space limitations, during the 1930s, R. Buckminster Fuller designed a prefab bathroom that only needed assembly. And in 1948, Add-a-bath offered an already assembled bathroom ready to simply add onto the house.

Plumbing Codes

With an increasing number of bathrooms, more regulations were necessary, which led Secretary of Commerce, Herbert Hoover to establish the 1924 Bureau of Standards for basic plumbing. Although these codes were not enforceable, they were effective and provided a technical solution to the plumbing aspects of safety and sanitation. Almost 20 years later, the 1940 Housing Census found that still only 50.9 percent of all U.S. houses were in good condition with a bath and flush toilet.

The plumbing situation improved by 1950 with more than 85 percent of urban homes having hot and cold running water; 92 percent, a flush toilet; and 89 percent, a bathtub or shower. In rural areas, however, more than half of farm homes lacked a bathroom. In 1951, the Department of Commerce established a National Plumbing Code, and in 1955, the American Standards Association distributed a list of basic plumbing principles that served as recommendations to municipalities.

Today, technological solutions, as well as strict plumbing codes, have made a safe water supply and sanitary disposal system available except for a very small portion of the American population. As new innovations emerge, care is taken to make sure they continue to provide the sanitation standards necessary for good health.

Today's Bathrooms

The bathrooms of today contain many of the basic elements of earlier bathrooms, but new technologies, materials, and lifestyles have made the bathroom into a more inviting, relaxing, and comfortable room to enjoy. Awareness of the need for universal and accessible design has been growing since the end of World War II, with the requirements of disabled veterans, polio patients, and the aging population.

Today the bathroom is undergoing a reinvention similar to the kitchen. No longer just a place to cleanse the body, the bathroom is also serving as a place to relax and become revitalized, a place to awaken the senses to a pleasurable experience.

IMPORTANT RESEARCH

Bathroom design today has also benefited from key research on anthropometrics, ergonomic design and universal design. Designers now have a better understanding of the human body, the design and space requirements to accommodate it, and the interface between humans and their interior space. The result has been fixtures and spaces that are more convenient, easier to use, and more versatile. Following is a summary of some major research that has impacted bathroom design.

Center for Housing and Environmental Studies

Perhaps the first extensive research into bathroom usage began in 1958 by Alexander Kira at the Center for Housing and Environmental Studies located at Cornell University in Ithaca, New York. The research was sponsored jointly by the Cornell University Agricultural Experiment Station, and the Plumbing and Heating Division of the American Radiator and Standard Sanitary Corporation.

The aim of the research was to thoroughly investigate what was then the unexplored area of personal hygiene, and establish basic criteria and parameters for design of facilities to accommodate these activities. The study included a laboratory investigation of the problems and needs posed by the principal personal hygiene activities.

The report covers such topics as the purpose of personal hygiene and the concept of dirt, attitudes about body cleaning, the anatomy and physiology of cleaning, and design considerations related to personal hygiene activities. The report describes each activity in much detail, including the motion and position of the body before and after, as well as during, the activity. It was this study that developed a rationalization for ergonomic design in bathrooms.

Space Standards for Household Activities

Another study, conducted from 1956 to 1957 by the University of Illinois Agriculture Experiment Station, in cooperation with four other state Experiment Stations, involved taking and recording basic body measurements, as well as the human measurements for body activities. The primary objective was to determine the floor space needed by people to perform various activities in the home. Measurements were taken to establish clearances needed for activities, as well as the basic movements involved in fundamental activities, such as reaching and bending, that are a part of many other activities. This study set some very basic parameters for human space needs in the home.

Human Engineering

Pioneers in the field of human engineering, which is the application of knowledge about human beings to design, are Henry Dreyfuss and Associates. This group was perhaps the first to take anthropometric measurements gathered through military and civilian studies and transform them into a form that could be used by designers. The first documents presenting these ideas were the innovative work of Alvin Tilley. *Measures of Man* (1960) and *Humanscale* (1974 and 1981) were followed by a more recent book, *The Measure of Man and Woman: Human Factors in Design*, published in 1993.

This book presents human body dimensions from birth to adulthood. For adult dimensions, it applies the concept of the percentile person to provide not only average body dimensions, but also the extremes. Sections of the book address the needs of the elderly and people with mobility aids, as well as space requirements for the home and other locations.

Human Body and Interior Spaces

The next major work that impacted bathroom design was assembled by Julius Panero and Martin Zelnik into a source book titled, *Human Dimension & Interior Space: A Source Book of Design Reference Standards*, published in 1979. The purpose of their book was to focus on the anthropometric aspects of ergonomic fit, or ergofitting, and apply the data to the design of interior spaces where people work, play, or live.

Early in their study of the relationships between the user and his or her space, the authors realized that most references for professionals dealt with general planning and design criteria. They found that very little information addressed the physical fit between the human body and the different components of interior space.

In their search for anthropometric data, the measuring of humans and their relationship to objects and spaces, they discovered that most of the previous human engineering had taken place in industry and the military sectors. An enormous boost to the database came during World War II, when the need arose to match human capabilities with new technologically advanced equipment such as airplanes. These sectors continue to generate anthropometric research today. One important civilian study prepared by the U.S. Department of Health, Education and Welfare contributed to their database as well.

In their sourcebook, the authors present numerous diagrams for human structural and functional dimensions. Structural dimensions are the static dimensions of the head, torso, and limbs in a standing or seated position. The functional dimension is the measurement of a working position or the movement associated with a task. As they continued their research, the authors found that it continually reinforced the need to use anthropometric data in the design process. This meant bath designers would now have a basis for design considerations related to fixture and storage use.

A 1995 version of this work by DeChiara, Panero and Zelnik titled, *Time-Saver Standards for Housing and Residential Development*, includes much of the same anthropometric measures and information as the earlier document, with additional planning guidelines, including dimensions for such spaces as exercise areas and hydrotherapy pools. This reference remains as perhaps the most comprehensive and primary reference for anthropometric measures.

ADDITIONAL HUMAN FACTORS RESEARCH

Human factors research is also being conducted at other universities, but with the focus on universal design, and accessible design related to specific populations. Three major programs conducting research in these areas include the Buffalo Rehabilitation Engineering Research Center on Universal Design at the State University of New York (SUNY) Buffalo, the Trace Research and Development Center at the University of Wisconsin–Madison, and the North Carolina State University Center for Universal Design. All three have conducted extensive research in the areas of universal design and are involved with projects specifically addressing accessible design. Major funding for these programs comes through the Department of Education and the National Institute on Disability and Rehabilitation Research (NIDRR).

The mission of the Rehabilitation Engineering Research Center on Universal Design program in the Buffalo School of Architecture and Planning program at SUNY Buffalo, which was established in 1999, is two-fold:

- To use research, product development, and information dissemination to create new resources for universal design practice.

- To facilitate a dialogue on the practice and delivery of universal design in order to build a national and international universal design community.

Three projects they have undertaken specifically addressed accessible design in the bathroom. The first was a Prototype Anthropometric Database project that gathered anthropometric measurements of 500 wheelchair users. Information from this study was used to develop a prototype database specifically for bathrooms and bathing facilities. The second was the Visit-ability Project which examined how to make homes more visit-able for people with disabilities, including bathroom entry and access. The third involved assessing the bathing needs and preferences of older persons with disabilities who lived at home. Data from this study was also used to design bathing facilities.

The Trace Research and Development Center, part of the College of Engineering at the University of Wisconsin–Madison, was started in 1971 and has primarily focused on finding ways to make information technologies and telecommunications systems more accessible and usable by people with disabilities. An additional research program was designed to gain an understanding of why and how companies adopt universal design, what factors are most important in making this decision, and what factors discourage or impede the adoption and successful practice of universal design.

Research activities at The Center for Universal Design in the College of Design at North Carolina State University began in 1989 and include applied research studies on human factors and user needs, usability of accessible and universally designed products and environments, and the impact of universal design. The bathroom is an important focus in this research.

As changes take place in bathroom usage and products, on-going research is needed to ensure the bathroom is a comfortable, safe, and efficient space. Universities and other institutions will continue to contribute to the body of knowledge that can assist bathroom designers.

MAJOR BATHROOM TRENDS

After becoming an integral part of the home early in the 20th Century, the bathroom has undergone many changes and experienced many design trends. Some reflect changes in lifestyles, while others came about with the development of new materials, products, and processes. Following is a summary, by decade, of select bathroom design trends.

BATHROOM DESIGN
TRENDS BY DECADE

Early 1900s

- Bathroom design was moving away from the lavish toward the convenient, family-style bathroom.

- A concern for sanitation and hygiene was paramount in bathroom design.

- An emphasis on maintenance and safety emerged, with consumers demanding products and materials that were easy to clean.

- Everything came in white, presenting the "antiseptic" look.

- Cabinetry was not popular because exposed pipes were considered more sanitary and easier to repair.

- A claw-foot tub, pedestal lavatory, and water closet with an elevated tank made up the standard three-piece bathroom.

- If the home had electricity, lighting most likely consisted of a shadeless, clear bulb, usually hanging from the center ceiling on a cloth-covered cord.

- The cage shower was introduced as a single shower fixture.

Figure 1.2 The claw-foot tub had legs with claws on its feet to allow cleaning beneath the tub.

1920s

- Sanitary plumbing was so widespread among the middle and upper class that attention turned to aesthetic considerations.

- The shower became common in the home.

- The closed-in, rectangular porcelain tub replaced the claw-foot tub.

- Faucets and shower controls lined up vertically under the shower head.

- Pedestal sinks were popular, as well as console sinks supported by metal legs.

- Sinks were often made of Monel, a corrosive-resistant, light weight, white metal containing a mix of copper and nickel.

- Nickel was used for bright work on faucets.

- Hand painted murals, mirrors, and cloth were common surface coverings for walls.

- White was still popular, but porcelain made it possible to add color.

    The color matching of vitreous china glazes and cast iron enamels was perfected.

    Although black fixtures appeared, they would not be popular on the market for four decades.

    Colors included blue, green, ivory, yellow, brown, lavender, and gray.

- Dressing table vanities were featured as more activities moved into the bathroom space.

- The bathroom continued to be viewed as a functional space, not for relaxation.

- Lighting consisted of a center ceiling lamp surrounded by milk-glass diffusers of various shapes.

- The first copper plumbing systems were installed late in the decade.

Figure 1.3 Rectangular tubs replaced the claw-foot tubs, and new colors, like this soft yellow, emerged on the market.

A FOUR-FIXTURE BATHROOM BUILT AROUND THE NEW *Cosmopolitan* BATH

One of the most interesting details of this colorful room is the new Kohler Cosmopolitan . . . the bath with flatter bottom, wider rim, lower sides, K-554-CV. Other matched fixtures which make up the foursome are the Claridge vitreous china lavatory, K-4946-F; Walcot vitreous china dental lavatory, K-5360-BA; quiet-performing siphon jet Integra closet, K-5580-A. The Kohler color is Tuscan.

The bathroom above measures 12′x11′ 4″. Floor and wainscot are 6″x12″ glazed tile. Upper walls are sand blasted plate glass. Glass linen cabinet doors. Indirect lighting above the tub and in lavatory recess. Plaster ceiling is painted.

The dental lavatory should be in every home, especially one with children, as it encourages regular brushing of teeth. Relieves bathroom congestion. Shelf at back. Hot-and-cold water. K-5360-BA.

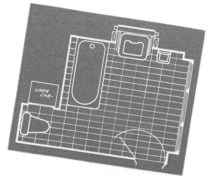

3

Figure 1.4 This console "boudoir" lavatory, supported by two cast metal legs, included a raised shelf and room for a dressing table bench under it.

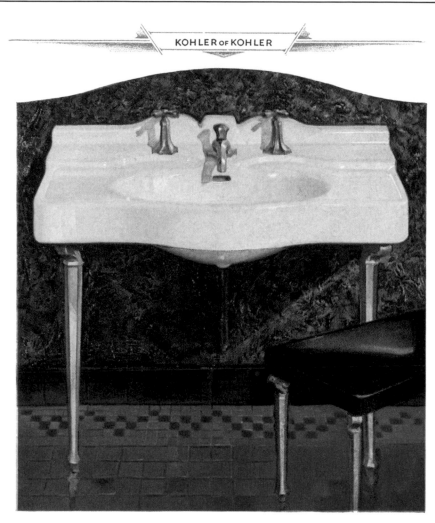

KOHLER of KOHLER

Kohler Bellaires Lavatory K-4915

AN artistic triumph in vitreous china is the Kohler Bellaires lavatory. A monument to the skill and craftsmanship of the Kohler artisans. The broad, massive slab is cast in one piece. The graceful curving back, the slightly raised shelf, the spacious tablelike end portions and generous bowl combine to give this boudoir lavatory a beauty, utility, and appeal never before approached.

The fittings, like two shining obelisks, are dainty and lovely with their coating of shining gold. Yet they are sturdy, and efficient as well.

The finely sculptured legs are cast of fine metal. They have all the grace found in fine furniture. Placed far apart, they allow the use of a dressing table bench such as is shown in the above illustration.

Fixture	Prices Size		Chromium Plated Fittings	Gold Plated Fittings
Bellaires K-4915	20 x 36 inches	White	$540.00	$700.00
Bellaires K-4915	20 x 36 inches	Colored	630.00	790.00

29

1930s

- The bathroom began to resemble the rest of the house with comfort emphasized.

- Small sinks called dental lavatories were marketed as a means to help children practice dental hygiene.

- The four fixture bathroom was now common—tub/shower, lavatory, dental lavatory, and toilet.

- Wall hung lavatories were shown, along with lavatories supported by metal posts that included towel bars on the sides.

- Disappearing steps were incorporated to help children reach the lavatory.

- The leak-proof, one-piece shower was developed.

- Pedestal lavatories were common.

- Late in the decade, plumbing was hidden and fixtures were compartmentalized.

- Ads showed Americans how to design unused space (under stairs, dormer rooms, or large closets) into small bathrooms Kohler named the "lavette."

- Plans were available to show homeowners how to convert underused space to a bathroom.

- Although introduced in 1893, glass block was now heavily promoted for residential buildings.

- Bathrooms were lit by a single, flush-mounted ceiling fixture in the center of the room, which remained the norm until the 1970s.

- Influence of the Arts and Crafts Movement introduced more colors into the bathroom.

Figure 1.6 A wide side on the bathtub served as a bench where parents could sit to help children while bathing.

BATHROOM EFFICIENCY

In a Lively Setting

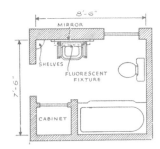

Centra lavatory fitting.

● If your bathroom is Kohler-equipped, which means that the fixtures have Kohler fittings as well, your reward is a smooth-working, matched set of which you can feel proud.

In the bathroom shown, the 5'6" Cosmopolitan Bench Bath, K-526-F, with seat at front, has a popular feature in the Triton shower and bath fitting. The dial mixer tempers the water for either the shower or the tub. After the correct temperature is obtained, raising the knob on the spout diverts the water to the shower head.

The lavatory is the K-1740-C vitreous china Chesapeake, 24 x 20", with compact Centra fitting illustrated, and the closet indicated in the floor plan is the K-3665-EB close-coupled Bolton.

3

Figure 1.7 One of the popular bathroom colors in the 1940s was pink.

Matched Styling AT ITS BEST

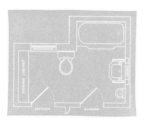

Fixtures: Cosmopolitan K-526-CF recess Bench Bath; Gramercy K-1850-BA vitreous china lavatory with "neatness shelf," metal legs and Wall-free towel bars; Walcot K-2200-BA vitreous china dental lavatory; Integra K-3610-PB one-piece closet.

The problem of the two-door bathroom is here solved by grouping the fixtures closely, with all hot water outlets on the same inside wall to save on piping and protect from freezing. A Kohler Compact radiator, recessed under the window to meet cold as it enters, keeps the bathroom comfortably warm.

A true recess with dropped ceiling, lighted from above and faced with Vitrolite to ceiling height, focuses importance on the tub. Vitrolite continues around the room as a wainscot, drawing the other fixtures into the picture. Above the wainscot the walls are wallpaper, in which is repeated the Peachblow of the fixtures.

4

1950s

- Most new innovations came in the way of new materials.

- The 4 foot x 4 foot tub/shower became a solution for small spaces.

- Lavatory cabinets were common.

- The "Powder Room" idea developed.

- New innovations in the bathroom included a telescoping towel bar; ceiling fixtures with a light, heater, and fan; adjustable showers; and an electric heated towel bar.

- The plastic tub with glass fibers was patented.

- Pink and gray were popular colors.

- Stainless steel remained popular for sinks and countertops.

Figure 1.8 Smaller bathrooms incorporated smaller bath tubs. (Courtesy of Kohler Company)

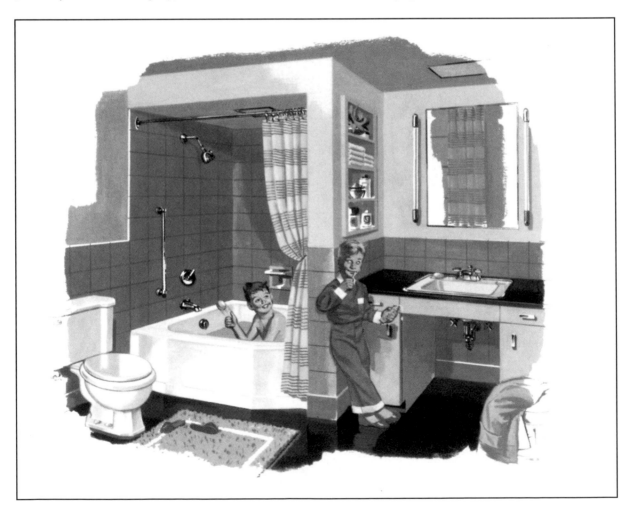

Figure 1.9 Bathrooms were now being shown with cabinets along with the lavatory, providing much needed storage.

1960s

- The idea of relaxation was finally coming back to the bathroom.

- Ads portrayed hometown girls and happy moms relaxing in the bathroom.

- Bold colors emerged, including orange, bright yellow, deep red, dark brown, dark green, as well as the colors so distinctive of the era—Avocado Green and Harvest Gold.

- New bathrooms were more luxurious and second bathrooms were promoted.

- The new self-rimming lavatory was incorporated into the vanity.

- The California hot tub and backyard pool were popularized.

- The claw foot tub disappeared.

Figure 1.10 The 1960s brought many new bold colors to the bathroom.

THE BOLD LOOK

KOHLER'S BOLD LOOK STARTS WITH
AVOCADO, THE "GO-WITH" COLOR

A bold new play of color for bathrooms and kitchens! Avocado fixtures go beautifully with any background—the more so with bold room accents to set off their timeless warmth. Add the crowning touch of new Flair fittings with the golden look: amber acrylic on polished brass. Bring Avocado into your kitchen, too, with Kohler's spacious new self-rimming sink, the Lakefield. Avocado! Want more information? Send 10¢ for our new brochure. Kohler Co., Kohler, Wis., Dept. BHG-3.

(kitchens, too!)

KOHLER OF KOHLER

the Bold Look for '67/Kohler Co., Kohler, Wisconsin

1970s

- Multi-person tubs for group soaks were popular.

- Hydromassage tubs, such as the whirlpool tub, were developed.

- New colors included sand, gray, black, and pink.

- Colored fixtures were an important part of the bathroom design.

- The double lavatory became an important selling point in new homes.

- The nostalgic look reappeared in a vintage toilet with elevated tank and chain pull, the ball-and-claw-foot tub, and pedestal lavatory.

- Theme designs were shown for the bathroom including the patriotic, desert Southwest, and Caribbean motifs.

- Solid surface countertops with integral lavatory were developed in 1968, but were not introduced to the builder market until 1971. Four colors were available.

- Later in the decade, bathrooms were becoming a place of leisure with larger tubs for relaxation.

- Homeowners switched to fluorescent lamps to save energy, and to track lighting to increase the amount of light.

1980s

- Bathrooms increased greatly in size.

- Softer pastel colors returned.

- Designs appeared on the surface of bathroom fixtures.

- More high-end homes incorporated hydromassage tubs.

- Large tubs that accommodated group soaks remained popular.

- Faucets and controls moved from the sink to the counter.

- Pedestal lavatories and claw foot tubs remained popular.

- There was a significant increase in the use of appliances in the bathroom.

- New toilet designs included models with reduced water usage.

- Glass block enjoyed a resurgence.

- Recessed down lights were part of the lighting plan.

- In 1980, the American National Standards Institute standards were revised to include residential bathroom applications.

- In 1984, the Uniform Federal Accessibility Standards were published, providing accessibility guidelines for Federal buildings and government-funded apartment buildings.

1990s

- Sculptured fixtures added softer lines and new interest to the bathroom fixtures.

- Lavatory faucets appeared on the walls, as well as on the lavatory surface and counter.

- Many new types of vessel-style lavatories were introduced in a multitude of materials.

- Whirlpool and jetted tubs were common, especially in the higher end market.

- Spacious bathrooms incorporated room for many activities including meditating, exercise, and relaxation.

- Clothing storage and a dressing area were incorporated into larger bathrooms.

- Metallic finishes were added to lavatory surfaces.

- Detailed designs covered the surface of vitreous china fixtures.

- His and her spaces were beginning to emerge.

- Fine furniture was used for a vanity.

- New types of lighting were incorporated, including recessed, low voltage, and compact fluorescents.

- In 1991, Fair Housing Laws required that all new multifamily buildings have adaptable units.

- New Federal mandates required 1.6-gallon flush toilets in all new residential applications.

THE 2000s DEMOGRAPHIC AND POPULATION TRENDS

With each era, new design trends emerge that incorporate the lifestyles and technologies of the time. In this new millennium, we see many factors influencing bathroom design, the most important being the changing demographics of North America. There are two major trends emerging in the population: an increasingly more diverse population and a larger number of older people. Another long-term trend affecting bath design is changing household composition.

Population Diversity

According to the *State of the Nation's Housing 2002*, a publication of the Joint Center for Housing Studies of Harvard University, almost two-thirds of the household gain in the U.S. involved minorities, and one in five U.S. households are headed by either a foreign-born individual or a first generation American. The disproportionately large increase in minority households is primarily due to immigration.

An Aging Population

- U.S. Census figures indicate that the number of Americans aged 65 and older increased to over 34.9 million in 2000, compared to 3.1 million in 1900.

- One in eight Americans fits into this over 65 category, and this trend is expected to continue as the Baby Boom generation ages.

- It is projected that by 2030, 22 percent of the American population will be 65 years of age and older, and 25 percent of that population will be minorities.

- Thirteen percent of the Canadian population is 65 years of age or older, an increase of 10.2 percent since 1996. This is twice the growth of other age groups.

Increased life expectancy is credited with some of the increase. When our nation was founded, the average American was expected to live to the age of 35, but by 1997 that increased to 76.5 years of age. These demographic trends open up a large market of individuals who will have an increased interest in bathrooms that are safe, comfortable, and ergonomically designed. Of course, accessible design will be critical for those aged individuals with disabilities. See Chapter 9 for additional characteristics of this population and design applications appropriate for them.

Household Composition

Other demographic changes noted by the National Association of Home Builders and the Joint Center for Housing Studies of Harvard University that could impact the design market include changes in household composition.

- From 1974 to 2000, the number of dual-employed couples increased from 43 percent of the household population to 57 percent. Busier households, where two adults may be showering, grooming, and dressing at the same time in the morning, need bathrooms that have the space and facilities to easily accommodate two individuals.

- The number of non-family households, with either two unrelated individuals or a single person, rose 11 percent between 1996 and 2001.

- Family households headed by an unmarried person, typically a single parent, increased eight percent. These population groups may not need as large a space, but they may desire more personal touches that fulfill their needs.

- The one household category that experienced the smallest increase was married-couple families, which grew by three percent between 1996 and 2001.

DESIGN TRENDS

These changing demographics all affect how consumers use their baths, the products they demand, and the looks and styles they favor. The retail markets of today offer the consumer and designer an unlimited array of choices for bathroom design. Although certain styles may go in and out of fashion, today's selection of colors, materials, styles, sizes, and textures allows the designer to create a room to fit every preference and situation. As new trends are incorporated into the bathroom, you, as the designer, must always keep in mind that the bathroom is a very complex space to plan, and the fundamental characteristics of sanitation, ergonomics, and safety should always be considered.

Here are some of the key directions in bathrooms today.

Space Usage Trends

- **Open Spaces**. Most bathrooms of the past were minimal in size and looked upon as very private and somewhat hidden spaces. Today's bathrooms incorporate a feeling of openness by expanding space both visually and physically, through the size of fixtures and the use of mirrors and glass.

- **Outdoor Access**. Today's consumers have a love for the outdoors, sunshine, and fresh air, so this feeling can be created in the bathroom by physically opening the space to the outside, allowing access to a private deck or patio.

- **Suites**. A popular idea is merging the bedroom and the bathroom or providing access through a dressing area to create the bathroom suite. Bathroom designs are moving away from the bathroom as a confined area into one that is a fluid living space that blends the public with the private.

- **Dressing**. Dressing areas and closets are moving into the bathroom (Figure 1.11) from the actual bedroom space. The closet may include hanging and drawer space, as well as a cedar lined compartment.

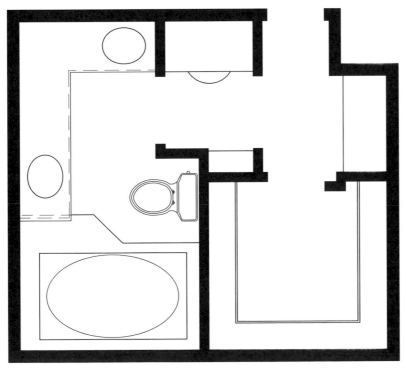

Figure 1.11 Closets in the bathroom area form a dressing area that is convenient to the grooming area in the bath.

Figure 1.12 A compartmentalized bathroom will more easily allow multiple users at one time. (Courtesy of Porcher)

• **Two Users**. Designing a bathroom with two simultaneous users in mind is essential for many households. The double lavatory has been used for some time as a means of eliminating the morning wait, and compartmentalized areas (Figure 1.12) have also helped provide privacy for one individual while another is using the space.

• **Laundry**. Laundry equipment and facilities are moving to the bathroom or master suite.

Color and Theme Trends

- **More Color**. The standard all white, institutional bathroom of the past is no longer the norm. Today's bathrooms come in an endless variety of colors and include as much ornamentation as other parts of the house.

- **Nature**. The natural look with colors and textures to match the surrounding outdoor environment is gaining favor among designers and consumers. The nature-inspired designs might include natural stone or warm woods for a soft natural beauty.

- **Contemporary**. There has been a move to the clean lines of contemporary styles (Figure 1.13). Some designers would call this a minimalist design with an Asian influence or a desire for simplicity. Even traditional designs are including contemporary elements like the vessel bowls and stone.

Figure 1.13 One of the most popular looks in bathrooms today is a more minimalist contemporary design, with a bit of Asian influence. (Courtesy of Duravit)

- **Historic Themes.** With the abundant choices of fixtures and materials in the market place, designers are unlimited in their ability to create a bathroom that incorporates any number of themes or atmospheres, from a traditional Victorian look to a whimsical Elvis Presley motif.

- **Group Themes.** Bathroom themes can also center on a certain population, like children, where child sized fixtures and novelty designs within fixtures accommodate the needs of young people.

Multicultural Influences

- **Culturally sensitive design.** As our nation becomes more culturally diverse, demands for culturally sensitive bathroom spaces emerge. Designers are often asked to incorporate culturally specific design features.

- **Multiple generations.** For many cultures, one home may accommodate many generations. Therefore, designers need to plan spaces that will accommodate this multi-generational family.

- **Feng Shui.** The Ancient Chinese practice of "fortuitous placement" is known as Feng Shui. It is a way of creating harmony and prosperity in someone's life through the arrangement of their environment. By introducing the most pleasing organization of the elements in one's surroundings, it is thought that Feng Shui can influence the events in a person's life.

Fixtures

- **Luxury.** In today's luxury bathrooms, fixtures make a statement. They can dominate, like with the use of large tubs and massive stone pieces, or they can present a soft look of sculptured fixtures with delicate lines. Bold colors and unique designs can also attract immediate attention. There are fixtures of all sizes, colors, materials, and styles from which to choose to make a design statement.

- **Vessel and wet surface lavatories.** New trends are emerging in fixture design. In the place of a standard lavatory, we find a vessel or bowl used for a wash basin. These vessels, which can be made of many different types of materials, often sit on a flat, wall hung base, with plumbing exposed below, but can be placed on a vanity cabinet as well. Other styles hardly resemble a standard lavatory, like the marble wet surface lavatory. Counter and wall mounted spouts and controls are commonly used with these fixtures.

Figure 1.14 Some of the newer lavatory styles for bathrooms hardly resemble a standard fixture. (Courtesy of Kohler Company)

- **Whirlpool tubs**. Whirlpool and jetted tubs are no longer restricted to the luxury bathroom. These tubs come in many sizes, and may be designed to fit the space occupied by a standard sized tub.

- **Universal design**. Universal design considerations are incorporated into bathroom fixture selection and placement. Vanities with a knee space, single-lever plumbing fixtures, comfort-height toilets, larger showers with flat thresholds, and illuminated thresholds and doors all make the bathroom a place that accommodates everyone's needs.

- **Walk-in shower**. For daily uses, the shower is becoming the preferred method of bathing. Many consumers desire the large walk-in shower instead of a tub, for that quick morning getaway. Some of these showers have no doors for easier access.

Figure 1.15 Larger bathrooms allow for spacious showers with multiple shower heads. (Courtesy of Grohe)

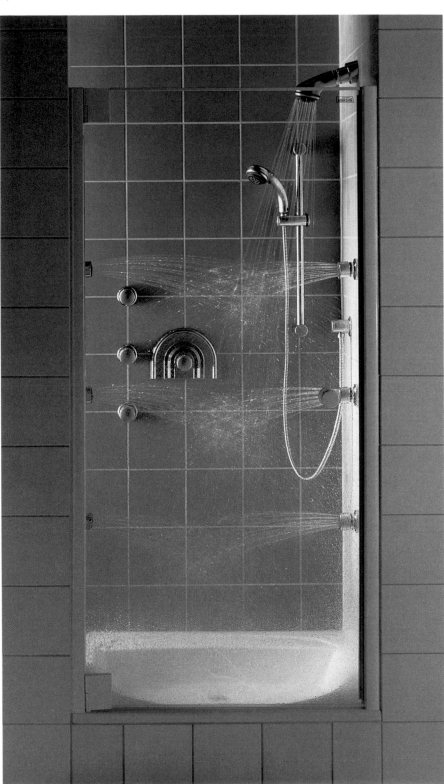

Furniture

- **Furniture replaces cabinetry**. Furniture is being introduced into the bathroom much like it has been in the kitchen. There is a trend towards less use of cabinetry and more furniture items, like the console lavatory, to create a look that is unified with the bedroom.

Figure 1.16 The new look in console lavatories includes wooden bases that resemble furniture. (Courtesy of Decolav)

- **Contemporary look**. Contemporary lines are echoed in the freestanding furniture pieces.

- **Floating cabinets**. Many cabinets are taking on the "floating look" when they are attached to a wall instead of grounded on the floor.

Environmental Awareness

- **Environmentally Friendly Products**. Clients may be very pro-environment and looking for environmentally friendly products, including those made of recycled and renewable materials, to use in their homes.

- **Water and Energy Saving Fixtures**. In addition to water and energy saving features, consumers want products that are low maintenance to reduce cleaning and the use of chemicals. They also want durable materials so they will not need to be replaced frequently.

- **Chemical Sensitivity**. Many people are very sensitive to chemicals, so selecting products with low or no chemical emissions is important in these cases.

ACTIVITY TRENDS

Grooming

Providing a place for applying make-up no longer means just an open space with a stool at the lavatory counter. Larger, more luxurious bathrooms include a special vanity area designed with adequate lighting, storage, and multiple mirrors for special grooming activities.

Relaxation

The idea of using the bathroom as a retreat for relaxation has hit new heights in American homes. The reemerging interest in health and spirituality has brought new attention to the "bath". Spurred by the popularity of the hot tub and hydrotherapy, the home spa concept has evolved into a spa bathroom that includes multiple ways to slow down the pace of life, relax, and soothe away the stresses of the day. Spa bathrooms might include a spa tub, whirlpool/jetted tub, sauna, and steam shower.

Figure 1.17 Larger bathrooms can turn into a spa with the inclusion of a whirlpool and deluxe shower. (Courtesy of John A. Petrie, CMKBD – Mechanicsburg, Pennsylvania)

In addition to using water for relaxation, the bathroom can be an intimate and private space that has an emotional and mental feel like no other in the home. Linking the bedroom, library, and bath creates a space to relax and read. A fireplace brings back the intimate sitting room of the past, where the tub was brought into the bedroom and placed near the fireplace for warmth.

Comfort Station

In creating an inviting and relaxing space, comfort is a top priority, and new materials and technologies are used to design these elements of comfort.

- Tubs not only contour to the body, but are made of a soft, resilient material to cushion the body as the bather enjoys the relaxing hydrotherapy.

- Cushioned and heated toilet seats have been available in other parts of the world for many years, and have made a fairly recent appearance in the North American market.

- Additional comfort is added through heated floors so people no longer step out of the tub onto an icy, cold surface.

- Warm towels are very comforting to people as they step out of the shower, or to warm up muscles before beginning exercise. In addition to the reintroduction of towel warmers, warming drawers are now available.

Figure 1.18 Towel warmers are just one way of adding comfort to baths today. (Courtesy of Mr. Steam)

Meditation

Meditation rooms or spaces provide a quiet place to relax and reflect. Japanese rock and sand gardens allow the user to create a peaceful setting. A space devoted to exercises like yoga helps with a relaxing end to a busy day.

Health and Wellness

An interest in healthy routines and health monitoring among an aging population has made its way into the design concept of more luxury bathrooms. Designers are including massage tables for treatments at home. The bathroom may also include a gym or exercise studio.

With the newest technologies, consumers can also use the bathroom for health monitoring. Fixture companies are marketing toilets that monitor waste for various health-related indicators. A concern for health has also fostered the development of antimicrobial finishes to deter bacterial growth.

Technology and Electronic Devices

The modern bathroom is not lacking in technology and electronic devices. Equipped with radio, CD/DVD players, televisions and speaker systems, consumers can stay abreast of the current world news while dressing, or listen to music while relaxing in the whirlpool tub or sauna. Not only are flat screen televisions incorporated into some whirlpool/jetted tubs, but showers also can have a waterproof television screen, blended into the tile wall, controlled by a waterproof remote, and heard on ceiling speakers.

LOCATION TRENDS

Outpost Kitchen Area

As part of the master bathroom suite, many households are incorporating a mini kitchen, outpost kitchen, or morning kitchen to handle food, drink, and health needs. Households are finding these outposts a very convenient solution to the morning rush and an enhancement for evening relaxation. Often included are a coffeemaker, a small refrigerator or refrigerator drawers, and a small microwave oven.

Once thought of as a luxury, these auxiliary kitchens can also serve as support stations when a family member is injured or ill, or when a caregiver is involved. Medications may need to be refrigerated. Storing and warming bottles for a baby is another function of this kitchen area. The bedroom suite does not need to be extremely large to accommodate a few of these appliances.

Multipurpose Space

Just as the kitchen has evolved into the "hub" of family activities, the bathroom is now taking on a similar role in some homes, with parts of the bathroom space providing a place for family members to gather, share time together and communicate about the day's activities. Compartmentalization provides the privacy needed, so that open spaces can be enjoyed by many.

Figure 1.19 Family members might gather in the seating area adjoining this bath, which serves as a multi-purpose space. (Courtesy of Erica S. Westeroth, CKD and Co-Designer Tim Scott – Toronto, Ontario. Photography by Donna Griffith Photography)

- **Master Bath**. The master bath has become a sought-after addition to homes and a standard in much of the new construction today.

- **Guest Suite**. The idea of a guest suite is gaining in popularity. A second bathroom with more than one entrance (Figure 1.20) provides a means for establishing a guest suite without adding another bathroom. Examples include an entrance from one bedroom and the hall, or a bathroom between two bedrooms.

Figure 1.20 Double entry bathrooms make the room available from two different areas, such as two bedrooms or a bedroom and a hall.

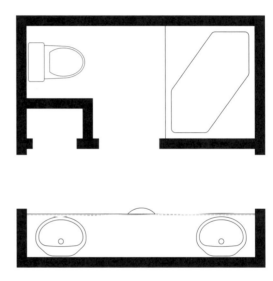

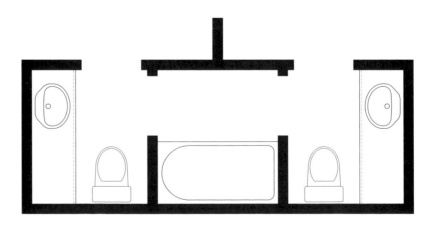

- **Laundry Area**. Because most laundry is produced in bedrooms and bathrooms, designers and builders are incorporating a laundry area, or even a second laundry area, into or near the bathroom and bedroom area. Two appliance manufacturers now have personal clothing care systems that can also be incorporated into this area. These units may dry and/or freshen clothing.

STORAGE TRENDS

- **Multiple types**. Once almost devoid of storage, the bathroom now contains multiple types of storage to handle the variety of activities that take place there.

- **Clothes storage**. In larger bathrooms, there is now more clothing storage, both folded and hanging, as part of a dressing area. These dressing areas can be entire rooms, taking all clothes storage out of the bedroom space.

- **Open storage**. In the form of open shelves, open cabinets, or poles with wire baskets attached, these provide visual appeal as well as convenience.

- **Appliance storage**. An increase in the use of portable electric appliances in the bathroom calls for more storage for these items, as well as consideration for utility connections. Not only are the appliances requiring storage space in cabinets and drawers, but on the counter as well. Built-in appliances, like refrigeration units, may need special circuits and electrical connections incorporated into the plan.

- **Electronics**. Designers are also providing storage for electronic equipment incorporated into the bathroom. A television, video equipment for the exercise room, a radio, a CD player and speakers need space out of the traffic pattern, yet positioned so they can easily be used during bathroom activities.

CONSUMER BUYING TRENDS

In addition to population and demographic changes that may affect bathroom design, specific consumer preferences can greatly impact the bathroom projects your clients request. Surveys conducted by national trade magazines, associations and manufacturers, can give designers an idea of what consumers prefer in their bathroom. Just remember, tastes change quickly today.

As a professional designer, you will find it beneficial to stay up-to-date on ever-changing consumer preferences, and style, material and color trends, by reading consumer and trade magazines, visiting industry-related websites, and attending trade shows.

Nevertheless, surveys consistently show that bath remodeling remains one of the most popular remodeling projects. The primary goals of households who are remodeling a bathroom vary somewhat from survey to survey, but generally include updating appearance, adding new fixtures and often, making the bath larger if possible.

Increasingly, consumers buying or building a new house are looking for more bathrooms to accommodate their larger homes and busier lifestyles.

As for what consumers feel are the most desirable features in a bathroom, the responses also vary by survey. The top features considered essential or desirable by many include a linen closet, and an exhaust fan, as well as more storage and compartmentalized spaces. Also high on the list are dual sinks/grooming stations.

The two key features many respondents want in their dream bathroom are a whirlpool tub and a shower system. Listed as key accessories desired in a dream bathroom in one survey were: a skylight (45 percent), heated tile floor (38 percent), a stereo system (32 percent), a heated towel bar (19 percent), TV/VCR (14 percent), fireplace (11 percent), and a coffee/cappuccino maker (6 percent).

CHAPTER 2: Infrastructure Considerations

Before beginning a bathroom project, you will need to consider the infrastructure of the bathroom space and related areas in the home. In Chapter 5, a checklist is provided to help you carefully examine the structure of the home, and particularly the areas where the bathroom project will take place. No matter what types of structural changes are made, from remodeling a bathroom to designing a new one, you must take time to carefully plan infrastructure needs and double check your list so that nothing is forgotten. Forgetting or miscalculating some aspect of the installation may not only be difficult to change later, but most likely expensive as well.

This chapter provides an overview of the structural and plumbing infrastructure considerations that may impact your decisions while designing a bathroom project. The National Kitchen & Bath Association's book *Kitchen & Bath Systems*, part of the *Professional Resource Library*, covers building codes and the actual plumbing, electrical and mechanical systems, so refer to it for the specifics that this chapter does not detail. *Residential Construction*, also from the NKBA, covers codes and overall interior and exterior home construction.

CODES

The fundamental regulations which govern the types of materials that can be used in construction, as well as how they may be used, are called building codes. Although you may be working with a plumber or contractor who is very familiar with these codes, having a working knowledge of the codes yourself will help you be more aware of restrictions or requirements that must be followed as you develop a bathroom design. Building codes are legally binding, and inspection may be required to assure compliance.

Although a new international building code, called the International Residential Code (IRC), has been developed to form a set of consistent, correlated, comprehensive, and contemporary building code regulations for homes throughout North America, the code must be adopted by state and/or local governments. So becoming familiar with the state and local codes in your area is essential. A few specific items to be aware of are included here. The NKBA Bathroom Planning Guidelines in Chapter 6 and 11 reference IRC code requirements.

Plumbing, Electrical and Other Codes

Plumbing codes regulate the types of materials and structural makeup for components used in the house plumbing system and the methods for installing them. Although some codes may vary by area of the country, one water conservation code that has been mandated nationwide is the 1.6-gallon single flush on toilets.

For new construction, complying with the codes is just a matter of your plumbing contractor selecting the materials and methods allowed for your area. For remodeling projects, however, it may take a little more planning to evaluate the situation, decide what is feasible, and make certain the changes reflect the current plumbing codes.

Electrical code considerations are discussed in Chapter 7—Mechanical Planning.

If you are remodeling a fairly old bathroom, you many find that codes require other updates to your bathroom materials and structure. Some other common code upgrades for safety and health require the use of a vent fan or operable window, safety glass, and scald prevention systems.

STRUCTURAL ISSUES

Whether you are working with new construction or a remodeling project, special structural considerations may be necessary for many different installations. Again, your building contractor may be well aware of these issues, but careful planning or a careful examination of the current structural components in the bathroom will be critical when making decisions about design options. You can begin with the original construction plans as a guide, but eventually you will need to verify that the structure is actually built as indicated on the plans. Following are some of the structural considerations to keep in mind.

Floor Structures

Whenever the floor will be changed in some manner during your remodeling project, it is important to know more about the floor structure and what is hidden within that floor. Once you have verified the direction and size of the floor joists or floor trusses, you have a better idea of how to proceed with plans for new plumbing, wiring, or heating components that need to be placed in the floor. An examination of structural components will also help you determine the floor strength. In addition, it is essential that you know what components are already within the floor structure so that you do not damage them during the remodeling process. Concealed air ducts or plumbing may be difficult and expensive to relocate.

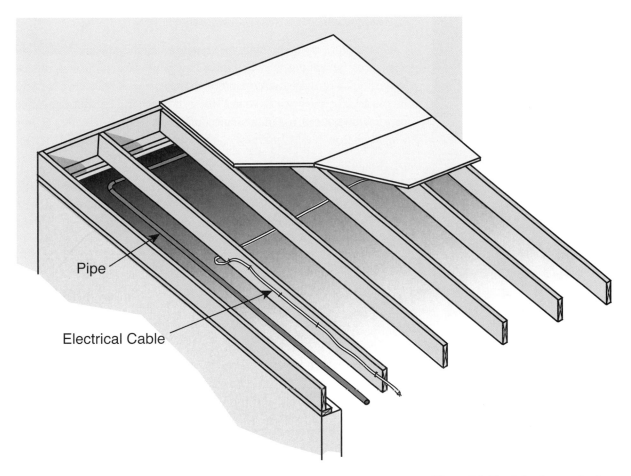

Pipe

Electrical Cable

Floor framing must also take into account the toilet placement so that the waste pipe can be properly installed between the joists in the floor. If only a small adjustment needs to be made in order for the toilet to line up with the waste drain, an off-set flange attachment can allow you to move the toilet as much as two inches, code permitting of course, in order to make use of the current waste drain. Roof venting may also need to be adjusted, so check to see what that may involve.

Figure 2.1 Check for ductwork, pipes, or electrical wiring hidden between the joists before drilling through floors or ceilings.

DAMAGE

Check for any water damage that may have weakened the floor structure. Leaking toilets or pipes can cause structural supports to deteriorate over time, and often this damage goes undetected because it is hidden by a floor covering. Lifting or removing the floor covering or checking for possible evidence of water damage on the ceiling directly below the bathroom will give clues to such damage.

If the damage is severe, sub-flooring materials or even floor joists may need to be replaced or reinforced. To prevent some of these problems in the future, seal the floors to prevent moisture from reaching the subflooring and joists. This is especially true around toilets, tubs, or showers.

The floor covering may serve as the seal if it is caulked at the joints and seams, or special concrete or other poured floors may be a better choice for sealing out water and providing stability. Along with the structural damage, you may find mold forming inside the floor area where moisture is trapped. Chapter 3 discusses mold in greater detail.

NO-THRESHOLD SHOWERS

If you are considering a no-threshold shower, the structural components of the floor will be critical in recessing the drain. For a complete explanation of the construction process, see the NKBA book *Kitchen & Bath Systems*. You will also find more details about no-threshold showers in Chapter 9.

OVERSIZED TUBS

If your client is considering the addition of a whirlpool, jetted tub, or soak tub, these fixtures can exert a great deal of pressure on a floor because of their weight when filled with water and people. In new construction, extra supports are fairly easy to add. In older homes, however, a careful evaluation of the floor structure is needed. Older floors were typically not built to hold these oversized tubs, therefore reinforcing the floor is necessary. Stripping the floor down to the joists will help clarify if the joists are large enough or spaced appropriately with enough support to hold these heavy tubs.

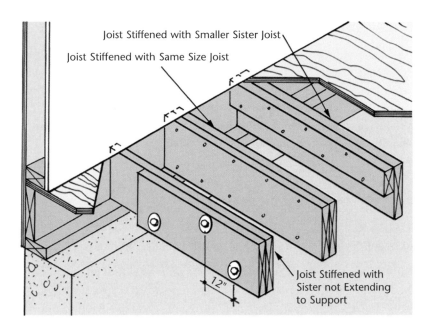

Joist Stiffened with Smaller Sister Joist

Joist Stiffened with Same Size Joist

Joist Stiffened with Sister not Extending to Support

12"

Figure 2.2 Extra floor supports may be needed when installing heavy bathroom fixtures.

STABILITY AND EVENNESS

Whether poorly constructed, weakened by time, or sagging because of a settling foundation, floors can become weak or uneven. Stable and even floors are essential for many bathroom applications, one being the toilet. As someone sits on the toilet, they would not want it to wobble or become unstable. Toilets are sealed at the floor with some type of seal, such as a wax ring, to prevent any water leakage from the drain. If the toilet does not fit flat on the floor, it could break the seal and create a major water leak.

Other installations require a sound and flat foundation on which to rest a product. Floor tile must have a flat and non-flexible surface to prevent the tiles from breaking and grout cracking with use. Tub and shower pans also must have a flat surface to be stable and prevent damage. Another consequence of unstable floors is squeaking. The constant squeak can not only be annoying, but make for plenty of uninvited noise.

LAUNDRY

Laundry areas on the second floor, or even above a finished basement, may also need special flooring considerations. Some manufacturers of laundry equipment with drums that rotate at high revolutions per minute (rpm) recommend extra floor support to handle the added vibration that could form. With standard construction, joist spacing may be far enough apart that it sets up a vibration that could travel to other parts of the home, like an echo, as the laundry equipment drum rotates. As an alternative to adding extra support to the floor joists, a thicker subfloor could be placed down to stop the vibration from forming.

The possibility of overflow from the washer should also be considered as the floor structure is evaluated. If a floor drain cannot be incorporated, a water pan of some type should be added to contain water that overflows.

Walls

If you are expanding the bathroom or reconfiguring the walls, be aware of the load bearing walls in your plan. Load bearing walls are those that support the weight of the structure above. Many times, in an effort to open up space, load bearing walls may need to be removed. As a general rule, you can identify which walls are load bearing by checking to see which direction they run. Exterior walls that run perpendicular to the ceiling and floor joists, as well as at least one interior wall, are load bearing. If the wall runs the entire length of the house, it is probably load bearing.

If load bearing walls need to be removed, local codes specify the type and length of header that needs to be used to span the opening for support. Usually wood beams will be sufficient for short spans, but steel I-beams or structural beams made of laminated timbers are needed for longer spans. Refer to *Residential Construction* for details.

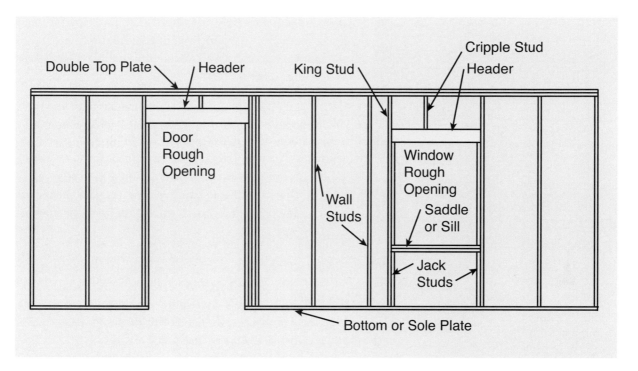

ADDED SUPPORT

Many bathroom designs today are incorporating features that hang from the wall, including cabinets, sinks, toilets, bars, and doors. In order to assure that these wall mounted items are securely attached, additional wall supports may be necessary.

Keep in mind that when specifying wall mounted cabinets, toilets, and sinks, not only does the mounting device need to be strong enough to support the weight of the fixture, but it must also be able to support the weight of people as well. Wall mounted toilets, logically, must support a person sitting on the toilet, within certain weight limits. Although we usually do not sit on cabinets and sinks, people may have the habit of leaning, or even lightly sitting on these fixtures and cabinets at times, which means these fixtures may also need to support additional weight.

Grab bars and some hinged shower/bathtub doors also need additional support inside the walls, often referred to as "blocking." Grab bars, usually incorporated to aid people as they move in and out of showers or tubs, or on and off toilets, must be able to support a person in the event they slip and grasp the grab bar as they fall. In addition to the manner in which the bar is attached to the wall, the necessary support must come from the bar itself. Standard towel bars

Figure 2.3 When openings are made in load bearing walls, headers are needed in each opening for support.

are not strong enough structurally to hold a person as they fall, and they are typically not designed to incorporate the hardware necessary to form a solid connection to the wall. More information on grab bars is located in Chapters 6 and 9.

Some glass door designs for showers or tub/shower combinations have the doors hinged directly to the wall rather than to the shower frame. This application does not typically call for special mounting considerations unless you select doors that are made of extra heavy plate glass. This type of glass is often used with the frameless glass door style. If your client decides to use this type of glass, it will be necessary to place additional studs on the inside of the wall for support.

UNEVEN WALLS

Uneven walls and the absence of square corners may make it difficult to properly install wall finishes, fixtures, and cabinets. This can be a problem in both new and older construction. Walls can become uneven for a number of reasons. Over time, old plaster walls crack, and in an effort to restore it, the surface is distorted. Drywall board may be damaged and not properly repaired. Or, walls may not have been installed square when initially built.

If these walls are to be retained in the new project, problems can arise whenever this uneven surface interferes with the installation of a product. For example, if you are adding tile or stone to the wall, the pieces may not lay flat to the surface. Uneven walls will not allow a plate glass mirror to make complete contact on the wall, or the edges of a glass door to fit flush or flat. If you do not plan to replace these walls, find surface treatments, such as liners or wall panels, that will help smooth them out enough to meet your purposes. If the walls or corners are off-square, you may find that pre-formed showers or other fixtures may not fit well into corners, so gaps may need to be filled in. Cabinet fillers may also be needed where gaps exist.

INCREASED WALL SPACE

Early in the planning process, consider where extra wall depth may be needed to accommodate items that are recessed into walls, as well as plumbing and/or electrical components that accompany bathroom fixtures. A 6 inch deep wall is typically needed for these items. Installation instructions for some equipment, like full body spray showers and wall mounted/hung toilets, specify a 2 inch x 6 inch studded wall to enclose valves and pipes.

INSULATION

Wall insulation can be beneficial in the bathroom for a number of reasons. The first is auditory privacy. This means privacy for the bathroom user as well as the occupants of adjoining rooms. If you are attempting to create a quiet and serene bathroom setting suited to relaxing or meditating, insulation will help stop outside noises from the street and other rooms. The bathroom also creates noises that can echo into adjoining rooms. The sounds of people, bathroom fixtures, noisy hair dryers, or humming shavers can be annoying to those trying to relax, listen to music, or sleep in nearby rooms. Laundry rooms or laundry spaces in bathrooms also need added insulation to deaden the sounds of laundry equipment. See Chapter 3 for more information on noise issues.

Insulation is also essential when it comes to controlling energy and moisture. Added insulation on the exterior walls will keep the room warmer and therefore more comfortable for users, especially when they are wet. A warmer room means less energy for heating. Details on insulating walls are covered in the NKBA book *Residential Construction*. Added insulation on the exterior also means a warmer wall. Because warm, moist air is attracted to cold surfaces, a warmer wall will attract less moisture and therefore mean fewer condensation problems. Moisture control is covered in more detail in Chapter 3.

If you do not plan to replace the wallboard on bathroom walls, you will probably need to use a foam type insulation to fill the walls. Professional installers can do this for you. If the wallboard is being replaced or you are working with new construction, consider adding insulation in all walls that adjoin another room and extra insulation on outside walls. For inside walls that have a closet or other built-in storage that can serve as a buffer for noise, wall insulation may not be necessary.

MOISTURE

Excess moisture is another issue present in bathrooms. Because of all the moisture producing activities, special measures must be taken when constructing the walls to prevent mold, mildew, and rot from forming. The shower, steam room, and tub all produce moisture that can come into contact with the walls. To prevent this moisture from making contact with the wall structure, cover all walls in these heavy moisture areas with water impervious wallboard. If you have a steam shower, the ceiling must also be waterproof, as well as sloped or curved to allow water to drain off. Refer to Chapter 3 for more information on moisture control and ventilation.

Doors and Windows

Doors and windows are very important components of the room structure and should be planned with consideration for other aspects of the room. For new construction, discuss with the client the type and amount of window space they desire, and the type of door that best fits their design and room configuration. For remodeling projects, examine the windows and doors carefully to decide whether they need to be replaced or just renewed. Information on window and door styles and choices can be found in *Residential Construction*.

Door Choices

When you decide to replace a door or modify the room entry, be sure the new plan fits with the other components of the room or other changes you plan to make. A new door size may mean a different size door swing that could interfere with the placement of fixtures.

Figure 2.4 One alternative to a pocket door is a sliding door with hardware that mounts on the outside of the wall. (Courtesy of inFORM by Beyerle)

Pocket doors are nice for opening up rooms and eliminating the door swing issue, but they require their own unique installation. First of all, pocket doors need adequate wall space to enclose the pocket free from plumbing, electrical, or HVAC (heating, ventilating, and air conditioning) components. Consider this possibility when this door style is being selected. Because they must move into the wall, pocket doors also may take away from the support in that wall. Historically, pocket door hardware has not been very good quality, but that has changed in recent years. If the wall contains plumbing or HVAC components that would be difficult or expensive to relocate, one alternative to the pocket door is a sliding door with hardware that mounts on the outside of the wall.

Many times other bathroom modifications can affect the door fit. For example, some floor covering applications like tile or stone, or floor heating systems, may raise the floor level enough that the door will need to be trimmed in order to clear the floor.

Changing Windows

Simply replacing a window with one of the same dimensions will not usually require any changes in the wall structure. However, if you decide a window needs to be moved or increased in size, carefully examine the wall space on which the changes will be made. Be aware of any structural issues, such as studs that need to be removed or moved, vent stacks that might be present, or headers that need to be modified. Also check for any specific code requirements related to the type of window glazing to be installed.

With any type of replacement window, consider the fenestration pattern of the windows on the exterior. You want it to blend with the other windows of the home, especially if it faces the street.

Energy Efficiency

The energy efficiency of the window area in the bathroom is extremely important for a number of reasons. More efficient windows will improve energy efficiency, as well as increase comfort and cut down on moisture accumulation on the window (those frosty windows we sometimes see on cold winter days). Windows that are energy efficient will have at least two layers of glazing (glass); a low-e coating (low-emittance); a good quality, insulating frame; tight fitting parts; and sometimes argon or other gas between the panes of glazing. One way to identify the most efficient windows on the market is to look for the Energy Star label.

Figure 2.5 Products that carry the Energy Star label are among the most energy efficient for that type of product.

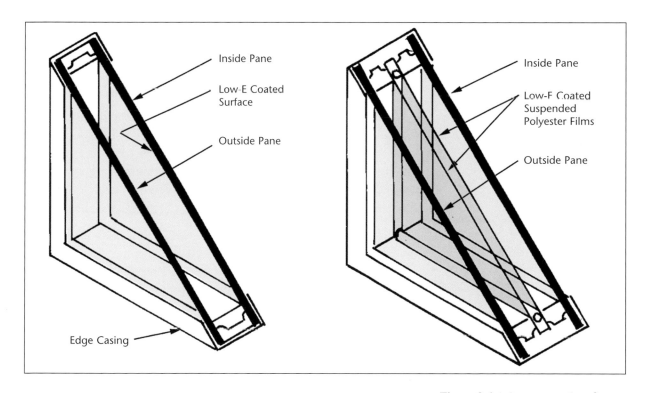

Figure 2.6 A low-e coated surface or low-e coated polyester films improve the energy efficiency of a window by limiting heat gain and reflecting heat back into the home.

Windows in older homes are many times extremely inefficient. First of all, they may have loose-fitting frames and poorly working components that allow air infiltration. If the client insists on keeping the current windows in place, the windows can be tightened up with caulking and weatherstripping. Another reason for poor efficiency is the type of frame and glazing present. Uninsulated metal frames and single glazed windows will allow warmth to conduct through the materials very easily. Adding full storm windows is one way to improve efficiency, but your client may not want to deal with storm windows every season. In the long run, if the client can afford new windows, that is probably the best solution.

PLUMBING

Of prime importance in any bathroom are the water delivery and drainage systems, including the water heating equipment. Many of the activities that take place in the bathroom rely on a dependable and adequate supply of both hot and cold water, so careful consideration should be given to structuring the plumbing system to meet the needs of the client and the fixtures they have chosen. Standing all lathered in a shower and having the water turn icy cold because the hot water ran out is not the most pleasant experience for anyone.

Most water systems, either public or private, should not have a difficult time keeping up with the water requirements of a standard bathroom. When high water-demanding fixtures like large tubs and multiple head showers are added to a system, there is a good chance demand can exceed supply, or the water pressure cannot provide the force or timely delivery expected.

Manufacturers' instructions should provide information on water delivery requirements. If there is a problem with water volume, water pressure, or the amount of available hot water, assist your client with investigating ways to remedy these issues to improve the entire home's water system.

Water quality related to water hardness can also impact water delivery when it leads to clogs in the shower heads or fills water heaters with sediment. Chapter 3 provides information on hard water and other water concerns, and how to remedy water problems in the home.

In new construction, the plumbing system can be planned with the new bathroom in mind. With today's new plumbing and connector technologies, plumbing can be placed most anywhere, so do not let it restrict your design. If you are working with a remodeling project, however, two questions must be answered early in the planning process:

1. Which fixture changes are economical to make?

2. How does the present plumbing structure affect plans for changing fixtures and fixture locations?

Fixtures

A new bathroom means selecting all new fixtures, but when a client is remodeling a bathroom they can make choices as to which fixtures they replace. If cutting costs is a goal, some of the fixtures may be able to be reused, especially if they have been replaced fairly recently. If the client chooses to keep some of the present fixtures, can they be successfully removed and relocated if the new plan called for a new location?

When new fixtures are desired, will they be able to be installed using the old plumbing or will new lines need to be added? This is discussed in more detail below. Another consideration with new fixtures is their fit in the old spaces. If the basic structure of the bathroom will stay, and the desire is to update the fixtures and look, work with your client to select fixtures that will fit in the old spaces with minimal changes. For example, find a new shower or tub to fit the previous space, or install a new lavatory into a vanity cabinet and counter the client wishes to reuse. With the use of many new finished wall materials, you may even be able to convert a tub space to a shower and vice versa. If you decide to relocate the water controls to the counter or wall, or offset for easier access, are there major problems with doing so?

For a new or remodeled bathroom project, talk with the client about the fixtures they have in mind, and the basic water and plumbing requirements for each. As an example, keep in mind that the type and location of pedestal lavatories or above-counter vessel bowls have specific requirements for drainpipes or wall mounted faucets. Corner designed fixtures, especially sinks and toilets, may also have special requirements. You should also discuss the implications of their choices. Larger tubs and high volume showers can use a tremendous amount of water which will increase water bills. And, in order to provide a sufficient spray for massaging showers, a specific water pressure level must be maintained, which may be an issue with some water systems.

Figure 2.7 A corner sink or fixture may require special techniques for installing and concealing the plumbing. (Courtesy of Porcher)

Water Delivery

Getting water to the fixture also has to be considered. Below are some factors to keep in mind.

- Beyond standard water requirements, bathrooms that include a spa tub, whirlpool tub, or high volume or multi-head showers not only require large volumes of water and adequate water pressure, but also different sized delivery lines. The standard $1/2$-inch pipe used for most plumbing installations may be insufficient for large water demands. Larger tubs and whirlpools should use a $3/4$-inch water supply line with a $3/4$-inch iron pipe size valve and bath spout to ensure proper water delivery. Also, if the home relies on a well or cistern for water, you may not be able to accommodate high water use fixtures in the design.

- To help cut costs in new construction or remodeling projects, locate the bathroom near another room with plumbing, like the kitchen, another bathroom, or the laundry room, to take advantage of existing plumbing lines.

- In cold climates, avoid placing water supply pipes on exterior walls if possible. If that cannot be avoided, be sure to insulate the wall well. Extremely cold climates may need to consider a double-wall construction in this area to make sure there is space for adequate insulation.

- New flexible water supply lines make it possible to easily reposition fixtures, such as a sink, along a wall. Before you count on using these, check local codes to make sure they are allowed.

- It would be a good idea to have a water shut off valve in or near each bathroom fixture for emergency shut off of water. Many times the only shut off valve for the home water supply is located in the basement or outside the house, which is a long way to go if you are on the second floor. Some valves are also difficult to access because they are hidden behind panels or doors that are semi-permanently attached. A good location for a valve would be where the water supply enters the area.

- Consider planning access to plumbing for as many bathroom fixtures as possible. Valves and water lines for showers or tubs that are permanently concealed behind walls or tile will require a major excavation and much expense if these lines need to be accessed. Cleverly disguised doors or removable tiles can serve as easy and replaceable access.

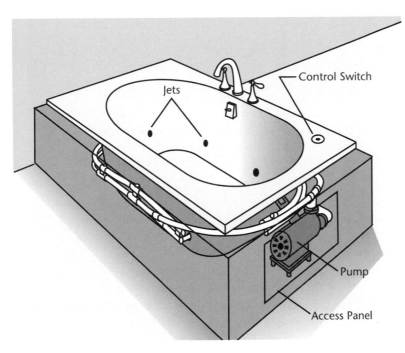

Figure 2.8 Conceal water shut-off valves (as well as other mechanical systems) with removable panels for easy access.

Drain/Waste/Vent Pipes

As you examine the plumbing in the bathroom you are remodeling, you may notice that current code requirements for the size, type, and/or height of plumbing components may require a few structural changes. For example, codes set a minimum diameter for stack and vent pipes in relation to the number of fixtures installed. If the home is quite old, a careful examination may find that the current configuration of pipes does not meet these codes, so you must decide what it will take to make the necessary changes. There is also approximately a five foot limit for relocating some fixtures before a new vent needs to be added.

Newer code requirements could also impact how some bathroom fixtures work with older plumbing systems. For example, if you are remodeling a bathroom in an older home, you may encounter problems with the new 1.6 gallon low flush toilet fixtures. Older waste pipes may be made of cast iron that has a rougher interior surface than the present plastic pipes, which could lead to back-ups and clogs. In this case, a power assisted flush may be needed if new waste pipes are not installed.

Following are other waste/vent considerations.

- If you are remodeling a bathroom, check to see if the new fixtures can make use of existing vent stacks and drains. If not, these could be costly to move because they may require major structural changes.

- High volume showers need enlarged drain lines.

- Be aware that changes in fixtures may require changes in the drain size or location. For example, the drain line size requirement may change if you replace a tub with a shower. In other cases, fixtures may be able to share a drain line, like two lavatories. When replacing old fixtures, it would be best if you could select a new fixture that would use the same drain location as the previous fixture to eliminate the need to relocate the drain. As an example, showers come with a drain opening at either the center or side. Select a new shower that will be compatible with the existing drain.

- When replacing an old freestanding toilet, drain location specifications on the new fixtures may be different. Many older toilets were mounted such that the distance from the center of the drain outlet to the stud wall was 10, 12 or 14 inches. Newer toilets are mounted with the center of the drain 12 inches from the wall. A flange can be used to adjust for this difference.

- If you are including a steam unit somewhere in the bathroom, be sure the contractor has planned a drainpipe for the steam generator.

- One other consideration in the waste/drain system, for clients who are not connected to a municipal waste system, is the septic tank. Septic tanks are sized based on the house and family size. If your client plans to install a whirlpool, full body spray shower, or other high water use fixtures that will place an increased amount of water into the waste system, you will need to check the capacity of the septic system to make sure it can handle the additional water. It may be that you will need to have the client add a larger tank, or additional tank, to accommodate the extra water. If too much water flows through a septic tank, the system cannot adequately deal with the waste products, leading to break down of the septic system and environmental consequences.

Below Grade Applications

If the house is built on a slab, reconfiguring plumbing will involve additional challenges. In order to move or add new pipes, you may need to chip into the slab's concrete.

Basement Bathrooms

Basement bathroom installations can also be challenging. If the basement is not pre-plumbed for a bathroom, considerable work will be needed to add the necessary water sources and drains. You can make the installation a little easier by locating the new bathroom next to existing plumbing, but adding the waste drain lines will be the most difficult. You will first need to locate the main sewer or septic line and determine its location below ground level.

Many sewer lines are actually quite deep, and with proper excavating you may be able to form the necessary quarter-inch per foot of slope that is required for good drainage. The sewer line depth may be recorded at the local city or county public works department. Septic lines may be recorded on the plan for the lot. If the records are not available, you may need to talk with an excavator who is familiar with the area or dig a test hole to locate the line.

Once the sewer line is located, you will need to compare it to the exact level of the proposed toilet installation. A plumber, contractor or excavator can help you make this comparison. If the sewer line level is sufficiently below the level of the toilet, you can simply install a 3-inch drain line from the toilet to the sewer.

Ejector Toilets

When the drain is below the main sewer line for the house, you cannot take advantage of gravity to remove waste and water. In this case, a sewage ejector toilet is needed to pump waste up to the main sewer line.

A typical ejector toilet has a pedestal made of polyethylene, which acts as a base for mounting the toilet. This pedestal, which is five to six inches high, can sit directly on the floor or recessed into the floor. Recessing the pedestal will place the toilet level with the floor. Inside the unit is a set of impellors and a sewage ejector pump, which processes the waste and pushes it up to the main sewer line.

Some models of ejector toilets are designed such that the pump, vent and pipes are located a distance behind the toilet. This makes it possible to build a wall between the toilet and the equipment, which allows for a cleaner installation and makes the pipes and equipment much less obtrusive. In some situations, a false or raised floor can be used to give space for plumbing lines if you have enough ceiling height to do so.

Figure 2.9 When toilets are installed below the waste line of the house, they must be hooked up to an ejector pump that grinds the waste into slurry and pumps it up to the waste line. The device can be mounted in a pit below the floor, as shown, or set behind the toilet, if the toilet is installed on a platform above the floor.

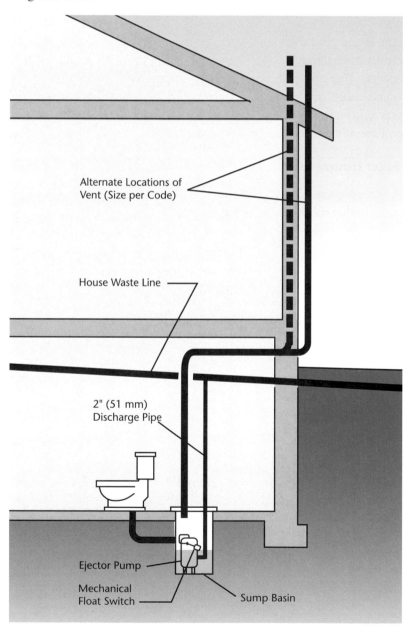

Composting Toilets

Another below grade option that eliminates the need for a pump and gives the environment a boost is the composting toilet. This fully self-contained toilet requires no water inlet, no connection to the sewer, and no chemicals in order to operate, but it does need an electrical connection and a vent to the outside. The composting toilet works much like a septic tank. About 90 percent of the waste material is actually water. A small electric heating grid and fan in the unit evaporate the liquids and send the vapor up the vent pipe. The solid waste material breaks down through normal bacterial action, converting it to a soil type residue. The residue filters down to a collection tray at the bottom, which needs to be emptied about once a year. These units can operate very efficiently if the usage isn't excessive, and odors should not be a problem if the toilet is operating properly.

Water Heaters

An adequate supply of hot water is essential for the bathroom, as well as other rooms in the home. Plan the hot water needs carefully to insure that plenty of water will be available during peak use times, such as early in the morning, when many family members may be getting ready for the day.

How quickly that hot water arrives to the bathroom fixtures can vary depending on the location of the water heater in relation to the bathroom. A somewhat common home design scenario is where the bathroom ends up on the opposite end of the house from, or two stories above, the home's water heater. Not only does this make for a long time lapse before hot water reaches the bathroom fixtures, but a large amount of water is wasted while waiting for the hot water to arrive.

If this appears to be an issue, a second water heater located near the bathrooms, would be a good idea. Other types of systems, like re-circulating hot water and on-demand or in-line water heaters, may also be good solutions for ensuring instant hot water, but they may require extra space for installation. These units vary in their capacity, however, so make sure they meet the water demands of the fixtures you have chosen.

As mentioned previously, if your client wants to install a whirlpool type tub or multi-head showers that require a large amount of hot water, a second or larger water heater would be recommended.

SUMMARY

Whether you are helping a client plan a new bathroom or remodel their current bathroom, carefully investigate the basic infrastructure components that are essential to a successful project. Floors must be structurally sound to accommodate the fixtures that will be installed. Walls need to not only be flat and square for cabinet, fixture, and surface finishes, but special wall supports may need to be added for some applications.

Windows are important for lighting and ventilation, but should also be energy efficient to add to the comfort of the area. Carefully examine the plumbing changes and needs for the new plan. Plumbing requirements and changes may pose problems related to meeting code requirements or altering structural components.

All of these considerations involve details that must be identified and dealt with before the finishing touches are applied. This overview of infrastructure considerations is expanded upon in *Residential Construction* and *Kitchen & Bath Systems*. The more knowledgeable you are about these issues, the fewer changes you will need later on and the more functional your plan will become.

CHAPTER 3: Environmental Considerations

Good design includes planning spaces that are environmentally friendly and healthy for the user. In this chapter, we will look at important issues of water quality, air quality and noise. We will consider these issues from the choices you, the designer, must make, as well as the impact on your client.

This section is a very brief review of environmental issues affecting bathroom design. More information on moisture, ventilation, and air quality is also discussed in the book *Kitchen & Bath Systems*, part of the NKBA's *Professional Resource Library*. If you as the designer, or your client, need further information on environmental issues, you can contact the U.S. Environmental Protection Agency (EPA). The website www.epa.gov is a good place to start. Another excellent resource is the Canadian Mortgage and Housing Corp (CMHC), which under the slogan "home to Canadians," provides information on many aspects of housing at its website www.cmhc-schl.gc.ca. Or contact the local office of your Cooperative Extension Service, health department or water authority. Additional resources are included at the end of this book.

WATER QUALITY

A bathroom is a wet place. Water is used for many purposes, both utilitarian and luxurious. In the process of using a bathroom, people may swallow, inhale and absorb water. For these reasons, the water used in a bathroom should be safe and healthy, as well as smell, taste and look good. Clients need water that works well for all bathroom uses and does not contribute to maintenance problems.

Chapter 2 of this book discussed issues of an adequate water supply, water pressure and the plumbing infrastructure necessary for a well-designed bathroom. This section discusses issues of water quality—water that is safe, healthy, and functional for use in the bathroom. It also covers water conservation.

Water Quality Standards

There are two types of water quality standards in the United States. The first type of standard is used to assure that water is *safe to drink or ingest*. These standards are called "Primary Drinking Water Standards" and are enforced by law. The second type of standard is to assure that water is *functional and aesthetic* for various uses such as bathing and washing. These standards are referred to as "Secondary Drinking Water Standards" and they are voluntary.

The EPA establishes drinking water standards. All municipal or public water systems are required to meet the primary standards. These systems must regularly test and, if necessary, treat their water to assure that they are meeting the primary standards. Individual or small private water systems (defined by the number of households connected to the water system) are not required to meet any water quality standards. However, owners of private systems are encouraged to use the EPA standards as benchmarks for testing and treatment of their water systems.

Primary Drinking Water Standards

The Primary Drinking Water Standards are based on the maximum contaminant levels (MCLs), or highest concentration, of pollutants allowed in public drinking water. The pollutants that are regulated by the primary standards are those that are known to cause adverse health effects and for which there is information available about chronic or acute health risks. There are three classes of pollutants for which there are MCLs.

- *Disease-causing organisms:* Most disease-causing organisms in water come from animal and human waste contamination, including bacteria and viruses. These organisms are very common in water supplies before treatment, especially if the water source is from surface water, such as lakes or rivers.

- *Toxic chemicals:* There are many toxic chemicals covered by the primary standards, including naturally occurring contaminants, such as arsenic and copper; heavy metals such as cadmium, lead, and mercury; agricultural by-products, such as nitrates; industrial and manufacturing by-products and wastes, such as asbestos, benzene, and xylene; and pesticides and herbicides, such as atrazine and lindane.

- *Radioactive contaminants:* Radium is an example of a radioactive contaminant. In addition, radon can be a radioactive water problem. Radon is a gas that is easily released when contaminated water is aerated, such as in a shower. Radon then is breathed into the lungs, which can be a health threat. Breathing radon gas is usually considered a greater problem than ingesting radon-contaminated water.

Under the provisions of the Safe Drinking Water Act, the Primary Drinking Water Standards are regularly reviewed. As new knowledge about health concerns, or new technology to detect water pollutants, is developed, the standards may be modified.

Secondary Drinking Water Standards

Secondary Drinking Water Standards are based on the Secondary Maximum Contaminant Levels (SMCLs) of pollutants that affect the aesthetics and function of water. These are contaminants that impact water qualities such as appearance, taste, odor, residues or staining. Examples of secondary standard contaminants are chloride, iron, manganese, sulfur and pH. While these contaminants might not present a health threat, they can be very important to water use in the bathroom. Secondary standards are voluntary and are not required. A public water system may choose to test and treat for some of the SMCLs.

Canadian Water Quality Guidelines

Health Canada is the ministry responsible for drinking water standards in Canada, and for educating Canadians about the importance of safe drinking water. The Healthy Environments and Consumer Safety division of the ministry (www.hc-sc.gc.ca/hecs-sesc/hecs/index.html) provides guidelines to assure that Canadian water is safe to drink, as well as functional and aesthetic for household uses.

Other Water Contaminants

Two other water contaminants are not covered by the EPA standards, but are a concern in bathrooms.

- *Water hardness:* "Hard" water is water with a high mineral content, usually calcium and magnesium. Hard water usually is found in groundwater sources, such as water from wells. Both private and municipal systems can use groundwater. Hard water creates problems with mineral deposits on fixtures and plumbing, which can reduce water pressure and lead to mechanical failures. Hard water also reduces the effectiveness of cleaning products, including shampoos and soaps, and increases soap scum deposits.

Figure 3.1 Water can be classified from soft to very hard, depending on the amount of calcium present.

Rating	Grains Per Gallon	Milligrams Per Litre (mg/L) Parts Per Million (ppm)
Soft	Less than 1.0	Less than 17.1
Slightly hard	1.0 – 3.5	17.1 – 60
Moderately hard	3.5 – 7.0	60 – 120
Hard	7.0 – 10.5	120 – 180
Very Hard	Over 10.5	Over 180

- *Iron bacteria:* Iron bacteria form a reddish brown slime that can clog pipes and fixtures. It is most likely to result when water is left standing. Typically, it is first noticed in the toilet tank or bowl. Iron bacteria are naturally occurring and more common with well water. They are an unpleasant nuisance and can cause staining. Cleaning products can treat iron bacteria, but will not eliminate the problem.

Water Quality Testing

As part of your design preparation and household assessment, you will want to find out if there are any water quality concerns. If the project is a renovation, you can look in the existing bathroom(s) for evidence of water concerns such as fixture staining or hard water deposits. Check to see if the household uses water filters in the kitchen for drinking water. You may even want to draw a glass of water and evaluate how it looks and smells.

If the home is, or will be, on a municipal water system, you can assume that the water is safe for drinking, and thus for bathroom use. If the home is on a private water system, ask your client about any testing or treatment. Regular testing is the best method to help maintain a safe water system. Most experts recommend that private water systems be tested annually for:

- Total coliform bacteria
- Nitrate
- Total dissolved solids
- pH

The first three contaminants on the list are considered "marker" pollutants, meaning that a problem with one of these contaminants is usually evidence of more extensive problems, such as sewage run-off. The test for pH measures the acidity or alkalinity of the water. Acidic water is more reactive, more likely to pick up pollutants, and corrosive to plumbing.

Other tests may be recommended, depending on the water source and recent water pollution problems in the area. A financial institution may require water testing before money is lent for any construction or home improvements. The local or state health department is an excellent place to contact for further information about water testing.

Additional testing of the water supply may be recommended if there are nuisance problems such as off-color, cloudy appearance, discoloration, unusual taste, odor or staining of fixtures. These problems can occur with both municipal and private water systems. If water problems are evident, and the home is on a public water system, start by contacting the local water authority. Some nuisance problems are temporary.

The local health department may test for nuisance pollutants, or may recommend a private company. An independent company that follows an EPA-approved testing procedure should always do the water testing. Never have a water test done by a company that sells water treatment equipment. Contact the water testing company and describe the water problem. They can recommend the necessary tests as well as the procedure for gathering the water sample.

Solving Water Quality Problems

There are many options for solving water quality problems. Some may be as complex as having to locate a new water source, such as drilling a new well. Others may be as simple as attaching a filter to a faucet. Figure 3.2 lists some of the common water treatment methods used in homes. More information on water treatment can be found in the NKBA books *Kitchen & Bath Systems* and *Kitchen Planning*.

Common Types of Water Treatment Methods

Water Treatment Method	Typical Contaminants Removed
Activated carbon filtration	Odors, chlorine, radon, organic chemicals
Anion exchange	Nitrate, sulfate, arsenic
Chlorination	Coliform bacteria, iron, iron bacteria, manganese
Distillation	Metals, inorganic chemicals, most contaminants
Neutralizing filtration	Low pH
Oxidizing filtration	Iron, manganese
Particle or fiber filtration	Dissolved solids, iron particles
Reverse osmosis	Metals, inorganic chemicals, most contaminants
Water softening (cation exchange)	Calcium, magnesium, iron

Figure 3.2 This table is a brief summary of water treatment methods for common contaminants in household water.

Some water treatment equipment, such as chlorinators, are typically installed to treat all water coming into the home. Equipment like this might be located near the well pump or storage tank. Other whole-house water treatment equipment such as water softeners, iron filters and neutralizers might be located in a utility area near the water heater.

Some water treatment equipment may be used to treat only the water that comes from a particular faucet. Examples include a reverse osmosis unit that might be located in a cabinet under a sink or lavatory, or a carbon filter that is actually part of the faucet fixture.

It is important to match any water treatment equipment to the water problem and the pollutant to be removed. Also, the amount of the contaminant in the water may determine the type of equipment, as well as the size or capacity. Finally, if more than one water treatment device is needed, the order of installation may be important for most effective operation.

Water Quality and the Bathroom Designer

It is important for you, the designer, to discuss water quality problems with your client. The water in a new bathroom should not be a health threat. New fixtures and fittings need to be protected from staining, deposits and other maintenance problems caused by water problems. Aesthetic problems with water can detract from the enjoyment of jetted tubs or luxury showers. Early in the design process, determine if water quality problems are a concern. Help your client get expert advice about water testing, and if needed, selection of appropriate water treatment equipment.

A large custom shower provides space for two people. A jetted tub full of hot water gives a stress-relieving water massage. A body shower pulsates with multiple streams of water. All these amenities in today's bathrooms, designed as private retreats and luxury spaces, don't seem to have much to do with water conservation, do they?

Precisely because so much water is used in the bathroom, the designer needs to be aware of, and plan for, water conservation. As populations expand, finite water resources need to be shared with more people. It is a major community—and taxpayer—investment to collect, treat and deliver high quality water to residents. People on private water systems may have to shoulder an expensive burden to maintain a safe water system.

Much of the water used in a bathroom is heated. Wasting it is also wasting the energy used to heat the water. Insulating hot water pipes, putting a secondary water heater in or near the bathroom, or installing an in-line or instant demand water heater in the bathroom are not really water conservation measures. However, they are ways to reduce the energy used to heat water and are part of an environmentally conscious home.

Efficient use of water in the bathroom means that water is not wasted, but can be used where it is most needed and appreciated.

Toilets

In most homes, the single greatest use of water is for flushing the toilet. Older toilets may use three, five, or more, gallons per flush. Toilets manufactured since the early 1990s have been Federally mandated to use 1.6 gallons of water or less. Toilet manufacturers have improved the technology for toilet flushing systems to make them more efficient, effective and quieter. An effective flushing system reduces the likelihood that a second flush will be needed to remove all the waste. In addition to saving water, efficient flushing systems reduce maintenance.

In a remodeling project, you may be replacing an older toilet that used more water in the flush. Make sure the water pressure is adequate for the new, more efficient toilet. Explain to your client that the new toilet may sound or operate differently. In some communities, the water authority may offer rebates for installing a more water-efficient toilet.

Manufacturers of toilets continue to look for technological improvements that reduce water use while increasing efficiency. Dual flush systems that let the user choose the amount of water per flush may become common. Alternatively, sensors are available to detect the presence or absence of solid waste and adjust the amount of water for the flush. Another development is toilet-flushing systems that do not have flapper valves—the point where water-wasting leaks often occur.

Showers

The early 1990s also saw new regulations limiting showers to 2.5 gallons per minute flow rate. Many fixtures offer even more efficient water use of 2.0 gallons per minute or less.

When designing shower systems with multiple showerheads, put individual controls on each fitting. The user can then adjust showerheads to provide only the desired amount of water, reducing waste, especially of hot water. This is particularly important in two-person showers that may be used, at times, by only one person.

Bathtubs

Water use in the bathtub is largely related to the size of the tub. A tub for soaking needs to have enough water to cover most of a person's body. Sometimes smaller, but deeper, tubs may use less water. In jetted tubs, the tub must be filled over the jets for operation, so consider the height of jets. Jets placed lower in the tub can provide an effective massage with less water.

Faucets

Aerators on faucets are important to water conservation. With an aerator, the air added to the water flow increases the pressure and makes the flow seem greater. Water use is reduced.

In the future, we may see an increase in new control systems in bathroom faucets that reduce water use. For example, a faucet with an electronic, motion-activator control may only turn on when the toothbrush or razor is under the faucet. Foot controls, already used in kitchens, make it easier to control the faucet to minimize water use.

Water Leaks

The type of fixtures and appliances selected affects water use and conservation. Another important factor is water leaks. Toilets or faucets that drip can waste tremendous amounts of water. For example, the EPA estimates a faucet that loses one drop of water per second can waste 2400 gallons of water in a year. Talk to your client about selecting quality fixtures, fittings and water-using appliances that will be easy to maintain and are less likely to develop leaks. This is not only a conservation measure, but also will save money and reduce maintenance for the client.

AIR QUALITY

Good indoor air quality makes a space pleasant to be in—and healthy for the user. Part of the design process is to ensure that the space is pollution free.

Providing good indoor air quality is a three-step process:

Source control – minimizing or preventing the sources of indoor air pollution in a room or building.

Ventilation – providing adequate air exchange, through natural or mechanical ventilation, to dilute the concentration of indoor air pollutants and assure that the space has a supply of fresh air.

Air cleaning – when necessary, using filters or other devices to remove potentially harmful indoor air pollutants.

Source Control

In the bathroom, there are a number of sources of potential air pollution. Excess moisture is the top of the list. Too much moisture can create a sticky space for the bathroom user and can also lead to structural damage. A high level of moisture in an enclosed space like a bathroom creates and/or fosters the growth of biological pollutants such as molds, viruses and bacteria.

Many grooming products used in bathrooms have the potential to be air pollutants, particularly those that are in aerosol form. Perfumed products may be pleasant to one person and annoying to another. As the designer, you do not control the use of grooming products. However, you can provide effective and easy-to-use ventilation to remove potential pollutants. Refer to Chapter 7 for more information on planning bathroom ventilation.

Indoor Air Quality and Construction

Some of the potential pollution in a bathroom can come from building and interior finish materials. New building materials such as paint, manufactured woods, varnishes, adhesives and plastics can off-gas or emit chemicals into the air, as the materials age or cure. This is especially true of products made from, or with, volatile organic compounds (VOCs) such as some paints, particleboards or wood finishes. The heat and moisture in a bathroom can increase off-gassing.

Choose building materials that have low amounts of VOCs. Many alternatives are available such as latex paints, water-based varnishes or low-VOC wood products. Some building materials can be ventilated for 24 to 48 hours before installation in the new bathroom, so that most off-gassing occurs outside your client's home. Increasing ventilation during and immediately after installation of new building materials is important to good indoor air quality.

Many building products such as grout, joint compounds, plaster and latex paints contain water. As these products dry and cure, water vapor is released. It is important that the bathroom be well-ventilated while these products are drying, to prevent moisture problems.

Renovation Hazards

New construction sometimes means removing old construction. Make sure your client is aware of possible air quality problems that can result from demolition. Some things to consider and discuss with the contractor and your client are:

- How will the demolition area be isolated from the rest of the home?

- Will the heating or air conditioning system be blocked in the demolition area, so that dust and debris are not circulated throughout the home?

- If the home was constructed before 1978, it is important to determine if there is any lead paint in the demolition area. Although lead paint was available until 1978, it was especially common in homes built before 1950. Disturbing lead paint can cause serious air pollution and health effects, especially to young children.

- Asbestos is another hazard in houses built before late 1970s. Disturbing asbestos-containing materials can create airborne health hazards.

- Sometimes demolition uncovers things like dead animals and insects in walls, attics and other spaces. This is part of the reason it is important to isolate the demolition area from the rest of the home.

- How will demolition waste be removed and disposed? Can any of the materials be recycled? Is any of the waste considered hazardous, such as asbestos-containing materials or preservative-treated wood? Are local regulations for disposal of construction waste being followed?

Air Cleaning

Air cleaners are often incorporated into the heating, ventilating and/or air conditioning system of the home, where they are used to filter heated or cooled air before it is returned, through ducts, to the house. Sometimes portable, tabletop, or larger console air cleaners are used in individual rooms. Air cleaners are most likely to be used to control particulate pollutants such as dust, pollen or tobacco smoke.

A typical air cleaner will use a fan to take air through a filtering medium, and then blow the air back into the room, or through ductwork. Because of the importance of exhaust ventilation in a bathroom, which removes moist and possibly polluted air to the outside, individual air cleaners are rarely used. In addition, the fan of the air cleaner may create objectionable noise in the small space of a bathroom.

If an air cleaner is desired, choose a filtering medium that is effective for the type of pollutant the client wants removed. Look for information that the air cleaner has been tested and rated against an efficiency standard, such as ASHRAE's (American Society of Heating, Refrigeration and Air-conditioning Engineers) standard for in-duct cleaners or AHAM's (Association of Home Appliance Manufacturers) and ANSI's (American National Standards Institute) CADR (Clean Air Delivery Rate) standard for portable air cleaners. Finally, make sure the capacity of the air cleaner is matched to the size of the room.

Moisture and Indoor Air Quality

The bathroom is a major source of moisture within a home—showering, soaking in the bathtub, running water in the lavatory, water evaporating from the toilet bowl, towels drying. Even in a very dry climate, excess moisture inside a building structure can lead to serious problems.

Prevention of moisture problems within the bathroom is part of the designer's responsibility. In addition, the designer needs to consider problems that might occur throughout the home due to moisture generated in the bathroom. The designer's goal should be to make it as easy as possible to control moisture in the bathroom, and to minimize the potential for problems from moisture that is not controlled.

Excess moisture is a potential problem for both the building and the people who live in it. Excess moisture in building materials leads to structural problems, such as peeling paint, rusting metal, and deterioration of joists and framing. Damp building materials tend to attract dirt and therefore require more cleaning and maintenance.

Damp spaces make good environments for the growth of many biological pollutants. Bacteria and viruses thrive, as do pests from dust mites to cockroaches. Wet building materials can also harbor mold, which leads to further structural damage. Mold can be a health threat. In addition, mold growing on interior finish materials smells bad and is ugly.

Moisture Basics

Water vapor is present in air in varying amounts, depending on the temperature. The warmer the air, the more water vapor it will hold. Humidity describes how much water vapor there is in air. Relative humidity, expressed as a percent, can be explained by the following formula:

$$\frac{\textit{Amount of water vapor in the air}}{\textit{Maximum amount of water vapor air can hold at that temperature}} \times 100 = \textit{Relative Humidity}$$

Note that the temperature of the air is important to understanding relative humidity. For example, on a winter's day, when the temperature is 20 degrees Fahrenheit and the relative humidity is 70 percent, the air will actually be much drier, and have less moisture, than on a summer's day, when the temperature is 85 degrees Fahrenheit and the humidity is 70 percent.

Condensation, the opposite of evaporation, occurs when water vapor returns to a liquid state. As air cools, it can no longer hold as much water vapor, so the water condenses into a liquid. The temperature at which condensation occurs is referred to as the dew point. Most everyone is familiar with the experience of taking a warm shower and then finding that water has condensed onto the cooler surface of the bathroom mirror.

The cycle of water evaporating and condensing in a bathroom can lead to moisture problems. A bathroom tends to be warmer than other parts of the home, which is desirable as it increases the comfort level when someone is naked or wet. However, because they are warmer, bathrooms tend to have higher humidity.

Many bathroom activities, such as showers and baths, further increase the temperature of the air as well as the moisture level. However, materials and surfaces in the bathroom tend to be cooler than the air—which leads to condensation. In addition, when the user finishes showering or bathing, the room tends to cool down, leading to more condensation.

As explained previously, wet materials result in increased maintenance, and eventually, deterioration. This is especially true of any that are absorbent and stay damp, such as drywall and fabrics.

Hidden Condensation

The air temperature inside the bathroom tends to be higher than the air temperature on the other side of the walls, floor and ceiling. This is especially true in winter of exterior walls, and a ceiling with an attic above it. There is a natural tendency for warm air to move to cool air. This is nature's way of trying to maintain equilibrium. In a bathroom, warm, moist air will tend to move through walls and ceilings, moving from warm to cool.

As the air moves through the wall or ceiling, it is cooled. When the dew point temperature is reached, condensation occurs. This hidden condensation inside walls and attics can be a particular nightmare for homeowners. As building materials get wetter, deterioration and mold growth can get extensive before the problem is noticed. A vapor retarder, shown in Figure 3.4, is used to help control condensation in walls and ceilings.

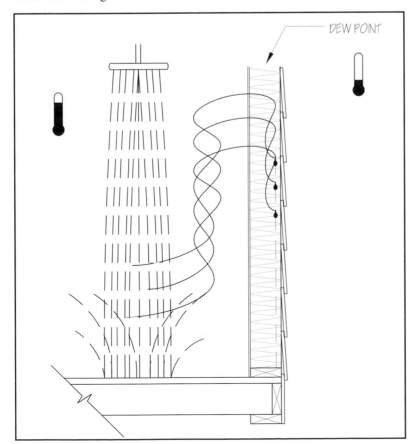

Figure 3.3 As warm, moist air moves through a wall, condensation will occur when the air is cooled to the dew point temperature.

Household Humidity

Managing the humidity level in a home is a balancing act between comfort of the occupants and protection of the structure. Excess moisture leads to many indoor air quality, structural and maintenance problems, and makes the home's occupants feel "sticky." Too little moisture dries out skin, nasal passages and throats, as well as wood in furniture and the house structure. Generally, a relative humidity level of 40% to 60% is a good compromise. At this level, most condensation and mold growth is prevented, but people are comfortable.

One method of controlling household humidity is through exhaust ventilation of moisture-laden indoor air. However, when the outside air is warm and humid, ventilation will not solve the problem. Mechanical air conditioning (cooling) of the air inside the home is effective in dehumidification by condensing water vapor from the air. If the air conditioner is oversized, however, it may cool the home's air quickly, but not operate long enough to provide adequate dehumidification.

Mechanical dehumidifiers may be used in the home to control humidity in moisture-prone areas. A dehumidifier operates on the same principle as an air conditioner. While dehumidifiers can be effective in controlling moisture, they do require regular maintenance, and generate heat and noise. A dehumidifier needs to be sized to the space in which it will be operating.

Molds, Moisture and Health

Molds are fungi. There are thousands of varieties of molds which reproduce by spores that are blown out into the air. The spores can be dormant for years. Then, given the right conditions of food and moisture, they can begin to grow.

At any given time, there are typically mold spores in the air around us. Molds are a natural part of the ecosystem, and play an important role in digesting organic debris, such as dead leaves, insects and wood. The problem is when there is an excess of mold growth, and the organic matter they are digesting is part of the building structure.

Molds require moisture, oxygen and food to grow. How much of each of these elements is required depends on the mold variety. However, most will start growing at a relative humidity of 70 percent or more. Molds can make food out of almost any organic matter, including skin cells and residues from shampoo.

Cellulosic building materials such as paper, wood, textiles, many types of insulation, carpet, wallpaper and dry wall make an excellent environment for mold growth. The cellulosic materials absorb moisture, providing the right growth conditions, and the materials themselves provide the food.

Molds grow fast. If cellulosic building materials get wet, mold growth will begin in 24 to 48 hours. Mold growth on the surface of non-cellulosic materials can start in the same time period, as long as food and moisture are present.

Molds can affect people in different ways. Some people are allergic to specific species. Molds produce chemicals that are irritants to most people, and can cause problems such as headaches, breathing difficulties and skin irritation, as well as aggravating other health conditions such as asthma. Molds can sensitize the body so that someone is more susceptible to health effects from future exposures. Finally, some molds produce toxins. The likelihood of health effects increases with the amount of exposure to mold, and also depends on the sensitivity of the individual.

Preventing Moisture Problems

Good ventilation is absolutely necessary to preventing moisture problems and mold growth in the bathroom. Exhaust ventilation removes excess moisture and prevents condensation. Ventilation systems are discussed in more detail in Chapter 7. The importance of moisture control in a laundry area that might be part of a bathroom is discussed in Chapter 8.

Finish materials can contribute to, or help prevent, moisture problems. After exposure to water and humidity, the more absorbent the materials, the longer they will stay damp. Specifying hard surface or non-absorbent materials such as glazed tiles, solid surfacing, vitreous china or engineered stone, reduces the likelihood of moisture problems. Materials that stay damp are much more likely to support mold growth. Specifying sealers for absorbent or porous materials, such as clay tiles, marble or grout, can also reduce moisture absorption.

It is especially important that wall and ceiling finishes or materials block the flow of moisture into wall cavities or attics. This can be accomplished by selecting materials that are not moisture permeable, such as glazed tiles or vinyl wall coverings. Alternatively, a vapor retarder material, such as plastic sheeting, can be used in the wall construction. There are special considerations about the placement of a vapor retarder, depending on whether the climate is dominated by heating or cooling. See the NKBA book *Residential Construction* for more information on vapor barriers.

Figure 3.4 Place a vapor retarder material on the warm or interior side of the wall, to help prevent moisture condensation inside the wall, in climates with cold winters. In hot, humid climates, where air conditioning is used most of the year, the placement of the vapor retarder may be different.

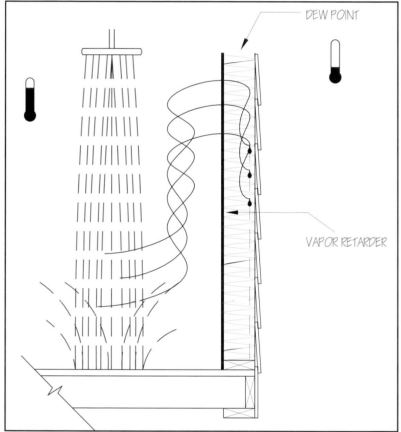

Low maintenance materials, fixtures and fittings are also important because materials that are kept clean are less likely to accumulate surface debris that can support mold growth. Avoid fixtures and fittings with cracks, seams, crevices and indentations that can accumulate residue from skin, body oils, grooming products and cleaning products—all organic materials that provide food for molds.

Anti-Microbial Finishes

New products are becoming available with various types of antimicrobial finishes or additives. Generally, an antimicrobial finish means that the material is treated with a pesticide of some sort to protect the material or product itself. For example, paints are available with fungicides to protect the paint from mold growth in the paint itself. This does not mean that mold will not grow on the paint, in a moist environment, if a food source such as skin cells or shampoo residues were to accumulate on the painted surface. Anti-microbial products may be desirable to minimize mold problems, but will not be an adequate substitute for good maintenance and moisture control practices.

Towel Bars

Damp towels can be ideal environments for mold growth. Plan adequate towel bars, rings and hooks for all users. Good air circulation around towels provides for quick drying. Consider placing towel bars near heat registers. Heated towel bars not only provide luxuriously warm towels after a shower or bath, but can also speed drying and prevent musty odors.

NOISE

Bathroom noise is an issue of running water, flushing toilets and people—well, you know what they are doing! Auditory privacy can be an important factor in designing a bathroom, especially in one that is centrally located in a home, or near the social or living areas. In addition, noises in a bathroom near a bedroom can seem especially loud and disturbing when someone is trying to sleep.

Noise is often defined as unwanted sound. Therefore, controlling noise is a matter of limiting the transfer of sound from one part of the home to another. Sound moves by vibrations which are transmitted through both air and building materials. Soft materials, like carpet and draperies, tend to absorb sound. Hard materials, like the ceramic tile and stone that are common in bathrooms, tend to reflect and/or transmit sounds. Bathroom noise is controlled, and auditory privacy provided, in several ways:

- Reducing the amount of sound or noise that is generated.

- Isolating and buffering the sources of noise through space planning.

- Using construction techniques to insulate and stop sound transmission.

Reduce Noise Generated

Many bathroom features that are otherwise desirable generate noise.

Bathroom ventilation fans are necessary to control moisture, yet motors and air movement can be noisy. The importance of selecting quiet bathroom fans with a minimum sone rating is discussed in Chapter 7 with other information about bathroom ventilation. A fan that generates too much noise simply will not get used.

Jetted tubs may offer stress-relief and rejuvenation, but are not silent in operation. As tub and motor size, and the volume of water movement, increase, the potential for noise grows.

Laundry areas (discussed in Chapter 8) are sometimes included in the bathroom. Noise transmission, especially to the sleeping area, should be a consideration in the placement and installation of washers and dryers.

Motors, such as those used in ventilation fans, jetted tubs and washing machines, may vary in pitch (hertz). Many people perceive lower pitch noises to be less annoying. However, it is important for your client to "test listen" to different motors to determine their reaction to the noise.

Pressure-assisted toilet flushing systems minimize the use of water while increasing flushing effectiveness, but the sudden rush of water can seem loud. Noise complaints about the mandated low-flush toilets have been frequent, but manufacturers continue to improve the product. However, toilets that use air pressure to assist the flush tend to be noisier.

Buffer the Noise

If you have the opportunity to influence the home design beyond just the bathroom space, you can help buffer the bathroom space, and reduce sound transmission. Look for ways to put sound-absorbing spaces between the bathroom and quiet areas of the home. For example, a closet between a bathroom and a bedroom is an excellent way to buffer bathroom noise and keep sleeping areas undisturbed. Other spaces that make good sound buffers are built-in cabinets, bookshelves, stairways and utility closets.

Another sound-buffering space planning technique is to back noisy area to noisy area. For example, put the toilet on the wall that is shared with the kitchen rather than the wall that is shared with the bedroom.

Sound-Insulating Construction Techniques

In new construction, or renovations that include building new walls, sound insulating construction techniques can be used to isolate bathroom noises. The simplest approach is to use acoustical materials such as acoustical tiles, cork, carpet and other textiles. However, these softer and absorbent materials may not be the best choices in the bathroom, where water-resistance, easy cleaning and mold-resistance are important. Therefore, look at wall construction techniques that reduce sound transmission.

Avoid air paths between the bathroom and other spaces to minimize sound transmission. Use resilient, non-hardening caulk to seal around receptacles, plumbing, light fixtures and other openings in walls and ceilings. Also, seal where the wall partition joins the floor and ceiling. If there are switches, receptacles and other openings on opposite sides of a wall, avoid locating them in the same stud space. If possible, separate these switches and receptacles, horizontally, by at least 24 inches.

There are several ways to construct the walls to minimize sound transmission. A standard stud wall can be insulated with fiberglass or a similar material, to absorb sound. A sound-deadening gasket can be used between the studs and the drywall, to minimize vibration and sound transmission. A double-stud wall, with the studs on separate plates, reduces sound transmission by separating the two wall structures and limiting vibration. A staggered-stud, double-stud wall will be even more effective. Insulating material can be added to any of the special wall constructions.

Figure 3.5 Different building techniques can be used to reduce sound transmission through walls which is measured in sound transmission units or STC.

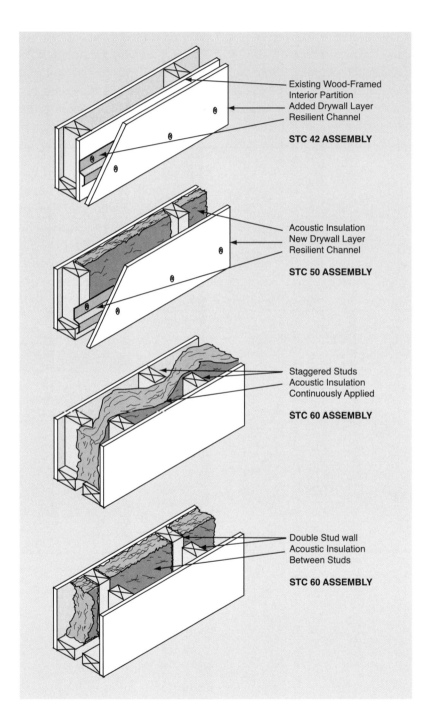

Existing Wood-Framed
Interior Partition
Added Drywall Layer
Resilient Channel

STC 42 ASSEMBLY

Acoustic Insulation
New Drywall Layer
Resilient Channel

STC 50 ASSEMBLY

Staggered Studs
Acoustic Insulation
Continuously Applied

STC 60 ASSEMBLY

Double Stud wall
Acoustic Insulation
Between Studs

STC 60 ASSEMBLY

Keep in mind that special sound-insulating wall constructions do have several drawbacks, and the trade-offs need to be considered. Cost is increased for extra materials and construction time. Floor space is lost, especially with the double walls. Also, the need to run plumbing, wiring and ducts in the walls has to be considered, especially with a staggered-stud, double wall.

SUMMARY

Environmentally responsible design benefits your client as well as the community as a whole. Increasingly, the public is asking for "green" design, and you have the opportunity to lead the way. See the resources at the end of this book for more information.

CHAPTER 4: Human Factors and Universal Design Implications

Like most principles and elements of design, universal design is an enduring approach that draws from both science and spirit. It is based solidly on human factors and along with this quantitative information, places equal value on the aesthetics of a space or product. Universal design responds to our growing appreciation and respect for diversity in the spaces we design, and in the stature, age, abilities, and culture of the people for whom we design.

The study of human dimensions, and the design of spaces and products around human factors are solid steps toward good universal design. Traditionally, human factors-based design seemed to center on two extremes. It was either one size fits all for the non-existent "average person" or totally custom design for each individual client's dimensions, abilities and needs. Universal design moves away from these extremes and builds on anthropometry and ergonomics in different ways. It embraces as broad a range of human factors as possible. One example is the placement of a wall switch that is dictated not by the reach range of the average height person, but by overlap of the reach ranges of the shorter and the taller among us. In addition, universal design places equal emphasis on aesthetics, acknowledging the importance of beauty and comfort in design solutions.

In this chapter, you will explore anthropometric and ergonomic information, as well as human factors studies that help guide design of spaces. Also covered are the basic concepts of universal design, which have become essential to good bathroom planning. Throughout this book, universal design concepts have been incorporated where applicable. Further information on access and specific user groups will be the focus of Chapter 9.

ANTHROPOMETRY

A basic understanding of the human body, including its limitations and capabilities, is helpful in any space planning, particularly in a room of such concentrated high activity as the bath. While you will often determine a client's particular dimensions and needs, there are general areas where standards, based on research, are useful. Anthropometry, defined as the study of human measurements such as size and proportion, and parameters such as reach range and visual range, is a good starting point. While not an exact science, anthropometry uses populations grouped according to specific criteria, such as age, gender, or ability, to collect data on bodies at rest (structural or static) and bodies in motion (functional or dynamic). Much of the information offered here on anthropometry is sourced from *Human Dimension & Interior Space* by Panero and Zelnik (1979) which is the generally accepted reference for interior space planning in the building industry.

In this chapter, we will discuss the various types of anthropometric information. In Chapter 5, which focuses on needs assessment, there is information about collecting anthropometric information on your specific clients. Included in Chapter 5 is FORM 1: *Getting to Know Your Client*, which provides graphics to guide you in collecting anthropometric dimensions (part 1.2), reach and grasp profiles (part 1.3), and anthropometric dimensions with mobility aids (part 1.5).

Structural Anthropometry

Also called static anthropometry, structural anthropometry includes many dimensions relating to the body at rest. Figure 4.1 illustrates those dimensions that clearly impact bathroom space planning and will be important to the design applications that will be detailed in Chapter 6.

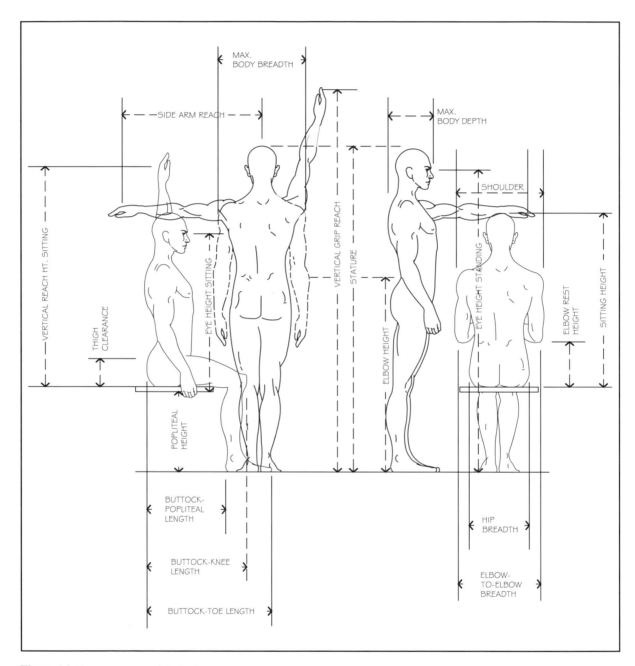

Figure 4.1 These are some of the body measurements that influence interior space planning. (Redrawn from *Human Dimension & Interior Space* by Julius Panero and Martin Zelnik [1979, Watson-Guptill Publications] pg. 30)

The dimensions presented in Figure 4.1 are defined as follows:

- Stature is the vertical distance from the floor to the top of the head. It impacts such spatial considerations as minimum height of door openings or showerhead heights.

- Eye height while standing is the vertical distance from the floor to the inner corner of the eye. It dictates and impacts such things as sight lines, or the height of wall sconces, mirrors, or wall art.

- Elbow height is the vertical distance from the floor to the depression formed at the elbow. This affects such things as comfortable counter heights, lavatory sink heights, and some grab bar heights.

- Sitting height is the vertical distance from the sitting surface to the top of the head when a person is sitting erect. This impacts the heights of such things as the privacy wall at a toilet or at the bath/shower area.

- Eye height while sitting is the vertical distance from the sitting surface to the inner corner of the eye with the person sitting erect. This dictates the sight lines that will influence makeup/dressing counter lighting and mirrors, or window heights.

- Mid-shoulder height sitting is the vertical distance from the sitting surface to the point of the shoulder midway between the lower neck and the acromion (outmost point of the shoulder). It will influence the location of neck or head rests in the tub.

- Shoulder breadth (width) is the maximum horizontal distance across the deltoid muscles. It is very important in determining needed clearance between lavatory sinks, for walk aisles, or in helping to determine shower sizes.

- Elbow to elbow breadth is the horizontal distance with the elbows flexed and resting against body. It is critical to the position a person might assume to groom or wash the hair, and influences shower width and depth, or the space between mirrors and returning walls.

- Hip breadth is the breadth of the body measured across the widest portion of the hip. It impacts bench or seat width, bathtub width, and clearance and passage.

- Elbow rest height is the height from the top of the sitting surface to the bottom of the tip of the elbow. It impacts such things as armrests, some grab bar placement and vanity counter heights.

- Thigh clearance is the vertical distance from a sitting surface to the top of the thigh at the point where the thigh and abdomen intersect. This is important when planning full-depth knee spaces, including the apron or drawer height.

- Knee height is the vertical distance from the floor to the midpoint of the kneecap and it is useful when planning a partial knee space.

- Popliteal height (behind knee) is the vertical distance from the floor to the underside portion of the thigh just behind the knee while a person is seated. It impacts the height of benches and seats, and should impact toilet heights.

- Buttock to popliteal length is the horizontal distance from the rearmost surface of the buttock to the back of the lower leg. It indicates the necessary depth for seats, benches, elongated or standard toilet seats, or bidets.

- Maximum body depth is the horizontal distance between the most anterior point, usually the chest or abdomen, to the most posterior point, usually found in the buttocks or shoulder. It influences shower sizes, clearance and passage. To accommodate people who use mobility aids, this measurement must include the aid.

- Maximum body breadth is the distance, including arms, across the body. It impacts the widths of aisles, doors and doorways, as well as shower and tub sizes, and the width of vanity areas at the sink. To accommodate people who use mobility aids, this measurement must include the aid.

Functional Anthropometry

Functional anthropometry is the measurement of the body in motion. It includes movement of body parts in relationship to one another and measures of strength. Because it is more complex, it is more difficult to accurately measure. However, certain measurements are very helpful to bathroom planning, mainly the reach range and the functional space of a person using a variety of mobility aids.

• Vertical reach height sitting is the height above the sitting
surface of the tip of the middle finger when the arm, hand, and
fingers are extended vertically. It impacts general overhead,
shower and bathtub controls, as well as storage.

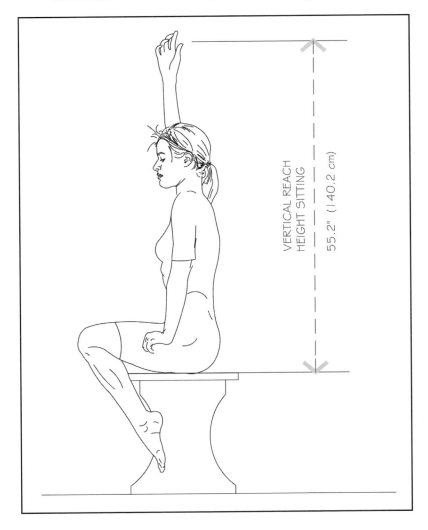

VERTICAL REACH
HEIGHT SITTING

55.2" (140.2 cm)

Figure 4.2 As a population, women
are shorter than men so we have
indicated the sitting adult female
vertical reach height. If a design
accommodated this shorter reach, it
would also include 95% of women and
others with a taller reach. (Redrawn
from *Human Dimension & Interior
Space* by Julius Panero and Martin
Zelnik [1979, Watson-Guptill
Publications] pg. 100)

• Vertical grip reach is the distance from the floor to the top of a bar grasped in the hand, raised as high as it can without discomfort, while the subject stands erect. It is important in planning the height of bookshelves, storage shelves or controls. Vertical grip reach from a seated position is also important in design that accommodates operating from a seated position.

Figure 4.3 The vertical grip reach is useful in determining maximum height for readily accessed storage. This drawing and related measurements are based on the adult female in the 5th percentile, this time in a standing position. (Redrawn from *Human Dimension & Interior Space* by Julius Panero and Martin Zelnik [1979, Watson-Guptill Publications] pg. 100)

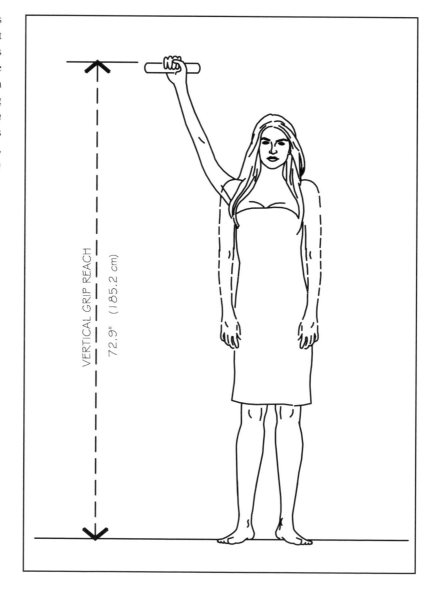

VERTICAL GRIP REACH

72.9" (185.2 cm)

• Side arm grip reach is the distance from the centerline of the body to the outside surface of a bar grasped in the hand, stretched horizontally without experiencing discomfort or strain, while the subject stands erect. This measurement helps determine a comfortable height for fixture controls and general storage. There seems to be more information available on this dimension for a standing person, but the data and its application involve the seated user as well.

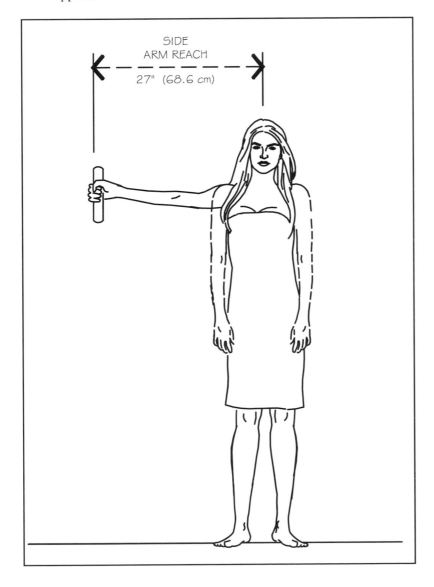

SIDE
ARM REACH

27" (68.6 cm)

Figure 4.4 Whether seated or standing, the side arm grip reach will influence placement of stored items and controls. These numbers are based on a standing adult female in the 5th percentile. (Redrawn from *Human Dimension & Interior Space* by Julius Panero and Martin Zelnik [1979, Watson-Guptill Publications] pg. 100)

• Forward grip reach or thumb tip reach is the distance to the tip of the thumb measured with the subject's shoulders against the wall, with the arm extended forward and index finger touching the tip of the thumb. This dimension influences depth and height of work counters and shelves above the counters as well as general storage.

Figure 4.5 Using the dimension for forward grip reach based on adult females in the 5th percentile is a good basis for planning within the reach of most people. (Redrawn from *Human Dimension & Interior Space* by Julius Panero and Martin Zelnik [1979, Watson-Guptill Publications] pg. 100)

FORWARD GRIP
OR
THUMB TIP REACH

26.6"

HEIGHT AND REACH RANGES

Height and reach ranges vary according to stature, physical ability and obstructions. The height range within a person's reach is useful for planning functional storage, fixtures, fittings and controls in the bathroom.

- The lower end of a forward reach range is 15 inches to 24 inches (38 cm to 61 cm) off the floor, depending on a person's ability to bend. The upper length can go as high as 72 inches (183 cm) depending on a person's stature and any obstruction, such as a counter or shelf.

- The average person who remains seated to maneuver in the bathroom has a forward reach range of 15 inches to 44 inches.

- A standing person who has difficulty bending may have a forward reach range of 24 inches to 72 inches (61 cm to 183 cm).

- A person who use crutches, walkers, or in some way needs their hands to maintain balance, has a slightly different reach range, depending on their mobility aid and physical ability.

Combining these reach ranges with the functional limits of reaching over a 25 inch (64 cm) deep counter, a universal reach range of 15 inches to 48 inches (38–122 cm) has been suggested. This range is generally accepted and used to guide placement of storage, controls and more.

	Seated User	Standing, Mobility Impaired Person	Standing Person 5' 3" – 5' 7"	Universal
Lower Limit–Bending	15"	15"	15"	15"
Lower Limit–No Bending	—	24"	24"	24"
Upper Limit	48"	72"	79 1/2"	48"

Figure 4.6 Working with the functional dimensions and reach ranges of a variety of people, universal design proponents use the universal reach range to accommodate most people.

RANGE-OF-JOINT MOTION

Range-of-joint motion is another aspect of human dimension that obviously impacts the design of the space and components within a bathroom. These include: movements of the hands, wrists, and fingers; movement and flexibility of the shoulders and elbows; bending or twisting at the waist or spine; and movement of the knees. Because no joint operates in isolation, it is difficult to generate accurate and useful information regarding range of motion of joints. However, understanding the areas to consider will help in developing a space that works for a specific client. If you can observe and estimate a client's range-of-joint motion, your design and specifications can more accurately meet the client's needs.

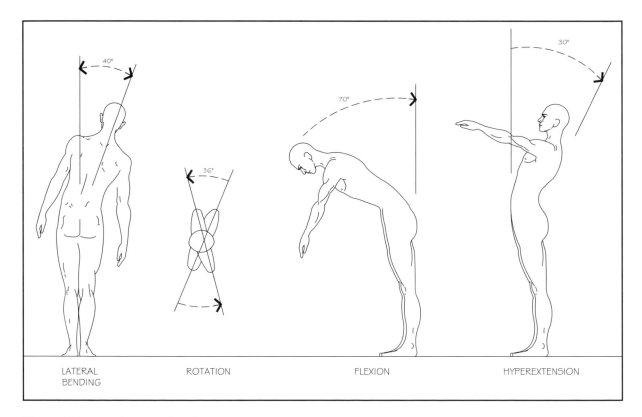

Figure 4.7 A person's range of motion in the spine and shoulders can impact the appropriate size of a shower and location of its fittings. (Redrawn from *Human Dimension & Interior Space* by Julius Panero and Martin Zelnik [1979, Watson-Guptill Publications] pg. 115)

MOBILITY AIDS

There is a growing amount of useful data related to movement and maneuvering, including information related to walking or moving with an assistive device. Although this data seems less plentiful, Panero and Zelnik do offer minimal parameters. Access guidelines such as those from the American National Standards Institute (ANSI) or Uniform Federal Accessibility Standard (UFAS) can be helpful. One critical rule is to consider the person and the aid as one. And, just as for a person who does not use a mobility aid, these figures increase when the person using an aid goes from a static position to motion.

Figure 4.8 These minimum allowances will help in planning spatial clearance. Note that in this case, using the larger dimensions of percentile of adult males provides clearances for any human of smaller dimensions as well. (Redrawn from *Human Dimension & Interior Space* by Julius Panero and Martin Zelnik [1979, Watson-Guptill Publications] pg. 54)

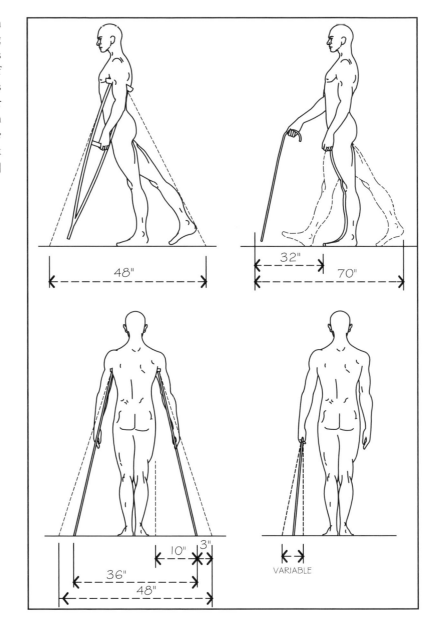

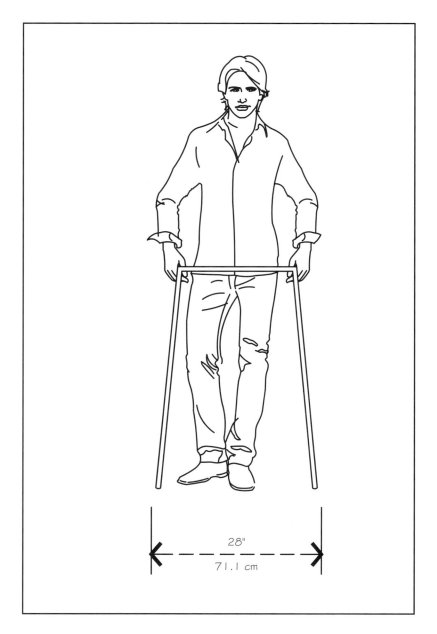

Figure 4.9 The width of a walker will determine the minimum clearance needed. (Redrawn from *Human Dimension & Interior Space* by Julius Panero and Martin Zelnik [1979, Watson-Guptill Publications] pg. 54)

Figure 4.10 In this case, the clearance dimensions must be based on the actual user and dog, but the given dimension of 30 inches could be used as an absolute minimum. (Redrawn from *Human Dimension & Interior Space* by Julius Panero and Martin Zelnik [1979, Watson-Guptill Publications] pg. 54)

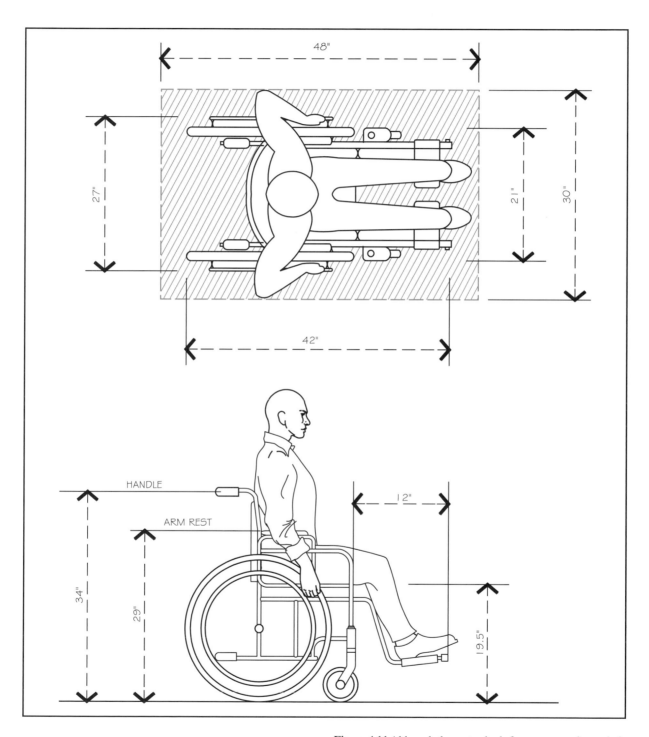

Figure 4.11 Although these standards for a person using a chair are useful in general, it is much better to measure the person in their chair. The variables are impacted by the person's size and ability as well as the design and fit of the chair.

COMFORT ZONE

Based on psychological factors, we can also identify a body buffer zone or comfort zone. We maintain this personal space between ourselves and others who are walking, talking or just standing with us. While we maintain a greater distance with strangers, the personal or close zone will be most applicable to bathroom design.

Figure 4.12 Based on a shoulder breadth of 24 inches and a body depth of 18 inches, a minimum area of approximately 3 square feet per person is a guide in planning a space to be shared. (Redrawn from *Human Dimension & Interior Space* by Julius Panero and Martin Zelnik [1979, Watson-Guptill Publications] pg. 41)

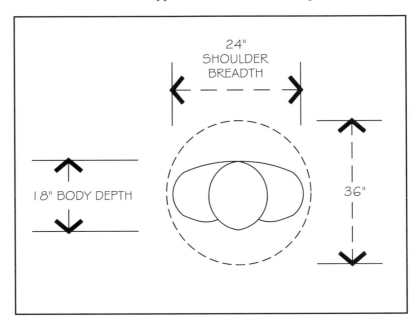

ANTHROPOMETRY OF CHILDREN

Historically there has been very little anthropometric data available regarding children. However, given the growing national focus on childhood health and safety, we can expect this to change. Although functional data would be most applicable, body dimensions of children are available and can be a starting point for the design of child-oriented spaces.

Figure 4.13 The height and breadth of children, both standing and seated, can be useful dimensions when planning a bathroom that must accommodate them as they grow. (Redrawn from *Human Dimension & Interior Space* by Julius Panero and Martin Zelnik [1979, Watson-Guptill Publications] pages 106-107)

Stature (Height)		6 years	11 years	Hip Breadth		6 years	11 years
95 Percentile	Boys	50.4	61.8	95 Percentile Boys		9.3	12
	Girls	49.9	62.9	Girls		9.3	13.3
5 Percentile	Boys	50.4	61.8	95 Percentile Boys		9.3	12
	Girls	49.9	62.9	Girls		9.3	13.3
Sitting (Height)				Popliteal Height (to knee from floor when sitting)			
95 Percentile	Boys	27.4	31.7	95 Percentile Boys		12.8	16.3
	Girls	27.1	32.8	Girls		12.6	16.4
5 Percentile	Boys	23.7	26.7	95 Percentile Boys		10.4	13.3
	Girls	23.1	27.4	Girls		10.2	13.1
Elbow to Elbow Breadth				Buttock Popliteal Length (wall to back of knee when sitting)			
95 Percentile	Boys	11.3	14.7	95 Percentile Boys		12.8	16.3
	Girls	11.1	14.7	Girls		12.6	16.4
5 Percentile	Boys	8.5	10.1	95 Percentile Boys		11.3	14.5
	Girls	8.3	9.6	Girls		11.3	15

(Measurements in inches)

ERGONOMIC AND UNIVERSAL DESIGN

Based on anthropometric data and other human factors, ergonomics is the study of the relationship of people to their environment. For us, ergonomic design is the application of human factors data to the design of products and spaces to improve function and efficiency. Universal design builds on ergonomics to improve the use of products, spaces and systems equally for people of a variety of size, ages and abilities. This basis for the design guidelines and applications are detailed in Chapter 6 and throughout the book.

Universal design is inclusive and equitable, meeting the needs of a great number and variety of people. It is much more than the misconception that it is design limited to medical solutions for access challenges.

HISTORY AND STATE OF THE ART

Since the end of World War II, awareness of the need for improved access and universal design has been growing. Currently, we are experiencing unprecedented interest, worldwide, in the design of environments and products that respect the diversity of human beings. Nowhere is this more true than in the bathroom (and kitchen) encompassing activities of daily life critical to everyone.

People are living longer, largely due to healthier lifestyles, better medicine, and vaccines and sanitation that have virtually eliminated many killer infectious diseases. We are redefining retirement to encompass active adult living, and our designs must include the support that will enable active lifestyles. In addition, more people are living with disabilities and they want to live better. There is a huge population of veterans with disabilities. Antibiotics and other medical advances have enabled people to survive accidents and illnesses that were previously fatal.

According to the U.S. Census Bureau, in 2000, 49.7 million people in the United States (19.3% of the population) had some level of disability, and approximately 31.2 million (12%) had a severe disability. In addition, the National Center for Injury Prevention and Control estimates that for every 100,000 people age 55 to 85, over 3,500 had an unintentional fall in the year 2000. For people age 65 to 85, that number jumps to 4,652 unintentional falls per 100,000 people.

In short, in response to our current society, universal design concepts must be applied to planning a bathroom so that it will function for, and benefit, all the residents of, and visitors to, a home.

Ron Mace, FAIA, known as the father of universal design, defined it as "the design of products and environments to be useable by all people to the greatest extent possible." From 1994 to 1997, Mace led a research and demonstration project at the Center for Universal Design at NC State University, funded by the U.S. Department of Education's National Institute on Disability and Rehabilitation Research (NIDRR), which included the development of universal design guidelines or principles.

Following is the Center for Universal Design's current list of the Seven Principles of Universal Design with design applications for the bathroom. You might find these principles a good checklist to use in the design process, as additional criteria when choosing between options.

1. Equitable Use

Design is useful and marketable to people with diverse abilities. Design provides the same means of use for all users: identical whenever possible; equivalent when not. It avoids segregating or stigmatizing any users. Provisions for privacy, security and safety should be equally available to all users. And the design should be appealing to all users.

Design applications include rocker light switches, an automatically-opening toilet, and motion-sensor lighting, ventilation or water at the vanity.

Figure 4.14 The most common example of universal design is the lever handle. This example does not stigmatize and appeals to all users. (Courtesy of Schlage)

2. Flexibility in Use

Design accommodates a wide range of individual preferences and abilities. It provides choice in methods of use and accommodates right- or left-handed access and use. The design facilitates the user's accuracy and precision. And it provides adaptability to the user's pace.

Design applications include a folding or built-in tub seat and reinforcement for, or installation of, multiple grab bars to support tub or shower use by a seated or standing user. Other applications include grab bars for use in a horizontal or vertical position, or that can be folded down out of the way.

Figure 4.15 A fold-up seat offers flexibility in use, providing for a seated or standing shower. (Courtesy of Hafele)

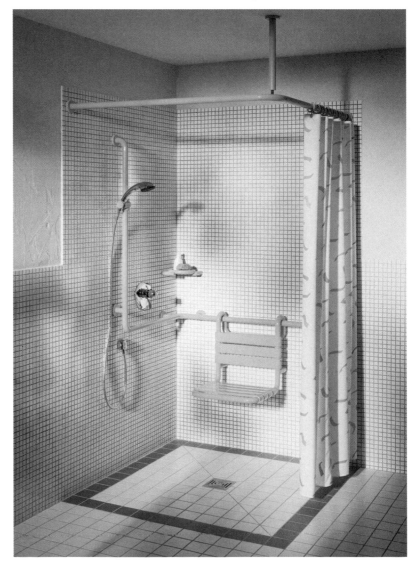

3. Simple and Intuitive Use

Design is easy to understand, regardless of the user's experience, knowledge, language skills or current concentration level. It eliminates unnecessary complexity and is consistent with user expectations and intuition. The design accommodates a wide range of literacy and language skills. It arranges information consistent with its importance. And it provides effective prompting and feedback during and after task completion.

Design applications include single-lever faucet operation that is left for hot and right for cool. Or the use of red to indicate hot and blue to indicate cold.

4. Perceptible Information

Design communicates necessary information effectively to the user, regardless of ambient conditions or the user's sensory abilities. It uses different modes (pictorial, verbal, tactile) for redundant presentation of essential information. The design provides adequate contrast between essential information and its surroundings. It maximizes "legibility" of essential information. It differentiates elements in ways that can be described (i.e., makes it easy to give instructions or directions). And it is compatible with a variety of techniques or devices used by people with sensory limitations.

Design applications include a digital temperature control that both makes a sound and blinks when temperature limits are reached. Or, lighting controls that light up in the "off" position and go dark when the light is on.

5. Tolerance for Error

Design minimizes hazards and the adverse consequences of accidental or unintended actions. It arranges elements to minimize hazards and errors, with the most-used elements being the most accessible, and hazardous elements eliminated, isolated or shielded. The design provides warnings of hazards and errors, and fail-safe features. It discourages unconscious action in tasks that require vigilance.

Design applications include GFCI receptacles that reduce risk of shock, temperature-limiting faucets that prevent accidental scalding, and timed automatic shut-offs on dryers, irons or ventilation.

6. Low Physical Effort

Design can be used efficiently, comfortably and with a minimum of fatigue. It allows the user to maintain a neutral body position and use reasonable operating forces. It minimizes repetitive actions and sustained physical effort.

Design applications include lever handles, remote controls for operating windows, and remote flushers, as well as motion-activated appliances and fittings, and conveniently located towel bars and toilet paper holders.

7. Size and Space for Approach and Use

Appropriate size and space are provided for approach, reach, manipulation and use, regardless of the user's body size, posture or mobility. Design provides a clear line of sight to important elements for any seated or standing user. Reach to all components is comfortable for any seated or standing user. Variations in hand and grip size are accommodated. There is adequate space for the use of assistive devices or personal assistance.

Design applications include full-height mirrors, movable (portable) storage, knee space at a vanity sink, and private toilet compartments that incorporate 30 inches x 48 inches of clear floor space.

Figure 4.16 Movable bath storage provides space for approach and use. (Courtesy of Villeroy & Boch)

The term "universal design" is sometimes inaccurately used as the politically correct description of compliance with the Americans with Disabilities Act (ADA) and other access standards or guidelines. While access standards and guidelines are important as a minimum, universal design is a broader approach that works to incorporate the needs of all users and is not limited to any one specific group. Universal design is an ideal, a way of thinking, whereas code compliance is often simply following a dictate.

A number of terms are used almost interchangeably with universal design.

- **Lifespan design** refers to the aspect of universal design that provides for the changes that may occur in the lifespan of household members, such as the birth and growth of children, or the return home after a skiing accident that results in a broken bone.

- **Trans-generational design** refers to design that acknowledges and supports the multiple generations commonly living under one roof today.

- **Barrier-free design** is an older term, first used to refer to solutions that removed barriers in the environment. While removing barriers is still one important aspect, in North America universal design has been embraced as a broader, more positive approach and term. Universal design seeks to eliminate building of architectural or structural barriers that will need to be removed at a later time.

- **Accessible design** or **accessibility** is a function of compliance with regulations or criteria that established a minimum level of design necessary to accommodate people with disabilities, i.e. "wheelchair accessible."

- **Adaptable design** refers to features that are either adjustable or capable of being easily added or removed to "adapt" the unit to individual needs or preferences.

- **Visit-ability** refers to basic accommodations that will allow people of differing abilities to visit a home. In terms of bath design, visit-ability requires at least one bath on the main floor, with a minimum 32 inch wide clear passage at the door. In some jurisdictions, it includes requirements for clear floor space and reinforcement for possible addition of grab bars.

- **FlexHousing** is a Canadian concept in housing that incorporates, at the design and construction stage, the ability to make future changes easily and with minimum expense, to meet the evolving needs of its occupants. FlexHousing is simply an approach to designing and building homes based on the principles of adaptability, accessibility, affordability and healthy housing.

  The FlexHousing concept of accessibility is user-friendly and its features add convenience and practicality to the functions of a home. Another consideration is the reduction of potential hazards. Although the initial cost of FlexHousing is slightly more than a conventional home, FlexHousing features recover their investment over the long-term because pre-engineered features allow for easy and inexpensive change and renovation. The integration of healthy building materials and innovative housing technology or Healthy Housing protects the health of the occupants and the environment.

Dispelling Myths

There are many misconceptions regarding universal design. Let's put an end to the most common ones.

Myth 1: Universal design is nothing more than design for people in wheelchairs.

Fact: The opposite is true. To be considered universal, a design will be accessible not only to people in wheelchairs, but also to people of most sizes, shapes and abilities. Universal design applies to people tall or short, young or old, left-handed or right-handed, visitors to an unfamiliar city or home, parents with children, people carrying packages, and more.

Myth 2: Universal design only helps people with disabilities and older people.

Fact: Universal design extends the benefits of functional design to many people including short or tall people, large people, frail people, pregnant women, children, or even people traveling with much to carry or where there is a language barrier — everyone eventually.

Myth 3: Universal design costs more than traditional design.

Fact: Many universal concepts are standard products and cost no more than traditional products. The degree of customization and quality of the products will have the greater impact on cost.

Myth 4: Universal design is stigmatizing because it looks medical.

Fact: The best universal design is invisible. When done well, universal design enhances both the appearance and personality of a space, as well as the function of that space, for a variety of users.

ACCESS CODES, LAWS, AND STANDARDS

In the U.S., most existing access-related laws, codes, and standards are intended as minimum criteria for access for people with disabilities. While this is not universal design, the related guidelines can serve as a starting point for universal thinking.

American National Standard for Accessible and Useable Buildings and Facilities (ANSI A117.1)

The first edition of the American National Standard for Accessible and Useable Buildings and Facilities (ANSI A117.1) was issued in 1961. Since then, the standard has been updated and revised several times; the last revision of the standard occurred in 2003.

Since the International Code Council (ICC) is the current secretariat for the standard, it is referred to as the ICC/ANSI standard and includes technical design guidelines for making buildings and sites accessible to, and usable by, people with disabilities. The ICC/ANSI standard is the referenced technical standard for compliance with the accessibility requirements of the International Building Code and many other state and local codes. Earlier editions of the ANSI standard are the referenced technical criteria for accessibility compliance required by the BOCA National Building Code, the Standard Building Code, the Uniform Building Code, and other state and local codes.

The 1986, 1992, and 1998 editions of the ANSI A117.1 standard are also U. S. Department of Housing and Urban Development (HUD) approved "safe harbors" for compliance with the technical requirements of the Fair Housing Amendments Act of 1988 (accepted in place of these requirements), a federal mandate for accessibility in multifamily housing. "Safe harbors" and the Fair Housing Act are further discussed here.

UNIFORM FEDERAL ACCESSIBILITY STANDARDS (UFAS)

First published in 1984, Uniform Federal Accessibility Standards (UFAS) includes criteria for the design and construction of federal buildings to provide access for people with disabilities. UFAS is the technical standard referenced by two federal mandates for accessibility: the Architectural Barriers Act (ABA) and Section 504 of the Rehabilitation Act of 1973 (Section 504). The ABA requires access to buildings constructed, altered, leased, or financed in whole or in part by the United States; and Section 504 requires that federally financed programs and activities be accessible to people with disabilities. Section 504 also requires access to federally financed newly constructed and altered buildings. The technical provisions of UFAS are largely the same as the 1980 ANSI A117.1 standard.

FAIR HOUSING ACT ACCESSIBILITY GUIDELINES

First published in 1991, the Fair Housing Act Accessibility Guidelines (the Guidelines) provide architects, builders, developers, and others, technical guidance for compliance with the accessibility requirements of the Fair Housing Amendments Act of 1988 (the Act). The Act covers newly constructed multifamily buildings containing at least four dwellings built for first occupancy on or after March 13, 1991.

"SAFE HARBORS"

In addition to the Guidelines, HUD has approved several "safe harbors" for compliance with the Act. A "safe harbor" is a standard that is legally recognized as compliant with the requirements of a code or guideline. The current "safe harbors" are:

- The 1986, 1992, and 1998 editions of the ANSI A117.1 standard, when used with the Fair Housing Act, HUD's Fair Housing Act regulations, and the Guidelines.

- HUD's The Fair Housing Act Design Manual (1998).

- The Code Requirements for Housing Accessibility 2000 (CRHA), published by the International Code Council in October 2000.

- International Building Code 2000 (IBC), as amended by the IBC's 2001 Supplement to the International Codes.

"Safe harbor" standards constitute safe harbors only when adopted and implemented in accordance with the policy statement that HUD published in the Federal Register on March 23, 2000. That policy statement notes, for example, that if a jurisdiction adopts a model building code that HUD has determined conforms with the design and construction requirements of the Act (such as the IBC 2000, as amended by the IBC's 2001 Supplement to the International Codes), then covered residential buildings that are constructed in accordance with plans and specifications approved during the building permitting process will be in compliance with the requirements of the Act.

If the building code official has waived one or more of those requirements, or the building code official has incorrectly interpreted or applied the building code provisions, then the buildings are not in compliance. In addition, adoption of a HUD recognized "safe harbor" does not change HUD's responsibility to conduct an investigation if it receives a complaint.

AMERICANS WITH DISABILITIES ACT ACCESSIBILITY GUIDELINES

First produced in 1991, the Americans with Disabilities Act Guidelines (ADAAG) are guidelines for compliance with the accessibility requirements of the ADA. The ADA addresses access to the workplace (Title I), state and local government services (Title II), and places of public accommodation and commercial facilities (Title III). It also requires phone companies to provide telecommunications relay services for people who have hearing or speech impairments (Title IV) and miscellaneous instructions for federal agencies that enforce the law (Title V). While not applicable to residential spaces, the ADA and the ADAAG are noteworthy as the action that brought our society to attention regarding access.

CANADIAN POLICIES AND PRACTICES

The National Building Code (NBC), developed by the Canadian Codes Center of the Institute for Research in Construction (a branch of the National Research Center), is the standard on which many of the provincial regulations are based. The Canadian Standards Association (CSA) developed B651, the Barrier Free Design Standards in 1975. This standard, now called B651-04 Accessible Design for the Built Environment, specifies minimum technical requirements, including a section that addresses kitchen and bathroom specifications. It has been revised many times. As is true in the U.S., this standard does not have the force of law unless mandated by a particular province. It is based on "average adult" dimension and to effectively use the concepts, a designer would need to consult with the end user.

Because of provincial jurisdiction, progress has been difficult in Canada in the development and enforcement of national civil rights or legislation related to housing, such as the ADA and the FHA in the United States. In 1982, the federal government enacted the Charter of Rights and Freedoms including Section 15 prohibiting discrimination on the basis of mental or physical handicap. However, the Charter of Rights has not been as thoroughly implemented into specific enforceable legislation as the FHA and ADA in the U.S.

In Ontario, the building code includes specific requirements for accessible buildings, and in 2001, the Ontarians with Disabilities Act (ODA) was passed. The purpose of the ODA is to improve opportunities for people with disabilities, and to enable them to become involved in the identification, removal and prevention of barriers faced by persons with disabilities.

Recognizing the difficulties in mandating change, the Canadian federal government, through Canada Mortgage and Housing (CMHC), has chosen to assist the development of housing through financial instruments such as grants, loans and insurance arrangements. CMHC assistance helps low-income and older Canadians, people with disabilities, and Aboriginals, with housing options and expenses.

For example, in 1986 the Residential Rehabilitation Assistance Program (RRAP-D) for Persons with Disabilities was developed to offer financial assistance to homeowners and landlords to undertake accessibility work to modify dwellings occupied, or intended for occupancy by, low-income persons with disabilities. Another example is the Home Adaptations for Seniors' Independence (HASI) program, which helps homeowners and landlords pay for minor home adaptations to extend the time low-income seniors can live in their own homes independently.

SUMMARY

There is a wealth of information available to plan bathroom spaces based on realistic human dimensions. Anthropometric studies give you basic dimensions for people of a variety of sizes and ages. Awareness of this information as you develop a plan for a client's bath will help to more accurately determine sizes and spatial relationships in each case.

In this chapter, you have also been presented with a quick summary of federal access laws, codes and standards. While this overview provides a level of familiarity, each bathroom you design may fall under specific local regulations, and you will need to work with your local officials for guidance and technical assistance.

For more information on housing accessibility, contact the U.S. Department of Housing and Urban Development (HUD). For ADA access issues concerning public facilities, contact the U.S. Access Board. To increase your awareness of local access laws, contact the building inspector and consult local homebuilder associations.

As one universal design leader noted, "It is questionable whether accessibility standards will ever encourage designers to practice universal design." However, considering the long-term demographic trends pointing to an increase in older age groups, access needs will not go away, and universal design is a broad and beautiful way to achieve improved access without mandates.

CHAPTER 5: Assessing Needs

A bathroom is a very personal and private space. People use the space in different ways and have different ideas about function, mood and ambience. To design a bathroom, your challenge will be to move past your own assumptions and learn about your clients' personal preferences.

This chapter focuses on assessing the needs of your client in preparation for developing a design. A needs assessment is the critical first step in the design process. Without knowing what your client wants and needs, you cannot know how to design the space.

Needs assessment includes both your client and their house. It involves gathering information about your client and their use of the bathroom, as well as inspecting and measuring the jobsite.

Design programming is the translation of the information about the client into a plan to guide the design process. Developing the design program allows you to make sure you have gathered—and understand—all the information you need to complete the design. In addition, the design program should be reviewed with your client to ascertain that both you and your client agree on the plan for the bathroom project. A design program can even be the basis of your contract.

Design programming is discussed further in Chapter 10, as part of the design process, and a sample program is shown there. However, a brief review of the parts of a typical design program is included here to help emphasize the need for careful and complete client information gathering.

ELEMENTS OF A DESIGN PROGRAM

Goal or Purpose. A statement that describes the project and the client, and defines the scope and the parameters of the project.

Objectives and Priorities. A list of the specific features, items, materials, layout or other details to be included in the design/project.

Activities and Relationships. A list of the different activities to be accommodated in the bathroom, and the fixtures, fittings, materials, cabinetry, lighting, furniture, storage and other details needed to support the activities. Also included is an explanation of how the different spaces of the activities relate, in terms of access, circulation or privacy. Some designers may include charts, matrices or bubble diagrams in this section to visualize the different spaces and the relationships among them.

INTERVIEWING THE CLIENT

From your first meeting with a potential client, you are gathering information. (For ideas on how to keep files on your clients, see *Kitchen & Bath Business Management,* part of the NKBA's *Professional Resource Library.*) Informal conversations can help you learn more about their household, who will use the bathroom, and their goals and dreams for a new bathroom. However, you will soon want a more structured needs-assessment interview and information-gathering session with your client.

Prepare for the Interview

You may want to interview your client in your office or showroom. Alternatively, you may set an appointment and go to your client's home, which provides the opportunity to observe it firsthand. Even if your client is building a new home, a visit to their existing home can help you better understand what your client wants. Your client may feel more comfortable talking in their home, and their existing bathroom(s) may give them clues about things to tell you. Finally, you may also be able to collect initial measurements during the same appointment.

Recording the interview on audio tape gives you an accurate record of information and avoids the need to take notes while talking to the client. However, after the interview, it can be time-consuming to transcribe information from the recording.

Needs Assessment Forms

Using a prepared interview format is helpful. This assures that you gather all the information that you need, and gives you a way to record and later, to organize, the responses to the interview. In some cases, you can give your client a checklist to complete and return to you.

The National Kitchen & Bath Association has a Bathroom Design Survey Form available to its members, and a completed example is included in the Appendix of this book. Familiarity with this Form is necessary for CBD certification.

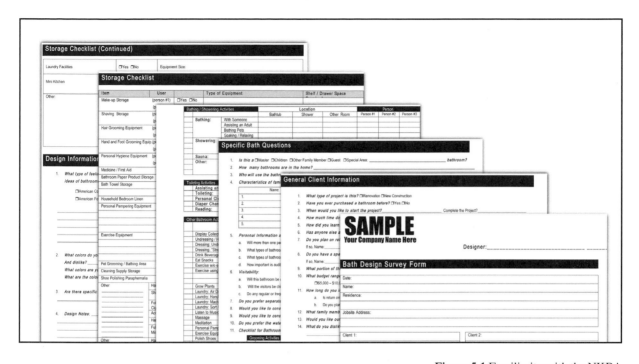

Figure 5.1 Familiarity with the NKBA Bathroom Design Survey Form is necessary for certification. A completed example appears in the Appendix.

In addition, there are twelve forms in this chapter created by the authors for use when gathering information about your client, their home and the bathroom design project. They provide an organized way to complete your interview and jobsite inspection.

You might want to adapt the forms in this chapter to develop an interview format that works well on a computer, and take a laptop with you to record information. All of these forms are found on the CD that comes with this book. The forms can be adapted as needed for your business, and used in either an electronic or a printed format.

The following forms are included:

Client Information Forms

Form 1: Getting to Know Your Client

Form 2: Getting to Know Your Client's Home

Form 5: Your Client's Bathroom Preferences

Checklists for Client Use

Form 3: Checklist for Bathroom Activities

Form 4: Bathroom Storage Inventory

Jobsite and House Information Forms

Form 6: Jobsite Inspection

Form 7: Dimensions of the Bathroom—Floor Plan

Form 8: Dimensions of the Bathroom – Elevations

Form 9: Dimensions of Mechanical Devices

Form 10: Window Measurements

Form 11: Door Measurements

Form 12: Fixture Measurements

Additional forms for planning closets and exercise areas are found in Chapter 8.

Personal Information

In order to complete a client interview, you need to ask some questions about intimate and personal activities related to the bathroom. To put your client at ease, adopt an open and frank approach. Use the correct terms for body functions and avoid euphemisms. Explain that some of the questions may seem personal, but the more information you have, the more successful your design.

During the interview, you will be asking about physical abilities. This can also be a sensitive subject. A client who is getting older may not recognize or accept the physical changes of aging. People with degenerative conditions may not be willing to yield to the impact of the disease on their bodies. Physical limitations can sometimes be hidden for short periods of time, especially with a relative stranger. Again, be open and stress the importance of fully knowing the client's physical situation, in order to develop the most supportive design. For more information on working with clients with special needs, refer to Chapter 9.

GETTING TO KNOW YOUR CLIENT (FORM 1)

The first thing you want to know is who uses the bathroom? Gather information about the users of the bathroom, their physical profiles and any specialized needs they have. For instance, who are the primary users of the bathroom? How old are they? How tall are they?

You will want to collect anthropometric (human measurement) information about your individual clients. This is especially important if your clients have any physical limitations or concerns about access to bathroom activities.

Review Chapter 4 to learn more about the importance of anthropometry and ergonomic design. *Form 1: Getting to Know Your Client* is a tool you can use to collect anthropometric information about your client. *Form 1* is also designed to help you collect information about any of your client's special needs with respect to the bathroom space. For example, do any of the users have special physical needs or situations? Do any of them require a mobility aid, such as a wheelchair or cane?

In addition to the anthropometric information and other special needs, you need to learn a little about your client's attitudes toward bathroom use and activities. It will be important to determine issues such as: will more than one person be using the bathroom at the same time? What are they comfortable doing in a shared bathroom space? *Form 1* can assist you in gathering this information.

Your Client's Home: Location, Location, Location

Start with the big picture. Where is the home located? How will the location influence the design of the bathroom? Location determines climate, telling you whether there are cold winters, hot summers or long seasons where the windows might be open to the outside air. Will there be views of the ocean, a lake, mountains, trees or a city skyline, to be captured in the design? Or does the location determine that the bathroom needs to be more inwardly focused, sheltered from things such as traffic noise or close-by buildings?

Location of the home can also give you a clue to your client's lifestyle. A bathroom in an urban apartment, a large ranch home in a rural area, or a condominium in a resort community represent different types of homes as well as lifestyles, and thus different types of bathroom design needs.

Finally, different countries, as well as different regions of the same country, can have variation in design trends. Vernacular housing describes housing styles that are typical of, or common to, a region, and that have been influenced by factors such as climate, available building materials, and cultural heritage. Knowing something about the vernacular housing of the area of your client's home may give you some ideas about style, color or materials to use in the bathroom design.

What Type of Home?

Most bathroom designers work on projects in single-family homes—but not always. Especially in urban areas, a designer may work on a home that is an apartment, townhouse, or other type of multi-family structure. There may be some unique concerns in this type of home. For example, in many multi-family housing communities, plans for remodeling must be approved by a group such as the homeowners' association. You may be limited in making changes affecting the home's exterior. Likewise, plumbing changes may be limited. Carefully consider any possible factors that could occur in a multi-family project.

Sometimes, single-family housing may be in a community with a homeowners' association with rules affecting renovations. In addition, sometimes there may be covenants in a property's deed that could affect a bathroom remodeling project, such as the size of an addition or the style and placement of windows.

While you are considering these special and legal situations that can affect your design for the bathroom, be sure to consider the impact of the building permit process. The books *Residential Construction* and *Kitchen & Bath Systems* discuss building codes and permits in more detail. Both are part of the NKBA's *Professional Resource Library*.

GETTING TO KNOW YOUR CLIENT'S HOME (FORM 2)

Another part of the big picture is the total home. If you are working on a remodeling project, ask to take a tour of the existing home. Observe the size of the home, the number of bedrooms and other bathrooms. How will traffic flow to the bathroom you will be designing?

A tour of your client's home will also be useful to get a sense of style and color. Ask your client to describe what they like and do not like about other rooms in the home. Use this information to give you clues about design preferences.

During the home tour, note what rooms are on the other sides of the bathroom walls. This information might be useful as you think about factors such as "borrowing" space from another room, planning for sound insulation or reconfiguring plumbing. Look for details that might give you valuable information and prevent surprises during the construction phase, such as the presence of heating or cooling ducts. You might want to make a sketch of the bathroom space, or do this as part of the jobsite inspection (See *Form 6*).

Take along a copy of *Form 2: Getting to Know Your Client's Home* when you do a home tour. This form can be used to gather information about the "big picture" of your client's home and their bathroom.

A camera can be a useful tool during a home tour. Be sure to ask permission first. Use the camera to make visual notes of features that will be useful to remember during the design process. A digital camera is particularly helpful for this type of documentation, as pictures are easily transferred to a computer file. Also, take pictures of family members, favorite accessory items or views from windows. Later, you may be able to incorporate these into presentation drawings for a wonderful personal touch.

The Home of the Future

Finish your understanding of the big picture by talking to your client about future plans for the home. Is this a home in which they plan to retire? Will they be likely to remodel or expand this home in the future? *Form 1: Getting to Know Your Client* and *Form 2: Getting to Know Your Client's Home* can guide you in gathering this type of information.

While you are learning about future plans for their home, you can ask about the future of their family or household. "Expanding" households are typically younger, and are at the life stage where they can expect to add new household members, such as by marriage or birth. Sometimes a new household member is an older relative. "Launching" households are more likely to be older, with children that will soon be leaving. Future changes in household size or composition can influence who uses a bathroom, as well as the activities that take place in that space.

ACTIVITIES IN THE BATHROOM (FORM 3)

You now know something about who is using the bathroom, so you want to gather information about what they actually do there. Major bathroom activities fall into three categories: grooming; bathing/showering; and toileting. Using these categories will help you design the bathroom centers presented in Chapter 6. There are many different activities that fall into these three categories. In addition, there are other activities that can take place in the bathroom, such as dressing, exercise and laundry.

Since the potential bathroom activities are numerous, you can give your clients an activity checklist to complete (See *Form 3*). This can save time and may get you more complete information. You may want to review the checklist with them and then ask them to complete it at home. Alternatively, you can mail (or email) the checklist to them in advance and then review it during the interview. *Form 3: Checklist for Bathroom Activities* is written for your client to use. It also asks about location and frequency of activities—information that is very useful during the design process.

In addition to the information provided on the checklist, you may need clarification on certain activities. For instance, ask about activities that your client prefers to do while seated or standing. When is privacy important for an activity? What activities might be done in shared space? If your client has completed the checklist in advance, these issues can be discussed at the interview. *Form 3* gives you space to make notes after the client has completed the checklist.

STORAGE IN THE BATHROOM (FORM 4)

Talking about activities in the bathroom can easily lead to discussing your client's storage needs. What does your client want to keep in the bathroom? Where will they use the different items stored in the bathroom? How frequently do they use each item? These are some examples of information that is useful to you, the designer, in planning bathroom storage.

The users of the bathroom space can complete the storage inventory checklist in *Form 4: Bathroom Storage Inventory*. This inventory is divided into several sections, by location of storage: near the vanity/lavatory/grooming center; near the bathtub/shower; near the toilet/bidet; and other; as well as for display only. In addition, your client is asked to identify frequency of use and type of storage. The *Form 4* checklist has many common bathroom items already listed to make it easier to use. This checklist will be very helpful in the design process, so encourage your client to be thorough in completing it. Also, it is helpful if the client has completed this inventory in advance of the interview.

If you are going to design a clothes closet adjacent to, or integrated into, the bathroom, you may need more detail than is provided in the bathroom storage inventory. *Form 13: Clothes Storage Inventory for Hanging Clothes, Form 14: Clothes Storage Inventory for Folded, Rolled, and Other Types of Clothes*, and *Form 15: Worksheet for Folded or Rolled Clothing* are available to gather specific information for designing closets. If you will be incorporating an exercise area in or near the bathroom, you may want to use *Form 17: Assessment for Exercise Area* to help in planning the space. These forms are provided in Chapter 8 along with more information about planning closets and exercise areas.

For the bathroom itself, you will want to compare *Form 3: Checklist for Bathroom Activities* with *Form 4: Bathroom Storage Inventory*. Are there supplies needed for an activity that are not included on the storage inventory? Do some of the storage items suggest activities that are not included on the checklist? You may need to go back to the client for clarification.

Towels

Towels need special consideration when designing a bathroom. In addition to the storage inventory information on towels, you need to consider the regular users of the bathroom, their activities, and the size towels they use, to determine how many towel bars are needed. Do not forget to ask about special towel storage features, such as heated towel bars or towel warmers.

Your client may want a linen closet in, or adjacent to, the bathroom. Refer to Chapter 8 for *Form 16: Linen Closet Storage Inventory* for more information on planning linen closets.

YOUR CLIENT'S BATHROOM (FORM 5)

After determining bathroom activities and storage requirements, you need to ask your client what they do and do not like in a bathroom—and what is feasible for their space and budget.

Begin with their current bathroom(s), even ones they are not planning to remodel (at this time). Ask what they do not like about the space. Be very specific. Let your client volunteer information first, such as:

- There is not enough light over the vanity.
- The space feels crowded.
- There are not enough towel bars.

Then ask what they do like, such as:
- The bathtub is comfortable for soaking.
- The towel racks are convenient to the shower.

Ideas suggested by your client, positive or negative, can indicate areas of strong feeling. Remember these as you develop your design.

Next, ask your client to talk about what they want in a bathroom. Let them suggest ideas, but be sure to cover the major features. *Form 5: Your Client's Bathroom Preferences* can help you collect and organize this information.

Client's Preferences and Specifications

Many clients think and dream about a bathroom project before it becomes a reality. They read shelter magazines, visit showrooms and surf the Internet. Many have a file of ideas about design, products, fixtures, materials and other features. By asking questions about preferences—or definite specifications—you are moving from general ideas to specific decisions to be made about the design.

In some cases, your client may have a specific item from the current bathroom to be included in the new one. Or, they may have a salvage piece, such as cabinet or door hardware, to include in the new design. Be sure to determine if there are any pieces like this. Get detailed information such as size, and any mechanical requirements such as plumbing connections. *Form 5: Your Client's Bathroom Preferences* will prompt you to collect this information.

Some clients may prefer to shop for, and select, certain pieces such as a mirror or a faucet, on their own. If the client is going to provide items for the new bathroom, this information will need to be specified in your contract. You and your client will need to agree on the specifications of the items they will provide. Timing will be important as well, so that the installation of the new bathroom is not delayed waiting for a client-provided item.

Budget

At some point, you will need to discuss the project budget. Unless your client has carefully researched the issue before meeting with you, there is a good chance that their budget amount is not in the same range as their ideas. You will probably want to get an idea of the client's budget at the time you are gathering the information you need to develop the design. The farther their ideas are from their pocketbook, the more you will need to focus on priorities. Help your client think about what they really need, want, and would like to have, in their bathroom. The clearer these ideas, the easier it is to make budget decisions.

THE JOBSITE

Before you can begin the actual design, you have one more major assessment. This is of the jobsite. Structurally and mechanically, you need to know if you can make your design ideas work.

If you are not familiar with structural and mechanical systems in a house, review the books *Residential Construction* and *Kitchen & Bath Systems*, both part of the NKBA's *Professional Resource Library*.

Until you are more experienced in "reading" a house and understanding its systems, you may want to enlist the help of a contractor or other knowledgeable person to assist you.

New Construction

If your bathroom project is new construction or an addition, get involved in the planning before construction begins. Get a copy of all drawings that impact your bathroom design. Make sure that you have all dimensions and mechanical information that relates to the bathroom.

Study the plans for the new space. Find out what is fixed and what is flexible. For example, can an entry door be moved or a window relocated? Or, can an interior wall be increased in width to make it work as a plumbing or "wet" wall?

REMODELING (FORM 6)

If you are working on a project that is a remodeling, you need to know all the structural and mechanical information as well, but it may be harder to find. A thorough and detailed inspection of the area and surrounding rooms will be necessary. If your client has plans or drawings of the space, this will be very useful and can save you time. However, you will need to verify that the rooms were actually built as drawn. You may want to make copies of client drawings, so that you can mark them up as needed.

Prepare for your jobsite inspection by making an appointment with your client. Give them an idea of what you need to do, and make sure that you have access to all the areas of the home. You may do the jobsite inspection at the same time you do the client interview, especially if you have to travel a distance to your client's home. Wear comfortable clothes that allow you to bend and stretch. Bring a sturdy measuring tape, graph paper, pencils and flashlight. A camera will also be useful.

Your jobsite inspection needs to cover several areas: overall knowledge about the bathroom and its relationship to other spaces in the home; structure; mechanical systems; access; construction/ installation planning; and dimensions (discussed in the next section). As with the client interview, if you use a prepared form or outline, you will be more likely to get all the information you need. You can follow *Form 6: Jobsite Inspection* to gain a thorough analysis of the needed information.

DIMENSIONS
(FORMS 7 THROUGH 12)

To collect dimensions of the jobsite, use:

- *Form 7: Dimensions of the Bathroom – Floor Plan*
- *Form 8: Dimensions of the Bathroom – Elevations*
- *Form 9: Dimensions of Mechanical Devices*
- *Form 10: Window Measurements*
- *Form 11: Door Measurements*
- *Form 12: Fixture Measurements*

Information on measuring both remodeling and new construction projects, as well as how to prepare project documents, can be found in the book *Kitchen & Bath Drawing*, part of the NKBA's *Professional Resource Library*.

Following are suggestions on how to collect accurate and complete measurements:

- Measure each wall. Take at least two measurements, one low and one high on the wall, to help determine variations in corners. Use these measurements to make a to-scale ($^1/_2$ inch = 1 foot) drawing of the bathroom space (See *Form 7*).

- Measure the ceiling height in several places. Layout a basic elevation of each wall (See *Form 8*).

- If needed, prepare a reflected ceiling plan to note features on the ceiling, such as heat registers, beams or lighting.

- Locate each mechanical connection, such as the soil stack, plumbing supply pipes, and electrical receptacles. (*Form 7*).

- Measure any architectural features in the space, such as columns, arches or beams. Locate these features on the floor plan (*Form 7*) or the elevations (*Form 8*), as appropriate.

- Measure the location and size of each heat register, radiator or other mechanical device. Include items on the walls, floor and ceiling. Record these measurements on *Form 9*, and locate these features on the floor plan and/or elevations.

- Measure each window. Measure the size of the window, frame, and overall size of the window including the trim. Measure the location of the window from the floor, ceiling and corners of the room. Include the height of the sill (See *Form 10*). Note the location of each window on the floor plan and elevations.

- Measure each door, similar to how you measured the window. Locate the height of the door handle. Note the location of doors on the floor plan and elevations. Indicate the door swings (See *Form 11*).

- Measure the size of any fixtures to be removed. Include height, width and depth. Note any potential problems with removal (See *Form 12*).

- Measure the size and location of any fixtures to remain. Include centerline dimensions to determine clearances (See *Form 12*).

PREPARE THE CLIENT

This chapter has detailed a process for assessing the needs of your client and gathering information necessary to design their bathroom. The process is extensive, but time spent on preparation will increase your success. Now that you are prepared, it's never too early to start preparing your client. At the end of the interview and/or jobsite inspection, or when you present your design proposal or contract, spend a few minutes discussing both the design process as well as the construction phase.

First, discuss the time frame of the project. Present a realistic plan for each phase of the project. Indicate to your client what factors may delay the project, and why. Discuss what you will do to keep the project on target. Suggest what your client can do to keep the project on time, such as minimizing change orders.

Talk to your client about what you will need from them. If they are going to do any of the work themselves, such as tearing out or painting, be very clear as to the time frame. At what point will they be needed to review plans and make color or design choices? When will they need to make decisions about fixtures and accessories? When will they need personal items removed from the workspace?

In a bathroom project that involves an addition or remodeling, there will be disruption in your client's home. Emphasize this with your client and reassure them you will do whatever you can to minimize that disruption.

Preparing the client requires continuous communication, starting at the interview stage and continuing throughout the project. Complete information on managing the installation process, including preparing your client, is in the book *Kitchen & Bath Project Management*, part of the NKBA's *Professional Resource Library*.

READY FOR THE DESIGN PROGRAM?

You now have a detailed picture of your client and their ideas about their new bathroom. In addition, you know about the users of the bathroom, activities in the bathroom, and storage needs. You have very specific information about the jobsite. It might be tempting to rush in and begin laying out your ideas. But first, you need to think about the next step in the design process. You need to develop a design program, which is discussed in detail in Chapter 10.

As you develop the design program, you clarify your client's priorities. The forms presented in this chapter can assist you in the process. What do they need or require in the bathroom project? What do they want to have, and what would be desirable? Your goal is to provide all the needs and requirements, most of the "haves", and some of the "desirables". If you and your client are clear on priorities, then it is easier to make compromises or trade-offs due to factors such as budget limitations, product availability or structural problems.

Consider the design program a working document. After you review the program with your client, you may need to make changes as you fine-tune the project plan. Once you and your client agree on the design program, you may ask the client to sign off on the program. This will give you a firm basis for negotiating any change orders as the bathroom project progresses.

You and your client are now prepared for a successful bathroom project.

FORM 1: GETTING TO KNOW YOUR CLIENT

This form collects information about your clients. Use the parts that are appropriate to your design project. A custom design project, or a client with special needs, may require more detailed information.

1. Users of the bathroom:

   Name: _____ Age: _____

   Height: _____ Weight: _____ Handedness: ❑ Right ❑ Left

   Special needs or concerns: _____

   _____

   Name: _____ Age: _____

   Height: _____ Weight: _____ Handedness: ❑ Right ❑ Left

   Special needs or concerns: _____

   _____

   Name: _____ Age: _____

   Height: _____ Weight: _____ Handedness: ❑ Right ❑ Left

   Special needs or concerns: _____

   _____

   Name: _____ Age: _____

   Height: _____ Weight: _____ Handedness: ❑ Right ❑ Left

   Special needs or concerns: _____

   _____

   Name: _____ Age: _____

   Height: _____ Weight: _____ Handedness: ❑ Right ❑ Left

   Special needs or concerns: _____

   _____

FORM 1: GETTING TO KNOW YOUR CLIENT (CONTINUED)

2. Anthropometric Information

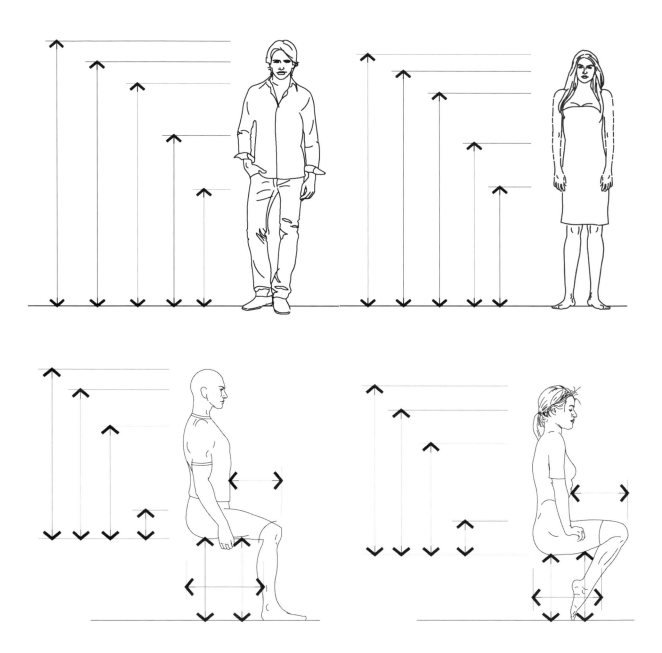

FORM 1: GETTING TO KNOW YOUR CLIENT (CONTINUED)

3. Reach and Grasp Profile

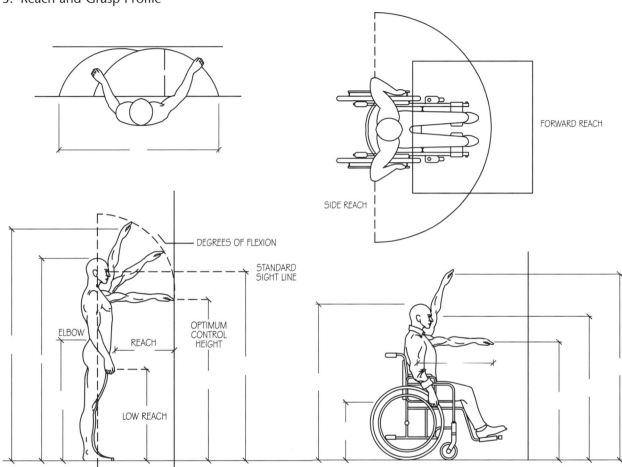

4. Physical Profile

   Physical characteristic(s) affecting activities in the bathroom:

   A. Sight: _____

      Do you wear glasses for: ☐ Reading ☐ Distance

      Are you taking medications that affect your sight? _____

      Are you sensitive to light? _____

   B. Hearing: _____

      What issues regarding your hearing will affect your activities in the bathroom?_____

      _____

   C. Tactile/Touch: _____

      Can you feel hot and cold? _____

FORM 1: GETTING TO KNOW YOUR CLIENT (CONTINUED)

D. Taste/Smell: _____

What issues regarding your sense of taste or smell will affect your activities in the bathroom?

_____

E. Strength and Function: _____

What can you lift? _____ Carry? _____

Do you have more strength on one side than the other? _____

Do you use both hands fully? _____ Palms only? _____

How is your grip? _____

Left side? _____ Right side? _____

F. Balance, Mobility and Assistance: _____

How is your balance: Standing? _____ Bending? _____

Does your mobility or balance vary by time of day? _____

Does an assistant help you: Sometimes? _____ All the time? _____

What adaptive equipment do you use? _____

_____

_____

G. Prognosis: Is your condition stable? Is further deterioration anticipated? Is improvement anticipated? _____

_____

_____

H. Other Physical Concerns: _____

_____

_____

I. Special Safety Concerns: _____

_____

_____

FORM 1: GETTING TO KNOW YOUR CLIENT (CONTINUED)

5. Mobility Aids

If a mobility aid, such as wheel chair, walker, or cane is used, it is important to collect information on the size of the mobility aid, as well as anthropometrical information about the client when using the mobility aid.

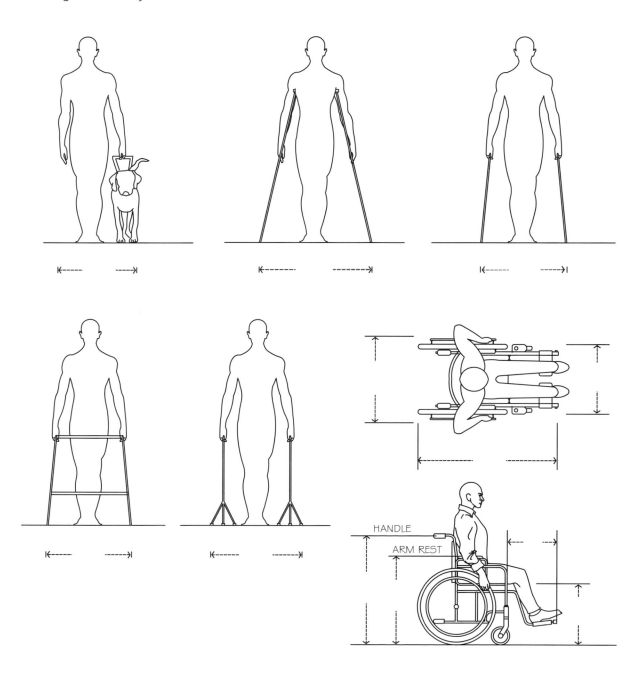

FORM 1: GETTING TO KNOW YOUR CLIENT (CONTINUED)

6. Personal Information about the Bathroom

❏ Will more than one person be using the bathroom at the same time? How often?

_____

_____

❏ What types of bathroom activities can be done in a shared bathroom space?

_____

_____

_____

❏ What types of bathroom activities need to be done in private? _____

_____

_____

_____

❏ How important is auditory privacy? Are bathroom noises a problem? _____

_____

_____

7. Visit-ability

❏ Will this bathroom be used by visitors to the home? Overnight or just for social occasions?

_____

❏ Will the visitors be children or adults? _____

_____

❏ Do any regular or frequent visitors have any physical limitations? _____

_____

_____

FORM 1: GETTING TO KNOW YOUR CLIENT (CONTINUED)

8. Future Plans

   ❏ How long do you plan to live in this home? _____

   _____

   ❏ Do you anticipate changes in your household size or make-up? _____

   _____

   _____

   ❏ Will this affect who uses the bathroom? _____

   _____

   ❏ Is resale value of the home important? _____

   _____

FORM 2: GETTING TO KNOW YOUR CLIENT'S HOME

This form can be used to collect general information about your client's home to help in developing your design. Specific structural and mechanical information is collected in other forms.

Location of home: _____

Type of neighborhood: _____

Type of home: ☐ single-family home ☐ duplex ☐ townhouse ☐ apartment/flat

    ☐ other _____

Structure of home: ☐ one-story ☐ two-story ☐ three-story ☐ ranch ☐ split-level

    ☐ split foyer/raised ranch ☐ other _____

Approximate size of home: _____

Number of bedrooms: _____ Number of bathrooms: _____

Style of home (exterior) _____

Is the home historic? What time period? _____

    Are there historic covenants or restrictions affecting the home? _____

    _____

    _____

Is the home part of a homeowner's association? _____

    Are there any covenants or restrictions affecting the home? _____

    _____

    _____

    Are there any deed restrictions? _____

    _____

    _____

Style of home (interior): _____

_____

_____

FORM 2: GETTING TO KNOW YOUR CLIENT'S HOME (CONTINUED)

Colors? _____

_____

Materials?_____

_____

Furniture?_____

_____

Accessories? _____

_____

Future plans for resale or remodeling? _____

_____

FORM 3: CHECKLIST FOR BATHROOM ACTIVITIES

Directions: Review the list of activities in each section. If it is an activity that you do or want to do in the bathroom, place a check in the first column. Then check the appropriate location and frequency column. Extra lines are left in each section for you to add activities as needed.

Grooming Activities								
✓ Activity	Location						Frequency	
	Vanity/ Lavatory	Toilet	Bathtub	Shower	Other (Specify)		Often	Sometimes
Body: apply lotion								
Cosmetics: apply, remove								
Face: skin care								
Face: wash								
First aid: treating cuts and burns								
Hair care: blow dry, curl								
Hair care: brush, style								
Hair care: color								
Hair care: cut, trim								
Hair care: shampoo, condition								
Hands: apply lotion								
Hands: wash								
Medicines/vitamins								
Nails (finger): clip, file, polish								
Nails (toe): clip, file, polish								
Shave: face								
Shave: legs, underarms								
Teeth: brush, floss								
Other grooming activities:								

Notes:

FORM 3: CHECKLIST FOR BATHROOM ACTIVITIES (CONTINUED)

Bathing/Showering Activities

✓	Activity	Location					Frequency	
		Vanity/Lavatory	Toilet	Bathtub	Shower	Other (Specify)	Often	Sometimes
	Bathing pets							
	Bathing in tub							
	Bathing: assisting an adult							
	Bathing children							
	Bathing: soaking, relaxing							
	Douching							
	Sauna: relaxing							
	Showering							
	Showering: assisting an adult							
	Showering with someone							
	"Sponge" bath							
	Steam showering							
	Whirlpool soaking							
	Other bathing/showering activities:							

Notes:

FORM 3: CHECKLIST FOR BATHROOM ACTIVITIES (CONTINUED)

Toileting Activities								
✓	**Activity**	**Location**					**Frequency**	
		Vanity/ Lavatory	Toilet	Bathtub	Shower	Other (Specify)	Often	Sometimes
	Defecate							
	Diapers: change infant/child							
	Diapers: change adult							
	Diapers: rinse out							
	Personal cleansing-bidet							
	Tampons/pads: change							
	Urinate							
	Other toileting activities:							

Notes:

FORM 3: CHECKLIST FOR BATHROOM ACTIVITIES (CONTINUED)

✓	Activity	Location					Frequency	
	Other Bathroom Activities	Vanity/ Lavatory	Toilet	Bathtub	Shower	Other (Specify)	Often	Sometimes
	Display collections							
	Dressing: underwear, sleeping clothes							
	Dressing: "street" clothes							
	Drink beverages							
	Eat snacks							
	Exercise							
	Exercise using equipment							
	Grow plants							
	Laundry: air dry							
	Laundry: hand wash							
	Laundry: machine wash							
	Laundry: sort, fold							
	Listen to music							
	Massage							
	Meditation							
	Personal pampering							
	Polish shoes							
	Read: books, newspapers							
	Supervise children							
	Talking on telephone							
	Talking with people							
	Tanning/sunning							
	Undressing							
	Watch television							
	Other activities:							

Notes:

FORM 4: BATHROOM STORAGE INVENTORY

Instructions: This inventory is divided into sections representing areas in the bathroom. Many of the typical items found in bathrooms are already listed. Check those items you want to store in the bathroom. Add any additional items needed. Complete the form, indicating how many of each item you have, how frequently you use it, and the type of storage you would like. Blank lines are included for items you have that are not listed. A space for notes is at the end of each section. Include information about special size or space requirements, items that need to be stored away from children, or other important details.

Items Stored Near the Vanity/Lavatory/Grooming Center							
✓	**Item to Store**	**How Many?**	**Frequency of Use**		**Type of Storage**			
			Often	Sometimes	Cabinet	Open Shelf	Drawer	Other (describe)
	Barrettes, pins, clips							
	Contact lens supplies							
	Curlers: electric							
	Curling iron							
	Hair brush, comb							
	Hair care products, e.g. mousse, gel							
	Hair dryer							
	First aid supplies							
	Glasses: drinking							
	Lotion							
	Make-up/cosmetics, e.g. mascara, lipstick							
	Medicines, vitamins							
	Nail clippers, files							
	Nail polish, manicure supplies							
	Perfume, cologne							
	Razor							
	Razor, electric							
	Shaving cream, after shave							
	Soap							
	Tissues							

FORM 4: BATHROOM STORAGE INVENTORY (CONTINUED)

✓	Item to Store	How Many?	Frequency of Use		Type of Storage			
			Often	Sometimes	Cabinet	Open Shelf	Drawer	Other (describe)
	Toothbrush							
	Toothbrush, electric							
	Toothpaste, dental floss							
	Towels, face							
	Towels, hand							
	Tweezers							
	Additional vanity/lavatory/ grooming items:							

Items Stored Near the Vanity/Lavatory/Grooming Center (Continued)

Notes:

FORM 4: BATHROOM STORAGE INVENTORY (CONTINUED)

Items Stored Near the Bathtub/Shower

✓	Item to Store	How Many?	Frequency of Use		Type of Storage			
			Often	Sometimes	Cabinet	Open Shelf	Drawer	Other (describe)
	Bubble bath							
	Cleaning supplies							
	Clothes: dirty							
	Clothes: robe, pajamas or sleeping clothes							
	Clothes: underwear							
	Douching equipment							
	Lotion							
	Powder							
	Radio, CD player							
	Razor							
	Scale							
	Shampoo, conditioner							
	Shower gel							
	Soap							
	Sponges							
	Squeegee							
	Television							
	Towels, bath							
	Towels, bath sheets							
	Towels, face or hand							
	Towels, guest							
	Toys							
	Additional bathtub/ shower items:							

Notes:

FORM 4: BATHROOM STORAGE INVENTORY (CONTINUED)

✓	Item to Store	How Many?	Frequency of Use		Type of Storage			
			Often	Sometimes	Cabinet	Open Shelf	Drawer	Other (describe)
	Books							
	Diapers: clean							
	Diapers: soiled							
	Magazines, newspapers							
	Medicines							
	Sanitary napkins, tampons							
	Soap							
	Toilet bowl brush							
	Toilet bowl cleaners							
	Toilet paper							
	Towels							
	Wet wipes							
	Additional toilet/bidet items:							

Notes:

FORM 4: BATHROOM STORAGE INVENTORY (CONTINUED)

Other Items to Store (if a separate linen or clothes closet is planned, additional information may be needed)

✓	Item to Store	How Many?	Frequency of Use		Type of Storage			
			Often	Sometimes	Cabinet	Open Shelf	Drawer	Other (describe)
	Accessories, e.g. scarves, belts							
	Clothes: folded clothes							
	Clothes: rod storage (specify height)							
	Clothes: rod storage (specify height)							
	Coffee maker							
	Coffee or tea supplies, e.g. cups, spoons							
	Exercise equipment							
	Household linens, miscellaneous							
	Household linens, pillows							
	Household linens, pillow cases							
	Household linens, sheets							
	Jewelry							
	Laundry products							
	Robe, pajamas, nightgown							
	Shoes, slippers							
	Additional items:							

Notes:

FORM 4: BATHROOM STORAGE INVENTORY (CONTINUED)

✓	Item to Store	How Many?	Frequency of Use		Type of Storage			
			Often	Sometimes	Cabinet	Open Shelf	Drawer	Other (describe)
	Antiques							
	Baskets							
	Bottles, jars, bowls							
	Decorative items, miscellaneous							
	Pictures, artwork							
	Plants							
	Additional display items:							

Items For Display

Notes:

FORM 5: YOUR CLIENT'S BATHROOM PREFERENCES

Use these questions to get general ideas about your client's preferences, and then as a check to make sure you have the specific details needed.

Features

Are there specific materials, fixtures, cabinetry, or other features that have been preselected by the client that are to be included in the project?_____

_____

Do they want a shower or bathtub? If they want both, will they be separated or a combination?

_____

Do they want a toilet, a urinal, or both? _____

Do they want a bidet? _____

How many lavatories do they want? Do they have ideas about the style? _____

_____

Do they want luxury features, such as a jetted tub or spa, soaking tub, steam shower, or sauna?

_____

What about clothes storage? Will this be adjacent to or included in the bathroom space?

_____

Do they want a linen closet in the bathroom? Will it be used to store household linens or just towels? _____

Do they want to include a laundry area? What about a washer or dryer? _____

_____

Do they want an exercise area? _____

_____

Do they want a food or drink area, such as for coffee, tea, or snacks? Will this area include appliances, such as a coffee maker, refrigerator, or microwave? Should this area include a separate sink? _____

_____

_____

FORM 5: YOUR CLIENT'S BATHROOM PREFERENCES (CONTINUED)

Layout

What ideas do they have about arrangement of the bathroom? _____

_____

Do they have ideas about areas that should be spacious or compact? _____

_____

What areas should be open to another? _____

_____

Do they want a compartmentalized bathroom? If so, what areas should be separate?

_____

Windows

Will the bathroom have windows? _____

_____

Should the window(s) be operable? _____

_____

What style of window is preferred? _____

_____

Is there a view to be considered? From where in the bathroom should the view be visible – such

as the bathtub or vanity? _____

_____

What about window privacy? _____

_____

FORM 5: YOUR CLIENT'S BATHROOM PREFERENCES (CONTINUED)

Doors

From what rooms will they enter the bathroom? _____

_____

Should the doors swing in or out? Or is a pocket or folding door preferred? _____

_____

Is a locking door preferred? _____

_____

General Preference

Style? _____

_____

Color? _____

_____

Architectural details retained in existing space? _____

_____

Architectural details added in new bathroom design? _____

_____

Cabinetry:

    Door style? _____

    Type of wood or face material? _____

    Color? _____

    Hardware? _____

Fixtures – style, color, material:

    Lavatory? _____

    Bathtub? _____

    Shower? _____

    Toilet? _____

    Urinal? _____

    Bidet? _____

    Other fixtures? _____

FORM 5: YOUR CLIENT'S BATHROOM PREFERENCES (CONTINUED)

Fittings:

    Material or color? _____

    Style? _____

Countertops:

    Material? _____

    Color or pattern? _____

    Backsplash? _____

    Edge treatment? _____

Finish materials:

    Floors? _____

    Walls? _____

    Ceilings? _____

    Doors, windows? _____

    Mouldings and trims? _____

Lighting:

    Style? _____

    Control features? _____

    Type of light sources? _____

Furniture? _____

_____

Accessories:

    Towel bars or warmers? _____

    Toilet paper holders? _____

    Mirror? _____

    Full-length mirror? _____

    Other items? _____

FORM 5: YOUR CLIENT'S BATHROOM PREFERENCES (CONTINUED)

Appliances? _____

_____

_____

Other materials or fixtures to include? _____

_____

_____

Scope of the Project

What is the potential for structural changes in the bathroom, including:

Can the location of the bathroom be moved?_____

_____

Is an addition to the home being considered?_____

_____

Is there opportunity to incorporate space from within the home, such as a closet,

hall, or bedroom? _____

Is relocating the plumbing an option? _____

_____

Will there be other building or remodeling projects that will be happening at the same time as

the bathroom? _____

_____

Are there specific construction parameters or limitations, such as walls or doors that cannot

be moved? _____

_____

What part of the project, if any, do the clients want to do themselves?_____

_____

Is there any part of the project to be done by another professional designated by the client? ____

_____

Contact Information: _____

_____

FORM 5: YOUR CLIENT'S BATHROOM PREFERENCES (CONTINUED)

What is the time frame of the project? _____

Are there specific events that affect the project schedule?_____

_____

Is there another bathroom in the home? _____

_____

Are there specific times when the workers cannot have access to the bathroom space?_____

_____

FORM 6: JOBSITE INSPECTION

The information on this form needs to be collected through a thorough inspection of the existing structure and/or construction documents. You are looking for detailed information! Some information may appear to repeat some of the questions on other forms, which were asking for client ideas and preferences. However, use this form to verify specifics at the actual site.

Overall Bathroom

Begin with a floor plan sketch to understand the relationship of spaces and to make notes about structural and mechanical details. See the following questions for additional information to add to your sketch.

FORM 6: JOBSITE INSPECTION (CONTINUED)

Note the following information on your bathroom sketch.

- What rooms are above, below, and around the existing bathroom space?

- Can any of the surrounding space be incorporated into the new plan? If so, how much – exactly?

- What walls can be changed – moved, removed, or otherwise altered?

- Which windows and doors are to remain or be reused?

- What doors and windows can be changed – moved, removed, or changed in size or type?

- What fixtures are to remain? Are they to be left in the same location, or can they be moved?

- Is there cabinetry that is to be left in place or reused in the new design?

- Which way do the floor joists run? Does the floor seem sturdy and stiff?

- Are there load-bearing walls to consider?

- Where does plumbing come into the space?

- Where are the soil stack and other drain/waste/vent pipes?

- Where are existing ducts and registers located? Can these be moved?

- What is the condition of finish materials – floors, walls, and ceilings? Are any of the finish materials to remain unchanged?

- Is there a view from the bathroom? Is the view from the bathroom important?

Determine the following additional information about the bathroom.

Bathroom is on: ❏ north ❏ northeast ❏ east ❏ southeast ❏ south

❏ southwest ❏ west ❏ northwest

If new fixtures are to be installed, are they to be
put in the same location as the old fixtures?_____

_____

If the remodeled bathroom project will impact on the exterior of the home, are there
any restrictions to be considered? Will existing siding or roof materials be easy to match? _____

_____

Are there any home improvements or repairs to be incorporated into
the bathroom project, such as new siding or a roof replacement? _____

_____

If the home is older than 1978, could there be
lead-based paint or asbestos in the existing space?_____

_____

FORM 6: JOBSITE INSPECTION (CONTINUED)

Structure

What is the construction of the house? _____

_____

What is the condition of the existing structure? Look for sound and level floors,
squareness of corners, and materials in good condition. Do floors squeak? _____

_____

Is there evidence of water leaks or pest damage? _____

_____

What size are the joists and will they be adequate support for the new fixtures? _____

_____

Are windows and doors in good repair and do they operate smoothly? Are new or replacement
windows and doors to match the existing windows with respect to type, size, style, and material?

_____

Is the home well insulated? Are doors and windows energy-efficient? _____

_____

Mechanical Systems

Can you relocate any plumbing pipes? _____

What is the capacity of the plumbing system? _____

What size are the supply pipes? Is there adequate water pressure? _____

_____

Is the water of good quality? _____

Will you be able to add additional fixtures, or higher-capacity fixtures to the existing plumbing? __

_____

Where is the water heater? What is its capacity? _____

_____

Can the soil stack and other drain/waste/vent pipes be relocated if needed? _____

_____

FORM 6: JOBSITE INSPECTION (CONTINUED)

Where are the traps, and what type are they? _____

_____

Is the home on a municipal or private sewage system? Are there any concerns about system capacity
if the amount of wastewater is increased? _____

_____

How many electrical circuits come into the space, and what is the capacity? _____

_____

Do the circuits have GFCI (ground fault circuit interrupter) protection? _____

_____

Is the wiring in good condition? _____

_____

Can existing receptacles be moved? _____

_____

If needed, are 240-volt circuits available? _____

Where is the electrical service panel for the house? _____

Can additional electrical circuits be added if needed? _____

_____

How is the existing space heated and cooled? Is the current HVAC (heating, ventilating and air
conditioning) equipment in good condition and adequate in size? _____

_____

If there will be an increase in the size of the bathroom, will the HVAC system be adequate? _____

_____

Is there an exhaust ventilation system? Is it adequate in size? How is make-up air provided? _____

_____

Does all or part of the ventilation system need replacement? _____

_____

FORM 6: JOBSITE INSPECTION (CONTINUED)

Access

What size are any doors between the bathroom and the exterior of the home? Are there narrow hallways or sharp turns? Will there be any problems in removing or bringing in large, bulky, and/or heavy fixtures? _____

_____

Is there finished living space above or below the bathroom? Will you be able to open up floors, ceilings, or walls to get access to plumbing, electrical, and HVAC systems? _____

_____

Construction/Installation Planning

Can fixtures, cabinetry, and materials be stored at the jobsite? How much space is there? Is the storage secure and protected from the weather?_____

_____

Where will trash be collected? _____

How will workers get into and out of the jobsite? Is there carpeting or furniture that needs to be protected? _____

_____

Where can workers park? Where can they take breaks or eat lunch? _____

_____

What about smoking, playing music, eating, and drinking at the jobsite? What about bathroom facilities for worker's use? _____

_____

FORM 7: DIMENSIONS OF THE BATHROOM – FLOOR PLAN

Carefully measure the bathroom space and prepare a dimensioned drawing. Be sure to include wall thickness. Note the location of all mechanical connections, including electrical and plumbing information. Double check each dimension and record your numbers carefully.

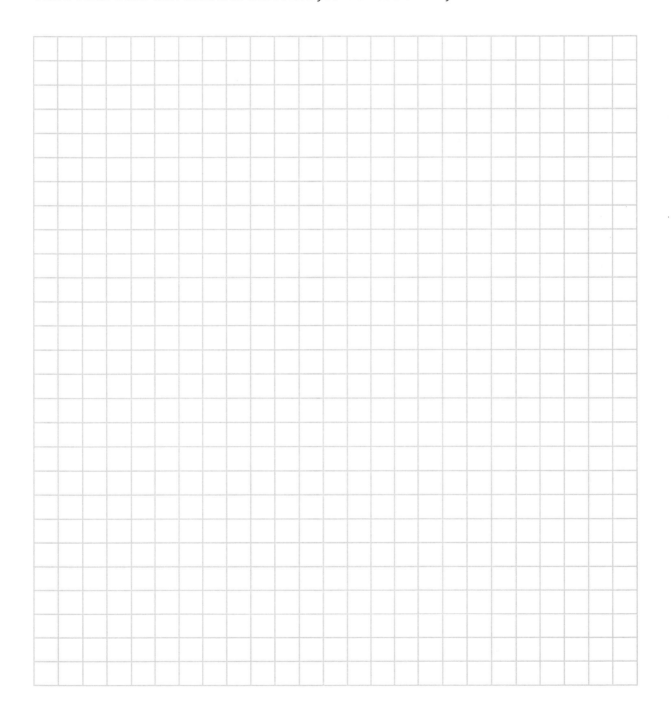

FORM 8: DIMENSIONS OF THE BATHROOM – ELEVATIONS

Project an elevation of each bathroom wall, verifying the dimensions of each wall. You will use these elevations to note the location of architectural features, mechanical devices (FORM 9), windows (FORM 10), doors (FORM 11), and fixtures to remain (FORM 12).

FORM 9: DIMENSIONS OF MECHANICAL DEVICES

Measure and locate each heat register, radiator, or other mechanical devices. Note whether the location of these items are fixed.

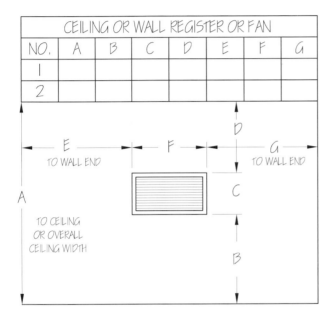

CEILING OR WALL REGISTER OR FAN						
NO.	A	B	C	D	E	F	G
1							
2							

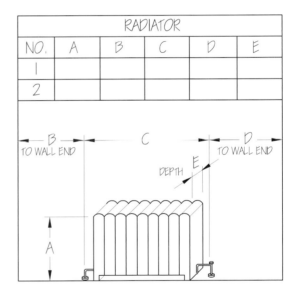

RADIATOR					
NO.	A	B	C	D	E
1					
2					

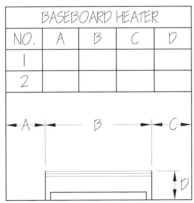

BASEBOARD HEATER			
NO.	A	B	C	D
1				
2				

FORM 10: WINDOW MEASUREMENTS

Note that the location of the window is determined in relation to the floor, ceiling, and both wall corners. Include the size of the window frame.

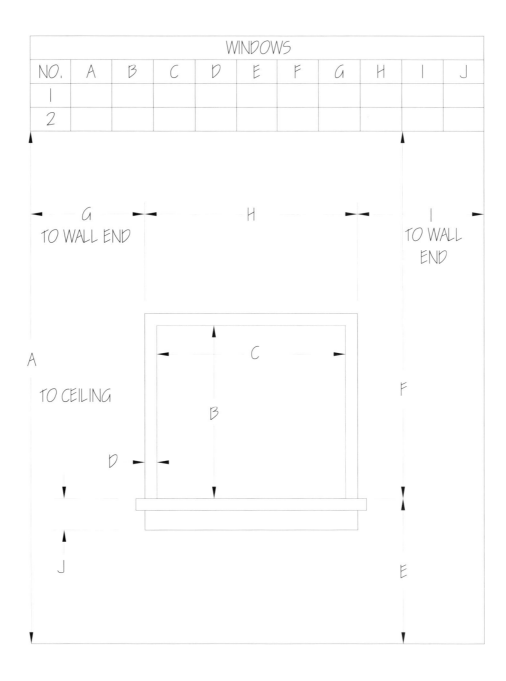

NO.	A	B	C	D	E	F	G	H	I	J
1										
2										

FORM 11: DOOR MEASUREMENTS

Note the location of the door in relation to both wall corners and the ceiling. Include the size of the door and the casing. Note the location of the handle.

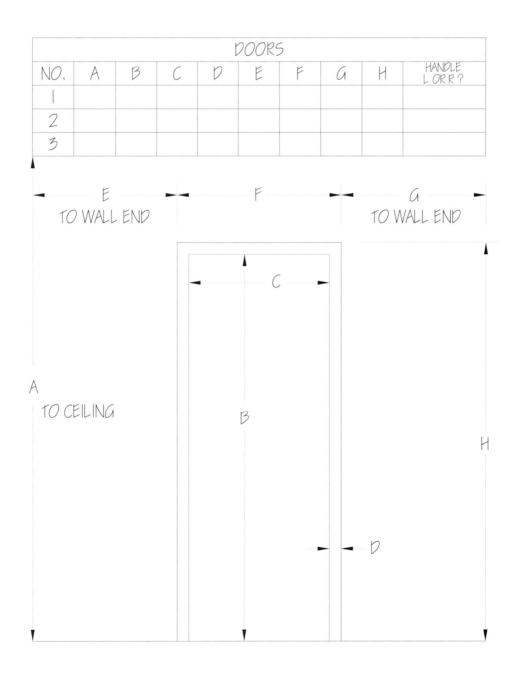

FORM 12: FIXTURE MEASUREMENTS

Existing fixtures that will remain need to be measured carefully, including centerline dimensions.

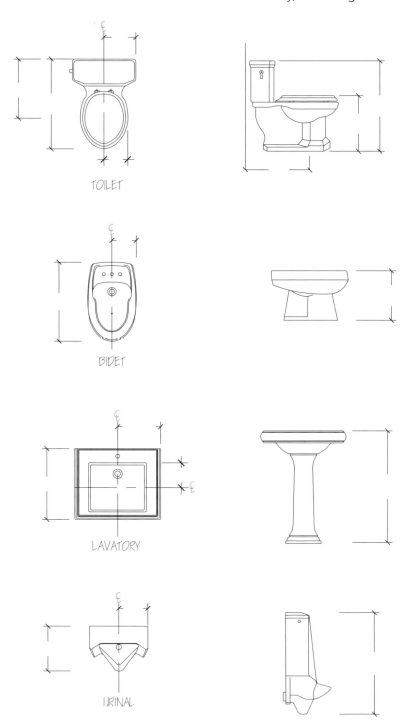

TOILET

BIDET

LAVATORY

URINAL

CHAPTER 6: Bathroom Planning

Planning a bathroom requires knowledge about many concepts related to people and their houses. The designer must draw on information about plumbing and electrical systems, bathroom fixtures, finishes, and the people who will be using the space.

This chapter presents background information about the type and location of bathrooms within the home, and gives key information about specific planning issues for various bathroom centers. Information about planning for different types of users is integrated into each section. The National Kitchen & Bath Association Bathroom Planning Guidelines and related Access Standards are presented as they relate to the bathroom centers. Chapter 11 presents these guidelines and standards in summary format.

TYPES AND LOCATIONS OF BATHROOMS

How the bathroom will be used affects the selection of fixtures and determines the type of bathroom needed. Following are brief descriptions of the types of bathrooms found in today's homes:

- **Half bathroom/powder room** – includes only a lavatory and toilet. It is usually located close to a social area for guests or close to family activity areas, such as the kitchen or outdoors.

- **Full bathroom** – includes the lavatory, toilet, and a tub and/or shower. It is usually located close to privacy areas of the home.

- **Compartmentalized bathroom** – includes lavatory, toilet, and tub and/or shower, but one or more of these has been separated into its own compartment. This allows the bathroom to be used simultaneously by more than one person. It can be located close to social and private areas or between two bedrooms.

- **Bathroom suite** – includes one or more lavatories, toilet, tub, shower and various other fixtures and features such as a bidet, vanity and dressing areas. It is located adjacent to a bedroom, such as the master or guest bedroom suites.

Figure 6.1 A variety of bathroom types are found in homes today.

• **Bathroom spa** – includes fixtures similar to the bathroom suite as well as one or more spa fixtures, such as a whirlpool or jetted tub, soaking tub, spa tub, sauna or steam bath.

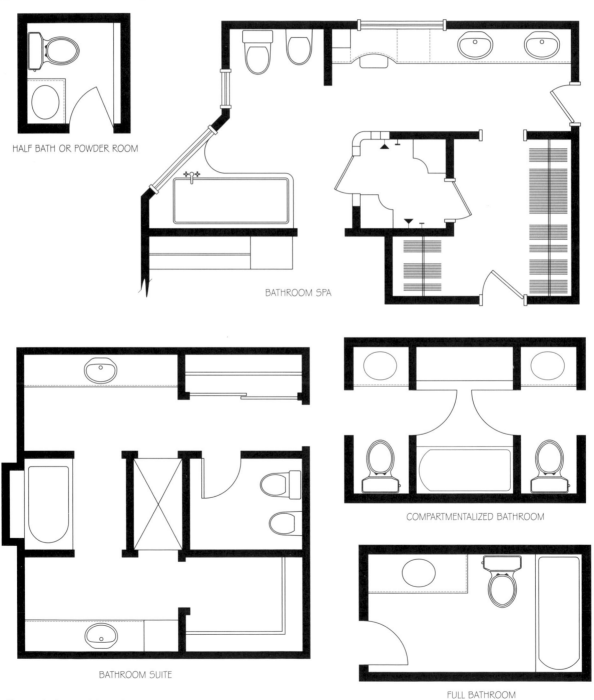

HALF BATH OR POWDER ROOM

BATHROOM SPA

COMPARTMENTALIZED BATHROOM

BATHROOM SUITE

FULL BATHROOM

Concept plans not to scale

Location in the Home

Using the bathroom is considered a private activity in the homes of most North Americans. Whether it is bathing or toileting, we often want these activities shielded from guests and other family members. Therefore, the bathroom is most commonly located in a private part of the home, usually close or adjacent to the bedrooms, which are also considered private spaces.

Getting ready for a day of activities or a night's sleep requires some personal grooming and preparation, and locating the bathroom close to the sleep areas is convenient for the user and the rest of the household. In older homes, one bathroom centrally located to all the bedrooms may be typical, but today we often find multiple bedroom or privacy areas, such as master suites, guest suites and children's areas. This suggests the need for bathrooms to be located in all of these areas.

Figure 6.2 Today we often find bathrooms as part of master suites in the privacy area of the home. (Courtesy of Holly Rickert – Ridgewood, New Jersey. Photography by Peter Rymwid)

Separating private and social areas can be handled in many different ways. In some homes, all social areas are on the first floor and all bedrooms are on the second floor. While this provides good separation of private and social activities, some difficulties may arise. A bathroom will still need to be planned on the first floor. A first floor bedroom, or room that can adapt to a bedroom, should be considered in order to provide private spaces for anyone finding stairs to be difficult or a barrier.

Another way to separate private and social areas is to locate bedrooms and bathrooms to one side of a social area. In some homes, all private spaces are together. In others there are separate primary (master suite) and secondary bedrooms, and even a third area (guest suite). All of these would have bathrooms. Plus, the home may have other bathrooms for special activity areas like pools and mudrooms.

Because guests may need to use the toilet and "freshen up," a small bath or powder room is often planned close to social spaces. It is particularly important that this bathroom be planned with universal design in mind so it can be used by any guest. Guest bathrooms may be located close to formal and informal living areas, outdoor social areas and the kitchen. Sometimes these bathrooms will serve two purposes and be located near, or between, social areas and privacy areas, such as secondary bedrooms or guest rooms.

Wherever the bathroom is, consider the relationship between it and the adjacent spaces. Visual and auditory privacy should be maintained. A guest bath opening directly into a social area or kitchen may present a view of the toilet, making guests feel they are announcing their private activity to everyone, and causing them to feel uncomfortable. Going through a private bedroom to get to the only bathroom is also uncomfortable for guests, as well as the bedroom occupant. Even sharing a bathroom with doors opening into two bedrooms can leave overnight guests feeling uncomfortable about their privacy.

Private Spaces

Within the private areas of the home, a bathroom that opens off a hallway is common in older homes. The hall is usually serving several bedrooms. However, if it is the only bathroom, or is also serving as the guest bathroom, it may also be close to social areas. In homes with more than one privacy area, the hall bathroom may serve the needs of occupants in secondary bedrooms. Traditionally, the hall bathroom includes a lavatory, a toilet, and a bathtub with shower.

Shared or compartmentalized bathrooms are also suitable for private spaces of the home. These bathrooms are divided so more than one person can use the space and still have privacy. In one version, the lavatory and toilet are in the same room, and the tub or shower is in a separate compartment. In another configuration, the lavatory is placed in the forward area, and the tub and toilet are placed together. These designs allow one person in the household to use the lavatory and/or toilet, while another is bathing. If visitors will also use the space, the lavatory and toilet compartment might be made available as a powder room.

Another version of the shared bathroom is one located between two bedrooms, and only available for the bedroom occupants. This type of bathroom might have three compartments: a lavatory and toilet room on each side, with a tub and/or shower in the middle (Figure 6.3a).

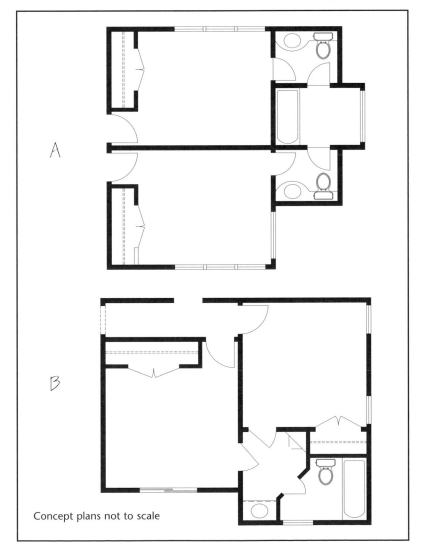

Concept plans not to scale

Figure 6.3 A bathroom shared between two bedrooms can provide privacy for one occupant to use a grooming area, while another can bathe or use the toilet.

All shared bathrooms provide the opportunity for more than one person to use the space at once, a real timesaver for families on a busy morning. The designer should determine the household's privacy comfort level with this type of arrangement, and be aware that extra space will be needed for circulation paths and doorways.

It may work better to provide two small bathrooms in the same area, so that each person has their own space. If guests and family members share a compartmentalized bathroom, it is best to have only one door in order to control access (Figure 6.3B).

Private Bathroom

Having a private bathroom for each bedroom is an option that offers the most privacy for occupants. Instead of one hall bathroom serving several bedrooms, each bedroom has a bathroom connected to it. In secondary bedrooms, this might be a small bathroom with a lavatory, toilet and bathtub or shower. However, the primary or master bedroom often has a more expansive master bathroom.

The master bathroom is often part of the master suite, an area that might be envisioned as the retreat for the homeowners. In its simplest form, the master bathroom has a lavatory, toilet and bathtub/shower. However, more expansive options are often planned into the space: double lavatories, separate vanities, separate tub and shower, oversized showers, whirlpool tubs, compartmentalized toilets, double toilet spaces, dressing areas and closets. Luxury master bathrooms might include exercise spaces and spa areas, discussed in detail in Chapter 8.

Some couples prefer two separate bathrooms, so that each person has their own space. Depending on the size, the two spaces might have each of the basic fixtures. In some arrangements, a tub might be in one bathroom and a shower in another. However, some might have both fixtures in both bathrooms. These "his and her" bathrooms might be adjacent to separate closets and dressing areas, to provide complete grooming areas tailored to each individual.

Many homes have a guest room that is part of the secondary bedroom area. In those cases, guests are expected to use the hall bathroom or the private bathroom adjacent to their room. Occasionally, a separate suite with many of the features of the master bedroom and bathroom may be planned to provide guests with a more luxurious experience. This arrangement can be comfortable for short-term and long-term guests. It can also serve as a second master suite, should a family member find that differences in nighttime and sleep patterns indicate a need for separate sleeping areas. It might also serve as a caregiver's suite if the need arises.

Figure 6.4 In this shared bath, the openness of the design with the facing vanities allows the couple to talk to each other while having their own space. (Courtesy of Lori Carroll – Tucson, Arizona. Photography by William Lesch Photography)

Children's Bathroom

Bathrooms planned specifically for children require consideration of their ages and needs. This bathroom may be located in the hall of the secondary bedroom area or connected to the child's bedroom. A private bathroom may allow for the selection of fixtures and the design to most accurately reflect the age-specific needs of the child. But a hall bath that will be used by others may require consideration for both the child and other users. Lower, adjustable or tilting mirrors, adjustable showerheads, and stepstools can help to make an adult-sized bath fit children. Remember that children grow quickly. Further information about designing for children is found in Chapter 9.

Public and Social Areas

Whenever possible, visitors to the home should be able to use the bathroom without having to invade the household's private spaces. Therefore, a bathroom should be planned within the social area of the home. However, placing the visitor bath at the front door or in the entry hall is not a good idea, since this is a very public location and does not provide for visual or auditory privacy.

In order to effectively plan guest or visitor bathrooms, it is important to understand the type and frequency of social activities that are typical of the client. The visitor bathroom should be consistent with the plan for the social areas. Is there formal sit-down dining? Informal open spaces? Basement recreation room? Outdoor living areas?

Considering the social activities and the spaces that accommodate them will help determine the location and type of the visitor bathroom. In some homes, one bathroom might accommodate all of these activities, but in others, several visitor bathrooms might be desired in the various social areas.

Social areas are usually planned on the first floor of the home. If no private spaces are planned on this level, then the visitor bathroom may be the only one convenient to guests and household members using the first floor spaces. As indicated previously, this might be a half-bathroom or powder room, with only lavatory and toilet fixtures (Figure 6.1). If there are bedrooms that will also use the visitor bath, then a tub or shower should be included. Its placement should be convenient to the bedroom occupants as well as visitors.

Figure 6.5 In this dramatic powder room, a decorative vessel sink in a vanity with display space becomes the focal point, accented by a long mirror. (Courtesy of Holly Rickert – Ridgewood, New Jersey. Photography by Peter Rymwid)

Outdoor Baths

If a focus of social or household activities is on the outdoor living areas, then ideally there should be a bathroom adjacent to them. For example, a bathroom and dressing area adjacent to a pool or hot tub would provide a convenient space for toileting, showering and changing without dripping water throughout the house. Some households enjoy an outdoor shower to rinse off beach sand or pool chlorine. Outdoor showers might also be part of a master bath with a private garden area.

Families who use outdoor play spaces for children, or who spend time outdoors gardening, find a bathroom or mudroom close to the backyard is convenient for cleaning up before going into the house, or for using while outside. If outdoor kitchens and dining are part of the way the household entertains, then a bathroom close to this area provides a convenience to guests.

Visitors' Needs

The needs of users are always critical to the decisions you will make in designing a bathroom. However, it is not always clear who the visitor in the home will be. Planning the visitor bathroom to be a universally designed space assures that most people will be able to use it.

Several communities and states are adopting visit-ability requirements for new homes. These indicate that as a minimum, there should be a doorway into the home that is accessible, and that doors and passage ways on the first floor should be wide enough for everyone to use. In addition to a door opening that is wide enough, the first floor bathroom should have adequate floor space and reinforcement in the walls for grab bars in case they are needed in the future.

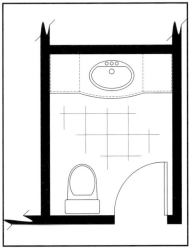

Figure 6.6 This powder room has a wide door and enough floor space that it would meet the criteria for a visitable bathroom. Grab bars and a clear space under the lavatory would enhance its accessibility even more. (Courtesy of Martha Gargano and co-designer Karen Sciascia – Cheshire, Connecticut)

THE CENTER CONCEPT

There are many different ways to approach designing bathrooms. This book focuses on the center concept. A center is an area where a particular task occurs. The user, space, fixtures and other components are all analyzed in order to design a center for a particular task. The basic tasks and corresponding centers in the bathroom are Grooming, Bathing/Showering and Toileting.

Each bathroom center is described here separately, the tasks and activities are identified, and requirements associated with completing tasks safely and conveniently are detailed, followed by design recommendations. The Bathroom Planning Guidelines important to the safe and comfortable use of the center, and related Access Standards are also discussed. For a quick reference, summary listings of the NKBA Bathroom Planning Guidelines, with the Access Standards, are in Chapter 11.

Universal design concepts and ideas are presented and integrated throughout this chapter to encourage you to think about various user needs while planning the space. Thinking broadly about clients' needs, now and in the future, can help you develop a thoughtful design that anticipates changes that will occur over their lifespan. In Chapter 9, you will find expanded ideas and recommendations for designing for specific user groups.

NKBA Guidelines and Access Standards

The National Kitchen & Bath Association has been providing information on the design of bathrooms since Ellen Cheever's book *The Basics of Bathroom Design ...and Beyond* was published in 1989. The Bathroom Planning Guidelines, which first appeared in 1992, have always had a strong focus on safety and building code requirements. The Guidelines have been reviewed and updated periodically to include new information, such as universal design, and in 2003 an NKBA ad hoc committee developed the current Guidelines incorporated in this book.

The update of the Guidelines incorporated a review of housing trends and an analysis of the 2003 International Residential Code (IRC). Space recommendations are based on documented ergonomic considerations, and code requirements are highlighted. The IRC has been adopted by many states and localities, but designers should check the local building codes to make sure they are in compliance. The Bathroom Planning Guidelines are intended to serve as a reference tool for practicing designers and an evaluation tool for bathroom designs. Designers taking the Certified Bath Designer Exam will be expected to know the Guidelines and apply them to the designs they create for the exam.

NKBA has led the kitchen and bath industry in promoting universal design. Its 1996 Bathroom Planning Guidelines included recommendations that would make the bathroom universal and accessible, many based on ANSI 117.1 guidelines and the Uniform Federal Accessibility Standards (UFAS). Many of the universal design points included in the 1996 Guidelines continue to be incorporated in the updated Guidelines.

In this book, Access Standards have been included as planning information that will improve a client's access to the bathroom. Because the International Building Code (IBC) references it, the *Accessible and Useable Buildings and Facilities* (ICC/ANSI 117.1) has been used as the basis for the Access Standards. The 1998 ICC/ANSI standards serve as one of several "safe harbors" for designers and builders of multi-family housing who must be in compliance with the Fair Housing Accessibility Guidelines. If you are designing bathrooms that are covered by the Fair Housing regulations, please check the sources mentioned in Chapter 4 to make sure you are in compliance with these federal standards.

An NKBA Access Standard follows each NKBA Bathroom Planning Guideline when appropriate. While these Access Standards and the ANSI standards on which they are based provide a great starting point, designers should closely examine the needs of each individual client to assure that the bathroom is truly useable, not just meeting minimum requirements. The assessment forms presented in Chapter 5 should be used to gather information about the client's needs.

GENERAL BATHROOM DESIGN

As you examine the space of an existing bathroom or the plans for a new one, there are several general things that should be assessed. Not only are the dimensions of the space important, but the form of the space needs to be considered. How will the space join to adjacent rooms or areas? Are there other openings, such as windows? Is the space a basic rectangle shape or are there curves or angles? How will the user(s) move about the space?

Entry

One of the first decisions for the design is how to get into the bathroom. Door placement can make a real difference in the available space and in the circulation to adjacent rooms. If a major remodeling or new construction is taking place, look carefully at the entry and examine all possibilities for its location. In more modest remodeling, there may not be space or budget to allow for a change in location.

It is recommended that the entry to the bathroom have a 32-inch clear opening between the door jambs. This can be accomplished by specifying at least a 2 foot 10 inch door. While this is larger than what has been typical in the past, consumers are requesting this enhancement.

Not only will it make the bathroom more spacious, it will accommodate larger people, some people with assistive devices, and a large tub or shower installation. If a doorframe of a remodeled bathroom cannot be modified, NKBA allows a door as small as 2 feet 0 inches, but it will be difficult for many people to use and will not meet basic visit-ability or access standards. It will allow you to get a 21-inch vanity into the room, but not larger cabinetry or fixtures.

Figure 6.7 A 32-inch clear opening is recommended for bathroom entry (Bathroom Planning Guideline 1).

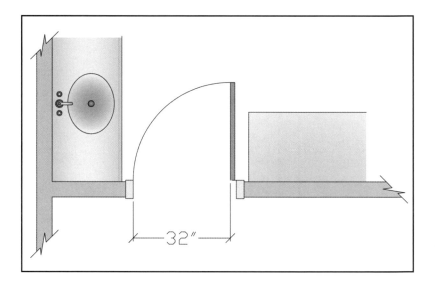

In many cases, a 3 foot 0 inch door is preferred as it provides 34 inches of clear opening for even greater clearance. When the clear space of a door is less than desired, a swing-clear hinge may be used to gain clear passage by moving the door out of the opening. For a person using a wheelchair or mobility aid, a minimum of 18 inches on the pull side of the door is recommended to allow room for the person to maneuver around the swing of the door. Actual clearances are impacted by a person's approach and the door configuration. Several of these are detailed in Chapter 9.

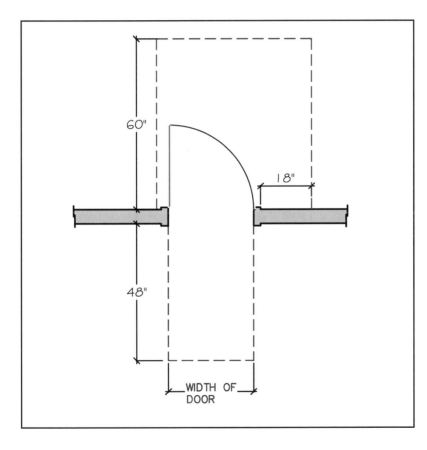

Figure 6.8 For a door to be useable by a person with a mobility aid, there should be at least 18 inches of clear space beside the door opening (Bathroom Access Standard 2).

Many homes today have ceilings that are 9 feet, 10 feet or 12 feet high. These high ceilings can create wonderful spaces, but the designer should carefully consider the proportions of the bathroom space. Dropped ceilings, soffits and mouldings can help bring the volume into proportion.

Circulation

As you look at the options for placement of bathroom fixtures, you will use the information in the sections about the centers. In larger baths, maneuvering space is easier to attain, but careful planning is needed to arrange the fixtures so that they are convenient to use.

In very small bathrooms, the user can reach all fixtures with just a few steps, but clear space for maneuvering may be scarce. The designer has to weigh the needs of the client and the job parameters to reach the best solution.

If more than one person will be using the bathroom at the same time, consider the minimum 30-inch clearance needed for one person to walk behind another and plan accordingly.

If a person will be using a mobility aid, such as a wheelchair, plan a larger space for turning and maneuvering. A 60-inch turning circle should be included somewhere in the bathroom. If this turning circle is not possible, a 36 inch x 60 inch x 36 inch T-turn is a possible solution.

Figure 6.12 A walkway of 48 inches allows 18 inches for a person using a fixture and 30 inches for a person to walk behind them.

30″   18″

48″

AVERAGE WALKWAY CLEARANCE

Figure 6.13 A 34-inch clear opening and a space for a 60-inch turning radius are recommended for a universally accessible space (Bathroom Access Standard 4).

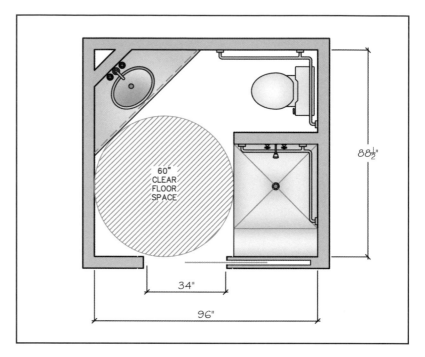

Figure 6.14 A person in a wheelchair can often turn and maneuver in a T-shaped clear space created by using a knee-space under the lavatory (Bathroom Access Standard 4).

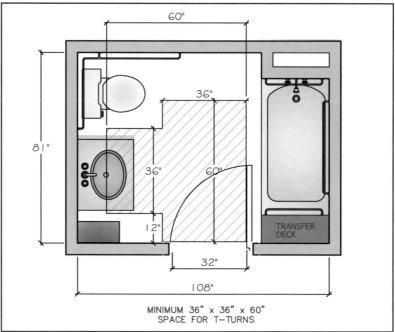

Guidelines and Access Standards

Bathroom Planning Guidelines and Access Standards that are important to the general design of the bathroom are 1, 2, and 3. For the complete Guidelines and Access Standards, see Chapter 11.

GROOMING CENTER

The Grooming Center should not be thought of as just the bathroom sink or the lavatory. While a water source and basin are critical components, many activities occur in this center and it should be designed to accommodate as many client desires as the space and budget permit.

- Washing hands after toileting is an important health measure and using soap is critical to assure that as many germs and bacteria are killed as possible. To effectively wash their hands, the user should be able to place their hands under the water spray while standing or sitting.

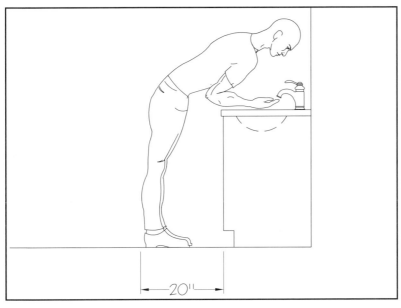

Figure 6.15 It takes about 18 inches of floor space for a person to stand to wash their hands, and about 20 inches for a person to bend to wash their face.

Figure 6.16 The space needed for a seated user at a vanity will depend on the chair and person. A wheelchair extends at least 30 inches beyond the vanity, while a small chair may require 18 inches to 24 inches beyond the vanity.

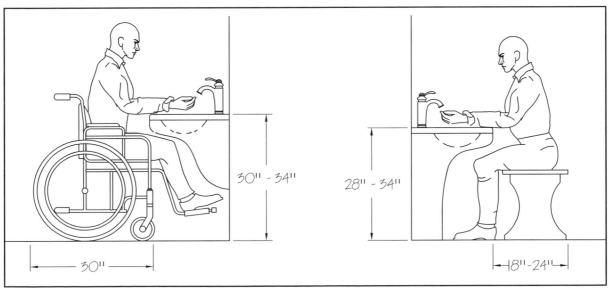

- Face washing is another important activity that occurs in this center. Usually people bend at the waist in order to place their face close to the water surface, especially if they wash by splashing water on their face. Other people may use a washcloth or cleansing pad and they may remain upright, wetting the cloth and bringing it to their face.

- Brushing teeth is another key activity, and people usually bend at the waist to rinse into the sink. They also stand upright and examine their teeth in the mirror. Other activities might be using mouthwash, flossing, and caring for dentures, braces or other orthodontic devices. A water source is needed for cleansing brushes and a cup is needed for rinsing.

- Facial care and makeup applications are very important in the grooming routine. The number of products and the steps involved in cleansing and conditioning the skin, and in applying face, eye, and lip makeup, are staggering.

  This activity may require the user to be in the Grooming Center for some time. Although a water source may be needed, some facial care can and does occur at a seated vanity with water close by. A place to store and access products, good lighting, and an appropriately placed mirror are important to successfully completing this task. Chapter 7 has more information about planning lighting.

- Facial shaving is a similar task. It may be completed with an electric razor (requiring an electric receptacle for use or when charging), or with a blade razor (requiring creams and a water source). As with other facial care, proper location of the mirror and good lighting will be important.

- Hair care may be as simple as combing or brushing hair in front of the mirror. More often, hair styling is done, using gels, mousse, crèmes and sprays. Several electric appliances may be used to accomplish styling as well: blow dryers, curling irons, electric curlers, crimpers and straighteners.

  Usually this activity will require an appropriately placed mirror, storage for the appliances, and electrical receptacles that can accommodate the requested appliances. Chapter 7 can provide information on planning for electrical receptacles.

- Some people store and use medicines and first aid supplies in the bathroom. If medicines are taken first thing in the morning or last thing at night, this may be a good place for this activity. Because some medications require refrigeration or must be taken with food, people also take and store medicines in the kitchen.

  Some clients might be interested in having a small under-counter refrigerator in the bathroom, perhaps part of a small "morning" kitchen, to avoid a trip to the kitchen. Some medicines should not be stored in moist and humid places, and may need to be stored away from the bathroom.

  First aid supplies might be stored in several places in the house, close to where they are needed, such as in the kitchen, hobby area or a first-floor bathroom. Storage for these supplies is needed, as well as a sanitary way to dispose of them. We often use the medicine cabinet for storage, although other storage may be more appropriate. Additional items needed for taking medicine might be good lighting, and a cup or glass.

- Nail care may be performed in the bathroom. Foot baths and massages might be undertaken. Manicures and pedicures require storage for supplies, good lighting and ventilation, and a seat with a counter area.

Households may have a wide variety of other activities that they complete in the grooming center of the bathroom, so completing an analysis and inventory as suggested in Chapter 5 is important for planning.

RECOMMENDATIONS

Considering all the possible activities, important planning considerations at the Grooming Center include clearance in front of, and beside, the lavatory; the height of the lavatory; amount and placement of storage; and mirror and towel placement. Lighting and ventilation will be important also, and are discussed in Chapter 7. To plan the Grooming Center effectively, it is important to review the anthropometric measurements of the user. In the past, the dimensions of standard fixtures and cabinets have often determined this space, but as a designer working with individual clients, you should plan for the needs of the users.

Floor Clearance

The amount of space the human body requires to use the lavatory includes room to stand or sit in front of it. Anthropometric data indicates that about 18 inches of floor space is required to stand and face the lavatory (Figure 6.15). It is also important to be able to bend at a comfortable angle when washing hands or face.

Figure 6.17 A clear space of 30 inches in front of the lavatory is recommended for comfortable use of the fixture. A minimum clearance is 21 inches (Bathroom Planning Guideline 4).

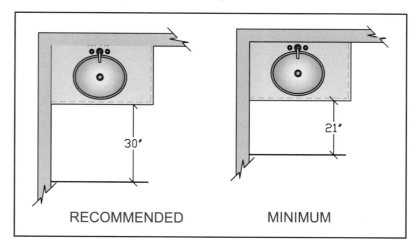

While 18 inches may allow some people to stand, it does not account for the movement of the standing user that might take place at the lavatory. NKBA recommends 30 inches of clearance in front of the lavatory for a more comfortable space. This would even allow a person to place a seat at the lavatory. Building codes will permit 21 inches of floor clearance in front of the lavatory, but this will be very tight.

However, 30 inches does not provide adequate clearance for two people to use the space and move around each other, since the average shoulder width is 24 inches. A floor space in front of the lavatory of 48 inches will accommodate two users comfortably. A minimum 30 inch x 48 inch space should be allowed in front of the lavatory for a user with an assistive device (Figure 6.18).

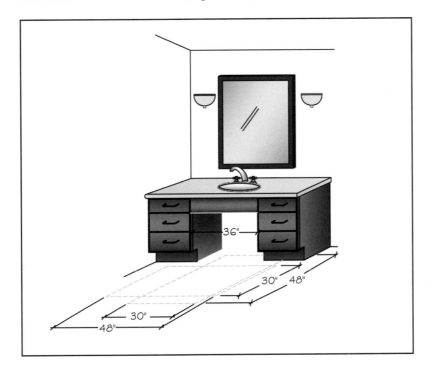

Figure 6.18 Accessibility standards require 30 inches x 48 inches of clear space in front of the lavatory (Bathroom Access Standard 4).

Side Clearance

Body size affects how much room a person needs on either side of the lavatory. To complete typical grooming activities, a person needs to be able to raise hands and elbows. The recommended distance from the center of the lavatory to a wall or tall obstruction is 20 inches. (Figure 6.19A).

This provides about 6 inches of clear counter space from the edge of the average lavatory to the wall or obstruction, but may not be adequate. Consider the breadth of the user and items placed on the counter to determine if more counter area is needed.

The minimum distance is 15 inches from centerline of the lavatory to the wall, according to building code, providing only about 2 inches from the edge of the average lavatory to the wall or obstruction (Figure 6.19B). If a wall-hung or pedestal sink is specified, allow 4 inches between the edge of the lavatory to the wall (Figure 6.19C).

Figure 6.19 Placing the center of a single lavatory 20 inches from a wall or tall object provides about 6 inches of counter space (**A**). The minimum distance is 15 inches on center (**B**). If a wall-hung or pedestal lavatory is used, make sure there is at least 4 inches from the edge of the lavatory to the wall (**C**) (Bathroom Planning Guideline 5).

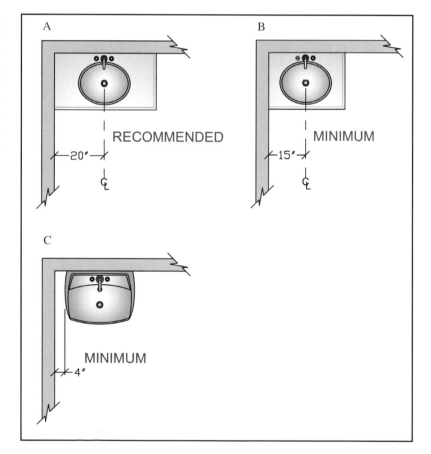

If two lavatories are being planned beside each other, 36 inches between the centerlines of the lavatories is recommended (Figure 6.20A). The code requirement for the centerline distance is 30 inches (Figure 6.20B). The IRC requires a 4-inch clearance between the edges of two freestanding or wall-hung lavatories (Figure 6.20C). These clearances also meet the Access Standards, but more generous spacing may be needed by many users.

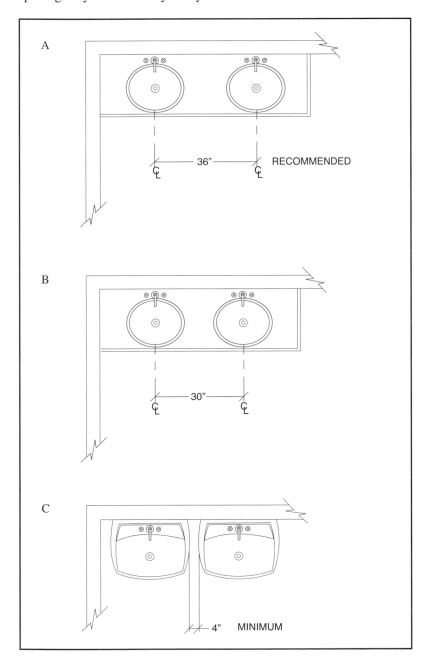

A

36" — RECOMMENDED

B

30"

C

4" MINIMUM

Figure 6.20 When planning a double lavatory configuration, it is recommended that the center of the fixtures be 36 inches apart. The minimum distance is 30 inches. If two pedestal or wall-hung fixtures are planned, make sure the edges are at least 4 inches apart (Bathroom Planning Guideline 6).

Lavatory Height

Traditionally, the lavatory has been 30 inches to 32 inches high, although recently higher cabinets have become available. Work surfaces in the bath, like those in the kitchen, should be about 3 inches below the users' elbow height. Subtracting 3 inches from the average female's elbow would place the comfortable height at 36 inches.

Panero and Zelnik (1979) recommend a range of heights. For men it is 37 inches to 43 inches; for women, 32 inches to 36 inches; and for children, 26 inches to 32 inches. When a knee space is planned for a seated user at a vanity, the height of the lavatory may range from 28 inches to 34 inches.

The recommended range of lavatory heights in the Bathroom Planning Guidelines reflects adult users and is 32 inches to 43 inches. Remember to plan the lavatory height so that the rim is 3 inches below the elbow of the user.

If two users will use the same lavatory, a compromise will have to be made and discussions with the client will help determine which height is most comfortable. Two lavatories of different heights may be the best solution.

Figure 6.21 The height of the lavatory should fit the user. For adults, this could range from 32 inches to 43 inches high depending on the user's height (Bathroom Planning Guideline 7).

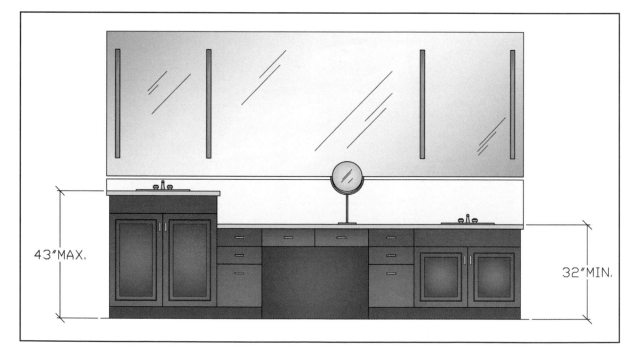

Figure 6.22 Lavatories at two heights can accommodate users with a wide range in their height. (Courtesy of Kohler Company)

There are many styles of lavatories, and the selection will impact how lavatory height is planned. Wall-mounted lavatories and those placed on wall-mounted counters offer flexibility in the height of the fixture. Pedestal sinks, wall-hung sinks and console-style vanities also improve the clear floor space in front of, and under, the fixture.

When using a pedestal sink, the designer will be limited by the height of the specified product. The pedestal may need to be placed on a platform to reach the appropriate height for the user. Finish the platform at the baseboard height, and in the same material as the floor, so that it blends.

Several styles of vanity lavatories can be placed in a counter: integral, self-rimming, under-mounted and rimmed. A vessel lavatory can be set on or cut into the counter. In all of these applications, it is important to estimate the actual height of the lavatory rim. A vessel lavatory will sit several inches above the counter, so add the height of the lavatory to the cabinet and counter heights, to get the finished height.

Figure 6.23 A vessel lavatory sits above the counter, so add both the height of the cabinet and counter, and the height of the lavatory together, to get the total finished height. (Courtesy of Porcher)

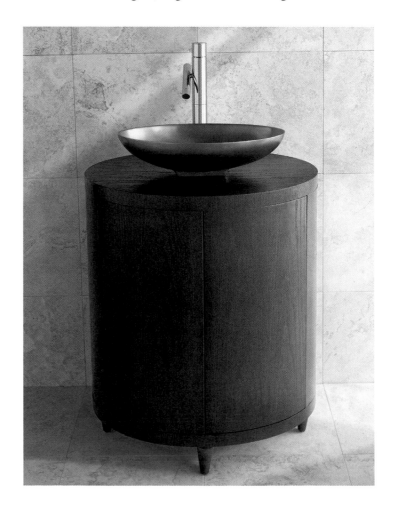

Because vanity bases are often low (30 inches to 32 inches), a cabinet or console may need to be adjusted to place the lavatory at the appropriate height. Although a 34 ^{1}/$_2$-inch cabinet with 1 ^{1}/$_2$-inch countertop might be the appropriate height, specifying a kitchen cabinet might be out of proportion to the specified lavatory. Standard kitchen cabinets are 24-inches deep, but many lavatories have been designed to fit in the typical 21-inch deep vanity cabinet.

To get the vanity cabinet at an appropriate height, specify a higher cabinet, or raise a standard cabinet by placing it on a deeper toe kick or mounting it on the wall and not using a toe kick. If the toe kick is raised, consider raising the baseboard dimension throughout the room for a clean line at the room base.

If the cabinet is raised, it creates a "floating" effect, which can be enhanced by decorative lighting. Plus, it improves access by increasing clear floor space. The same flooring material used throughout the bathroom should be used beneath the cabinet.

Figure 6.24 A floating vanity can be dramatic and convenient. (Courtesy of Gioi Ngoc Tran and co-designer Vernon Applegate – San Francisco, California)

Seated Vanity

People who wish to sit while using the lavatory can benefit from a knee space at the lavatory or at a vanity. If the opening is for a person in a wheelchair, the minimum code-related dimensions for the opening under the counter are 30 inches wide by 27 inches high by 19 inches deep. A 36 inch wide knee space is recommended, since the opening can then be used as part of a T-turn. The exact counter height for a specific client will be determined by the height of the client's knees and sometimes the wheelchair arm. When creating a knee space, support for the suspended counter should be planned.

Figure 6.25 A vanity near the lavatory can provide a place to apply makeup. (Courtesy of Belva Johnson, CKD, CBD – New Orleans, Louisiana)

Figure 6.26 A knee space should have clear opening 27 inches high and 36 inches wide (Access Standard 4).

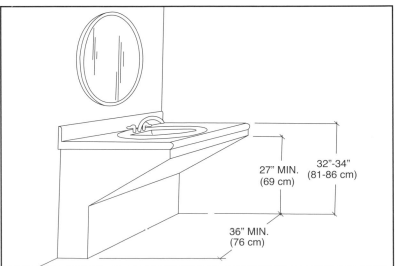

27" MIN. (69 cm)

32"-34" (81-86 cm)

36" MIN. (76 cm)

Counter Edges

In order to remove sharp edges in the Grooming Center, counter edges should be rounded or clipped if the counter projects into the room. This will help prevent injury if a person bumps into the edge or falls against it.

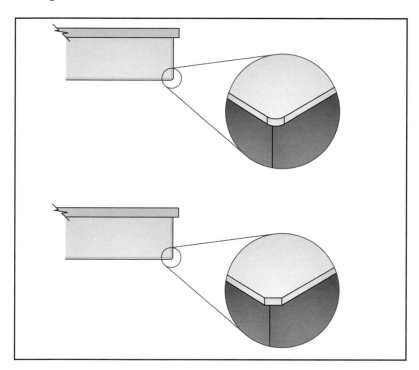

Figure 6.27 Counter edges should be rounded or clipped (Bathroom Planning Guideline 8).

Faucet

The type and placement of the faucet used with a particular lavatory design are important, and they should be looked at together. The faucet should have a water spray that stays in the sink and does not spray the user, the counter or the floor.

Water will be less likely to splash out of a larger bowl. The faucet should be high enough for users to get their hands beneath the spray. The length of the faucet spout should be proportional to the size of the lavatory sink, to avoid overspray.

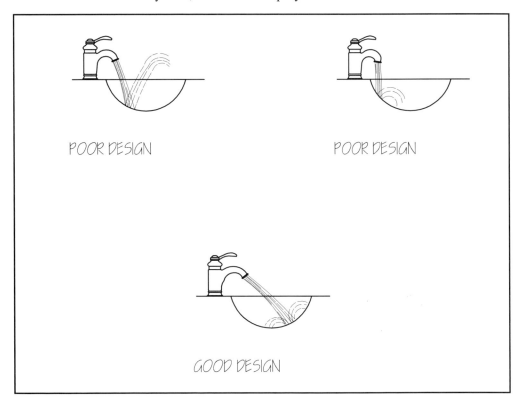

Figure 6.28 Plan the type and placement of lavatories and faucets so that the spray is accessible and stays within the sink bowl.

Center-set, widespread, mini-widespread, and single-hole faucets require different specifications for the placement of holes on the lavatory or counter. A deck-mounting of the faucet may require a deeper counter and a longer neck on the spout.

Wall-mounted faucets require a more difficult installation, since they are plumbed through the wall. The designer will need to identify the height and location of these types of faucets. The spacing of the controls should be planned with consideration for the user's handedness.

Lever handles or controls that are easy to twist and maneuver are recommended. However, any design of the handles other than smooth round knobs will improve function, as will single controls.

A

B

C

D

E

Figure 6.29 Faucet types and placements vary and should be considered in conjunction with the lavatory design. (**A**) This undermounted lavatory has a faucet mounted in the counter. (**B**) A self-rimming lavatory has the faucet mounted on the rim. (**C**) This self-rimming lavatory has a faucet mounted in the counter. (**D**) The faucet for a vessel lavatory is often mounted on the wall. (**E**) This unique faucet delivers water from a glass dish and is mounted on the back of the console lavatory. (**A**) Courtesy of Architectural Bath (**B and D**) Courtesy of Danze (**C**) Courtesy of Swanstone (**E**) Courtesy of KWC

Storage

With all of the activities there, many items could be stored at the grooming area. Many will be used daily, while others will only be needed occasionally. Either way, plan according to the following Storage Principles:

- **Store items at the first or last place of use.** Soap should be beside the lavatory.

- **Items used together should be stored or grouped together.** All make-up should be stored in one place.

- **Stored items should be easy to locate at a glance.** Place items so labels are easy to read.

- **Frequently used items should be within easy reach.** Keep the toothbrush convenient to the lavatory.

- **Store items in duplicate locations if needed.** Towels will be needed at the lavatory, shower, and bidet.

- **Store hazardous items out of the reach of children or others who might be harmed by them.** Medicines and cleaning supplies should be put in high locations or behind locked cabinets.

- **Store items in the appropriate environment.** Some medicines should be stored away from light, heat and/or humidity.

Consider if storage should be open or closed. Closed storage hides clutter, provides privacy and protects items from dust. But open storage is easier to see, reach and remember. It helps people with cognitive impairments. Generous and appropriate lighting improves access to storage, particularly for the aging eye.

Storage should be flexible (adjustable shelves) and efficient (maximize the space). When spaces are too deep, items just get lost in the back. Also consider that the most comfortable reach range while standing is 26 inches to 59 inches, and that the average maximum reach height for women is 69 inches.

Storage placed between 15 inches and 48 inches above the floor is most accessible and within the universal reach range. D-pulls on cabinetry are better for a person with limited use of their hands, wrists or fingers than other types of hardware.

Storage Ideas:

- An appliance garage makes a great place to store bathroom appliances—convenient and grouped together. GFCI receptacles and a kill switch help the careless or forgetful.

- Cabinet storage should include drawers and/or pull-out shelves to help make the storage convenient to reach. (Figure 6.30A)

- Shallow shelving will be useful for many items in the grooming area. (Figure 6.30C)

- Open shelving makes it easier to see where things are located. (Figure 6.30D)

- Laundry bins can be built into cabinetry. (Figure 6.30F)

- Hooks, pegs and racks can place items close to where needed.

- A turntable in deeper storage cabinets will make more space useable.

- A recessed storage area can be built into the wall. (Figure 6.30B)

- A pole with rotating and adjustable shelving might work in some spaces. (Figure 6.30E)

Figure 6.30 Many creative and convenient storage options are available including drawers, recessed shelves, using shallow open shelves, deeper open storage for towels, a pole, and a pull-out hamper. (Courtesy of (**A**) MasterBath (**B**) Anthony Binns, CKD, CBD – Toronto, Ontario, (**C**) Robern, (**D**) James P. Meloy, CKD – Roswell, Georgia, (**E**) Tim Scott and Erica Westeroth, CKD – Toronto, Ontario and (**F**) MasterBath)

A

B

C

D

E

F

Medicine Cabinet

The medicine cabinet is the old stand-by for storage at the Grooming Center. Its shallow depth makes it suitable for many small grooming items. There are many sizes and styles available, and this type of storage can be useful. Medicine cabinets can be recessed into the wall, partially recessed or surface-mounted. They can be placed centered over the lavatory, to the side, or on the returning wall, making contents easier to reach.

If the medicine cabinet is to be recessed, it is important to locate the studs as well as the plumbing, and place the cabinet within the framing. This decision must be made before construction begins.

A surface-mounted medicine cabinet can be placed anywhere, but may need to be secured into the studs to assure the weight does not pull it off the wall. The medicine cabinet can be moved to the side of the lavatory, which puts it within the reach of more users. Other items such as a large mirror, window or decorative design can be placed above the lavatory.

Figure 6.31 A medicine cabinet can be placed to one side of the vanity, leaving the wall behind the vanity for a mirror or art. (Courtesy of MasterBath by RSI)

Mirror

The mirror is an important feature of the Grooming Center. Several of the center's activities—applying make-up, hair care, and shaving—require users to view themselves in a mirror. This typically means a mirror is placed above the lavatory, but placing the mirror adjacent to the lavatory, in a vanity space, might also work.

It is recommended that mirrors be placed with consideration for the users' eye height and line of sight. To minimize glare, lighting should be selected and placed on either side of the mirror in a position that shields the light source from the naked eye. Refer to Chapter 7 for more information on lighting placement.

Placing the bottom edge of the mirror at a maximum 40 inches above the finished floor will make it useable by many seated or shorter people, but don't forget to extend the height so that it fits the taller user, as well. Small children might still need to stand on a stepstool. When possible, a full length mirror somewhere in the bathroom will function for users of all heights.

Separate mirrors placed at each user's height can also provide a custom fit, and an adjustable height or tilting mirror might also provide a solution. A full-length mirror in the bathroom can serve the needs of people of all heights and provide a final check after dressing.

Figure 6.32 The mirror at the vanity should be placed at the user's eye level. (Bathroom Planning Guideline 23). This arrangement has counters and mirrors planned for a tall and short user with storage, including an appliance garage, separating the two areas.

Towels

Towels need to be planned throughout the bathroom so that they are convenient to the user when needed. At the grooming area, washcloths and hand towels are needed for face washing and hand drying. Guest towels might be stored and displayed in some powder rooms or guest baths.

Placement of all towels should be 15 inches to 48 inches above the floor. Towel bars and towel rings are typical devices for storage and should be placed close to the lavatory so that water does not drip on the floor. Figure 6.33 illustrates sizes of hanging and folded towels that might be used in the bathroom.

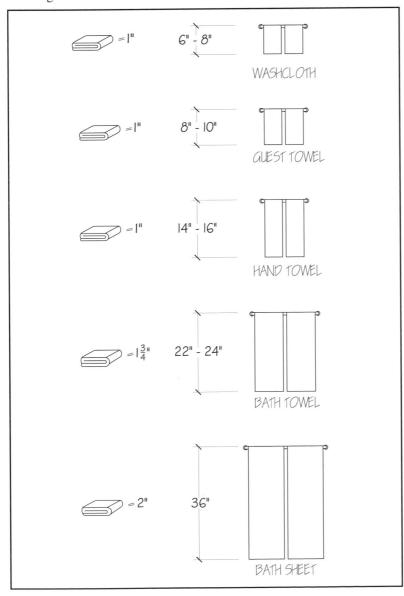

Figure 6.33 Towels should be placed where needed in the bathroom (Bathroom Planning Guideline 23). Make sure the hanging and folding space accommodates the size of towels used in an area.

BATHING/SHOWERING CENTER

Guidelines and Access Standards

The Bathroom Planning Guidelines and Access Standards that are important to planning the Grooming Area are 4, 5, 6, 7, 8, 22, and 23. For the complete Guidelines and Access Standards, see Chapter 11.

While the basic activity of the Bathing/Showering Center is cleansing the body, there is a wide range of associated activities that take place in this area. The bathtub, shower and tub/shower combination are the main fixtures, all of which have their own related planning considerations.

- Getting in and out of bathtubs is a serious safety issue, since falls can happen during transfer. Turning water on and off, and adjusting water temperature, are also key activities in bathing and showering. In addition to water and the fixture, soap and other cleansing products, washcloths and sponges are used in cleansing.

- Washing hair also occurs in the bathtub or shower. A faucet spray, shampoos, conditioners and a variety of other products will be needed for this activity.

- Shaving the face and legs might also take place in the tub or shower. A mirror may be needed to see the face, and a bench or ledge might make shaving legs safer and more convenient.

- The bathtub is also a place for relaxing, and is often therapeutic. Many people find that soaking in a warm bath can calm them and reduce stress. Tubs especially designed for relaxing might be deeper and jetted.

  Bubble baths, aromatic oils, bath salts and fragrant additives can enhance the effect of the warm water. Special sponges and loofahs help exfoliate the skin, and pulsating hand sprays can enhance the spa experience. Candles, soft lighting, a lit fireplace and music also add to the experience.

- Showering can also provide a sensual experience that goes beyond body cleansing. Pulsating showerheads and body sprays offer a variety of massaging actions that help to relax stiff muscles. Multiple showerheads from above, and jets from the side, can invigorate the body all over. Rain heads and waterfall heads may be more relaxing, offering a wide but gentle water flow from above.

- The amount of moisture created by bathing and showering will require specialized ventilation to remove some of the moisture and heat from the bathroom. Requirements for ventilation are covered in Chapter 7.

• Clothing will be removed before bathing and showering, and replaced with more clothes or a robe. The designer should think about how dirty clothes will be handled in the bathroom, and how clean clothes or robes will be stored. Hampers, laundry chutes and laundry rooms might help tackle the dirty clothes issue. Hooks, closets and a nearby dressing center could make fresh clothes more accessible. More information on these topics is in Chapter 8.

Bathing Recommendations

Bathtubs come in several sizes. The size of a traditional standard tub or tub/shower combination is 32 inches x 60 inches. This size will fit in most full bathrooms. However, it does not necessarily meet the needs of the user, so it is important to discuss tub size with the person(s) who will be bathing.

A tub bath may be taken by simply sitting in the tub. Knees might be outstretched or bent at an angle, but the back is generally perpendicular to the bottom of the tub. Leaning back and relaxing in the tub requires an angled contour to support the user's back. The appropriate length of the tub should be determined by the leg length of the user. A short woman might slide under the water if her feet do not reach the end of the tub. A tall woman may never be able to lean back and relax without her bent knees raised out of the water.

Longer and shorter tubs are available, and tubs come in different depths that might make the bath more comfortable. Smaller square tubs might also be appropriate for shorter people. If there are multiple users at different times, a compromise in tub size will be needed.

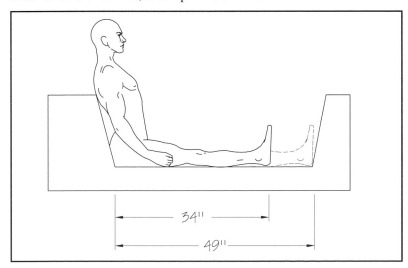

Figure 6.34 The buttock to heel measurement varies from 34 inches for small women to 49 inches for tall men. When selecting a tub for a client, consider the interior dimension, the angle of the back, and the depth of the tub to achieve an appropriate fit.

215

Two people may want to use the tub at the same time. Longer and wider tubs are available for this purpose. Sitting side-by-side requires a 42 inch wide tub. Sitting opposite requires a 36 inch wide tub. Often these will be jetted tubs, used sporadically. Soaking tubs which are often deeper, may not be jetted. See Chapter 8 for more information about specialized tubs.

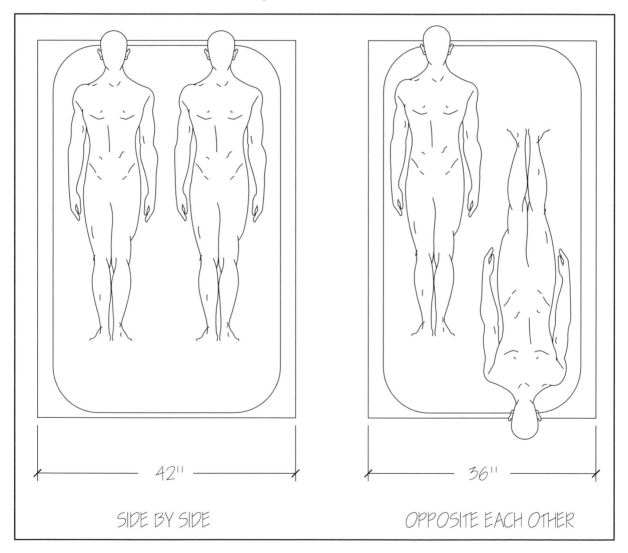

42"

36"

SIDE BY SIDE

OPPOSITE EACH OTHER

Figure 6.35 Bathtubs for two can accommodate side-by-side seating or an arrangement where bathers face each other.

Because of its size, the tub is often a dominant feature in the bathroom and is placed as a focal point. It may be viewed from the entry or placed in the center of the room.

Tubs that will be used for relaxing are often placed next to a window that offers an interesting and calming view. (Caution: Looking into the neighbor's breakfast room may not be relaxing to the user or the neighbor.) A privacy garden adjacent to the tub area may create the right atmosphere. If the window is placed so that privacy and view are compromised, a window treatment, a window of glass block, or a diffuser in the window, can be used to provide light without visual access. A window next to the tub (bottom edge less than 60 inches off the finished floor) should be made of tempered glass.

Figure 6.36 Often the bathtub is the central feature in the bathroom. (Courtesy of Kohler Company)

Floor Clearance

Wherever the tub is placed, it is recommended that at least a 30-inch clear space be planned along the side of it. If dressing occurs in front of the tub, more space is needed. A 42 inch to 48 inch dressing circle will allow room to dry off and put on undergarments.

Building codes allow a minimum of 21 inches in front of the tub, but this will be tight for many users. If a parent is helping bathe children, or a caregiver is assisting someone with a bath, extra floor space will be needed to accommodate them as well as the user.

If the bather will be transferring to the tub from a mobility aid or wheelchair, then 30 inches would be a minimum requirement, with more space preferred. When planning for a free-standing tub, consider which side(s) of the tub will be used for entering, exiting and passage, and allow the proper clearances.

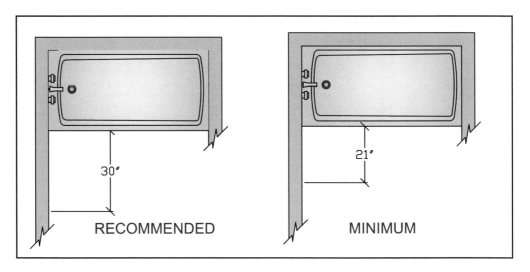

Figure 6.37 The recommended clearance in front of the tub is 30 inches. A minimum distance would be 21 inches (Bathroom Planning Guideline 4).

Getting in and out of the tub can be dangerous, but there are many things the designer can do to reduce the risks of falls. The typical method of entry is to stand on one foot and step over the side of the tub, which challenges anyone's balance. The danger is increased by wet and slippery surfaces, increased tub depth, and a tub bottom that is often not flat.

The ideal way to enter a tub is to sit on the edge, raise one leg at a time over the rim, and then ease into the water. Unfortunately, most standard tubs do not have an edge wide enough for most people to sit on.

With a standard tub, placing a seat at the head end provides a transfer seat. While 15 inches is the minimum recommended depth for a seat, even less depth can benefit some users. Attention must be given to the user's size and weight, so that the seat will support the intended use.

If a tub is placed on a frame or platform, a seating edge can be designed. Some accessible tubs have doors that open to allow the user to step in before the tub is filled.

When a deck cannot incorporate a seat, there are a variety of tubs that include integral or fold-away seats. For more details, see Chapter 9.

Grab Bars

Grab bars placed in the tub will give users something to hold onto as they enter and exit, thus alleviating some balance problems. NKBA recommends grab bars at the tub and shower to assist with this transfer. There are many decorative and attractive grab bars available to match other trim and accessories in the bathroom. It is critical that they be installed so they support at least 250 pounds. Some clients may need more support.

The wall behind the tub and shower should be reinforced to support the grab bar. The placement of the bar should be planned where it best fits the user.

Besides rails placed at the back and ends of the tub, a vertical bar at the front, and one on the back wall at a diagonal, are often helpful. Figure 6.39 illustrates where grab bars should be placed in the tub. See NKBA Bathroom Planning Guideline 14 and Access Standard for more detail on placement. Standard towel bars and soap dishes will not support someone in a fall and can be dangerous, since they protrude.

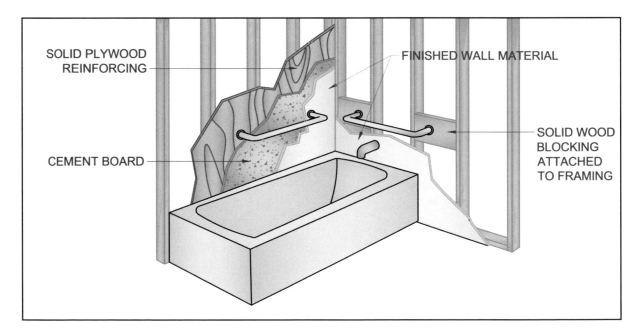

Figure 6.38 Providing blocking between studs or enclosing the entire tub surround with a solid plywood base will allow grab bars to be placed anywhere the user needs them (Bathroom Guideline 14).

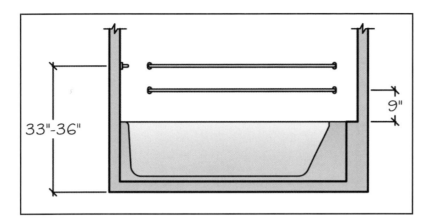

Figure 6.39 Grab bars should be placed according to user needs. A standard placement is along the back of the bathtub 33 inches to 36 inches high and vertically at the control end of the tub, 9 inches above the rim (Bathroom Planning Guideline 14).

No Steps

Tubs are most safely used if their floor is level with the bathroom floor, and the deck or top of the tub is approximately seat height (plus or minus 18 inches). Even one step into the tub creates a situation that can challenge balance and, therefore, is not recommended.

A tub sunk into the floor is even worse since it creates a situation where the user will step down from the floor level to the tub level. Or the person will need to sit on the floor to get into the tub, which is difficult for many. The sunken tub may also create a hazard if one were to trip and fall into it.

A tub placed on a high platform can require several steps to get up to, creating the same problem as the sunken tub. When users reach the top of the steps, they have to step down onto the bottom of the tub, more than 15 inches below them.

Even though it is clear that steps can cause a hazard, a client may insist on them. If you have to compromise, try to design so the step is strictly decorative and not actually used for tub entry. Use only one step designed in compliance with local building codes, or at least 10 inches deep and 7 1/4 inches high. A grab bar or handrail must be included for safety.

Figure 6.40 Plan the platform tub height so that no steps are needed to get into the tub with 18 inches being an ideal height for transfer (Bathroom Planning Guideline 17).

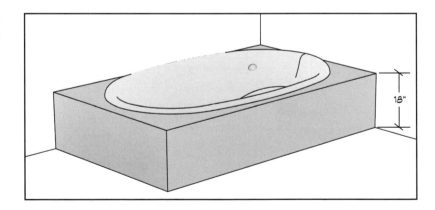

Access Panels

Whirlpool tubs and other equipment have motors and controls that need to be considered in the design of the bathroom space. Always follow manufacturers' specifications for installation. This equipment will need to be examined for maintenance and service, so it is important to plan for access. Removable panels should be easy to reach, and the equipment should be accessible for the installer and repair person.

Flooring

While no floor is completely slip-resistant, especially when wet, to help prevent falls, use slip-resistant surfaces on the tub floor, as well as the bathroom floor. Many tubs come with a slightly rough surface that helps the user grip the bottom of the tub.

Faucet Controls

Faucet controls should be accessible to the user before entering the tub. In an enclosed tub or tub/shower combination, the controls may be placed on the wall at 33 inches above the finished floor. In general, off-setting the controls toward the room improves access by reducing bending and stretching.

Placing controls within 6 inches of the front wall makes them more accessible. For a free-standing tub, or one placed in a platform, controls should be on the front side. The user should not have to lean across the tub to turn on the water and check temperature. Place the faucet and controls so they do not conflict with the transfer area.

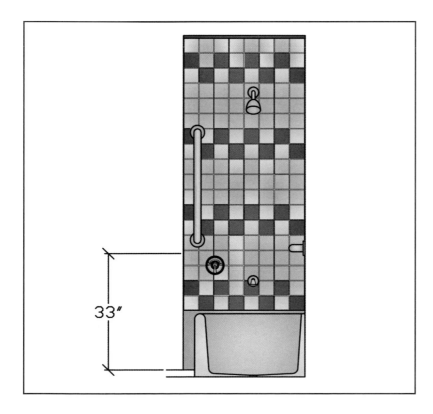

Figure 6.41 The centerline of the controls for the bathtub should be between the rim of the tub and 33 inches off the floor (Bathroom Planning Guideline 10). Offsetting the controls so that they are towards the front of the tub makes them accessible from both inside and outside of the tub.

33″

Figure 6.42 The controls on a platform tub should be to the side to allow for space to get in and out of the tub. (Courtesy of Jacuzzi)

Besides faucet placement, the type and design should be considered. A faucet with a hand spray and 60-inch hose allows a caregiver to assist with bathing. Controls should be easy to grasp and manipulate. Any design other than smooth round knobs improves function. A single control is easier to use than separate hot and cold controls. If a tub/shower combination is planned, the shower controls must be pressure balanced, have thermostatic mixing, or be a combination of both.

Storage

Storage is needed at the tub for the activities occurring there. Within the tub area, hair care products and shaving supplies may be needed regularly, and a shelf recessed within the wall to hold them would be preferred.

Storage should be provided for occasionally used items that help with a relaxing bath. Bath salts and oils, candles, loofahs and exfoliating sponges may be stored at the tub, on a shelf or in a cabinet. Items used regularly in the tub (sponges, tub toys) should be placed where they can dry out, to avoid a mold problem.

Figure 6.43 Shelving is recessed into the wall to the side of the whirlpool bathtub, creating a convenient place to store towels and bath accessories. (Courtesy of Joan Descombes, CKD – Winter Park, Florida)

Towels

Towels and washcloths should be stored close by the tub, and towel bars should be able to be reached from inside the tub. Hanging bath towels require a 22 inch to 24 inch high space on the wall, while bath sheets require a 36 inch high space (Figure 6.33). Towel bars, towel rings and hooks are all possible solutions in this area. Towel warmers or a warming drawer can be planned for a special drying experience.

Grab bars can be used in place of towel bars, but towel bars should not be placed where they will be used as grab bars. Towel bars have not been designed to withstand the weight of someone pulling on them. Accessible towel placement is between 15 inches and 48 inches off the floor.

Showering Recommendations

Showering is an increasingly common way to cleanse the body. The tub/shower combination is used in many simple bathrooms to provide both bathing and showering options. If the clients consistently take a shower, a separate shower may be preferred. It is easier to get into than a tub/shower combination because the user will not have to step over the tub rim. In large bathrooms, a separate shower and bathtub may be specified. If the shower is separate, it may be placed adjacent to the bathtub, or in a separate area.

Floor Clearance

At least 30 inches of clearance is recommended in front of the shower for comfortable access. Building codes require 24 inches of clear space in front of the shower, but this will be a limited area. A dressing circle of 42 inches to 48 inches might be needed for drying off and changing into clothing. If the bather will be transferring from a wheelchair or other mobility aid to the shower, a 36 inch x 48 inch space is a minimum requirement, with more space preferred.

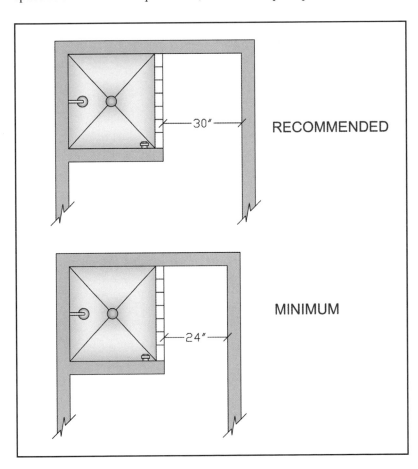

RECOMMENDED

MINIMUM

Figure 6.44 The recommended clearance in front of the shower is 30 inches. The minimum clearance is 24 inches (Bathroom Planning Guideline 4).

Shower Size

Most prefabricated showers come in standard sizes from 32 inches to 48 inches square.

- The recommended interior shower size for one person is at least 36 inches x 36 inches. This allows one person to comfortably stand in the shower with arms raised to wash their hair. Building codes state that the minimum interior shower size is 30 inches x 30 inches, but this is a tight space for most adults.

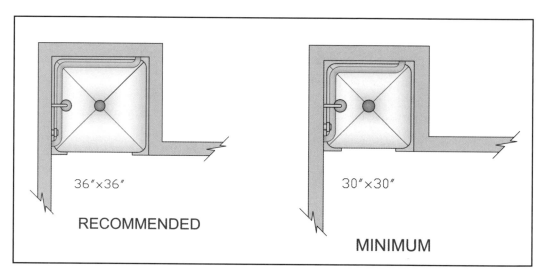

36"x36"

RECOMMENDED

30"x30"

MINIMUM

Figure 6.45 Plan a shower at least 36 inches x 36 inches. The minimum sized shower is 30 inches x 30 inches. If an angled or round shower is used, it should be large enough for a 30-inch disc to fit in the interior (Bathroom Planning Guideline 9).

- Check angled showers to make sure a 30-inch disc will fit into the shower floor. This will meet minimum code requirements. A larger disc area should be specified when user needs require more space.

- A 36 inch x 36 inch size is acceptable for a transfer shower to be used by a person transferring from a mobility aid. See Chapter 9 for more discussion.

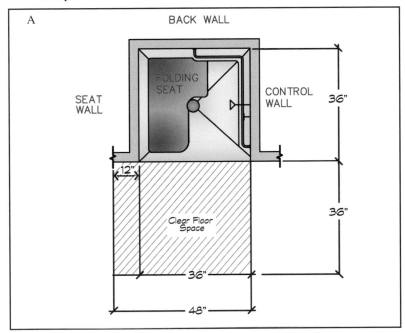

Figure 6.46 A transfer shower (**A**) is 36 inches x 36 inches and should have at least 36 inches x 48 inches of clearance in front of the shower with 12 inches extending beyond the wall opposite the controls. A roll-in shower (**B**) is at least 36 inches x 60 inches with a minimum 30 inches x 60 inches of clear space parallel to the open side of the shower (Access Standard 4 and 9).

- A roll-in shower used by a person with a bathing wheelchair should be at least 36 inches x 60 inches. Access standards suggest a 30 inch minimum width, but 36 – 42 inches makes it easier to contain the water in the shower (Figure 6.46B).

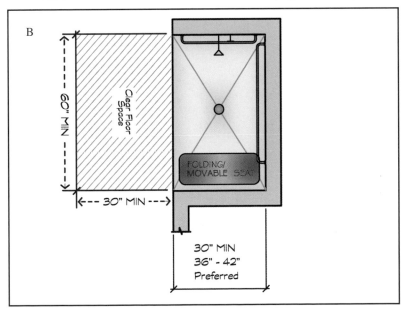

For a person to move out of the shower spray inside the shower, a 42 inch x 36 inch shower should be considered. Larger prefabricated showers are available, and custom showers can be designed to meet the needs of the user. (Check that any prefabricated shower will fit through the bathroom door.) In a shower at least 60 inches deep, it is possible to control the spray within the shower. In a two-person shower, make sure there is room for both people.

Figure 6.47 (A) A shower at least 36 inches x 42 inches allows one person to step out of the water spray. **(B–D)** Showers at least 60 inches wide can accommodate two shower sprays and two users comfortably.

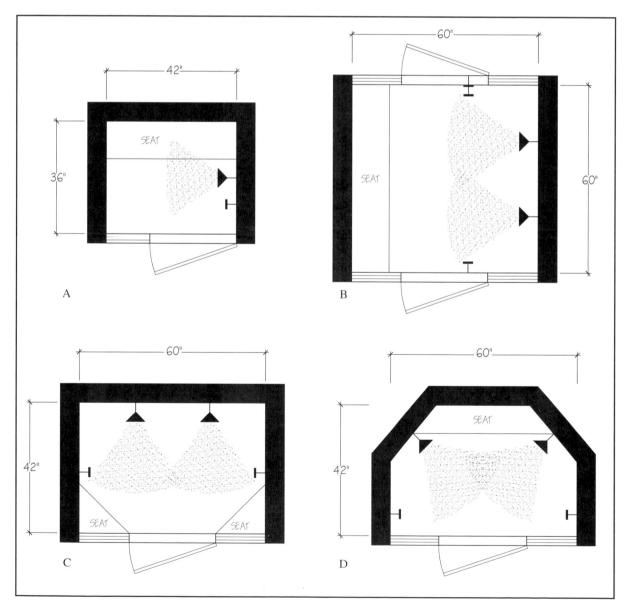

Getting in and out of the shower is somewhat easier than getting in and out of the bathtub, since the shower lip is lower than the bathtub rim. Curbless showers, showers with no threshold, can be planned if the water spray can be controlled, drainage planned, and flooring outside the shower included in the wet area. When possible, eliminating the shower door and threshold makes for easy entry.

Grab Bars

Because most users stand in the shower, the risk of falling is great. Grab bars are recommended for the back and sides of the shower (See Figure 6.48 for placement). The Bathroom Planning Guidelines and Access Standards found in Chapter 11 provide more detail on placement. As in the bathtub, the grab bars in the shower should be able to support at least 250 pounds.

The Guidelines and Access Standards recommend locations for grab bars. However, when possible, it is better to place reinforcement throughout the shower walls so clients can add support when and where they will use them.

Everyone is unique and their height and reach change as they age. A vertical bar at the shower entrance provides a helpful support when getting in and out. The surface and design of all grab bars should reduce the risk of a hand slipping on the bar.

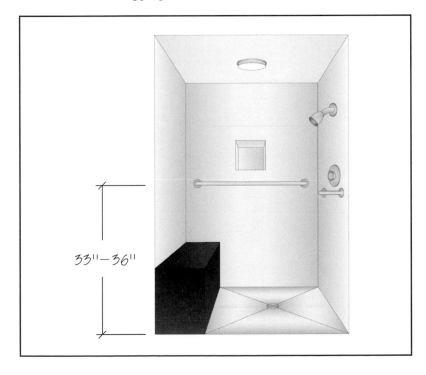

33"—36"

Figure 6.48 The walls behind the shower should be blocked or reinforced to support grab bars. Common placement of the grab bars is 33 inches to 36 inches above the floor on the back wall (Bathroom Planning Guideline 14).

Shower Seat

A seat is very helpful to many people as they shower. A person whose stamina is reduced due to age, pregnancy, injury, or too much physical activity, may not have the energy to stand throughout the shower. A woman may find a seated position the best for shaving her legs. A larger two-person shower usually has room for a bench. A seat or bench in the shower provides an opportunity to relax, assistance to people with limited strength or balance, and help with transfer.

NKBA recommends that a shower seat be planned. It should be 17 inches to 19 inches high from the finished shower floor and at least 15 inches deep, finished (Figure 6.49). Remember to allow for the thickness of the finishing material.

The bench should not interfere with the recommended minimum shower size of 36 inches x 36 inches of floor area, although codes will allow the minimum 30 inch x 30 inch size to be maintained. Just as in the tub area, when less than 15 inches is available, a narrower bench can benefit some users. Attention must be given to the user's size and weight so the seat will support the intended use.

Figure 6.49 A shower bench is recommended for the convenience and safety of all users (Bathroom Planning Guideline 12).

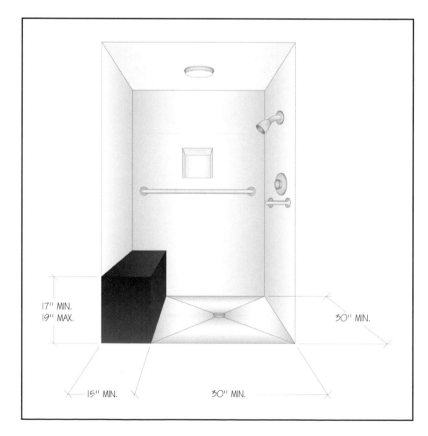

Shower Controls

The showerhead should be placed so it directs water toward the body, not the face or hair. A fixed showerhead, roughed in at 72 inches to 78 inches off the floor, is typical in many showers and tub/shower combinations. Plan the shower rough-in so that the bottom of the showerhead will be 72 inches off the finished floor or at a height appropriate to the user.

A showerhead on an adjustable bar, or a handheld showerhead, offers flexibility in a shower used by persons of different heights, or for different activities. When the adjustable height shower/hand spray is used, its lowest position should always be within the universal reach range (15 inches to 48 inches above finished floor).

The most convenient way for a plumber to install the shower control valves is to line them up under the showerhead. However, this is not most convenient for the user. Being able to reach the controls while standing outside of the shower spray is ideal. NKBA recommends that the controls be placed out of the water spray and between 38 inches to 48 inches above the floor. An accessible location is 6 inches from the outside of the fixture.

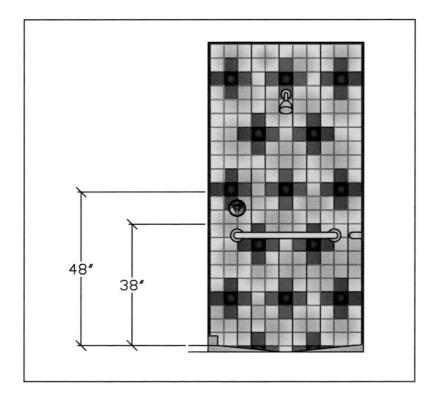

Figure 6.50 Shower controls should be placed 38 inches to 48 inches off the floor (Bathroom Planning Guideline 10). Offsetting the controls towards the front of the shower will make them accessible both inside and outside the water spray.

Codes require that shower control valves must be either pressure balanced, have thermostatic mixing, or have a combination of both, to prevent scalding due to changes in water-pressure. Hot and cold water controls should be easily identified with red and blue indicators. Consider a lever or loop handle control for ease of use. A handheld shower may be used in place of, or in addition, to the fixed showerhead to offer the user flexibility. This may be especially nice if the user will sit to shower.

If two people will be using the shower at the same time, there should be at least two showerheads, and each should be controlled separately. Design of the shower should take into account the number of body sprays, jets, control valves and diverters needed.

Figure 6.51 Water sprays and jets create a stress-relieving showering experience. (Courtesy of Grohe)

Shower Surround

The shower is a wet space so water resistant materials are critical. The surround of a shower or tub/shower combination should be of a waterproof material and extend a minimum of 3 inches above the showerhead rough-in. A typical rough-in is 72 inches to 78 inches. Codes require the waterproof wall materials extend at least 72 inches above the finished floor (Figure 6.52). The floor will be waterproof and should be slip resistant.

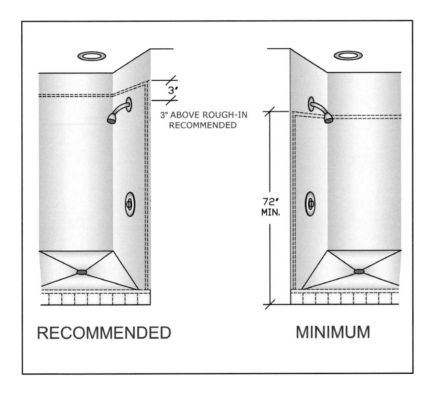

3" ABOVE ROUGH-IN
RECOMMENDED

72" MIN.

RECOMMENDED

MINIMUM

Figure 6.52 It is recommended that a shower surround be a water-proof material that extends 3 inches above the showerhead rough-in. A minimum surround should extend at least 72 inches above the floor (Bathroom Planning Guideline 13).

Prefabricated shower surrounds may be one piece, or divided into multiple pieces assembled onsite. Check the size of the room entry to make sure an installer can get a prefabricated unit into the room.

Shower Doors

Keeping the water in the shower, and not on the floor outside, is often a challenge to designers and users. A shower curtain will be easy to maneuver around. However, in smaller showers, the spray often extends beyond the shower floor and a curtain may not easily contain the water.

Enclosures and shower doors help to further seal the shower area and contain the water spray. In the case of a steam shower, the door opening will be sealed to the ceiling with a transom or a fixed panel.

The shower door should slide or open out towards the bathroom, a safety precaution to allow a helper to get into the shower if the user falls. Shower doors that swing both in and out, and curtains, can be easier for maneuvering. Ideally, door openings should be a minimum 32 inches wide to allow for easy circulation in and out of the shower.

Figure 6.53 A shower door should open into the room, so that it can be opened even if the bather falls against it (Bathroom Planning Guideline 16).

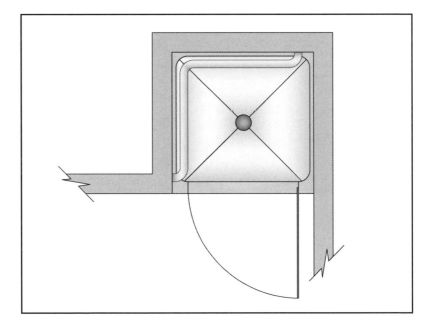

Creating a Shower With No Threshold or Door

A shower that does not require a threshold or a door has great appeal. It is a universal design that offers improved access and is popular in Europe. The water spray can be controlled in several ways. When a shower curtain is used, it will do a better job of water containment if it is made slightly longer than the height of the shower rod, and is weighted so that it drags. When not in use, the extra length can be draped using a tie back to enhance the appearance and allow for proper drying.

Sloping the floor towards the drain and sometimes adding a second drain can help to contain the water. A trough-style drain, separating the shower from the remaining wet area, can be used to collect any water that escapes. See Chapter 9.

A serpentine shower allows for an open entry with no threshold and no door. It can be beautiful and, when done correctly, is usable by a person with a mobility aid.

The ideal minimum size for this shower is large, 78 inches x 78 inches, to allow for minimum widths of 36 inches for any passage space. It includes a waterproofed wet area that helps contain the splash from the shower and doubles as a drying-off area.

Glazing

If glass is used in the shower surround or enclosure (including the door) it must be tempered glass. When using glass in this area, consider the sight-lines of the end users. Windows in the tub or shower area that are below 60 inches must be of tempered glass. Other glass windows or doors in the bathroom that are below 18 inches must be of tempered glass or an equivalent.

Figure 6.54 Tempered glass should be used in the bathroom wherever there is a chance that someone could fall against the glass, ie, in tub and shower doors and surrounds. It should also be used in windows at the bathtub or shower that are below 60 inches, and in windows or doors below 18 inches (Bathroom Planning Guideline 15).

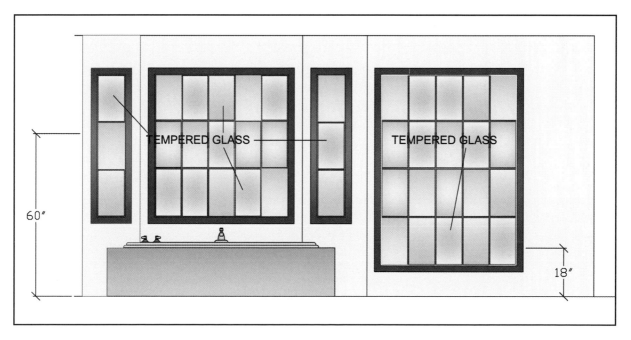

Storage and Towels

Since the shower is a convenient place to wash hair and shave, it is likely that numerous products will be used there, and storage for items used daily will be important. A shelf built into the shower wall or surround at a convenient height to the user is a good solution.

Towels should be placed within reach of the person in the shower and 15 inches to 48 inches above the floor. Extra towels will need to be stored close by. Refer to the previous section on towels and storage at the bathtub for guidance.

Guidelines and Access Standards

The Bathroom Planning Guidelines and Access Standards that are important in planning the Bathing and Showering areas are 4, 9, 10, 11, 12, 13, 14, 15, 16, 17, 18, 19, 22, and 23. For the complete Guidelines and Access Standards check Chapter 11.

TOILETING CENTER

Toileting is a universal activity of all bathrooms. It occurs in the master suite, as well as the powder room. In fact, "going to the bathroom" or "using the bathroom" often means using the toilet. But as with all the bath centers, there are many related activities to be considered in designing this area.

- The primary tasks taking place at the toilet are urination and defecation. Positions for urinating are culturally defined. A woman using a public toilet in Korea, for instance, may find that she is expected to stand over a receptacle in the floor. In North America, toilets have been designed so that women sit on the toilet and men stand when urinating, and both sit when defecating. Although Alexander Kira's research in the 1960s suggested that a squatting position is best for completing a bowel movement, this has not had an impact on the height of toilets in North America.

- The urinal is designed for a man to stand and urinate, and while common in commercial settings, it may also be a good idea in a house full of boys not known for accurate aim in using a toilet.

- Another activity that can occur at the toilet is feminine hygiene, especially during the menstrual cycle. Having supplies of tampons and/or pads close by will assist in this activity. Sometimes medications must be used vaginally or anally and often this is done at, or close to, the toilet.

- All of the toilet area activities mentioned previously will require cleansing afterward. Having toilet paper close by is standard in the United States. Bidets are also being used by clients wishing a more thorough cleansing of the perineal area. The need for, and benefit of, the bidet increases as people age.

A few other things might be considered when planning the toilet area. Some people read while sitting on the toilet, and having proper lighting and some reading materials stored in the area is helpful. Cleaning the toilet and surrounding areas should be done regularly to cut down on bacteria and odors, and having toilet brushes stored there will help make this easier. Ventilation should be planned in a toileting area to reduce odors.

Toilet Recommendations

The type and size of the toilet may affect the ability to meet some clearance recommendations, especially in small bathrooms. The two-piece toilet has a separate tank and bowl, while the one-piece toilet combines these and typically has a lower profile. The typical seat height of the toilet is between 14 inches and 17 inches, although 17 inch to 19 inch high toilets are growing in popularity. For a person who transfers onto the toilet from a wheelchair, the best height for the toilet is to match the wheelchair height, with the average being plus or minus 18 inches.

The toilet width ranges from 17 inches to 23 inches. A toilet with a standard bowl is about 25 inches deep, while one with an elongated bowl is about 30 inches. A wall-hung toilet with an in-wall tank will be about 22 inches deep. While not common, corner toilets are available for special applications. The fixture typically extends 33 inches from the corner and is about 15 inches wide.

Floor Clearance

Figure 6.55 Having at least 30 inches of clear floor space in front of the toilet allows for comfortable maneuverability. A minimum clearance of 21 inches is permitted (Bathroom Planning Guideline 4).

People using the toilet will need to stand, turn, sit, remove and replace parts of their clothing, and use nearby supplies like toilet paper. At least 30 inches of clear space is recommended in front of the toilet to allow for these activities, and perhaps more will be needed for larger people or persons needing assistance. Building codes allow this space to be reduced to 21 inches. This may allow leg room to sit on the toilet, but managing clothes may require moving to an area of the bathroom with more floor space.

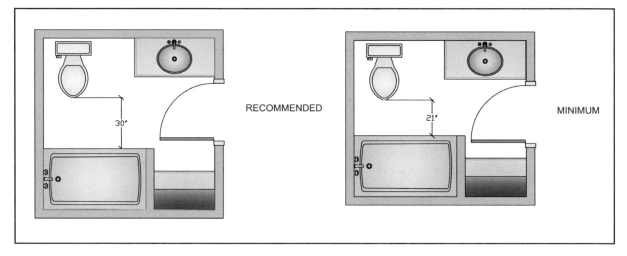

For a person approaching the toilet with a mobility aid, or transferring from a wheelchair, 30 inches in front of the toilet is a minimum clear space, but more is better. For a person approaching and transferring from the side, plan a minimum 30 inches clear floor space to the side of the toilet. Wall-hung toilets improve the clear floor space, making it easier to transfer onto the toilet and to maintain the floor around it.

Some users may need grab bars, so plan reinforcement around the toilet area so that they can be installed. Grab bars should be placed according to the user's requirements, including their method of transfer. Access standards suggest that the grab bars be placed behind the toilet and on the wall beside it. See Chapter 9 for more information on transfers and grab bars at toilets.

Toilet Placement

The toilet can be in several places within the bathroom and may be within its own separate area or compartment if space allows. There should be clearances on both sides of the toilet to allow the user to be able to sit comfortably and to move the upper part of the body without bumping into a wall or counter.

Placing the toilet at least 18 inches on center from the nearest wall or obstacle is the recommended distance. Building codes will typically allow the toilet to be placed 15 inches on center. Remember that this should be a clear space. Placing another obstacle in the space, such as a grab bar, towel bar or toilet paper holder, will interfere with the clearance.

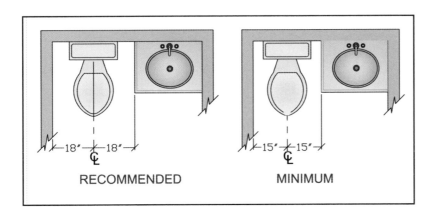

Figure 6.56 The toilet should be placed so that the center is 18 inches from a wall or other object. A minimum distance is 15 inches (Bathroom Planning Guideline 20).

Toilet Compartment

Placing a toilet in a separate compartment can be accommodated by following the previously recommended clearances. A 36 inch x 66 inch space measured from the inside wall will accommodate the recommended clearances. A 30 inch x 60 inch space will comply with building codes (Figure 6.57).

In both applications, the door to the compartment should open out toward the adjacent room; otherwise the door swing will interfere with the front clearance. A compartment is not recommended for people using mobility aids, since it limits options in transferring to a toilet. However, if one is used, it should be at least 60 inches x 59 inches. An exception to this is the toilet area planned for a client with limited balance or stamina, as this client could benefit from a space with support within reach on both walls of the approach to the toilet.

Figure 6.57 A toilet compartment that is 36 inches wide by 66 inches deep allows for a 32-inch clear opening at the doorway and comfortable clearances around the toilet. A 30-inch by 60-inch compartment will meet minimum requirements (Bathroom Planning Guideline 21).

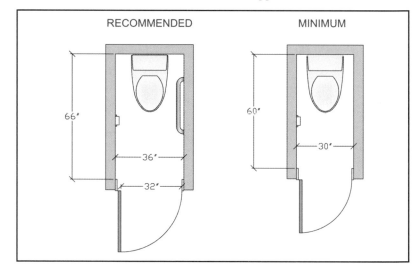

Figure 6.58 A toilet compartment that is 60 inches x 59 inches allows for a 30-inch x 48-inch clear floor space beside the toilet (Access Standard 21).

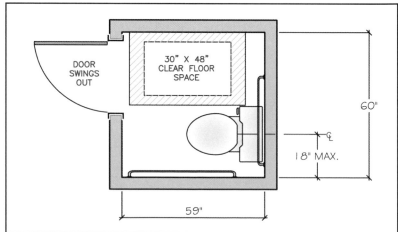

Toilet Paper Placement

It is important that the toilet paper dispenser be convenient to the user. The best location is on a wall or partition to the side, and slightly to the front, of the toilet. This allows the user to reach the paper while seated. Locations behind the toilet or across from the toilet will be difficult to reach without bending or stretching. The recommended location for the toilet paper is 8 inches to 12 inches in front of the toilet, centered 26 inches off the floor.

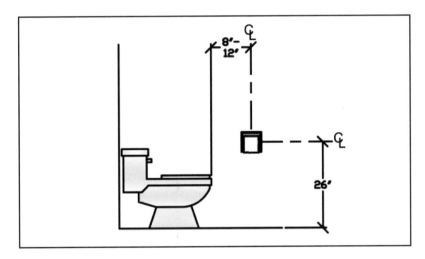

Figure 6.59 Place the toilet paper holder 8 inches to 12 inches in front of the toilet and 26 inches off the floor (Bathroom Planning Guideline 23).

Storage

It is convenient to locate storage close to, and accessible from, the toilet. Consider where extra toilet paper, feminine hygiene supplies and medications are stored. Cabinets close by, and within reach of the person seated on the toilet, would assist them in performing whatever task needs to be completed in the toilet area.

Bidet Recommendations

Bidets are used by straddling the bowl while facing the controls and the wall. Both hot and cold water must be provided. The bidet has a spray faucet spout (horizontal stream) or vertical spray in the center of the fixture (Figure 6.60). A pop-up stopper allows the bidet to be used more like a sink for a foot bath or hand washables. While the bidet looks similar to a toilet, it works like a sink.

The bidet provides cleansing for the pelvic area. Women may use the fixture for douching and cleansing during their menstrual periods. The bidet also provides a cleansing for both women and men that can help reduce irritation and heal rashes. The fixture may be especially useful for adults who have difficulty cleaning themselves. If a separate bidet cannot be included in the design, consider a toilet with an integrated bidet system or an add-on bidet system (Figure 6.61).

Figure 6.60 The bidet on the left has a vertical jet for the cleansing spray. The bidet on the right has an over-the-rim horizontal cleansing spray. (Courtesy of American Standard, Inc.)

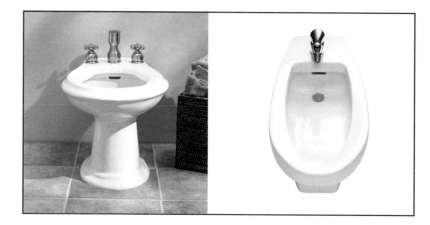

Figure 6.61 This toilet includes a washing system and uses sensors to control the toileting and cleansing actions. (Courtesy of Toto)

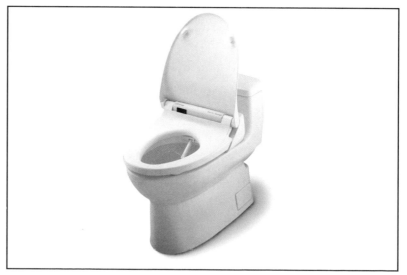

Clearances

The recommended clearances for the bidet are the same as for the toilet. That is, 30 inches of clear space in front of the bidet, with the bidet placed 18 inches on center from the nearest wall, obstacle or adjacent toilet. Minimum clearances are 21 inches of clear space in front of the bidet, with the bidet placed 15 inches on center from the nearest wall, obstacle or adjacent toilet.

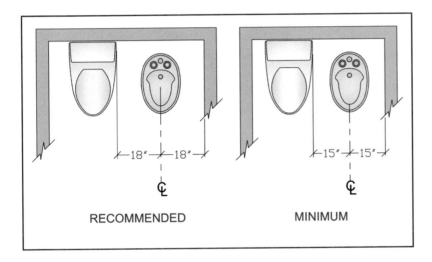

RECOMMENDED   MINIMUM

Figure 6.62 It is recommended that the bidet be placed 18 inches on center from a wall or other fixture and have a 30-inch clear floor space to the front of the fixture. Minimum clearances are 15 inches on center with a 21-inch clear floor space (Bathroom Planning Guidelines 4 and 20).

Storage and towels

Some storage should be supplied close to the bidet. It is important to have towels and soaps located next to this fixture.

Urinal Recommendations

The urinal can be a very practical fixture in the home. The toilet is designed for seating. However, when men stand to urinate at the toilet, the urine spray may not stay in the bowl. Spray on the floor and around the toilet area can cause discoloration, staining and odor. Men and boys of all ages can use the urinal with better control.

The height of the front of the urinal off the floor should be 19 1/2 inches for children and 24 inches for adults. In a custom installation, plan the lip of the urinal at 3 inches below the man's pants inseam.

It is recommended that the urinal be placed 18 inches on center from a side obstacle, such as a toilet or wall. The minimum centerline distance is 15 inches. Make sure at least 3 inches of clearance is allowed from the edge of the urinal to a side wall. A protective, durable wall surface material should cover at least 12 inches on either side of the urinal.

Flooring beneath, and in front of the urinal, should be of a durable material, as well.

The recommended clearance in front of the urinal is 30 inches, the same as for other bath fixtures. The minimum clearance allowed is 21 inches.

Guidelines and Access Standards

The Bathroom Planning Guidelines and Access Standards that are important to the Toileting area are 4, 14, 20, 21, 22, and 23. For the complete Guidelines and Access Standards check Chapter 11.

PLANNING THE
TOTAL BATHROOM

As you have seen, there are many decisions and details involved in creating a space plan for a bathroom that is functional and useable. Not only must you consider your client's needs and the physical space you are working in, you must consider the selection of product in relation to the spatial requirements. You may have to use a certain style of lavatory or bathtub because of space and planning restrictions. On the other hand, you may have to arrange the space to accommodate the desired fixture or activity. There may be several ways that the bathroom could be planned depending on the choices that you make.

Previous chapters presented assessment tools and background information to help you understand your client's needs and desires. In this chapter you have been presented with numerous NKBA Planning Guidelines that will further influence your design decisions. The Guidelines provide key criteria for effective space planning.

But you may not always be able to meet every one. Budget, time and space restrictions will influence how you incorporate the Guidelines within the parameters of each job. Of course, you will have to meet any requirements specified in your local building code. Particularly in small spaces, there will be instances where a building code may be relied on to determine your design decision.

Throughout this chapter and the rest of the book, universal access has been incorporated into recommendations and considerations. As a designer, you will work with clients whose needs are individualized. Refer to Chapter 9 for a more extensive list of universal and accessible design concepts arranged according to user groups. This is a great place to look for ideas that might be useful if your client is older, has children, has a unique mobility or handedness requirement, or has sensory or cognitive impairments.

Remember that infrastructure requirements also must be considered. There are also decisions related to mechanical systems. Lighting, ventilation, heat, and placement of receptacles have been referred to in this chapter, but in Chapter 7 there are more details (and Guidelines) related to these areas. Be sure you are familiar with these recommendations and requirements when you start to design a space.

More information about the design process and steps for the final layout of the bathroom are discussed in detail in Chapter 10. Until you have mastered the planning criteria, be prepared to refer to the Guidelines and information presented in this chapter throughout the design and planning process. A summary of all the Guidelines is at the end of this book in Chapter 11. These will provide you with a quick reference.

CHAPTER 7: Mechanical Planning

Electrical and mechanical components for the bathroom include the wiring for various electrical devices: heating, air conditioning, and ventilating equipment, and their placement; and lighting. Consider these early in the project, in order to assure the basic structure is in place before the installation of finishes and fixtures.

ELECTRICAL PLANNING

Whether building or remodeling, use the Needs Assessment Form in Chapter 5 to determine the electrical needs of the client. Then, consult current codes to see what must be implemented, and suggest additional ideas for improving the system to address future needs.

Codes

The National Electric Code (NEC) and the Canadian Electric Code (CEC), which are almost identical, help assure a safe electrical system, a major consideration in the bathroom where water and electricity are in close proximity. To improve safety, codes now require ground fault circuit interrupters (GFCI) in all bathroom receptacles. These devices reduce the hazards of electrical shock, by cutting the electrical flow quickly when they detect that the flow going out to an appliance is different than the flow that returns. GFCI receptacles fit in the same space as the standard receptacles, but need to be appropriately wired.

Codes also require that at least one GFCI receptacle be installed within 36 inches of the outside edge of the lavatory. Furthermore, no receptacles can be placed within the tub or shower space. No switches can be located within wet locations, or within reach of a person standing in the tub or shower, unless the switches are part of a listed tub or shower assembly.

For more in-depth information on codes, as well as technical details of electricity for the bathroom, see the NKBA book *Kitchen & Bath Systems*, part of the *Professional Resource Library*.

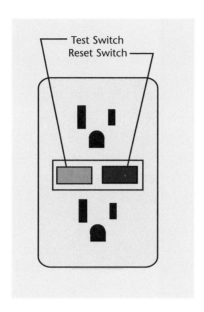

Figure 7.1 GFCIs are required in bathrooms by code.

Wiring

One component of older homes that is typically outdated is the wiring. Not only may the older wiring be in poor condition, it may also be made of unsafe materials like aluminum. In either case, it should be replaced. Signs of inadequate or outdated wiring include:

- The home is over 30 years old and installed without a ground.

- A fuse box is present instead of a circuit breaker box.

- The wiring system has only two wires, and therefore is not grounded.

- Aluminum wire is present.

- No GFCIs are present.

- Fuses blow or circuit breakers trip often.

- Too few switches, receptacles, and lights are present.

- Extension cords are frequently used.

- The electrical supply at the entrance box or main entrance is 100 amps or less.

Aluminum wire, which has been found to develop fire hazards, was frequently used for new construction and remodeling from 1965 to 1973. Copper wire is now the wire of choice, so if aluminum wire is present, the entire home must be rewired as part of the remodeling project. Updating the wiring will ensure that the electrical system is safe and meets current codes.

Adequate wiring for today's high tech homes is as essential in the bathroom as in other rooms. Consumers are bringing more electrical devices into the bathroom, so plan ahead to insure adequate wiring is available now and for future needs. Check to see if the room has an appropriate number of circuits. If not, can new circuits be added? Heaters for steam showers, saunas and tubs will demand a large amount of electricity and may need 240-volt circuits, not commonly specified in older bathrooms. Be sure these new circuits are in place before the finishing work is completed.

Special Wiring Needs

With the addition of more equipment in the bathroom, especially in larger luxury bathrooms, plan for the wiring needs before walls are finished. Here are a few examples:

- Hard wire electric towel warmers or lighted magnifying mirrors to eliminate dangling cords.

- Incorporate wiring for towel warming drawers, anti-fogging mirrors and heated toilet seats.

- Plan individual circuits for electric resistance heaters or electric floor heaters.

- Don't forget wiring for ceiling heaters and ventilation systems.

- Provide a line, and perhaps an individual circuit, to fixtures such as whirlpool tubs, steam showers, and some toilets and bidets.

- If a laundry area is being incorporated into the bathroom, plan a dedicated circuit for the clothes washer and/or clothes dryer. An electric clothes dryer will need a 240-volt circuit.

- Hard wire anti-fog mirrors behind the glass.

Receptacles

It seems that most rooms never have enough receptacles to cover electrical needs, and the bathroom is no exception. Today's consumers are using an increasing number of appliances and electric devices in the bathroom. In addition to the usual hair dryers and other hair care appliances, many families now have rechargeable appliances, like tooth brushes and shavers, that need to be connected on a continuous basis. Adding extra receptacles where these items are used would be advisable.

Consider including receptacles inside cabinets and on shelves for rechargeable appliances or other equipment like radios and televisions. It may also be a good idea to place a receptacle near the toilet for the possible addition of personal cleansing systems like a bidet or a fluid monitoring device. Some toilets also come with automated components like a pressure activated toilet seat.

Evaluate the receptacle needs in various areas of the bathrooms. Dressing areas may include space for ironing, clothes steamers, or the new clothes conditioning closets that steam and freshen clothing. Exercise and relaxation areas need receptacles for video players, stereo systems and televisions.

Figure 7.2 GFCI receptacles should be planned at each electrical point of use (Bathroom Planning Guideline 24). The correct electrical information on a mechanical plan will ensure that all electrical connections are included.

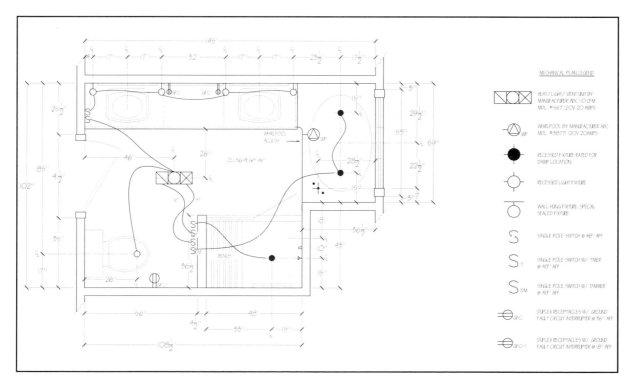

Communications

Communication devices are now coming to the bathroom, and the essential wiring for them should be considered in your design, especially in the luxury category. Linking the bathroom to the outside world and other parts of the house requires special wiring and planning. With new structured wiring bundles, many of the wires for communication link together to make installation easier.

Internal home communication networks such as intercoms are becoming common, and bathrooms are a logical link in them. They can be especially important if small children or older adults need assistance. Wiring needs to be incorporated early. Consider the users when deciding on the most appropriate type and placement of the intercom unit.

A telephone in the bathroom was once a luxury, but it can now be an easy addition. All it takes is extending another phone line. Although the phone is often found near the toilet, it can be located wherever the client finds it convenient to use, like near a sitting area. Help systems that use telephone lines for emergency calls may also be desired. Place the system where it can be easily accessed if someone needs help.

As families include more activities in the bathroom, the television becomes a regular feature. Linking the bathroom to the home cable or satellite system will allow family members to keep up with the news while they dress for work in the morning, view a program in the exercise area, watch television as they relax in a spa or jetted tub, and even view the television through the mirror.

Some whirlpool and jetted tubs now come with the television built in. Connections for a VCR, DVD player and sound system are also part of the entertainment package. If the client does not want electronic equipment in the bathroom space, an alternative is to install speakers in the ceiling or in the wall that connects to equipment elsewhere.

Although Internet connections are not common in bathrooms at this time, there is no doubt they will be coming, especially as medical monitoring and security systems gain in popularity. Wiring for the Internet now, in anticipation of new uses, would be wise.

Figure 7.3 Televisions and other entertainment and communications equipment are being incorporated into today's bathrooms. (Courtesy of Peter Ross Salerno, CMKBD – Wyckoff, New Jersey, Photography by Peter Rymwid)

HEATING

Stepping out of a shower or tub with wet skin can be very chilling if the bathroom air is not at a comfortable temperature. There are many ways in which to add heat to the bathroom. The first step, however, is to take measures to reduce heat loss by sealing leaks, improving insulation in exterior walls, and upgrading the windows. The NKBA book *Kitchen & Bath Systems* discusses heating systems in detail.

Heating Considerations

When selecting a heating system for the bathroom, keep in mind the following:

- Even if the bathroom is part of the central heating system duct network, consider adding supplemental heat, especially if the bathroom is at the end of the duct run, or the client tends to keep the house cooler than they would like in the bathroom.

- When ducting a central heating system into the bathroom, consider installing either a ceiling vent or a baseboard vent. Keeping the register off of the floor, especially in small bathrooms, will prevent users from stepping on the sharp vent with their bare feet.

- If converting a previously unheated area into a bathroom, or expanding it into an unheated area like a closet, be sure the central heating system can handle the additional load. If the new space is too far from a central heating system, a supplemental heater may be needed to deliver adequate heat.

- When multiple rooms need to heated, use a zonal system that allows the flexibility to control each area separately.

- Strongly discourage the use of portable heaters as an option for supplemental heating. They are dangerous to use near water and can be a tripping hazard.

- If the shower is oversized or designed with a door-less entry, additional heat may be necessary for comfortable use.

- If a tub/shower with a door is used, this enclosed area will benefit from added heat.

Types of Heaters

Heating systems for bathrooms come in a wide variety of types. They can vary as to installation needs, space requirement, responsiveness, comfort and heating mode. Some of the most common choices are listed below. Heaters are described in more detail in the NKBA book *Kitchen & Bath Systems*.

- **Infrared heat lamp**. Recessed into the ceiling, these lamps are among the least effective because they only heat what is directly below them. Because they heat objects, they do not make good room heaters. These lamps can be combined with a vent fan and light in a single ceiling fixture, or can be installed individually.

- **Ceiling mounted convection heaters**. These units have a small heater and a fan that blows the warm air down onto the user and into the room. They may also be combined into a single ceiling unit with a vent fan and light.

- **Wall heaters**. Wall heaters are typically recessed into the wall and include a grate or screen over the heating elements. Most wall heaters are now electric, but some older homes may have gas wall heaters. Typically located on the lower portion of the wall, they can be somewhat dangerous because users can easily back into them and be burned.

- **Ceiling or wall panel heaters**. Electric heating coils can be installed in the ceiling or in walls behind the drywall. Ceiling units are especially welcome over a bathtub to keep the air warm. For wall applications, do not install the heaters higher than 48 inches to leave room for hanging pictures without hammering a nail into the electric coils.

- **Electric toe kick heater**. A small electric heater installed in the toe kick below the cabinet can provide comfortable supplemental heat to the feet and floor area. Provision for this type of heater needs to be made when the cabinet is installed.

Figure 7.4 Small infrared or convection heaters can be mounted in the ceiling. (Courtesy of Hunter)

Figure 7.5 Small supplemental heaters located in the toe kick space can warm the feet while standing at the vanity.

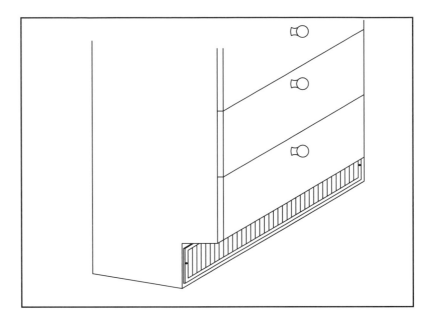

- **Individual baseboard heaters**. These are inexpensive to install and allow zonal control, but take up valuable floor space.

- **Floor heaters**. Floor heating systems can be either electric or hydronic. They give off an even heat that is comfortable to the feet. Children especially like the warm floors because that is where they end up most of the time.

Either type of floor heater will raise the height of the floor, so door clearances may need to be adjusted. It is not advisable to install them under wood floors that could be damaged by excessive heat, unless you use a product that is designed to be installed under wood flooring. Also, there are special products that are made to be installed under carpet.

Electric floor heating systems are typically easy to install during construction. Hydronic systems are a good choice if there is hot water heat in other parts of the home. Hydronic tubing can also be placed behind mirrors to prevent fogging, or used as the heating system for a towel warmer. Some towel warmers can also serve as supplemental heaters.

Towel Warmers

Stepping out of the shower or bath and into a nice warm towel can be very inviting. Most towel warmers come in the form of a wall- or floor-mounted rack, and they are designed to heat and dry bath towels as they drape over the rods. Some of these warmers, however, can also be used as the heater for the bathroom, serving two functions. Towel warmers come in both hydronic and electric models. The electric style can be either hard wired or plugged into a wall receptacle. To minimize the number of dangling cords, plan on hard wiring. Hydronic styles are used if there is already an hydronic system for other heating.

Another type of towel warmer is the warming drawer. It is designed more for heating dry towels; a towel bar is still needed for drying wet towels. A warming drawer requires additional wiring in the back of the cabinet. The drawer can be integral, so specify the cabinet and doors to fit with the warming drawer unit.

Figure 7.6 Electric or hydronic towel warmers can not only warm towels but heat the room as well. (Courtesy of Stephanie Tozzo – Clinton, New Jersey)

COOLING

Bathroom comfort is important all year around. When warm weather arrives, your client will expect measures to be incorporated into the bathroom that will ensure a comfortable environment that is void of excess heat and extreme humidity. Although cool air can be chilling when stepping out of a shower or bath tub, it might be welcomed in an exercise or grooming area, as well as the dressing area, to make clothing slip on more easily.

Climate will have a substantial impact on necessary cooling measures. In northern climates, little, if any, mechanical cooling may be necessary if summertime temperatures are not extreme. In warmer climates, mechanical cooling is essential for the most part.

In addition to cooling, some mechanical units can help remove excess humidity, which is important in the bathroom where so much extra moisture is added to the air during showering and bathing. Air conditioning units are not, however, a replacement for good ventilation.

Home orientation is another factor that can affect cooling needs. If the bathroom is located on the east or west sides of the home, windows on these walls, especially large windows or those unprotected by landscaping, can allow a large amount of heat into the space. More cooling will be necessary during certain parts of the day. Northern windows and properly protected southern windows should not have heat gain problems from direct sunlight.

Lastly, cooling needs are affected by the home's level of insulation. Just as good insulation will help keep a home warmer in the winter, it will also benefit it in the summer, keeping the entire home cooler and requiring less mechanical cooling.

There are two main types of cooling methods you might plan into the bathroom project: natural and mechanical. Depending upon the climate, you may decide to incorporate one or both methods.

Natural Cooling

The most basic method of natural cooling is to open windows to let in fresh air. Even on fairly warm days, allowing in cool night air and then closing windows during the heat of the day may be enough to keep a home or space comfortable. If it is possible to set up cross ventilation, opening windows on two walls will increase circulation. Select operable windows that open to the outdoors. Windows with low-e coatings can also assist with keeping out the heat from direct sunshine. More information on window choices is available in the NKBA book *Residential Construction*.

Surfacing materials can also assist with cooling. Ceramic tile, stone, concrete and other massive materials can provide a cool touch to the room. However, these materials will also feel cool in colder weather and may lead to discomfort during that time of year.

Mechanical Cooling

If natural cooling methods cannot give the comfort levels desired, then mechanical means are necessary. The most basic of mechanical devices is the fan. Although portable and window fans are available, they are not attractive and take up space. A ceiling fan may be a better option if the ceiling is tall enough to accommodate one. Ceiling hugger fans are available for standard height ceilings, but taller clients may have an issue with whirling blades just a short distance above their heads. More information about fans is included in the section about ventilation.

Mechanical cooling methods include refrigerated cooling and evaporative cooling and are discussed in the NKBA book *Kitchen & Bath Systems*. When incorporating either type, be aware of how the vent placement may affect the installation of fixtures, cabinetry and other components. Also evaluate how the vent location will affect the occupants. Cool air blowing directly onto people will not be very comfortable.

VENTILATION

Ventilation is critical in a well-designed bathroom and is necessary for moisture control and healthy indoor air quality, as discussed in Chapter 3. The designer's responsibility is to plan a balanced and efficient system that does not compromise user comfort. Importantly, the designer needs to provide a ventilation system that will be used.

Residential ventilation systems are generally designed with the assumption that indoor air is improved by mixing or replacing it with outside air. Air from outdoors is perceived to be fresher. Depending on the location of the home, this may not always be true. If the outside air is polluted, special ventilation systems may be needed that provide additional air filtration.

The minimum requirement for bathroom ventilation, specified by most building codes, is an operable window. If the window cannot be provided, mechanical ventilation is necessary. However, most experts including the NKBA, recommend an exhaust system for all bathrooms.

Windows

Although windows can be used to meet code requirements, relying on them for all bathroom ventilation can be a problem. It may not be practical or comfortable to open a window on cold or rainy days. An open window may compromise privacy or security. A single open window may not be enough to provide adequate air circulation to remove moisture.

Windows certainly can be used in a bathroom for light and view, and to supplement ventilation. If a window is being used for ventilation, place it high on the wall to take advantage of the natural tendency of warm, moist air to rise. For example, operable skylights or roof windows can provide ventilation in nice weather. However, be aware that the placement of an operable skylight or roof window is dependent on maintaining building code requirements for a horizontal and vertical clearance from a plumbing vent. For more information about selecting bathroom windows, read the NKBA book *Residential Construction*.

Figure 7.7 Windows can be used in a bath not only for light and view, but also to supplement ventilation. (Courtesy of Julie A. Stoner, CKD, ASID – Wayne, Pennsylvania)

Fan Systems

The most effective ventilation system for a bathroom is a mechanical one that exhausts air to the outside. This type of ventilation can be designed to remove moisture and control odors. Selecting the right fan is important, but only part of the decision. Bathroom ventilation must be considered as a system, including the fan, ducts, controls and installation.

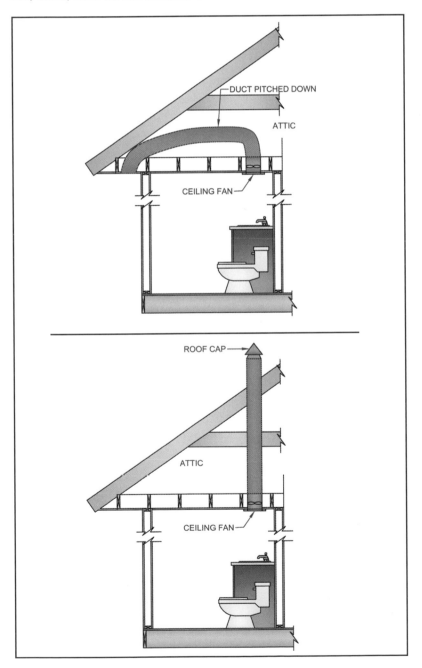

Figure 7.8 Plan for a mechanical exhaust system, vented to the outside, for each enclosed area of the bathroom (Bathroom Planning Guideline 26).

Many people resist using a bathroom fan because of the noise. A loud fan can be annoying, especially when using the bathroom as a stress-reducing retreat. The noise level of fans is rated in sones and fans vary in their sone rating. Generally, a fan rated less than 1.0 to 1.5 sones will be quiet enough to be considered background noise.

Choices in Bathroom Fans

Figure 7.9 A centrifugal fan can provide quieter operation. (Courtesy of Fantech)

Axial or propeller fans are common in bathrooms. This type of fan tends to be less expensive, but can be noisy. Centrifugal or "squirrel cage" fans are generally quieter, but can be more expensive.

The Home Ventilating Institute (HVI) classifies bathroom fans according to the following types:

- *Ceiling mounted fans.* Mounted in the ceiling between joists, this type of fan pushes air through ducts to the outside. Air can be exhausted vertically through the roof or horizontally out an exterior wall. If installing a fan in an insulated ceiling, specify a fan appropriate for this type of installation.

- *Fan lights.* This single fixture includes lights as well as the fan. If this type is selected, make sure that the location is optimal for both lighting and ventilation, and that the lighting is the type desired. Some fan lights may also include an infrared heater.

- *Exterior mount fans.* This type of fan mounts outside the room, in either a ceiling or wall, and air is pulled through the ducts to the outside. Because the fan is mounted outside the room, these types of fans tend to be quieter.

- *Inline fans.* In this type of fan, the motor is mounted in the duct system. Often, inline fans are part of a whole-house ventilation system where exhaust vents are in more than one location. Keeping the fan motor out of the living space results in quieter operation.

- *Wall fans.* This type of fan is located on an exterior wall, and exhausts air directly to the outside without using any ducts.

- *Whole house ventilation systems.* There are different types of systems that provide continuous ventilation of a house, exhausting air from it and bringing in outside air. Some systems have heat or energy recovery for increased efficiency. A typical system will have an air intake in the bathroom and the fan will run continuously. Changes in the size, moisture, or heat load from a new or remodeled bathroom will likely require an adjustment to the system.

There are toilets on the market that are direct vented to control odors and vapor spray from flushing. These are not likely to be adequate to control moisture from other bathroom sources. However, the exhaust venting capacity of the toilet needs to be considered in planning the total bathroom ventilation.

Fan Size

Bathroom fans are sized in CFM (cubic feet per minute) or L/s (Liters per second). These terms both describe the volume of air the fan can move in a period of time. A typical recommendation or building code requirement is to install a minimum size fan of 50 CFM. However, that does not consider the size of the room, the amount of moisture produced, or the efficiency of the installation.

A more effective way to consider fan size is to look at ventilation needs and then size the fan accordingly. The HVI recommends that the fan system should provide 8 ACH (air changes per hour). To determine what size fan is needed, follow this formula:

Step 1 – Determine the volume of the room in cubic feet

- Length x width x height = volume of room

Step 2 – Multiply the volume of the room by 8 ACH (air changes per hour)

Step 3 – Divide by 60 minutes in an hour to get CFM (cubic feet per minute)

Example: A bathroom is 8 feet 6 inches (8.5 feet) by 10 feet, with 8 foot ceilings

Step 1 – 8.5 x 10 x 8 = 680 cubic feet

Step 2 – 680 x 8 = 5440 cubic feet per hour

Step 3 – 5440/60 = 90.67 cubic feet per minute (CFM)

A short cut to this formula is to take the volume of the room (length x width x height) and divide by 7.5.

The fan size determined by the air change per hour method is effective fan capacity—or how much air the fan can actually move. Effective fan capacity is not the same as the mechanical size of the fan. The effective fan capacity will depend on a number of factors including:

- **Length of duct runs from the intake vent to the exhaust vent.** Generally, if the duct run is more than about five feet, the size of the fan should be increased to compensate for the resistance of a longer duct run.

- **Elbows or bends in the ducts.** Generally, if there is more than one elbow or bend in the duct, the size of the fan should be increased to compensate for the greater resistance.

Size of the Bathroom

Larger bathrooms may have additional fixtures, especially jetted tubs or both a shower and bathtub, which produce more moisture and increase the need for ventilation. The HVI recommends that for larger bathrooms (over 100 square feet), determine ventilation based on the fixtures. Add fan capacity as follows:

- Toilet: 50 CFM
- Shower: 50 CFM
- Bathtub: 50 CFM
- Jetted tub: 100 CFM

Fan Controls

Bathroom fans are available with different types of control systems. Whatever types of switches are chosen, make sure that they are easy to read and understand, and that clients can operate them.

Sensor controls are available that turn fans on and off based on humidity, and can provide excellent moisture control. Motion detectors turn a fan on when someone is in the bathroom, and then turn it off after they leave. However, motion detectors may not work effectively in some situations, such as when someone is soaking in a tub. Automatic timers can be convenient.

After showering or bathing, it may take 15 to 20 minutes for moisture removal from the bathroom and ventilation system. A timer switch can help provide moisture control without wasting energy. Electronic timers can be easy to use and accurate. Variable speed controls allow the user to match the speed of the fan to the need for ventilation. The ability to run the fan at a slower (and quieter) speed may encourage more frequent use of ventilation.

Some fans are wired into the same switch as the bathroom light, so that the fan comes on with the light. This is a good way to insure that ventilation is always provided. If this type of switching is selected, it is very important to use a quiet fan. Putting the light and fan on the same switch does have a drawback. To leave the fan running after bathing or showering, the light must also be left on—even if no one is in the bathroom.

Fan Location

Warm air tends to rise. In addition, the warmer the air, the more moisture it holds. Therefore, the warmest air, with the most moisture, tends to be near the ceiling. So the ceiling, or a high place on a wall, is the best place for a fan.

Another factor in fan location is having the air intake close to the source of air and moisture to be exhausted. Therefore, the best location for the fan is usually near the toilet, bathtub and/or shower. Some fans are designed to be located in the shower or directly over a jetted tub. They are usually described as "vapor proof" or "moisture proof."

In a larger bathroom, you may want to specify two exhaust fans, one over the toilet, and one over the bathtub or shower. The size of these two fans can be added together to determine the total ventilation capacity of the bathroom. An advantage of using two smaller fans is that the smaller fans are usually quieter than one larger fan, which might encourage their use.

If the toilet is in a separate compartment, it will need its own ventilation fan. This can be sized using the 8 ACH (air changes per hour) formula.

The relationship of the interior air intake and the exterior air exhaust needs to be considered in locating the fan. Minimizing the length of duct run, as well as the number of elbows or bends, will increase the efficiency of the fan system.

Fan Installation

Smooth ducts with sealed joints will offer less resistance to air movement and provide quieter, more efficient operation. Any duct that must go through spaces that are not heated or cooled should be insulated to help prevent moisture condensation. The ducts should not terminate in the attic, but continue to the outside. Warm, moist air being exhausted into the attic can lead to condensation and eventual structural problems.

A backdraft damper on the exhaust vent is important to the fan system. This prevents outside air from leaking back into the home when the fan is not operating. Also, the flap can prevent insects, birds and other animals from getting into the fan duct.

A fan that is installed on rubber gaskets or similar cushioning material is less likely to vibrate and will operate more quietly.

Make-up Air

When a bathroom fan is operating, it is exhausting or removing air from the room. This creates a negative pressure in the room—and replacement air must come from somewhere. If replacement air is not provided, the effectiveness of the fan is reduced. A bathroom door is often undercut slightly to allow air to flow into the room, even with the door closed. A louvered door is sometimes used, although it may be unsatisfactory from a privacy concern.

The bathroom fan is not just exhausting air from the bathroom, but from the whole house. Some of the replacement air may come from open windows, or from people moving in and out of doors. Some replacement air may come from leaks and cracks in the building envelope. However, in well-constructed, energy-efficient homes, there are few places for replacement air to leak into the home.

If replacement air is not provided, negative pressure can be created. Problems can occur with the operation of appliances that need to exhaust to the outside, such as gas furnaces or water heaters. This situation is referred to as back drafting. When back drafting occurs, dangerous combustion pollutants, such as carbon monoxide, as well as excess moisture and radon can be pulled into the home.

A simple solution to back drafting problems, and to providing replacement air, can be opening a window when operating exhaust fans. However, this is not always practical. Other solutions include a fresh air outlet into the home and a whole-house mechanical ventilation system that balances airflow.

LIGHTING

Quality lighting in a bathroom is essential for many reasons. It is very inviting and adds to the aesthetic appeal. Many grooming tasks, including dressing, take place in the bathroom and require a quality light source in order to complete adequately. Among the considerations for planning quality light is selecting sources that provide illumination that is flattering to skin tones and allows accurate matching of colors.

In addition, the lighting should be comparable to the light where your client will spend their day. As more activities move into the bathroom area, lighting must be more varied and flexible to accommodate them all. For example, the lighting needed for vigorous exercise will not be the same as desired for relaxing in a tub or meditating.

Your client will be the main source of information for determining lighting needs. Once you have determined the client's bathroom activities using the forms in Chapter 5, and made note of any special vision needs, or activities taking place in the bathroom space, you will have a better idea of where light sources will be needed and the type of lighting that will be most appropriate.

For design concepts that improve visual access specifically, refer to Chapter 9. For technical information about lighting, lighting sources, the color and temperature of light, fixtures and installation recommendations, see the NKBA book *Kitchen & Bath Systems*.

Natural Light

Natural light from windows, doors and skylights adds a warm, inviting quality to a room, as well as giving the room a feeling of openness. The following are tips for planning natural lighting:

- Determine when the bathroom is used most. Emphasizing natural light when the bathroom is only used at night or in the early morning may not lead to logical or cost-effective planning.

- Too much natural light can also lead to glare. If the window area faces a sunny direction, incorporate window treatments that can help control the bright sunlight during certain times of the day.

- Large windows and glass doors to the outside can provide adequate daytime lighting needs, plus visually open the room to the outdoors.

- Windows and doors below 18 inches will need to be made of tempered glass. Windows that surround a bathtub or shower should also be made of tempered glass. See information on Bathroom Planning Guideline 15 in Chapter 6.

- Skylights can add natural light without sacrificing wall space, but be sure to select high quality skylights and have them installed properly. Skylights provide about five times as much light as a comparably sized wall window.

- Select windows or skylights that have a high insulating value to keep the bathroom more comfortable year around. Also study air leakage rates, and select windows or skylights with a maximum of .07 cubic feet/minute/foot of perimeter.

Figure 7.10 Large windows provide an abundance of natural light. (Courtesy of Architectural Bath)

Privacy is another consideration when incorporating a large amount of glass. Privacy measures on the exterior of the windows, or adequate window treatments, are necessary to protect the privacy of the bathroom users. Glass block is a popular way to incorporate light without a need to be concerned about privacy.

General Lighting

Provisions for general lighting in each compartment or room of the bathroom are necessary, and can be accomplished through a variety of sources including: ceiling fixtures, lights in vent/heater/light combination ceiling units, lamps, wall fixtures, recessed lights, and indirect or cove lighting. Keep these points in mind:

- Recessed lights are less obtrusive and can distribute light in a wide, medium or narrow spread, depending upon how the fixture is designed. Select the type that gives the desired effect.

- Adding dimmers to spa, exercise or meditation areas will help set the desired light level or mood for the activity.

- Some types of lighting produce a lot of heat. The heat may feel comforting in the winter, but during the summer it will add to the cooling load and to the discomfort in exercise areas.

- Consider the surface finishes and colors when determining lighting. Shiny surfaces will produce glare, and dark surfaces will absorb more light.

Accent Lighting

In conjunction with general lighting, accent lights can enhance the visual texture of surfaces, objects or architectural features. Use small accent lights to highlight special features in the bathroom, such as a vanity toe kick or a special wall feature. Accent lights for shelves, soffit areas and glassed cabinets will add aesthetic appeal.

Task Lighting

Task lighting provides light at an area to help users see what they are doing. Task lighting should be provided for each functional area of the bathroom, such as grooming, showering and bathing. Some points to remember:

- Most of the task lighting in the bathroom is needed for grooming. Place the lighting where your client typically performs grooming activities, which might be either standing or seated. Each bathroom user may perform grooming activities in a variety of locations, so include the proper task lighting for each.

- Light fixtures for grooming should be located to each side of the user's face for optimum quality. Use the user's eye height measurement to guide where side lighting is placed. The light lamp should not be visible to the user. Fixtures located above a mirror cast shadows onto the user's face, whereas lamps at the sides of the mirror eliminate such shadows.

- Plan for additional lighting at mirrors used for shaving and applying make-up. Wall-mounted magnifying mirrors are often lighted, so a hard wire connection should be included to eliminate another cord.

Figure 7.11 Grooming lights placed on each side of the mirror prevent shadows from forming on the face.

- If you are incorporating a reading area into the bathroom, plan to add a quality reading light or an receptacle for a lamp in this area.

- Place lighting for someone reading while sitting on the toilet.

- Dressing areas may include mirrors for dressing and some grooming. Good lighting at these mirrors will help the users be better able to perform such tasks as tying a tie, arranging jewelry, checking clothing for soiled spots or wrinkles, and combing hair.

- Placement of the mirrors and related lighting should consider people of various heights. A full length mirror is appropriate for children and adults, standing and seated. Plan lighting that will illuminate the person in front of the long mirror.

- Include lights in closets and deep cabinets.

- If a pressing area is included in the dressing area, a light directly over the ironing table will aid the process.

LIGHTING FIXTURES

Lighting fixtures come in a wide variety of styles, mounting types and sizes. When deciding which type to use, consider the size of the space you are lighting, the type of light you want emitted, the design theme of the space, and the tasks that must be illuminated. Following are a few important points to consider concerning light fixtures.

Location

Locate the fixtures where they can deliver the maximum amount of light for their purpose. When you are lighting a task area, the fixture should be mounted so it casts light onto the task area without creating a shadow or causing glare. For grooming and shaving, light sources should be mounted on both sides of the face to eliminate shadows. The light fixture should be installed at the user's eye level, whether standing or seated.

General lighting might involve one or two lights in the center of the room, or a number of lights around the perimeter. Provide enough light so that dark corners do not form. Do not use fixtures that can get into the way of the users. For example, wall sconces in the walkways of very small bathrooms, or central ceiling fan lights in average height ceilings, may be easily bumped by the user.

Don't forget to place some general lighting in all compartments of the bathroom, as well as in the shower and over the tub. According to Bathroom Planning Guidelines and building codes, hanging fixtures cannot be located within a zone of 3 feet horizontally and 8 feet vertically from the top of the bathtub rim. Lights in the tub and shower areas should be marked "suitable for damp/wet locations."

Lighting Controls

Controls for general lighting should be located where a person enters the room, so they do not need to walk into a dark room to find the control. Place the light switch no higher than 48 inches above the floor for ease of access. If a bathroom has two entrances, such as one door in the hall and one from a bedroom, use a three-way switch so that general lighting can be controlled at either door. Additional compartments within the bathroom typically have the light controls at the compartment entrance rather than at the entrance to the main portion of the bathroom. Controls for other lights need to be close to where the light is being used.

Because every bathroom has a number of lights that need switches, try to consolidate them into banks, as much as possible, to avoid having the wall dotted with switches. Some switches may be needed to control vent fans and heaters. If you use banks of switches, three or four switches are perhaps all you would want together in one place.

Try to make it easy for your client to remember which switch controls which fixture. Try putting them in some logical order so that the light switch is nearest that light fixture. You can also mark them to avoid confusion. For example, if the two middle switches in a bank of four operate the vent fan and the overhead heater, a red marking on the heater switch will give the client a clue to its use.

Figure 7.12 Bathrooms should include general and task lighting (Bathroom Planning Guideline 25). All of the bathroom's lighting needs should be illustrated on the mechanical plan.

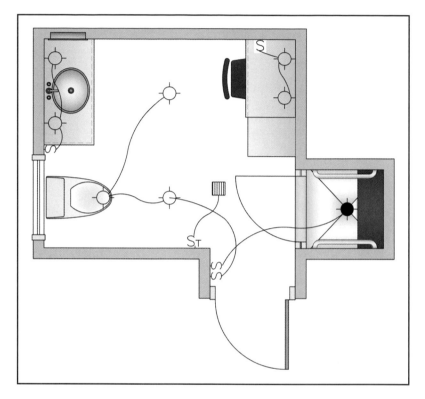

Many different types of controls are now available for lighting. Select the type your client can use easily, as well as the style they prefer. The flip or rocker switches are perhaps the most common. You may also choose a toggle switch, a motion sensor switch, or even a remote control switch for lights on elevated ceilings. Locate these controls in a convenient place for access by all users. Eliminate the need for controls by using motion-sensor light switches that do not require the use of hands in operation.

Controlling the amount of light is important in some areas of the bathroom. For spaces like the exercise area or near a spa tub, consider adding a dimmer switch so that the client has complete control over the light levels. Locate the controls, however, out of the reach of the bathers so they do not receive an electrical shock if they touch the control while standing in water. Or, use remote lighting control devices.

Low Voltage Lighting

Low voltage systems use a transformer, either as a separate unit or built into the lighting fixture, to transform the 120-volt service to around 7 – 10 volts. The capacity needs to be matched to the lamp wattage, and the transformer should be in a central location. The very small low voltage bulbs have a separate transformer you will need to hide in or above a cabinet. Transformers incorporated into a fixture increase the size of the fixture, making the light source more difficult to hide.

Low voltage lights come in a large variety of styles and offer many advantages. They are easy to wire for remodeling, and provide a very white and crisp light that can serve as an accent or create a sparkle. In addition to small track and recessed lights for general lighting, low voltage bulbs can fit very small places providing light for cabinets, shelves, mirrors, floors and art work. Low voltage lights can also make good night lights. Drawbacks include high cost and limited availability in some areas.

Low voltage lights come with either halogen or xenon bulbs (technically called lamps), which last much longer (2,000–3,500 hours) than standard incandescent lamps. Halogen lights burn at a very high temperature, and even though the low voltage bulbs are small, added together they can still produce a significant amount of heat. Therefore, keep them out of reach of users and flammable objects.

Lighting Safety

Although most lighting systems are generally tested and safe to use, following proper installation instructions and placing fixtures in locations away from contact with people, are extremely important steps to preventing light fixture hazards.

Safe installation is particularly important with recessed lights. If installed too close to construction members or smothered by insulation, these fixtures can reach very high temperatures and ignite materials around them. Many recessed fixtures are designed with built-in air spaces to help cool the bulbs.

Installing the incorrect bulb into a particular fixture can also increase the chances of a fire. Many times when a fixture is selected, it is difficult to tell how much light it may emit within a room. The size of the room, the colors used, and the textures present can all make a difference as to how much light is available.

If your client finds the fixture is not producing the amount of light they desired, they may increase the wattage of the bulbs inside it. This will indeed provide more light, but in the meantime the larger bulbs will give off more heat than the fixture can handle. The fixture can become hot to the point where it can crack or ignite. Think through the lighting needs carefully to avoid this.

Another safety precaution is to avoid contact with the light bulbs. Many types, like incandescent and halogen bulbs, produce a significant amount of heat as they produce light. Be careful to locate these bulbs where your client cannot easily come into contact with them, such as walking through the room or reaching for something.

SUMMARY

Planning for electrical and mechanical equipment is more essential than ever. Changing lifestyles, a surge in technology, and an increase in the number of activities, fixtures, and electronic devices in the bathroom, all create a space that demands attention to the systems that form the structure for this equipment. Without a clear and detailed plan and an attention to local code requirements, necessary components of such a system can be easily overlooked, leading to disappointment on the part of the client, or added costs if features need to be redone.

CHAPTER 8: More Than A Bathroom

Often a bathroom design or renovation may include the opportunity to plan and design other areas of the home. Typically, these spaces are still located in the private area of the home, and are often within the bathroom or adjacent to it. Designers may need to help the client rethink such functional spaces as clothes storage and laundry areas that are being incorporated into the new design.

Clients may also be looking for space within, or next to, the bathroom to address their interest in health and wellness. Exercise spaces and luxury home spas may be requested by clients who see these areas as important to their ability to take care of themselves or to pamper their mind and body. This chapter provides some guidance in how to consider and plan closets, laundry, and health and wellness areas, so you can offer the client functional and beautiful spaces.

CLOTHES CLOSETS

Given that a bathroom is a place for people to take off—and put on—clothing, then including a clothes closet in or near it makes a lot of sense. As a bathroom designer, you are likely to be involved in designing clothes storage of some type. This may range from temporary clothes storage during bathing or showering, to a complete walk-in closet. You may design an area for hanging clothes, or include drawers and shelves for all types of clothing.

During your initial client interview and assessment of needs (See Chapter 5), you will learn about clothes storage requirements. This section focuses on designing a full clothes closet, but includes useful information on all types of clothes storage. You may need to adapt the information to the situation of your particular client.

Moving Clothes

Start designing a clothes closet by thinking about how clothes are moved from one place to the next. They are moved from the laundry area to storage, such as in a closet. Then they are removed from storage when a person gets dressed. Sometimes clothes need to be moved from the storage area to the dressing area, or to temporary storage, while a person is bathing, showering or grooming. When a person gets undressed, clothes may move to temporary storage in a "dirty clothes" container or go directly to the laundry area. Sometimes clothes are taken outside the home to a dry cleaner or laundry.

Placement of the closet needs to consider this movement of clothes and its relationship to clothes-related activities. Where will dressing and undressing occur? Does your client want centralized storage of all clothes in one area? Or will clothes be stored in several areas? For example, a decentralized option might be to keep only underwear or nightclothes near the bathing/showering area, and others in the bedroom.

If more than one person regularly uses the bathroom area, access to both clothes storage and bathroom fixtures needs to be considered. Adequate room for multiple activities and users is needed. Plan for desired privacy for both bathroom and/or dressing activities. Will one closet area be provided or will there be individual clothes storage for each user?

Closet Placement

The movement of clothes, the dressing/undressing activities, and circulation through the space are important determinants of the location of clothes storage in relation to other parts of the bathroom. There are other factors to consider as well.

Moisture is produced in the bathroom, and excess humidity can be damaging to stored clothes. The clothes storage area should be separated from damp areas of the bathroom by a door or partition. Good ventilation in the closet area reduces moisture problems and helps keep clothes fresher.

Consider what is on the other side of the closet wall. A closet on an interior wall can be used to advantage by providing sound insulation. For example, a bedroom closet can reduce sound transmission, keeping peace among late night snackers, early risers and late sleepers in the household.

If the closet will be on an outside wall, it is important to determine that the wall is energy efficient. With the clothes in the closet acting as insulation from room heat, the outside wall will be cooler. In cold climates, this could lead to condensation problems and even mildew on clothes.

A Place for Everything

A well-planned and organized clothes closet begins with an inventory of everything that will be stored in it. The storage inventory in Chapter 5 is a place to start. However, if you are designing a complete or custom closet, you will probably want to get more detail on clothes storage. Start by thinking about how clothes will be stored: hangers on rods; folded or rolled in drawers or on shelves; or on hooks. Think about all types of clothes from underwear to suits and include shoes, belts, scarves, ties and other accessories.

Form 13: Clothes Storage Inventory for Hanging Clothes and *Form 14: Clothes Storage Inventory for Folded, Rolled, and Other Types of Clothes* are inventories that you can use with your client to determine what needs to be stored in the closet. These inventory checklists can be given to your client to complete and return to you, or you can complete them with the client. The inventory checklists are found at the end of this chapter and are also available in an electronic form on the CD that comes with this book.

The storage inventories group clothing by type of storage and similar size. This is an example of application of an important storage principle: *like items should be stored together*.

Clothes Planning Dimensions

There are a number of commonly accepted planning dimensions that will be helpful as you design clothes storage. Keep in mind, however, that you may need to adapt these recommendations to allow for users of different sizes, ages or abilities.

Hanging Clothes Storage

Depth. A typical closet is 24 inches deep, with the rod placed 12 inches from the wall. However, suit coats or jackets are bulkier and need 26 inches to 28 inches to hang perpendicular to the rod. Outerwear, such as winter coats, may need 30 inches of depth. If closet rod depth is inadequate, clothes will hang at an angle, and additional rod storage will be needed. If a closet is too shallow, clothes may get jammed and wrinkled in storage.

Figure 8.1 A generous depth of closet rod storage will allow clothes to hang perpendicular to the rod, maximizing storage space, and will prevent wrinkling of clothing. (Courtesy of ClosetMaid)

Children cannot reach a full height closet rod. However, every parent wants to teach their children to hang up their own clothes! The solution might be adjustable rods that can be raised as children grow, their clothes get bigger, and they can reach higher (Figure 8.4).

Figure 8.4 Rod heights increase for children as they get older.

Age of Child	Suggested Rod Height
Preschool Ages 2 – 6	30" – 40"
Elementary Ages 6 – 12	40" – 54"
Teens Ages 12 – 16	54" – 63

Notes: After the age of 16, most children can reach rods as high as most adults.

Rod Span. The closet rod span, the distance between supports or brackets, typically depends on the diameter and material of the rod. Figure 8.5 shows commonly recommended spans for wood and metal rods supporting the weight of hanging clothing. If the manufacturer of a closet rod system provides different information, follow the manufacturer's instructions. Depending on the style and design of the closet rod, support brackets may take up rod space. This will need to be considered in the calculation of rod length.

Figure 8.5 The type of rod determines the recommended span.

Material Size	Recommended Maximum Span
Wood Pole	
1 1/8" diameter	36"
1 3/8" diameter	48"
1 5/8" diameter	60"
Metal Pole	
3/4" diameter	72"
1" diameter	96"
1 1/4" diameter	120"

Access and Clearances. Adequate space to access hanging clothes is important to a well-planned closet area. A clearance of 36 to 38 inches is recommended in front of hangers (Figure 8.6). This clearance gives room for activities such as turning, holding up clothes, or removing clothes from a hanger. If a shelf is placed above the rod, a clearance of 2 to 3 inches is needed to allow space to remove the hangers from the rod.

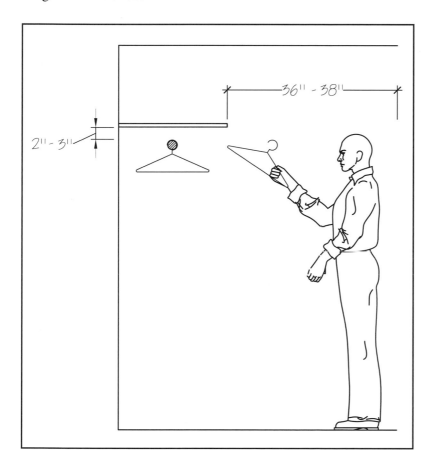

Figure 8.6 Adequate clearance space allows access to hangers.

Figure 8.7 Minimum dimensions are shown for different closet layouts, but more generous clearances are recommended. Figure 8.7A is a reach-in closet. Figure 8.7B is an edge-in closet. Figure 8.7C is a walk-in closet. Figure 8.7D is an alternative design for a walk-in closet, which has been adapted to work as a roll-in closet.

Closets layouts are often described in three different ways, based on the clearance for access to the hangers: reach-in, edge-in and walk-in. Figure 8.7 shows examples of these closet layouts. The dimensions shown are minimum access space. However, these minimums are very tight, and more generous clearances are recommended. For example, although a 24 inch opening is shown as the minimum, an opening of 60 inches to 72 inches is desirable for a clear view of, and access to, a closet. For a roll-in closet, include a 60 inch diameter clear space, which can extend 12 inches under one side, or 6 inches on both sides, of the hanging clothes (Figure 8.7D).

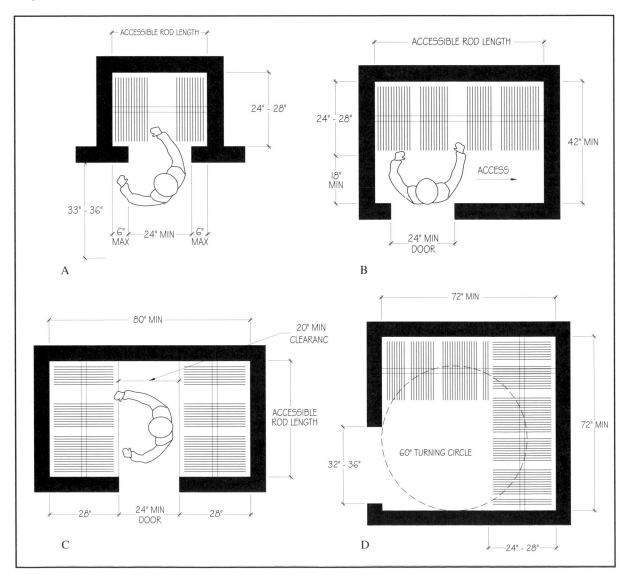

Other Types of Closet Storage

A clothes closet can hold much more than hanging clothes. A well-designed clothes storage area can include shelves, drawers, hooks, bins and other devices for storing clothes, shoes and accessories. The inventory checklist, *Form 14: Clothes Storage Inventory for Folded, Rolled, and Other Types of Clothes*, collects information about the number of other clothing items to be stored, as well as your client's preferred type of storage.

As you plan shelves, drawers and other types of storage in a closet, keep in mind the following storage principles:

- *Items used together should be stored together*. For instance, bras, underwear, socks and stockings might be stored near each other.

- *Like articles should be stored or grouped together*. For example, store all sweaters together.

- *Stored items should be easy to locate at a glance*. Deep shelves might violate this principle because items stored behind others could be "forgotten".

- *Frequently used items should be within easy reach*. An example is that T-shirts might be stored just below shoulder height, while an evening purse might be put on an upper shelf.

Shelf and Drawer Space. How much shelf and drawer space is needed? That can be a hard question to answer, depending on what items a person has to store in the closet, how they are folded or rolled, and how they are stacked. Recommendations vary from 8 square feet to 20 square feet of space per person. These recommendations assume a typical drawer depth or shelf clearance of at least 6 inches.

For a custom installation, you may want to count the number of garments and the amount of space they will need. Use *Form 14: Clothes Storage Inventory for Folded, Rolled, and Other Types of Clothes*, to get a complete inventory of the items to be stored on shelves or drawers. Discuss with your client how things will be organized. What items will be stored together? Then take some sample measurements of the amount of space the stored items require.

Form 15: Worksheet for Folded or Rolled Clothing can be used to determine how much drawer and shelf space is needed. Using the worksheet, you can determine the size of the various stacks of garments, which can then be grouped into requirements for drawer and shelf space. Be sure to allow room for expansion! The *Form 15* worksheet is found at the end of this chapter and on the CD.

Access and Clearance Space. When shelves or drawers are added to a closet, there needs to be adequate space for access. There are several concerns:

- Maximum reach to upper shelves (Figure 8.8).

- Bending or kneeling space to reach lower shelves (Figure 8.9).

- Depth of an open drawer added to bending or kneeling space (Figure 8.10).

To accommodate clients who are shorter or who use a mobility aid, lower the storage reach to 48 inches and increase the clear floor space. Alternatively, refer to the Reach and Grasp Profile and Mobility Aids information that is part of *Form 1: Getting to Know Your Client* in Chapter 5.

Figure 8.8 The typical maximum reach for a 12 inch shelf is illustrated here. A deeper shelf or obstruction (such as hanging clothes) will decrease the maximum shelf height.

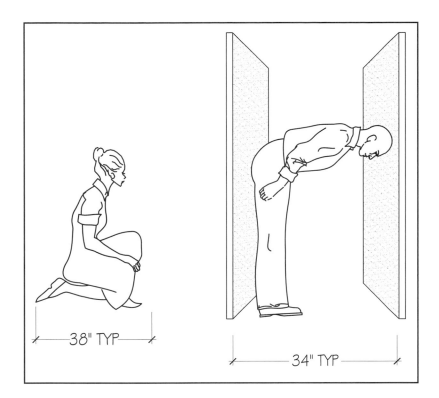

Figure 8.9 Minimum space allowances to bend or kneel, as if accessing a lower closet shelf, are shown.

38" TYP

34" TYP

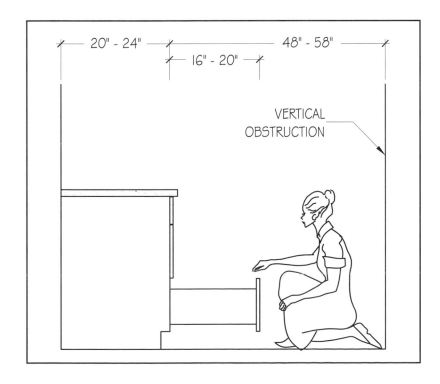

Figure 8.10 Bending or kneeling at an angle to the drawer will reduce the space needed for drawer access, but larger or deeper drawers will require more space.

20" - 24"

16" - 20"

48" - 58"

VERTICAL
OBSTRUCTION

Figure 8.12 A closet is a good location for a clothes care appliance. (Courtesy of Whirlpool Corp.)

Design Decisions

In our discussion about clothes storage, we have focused on capacity and clearances, for both clothes and the activities, such as dressing, that might occur in or near the closet area. Now it is time to make some design decisions.

Putting all the clothes storage requirements together, the goal is to maximize storage capacity, provide convenience of access and use, but minimize the total area devoted to clothes storage. Many storage accessories available today can help achieve this goal (Figure 8.13).

Closet storage systems provide double rods to increase storage capacity in the same floor space. Shelves, drawers, bins, turntables, pull-out or swing-out racks, and other storage devices can be put above, below or beside hanging rods to make sure every space is used while increasing the visibility of, and ease of access to, stored items. Mechanized systems, such as carousel rods and sliding racks, can increase storage capacity by increasing access to items stored in what would otherwise be dead space.

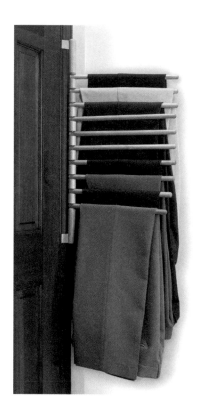

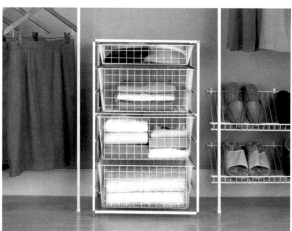

Figure 8.13 These are a few examples of the many closet storage accessories available today. (Courtesy of ClosetMaid and Easy Track)

New materials used in closet systems can increase storage function. For example, plastic covered wire mesh drawers, shelves and bins provide good ventilation and visibility of stored items.

Think about adjustability. Wardrobes change with the seasons, as fashions change and as lifestyles change. The mix of clothing may change. Therefore, think about adjustability of rod height, and the ability to increase or decrease hanging rod space. Adjustable height shelves are another plus.

Doors

Closet doors are an important part of the design. Think about the width of the door in relation to access. Although many experts recommend a 24 inch minimum, a 32-inch clear doorway (a 2 foot 10 inch door) is better to allow for universal access. Wider doors provide better visual access.

For any type of closet door, select good quality, durable hardware, handles, latches, tracks and/or hinges. Closet doors get daily use, and lots of wear and tear.

If a hinged door is used, consider where the door swing will be, and the potential for interference with circulation through the space. By-pass sliding doors eliminate the problem of accommodating the door swing. However, one panel of the sliding door always covers the closet opening. Triple-panel sliding doors are available. Also, by-pass mirrored sliding doors can provide a dressing area mirror and visual expansion of the space.

Pocket doors are similar to by-pass sliding doors, except that they slide into the wall. This type of door can provide good access to a closet, as long as there is adequate space in the wall cavity for installation.

Bi-fold doors come in different widths and styles. Because the door panel is hinged and folds out of the way, the space for a door swing is reduced while the opening in the doorway is increased. Accordion doors have multiple folds to move out of the way of the door opening without blocking the walkway in front of the closet door. With both bi-fold and accordion doors, some space in the door opening is lost to the stacked door in the open position.

A louvered door provides ventilation. Another common door, a flush door, permits storage accessories to be hung on it. However, a hollow-core flush door may not be adequate to support accessories, and reinforcing strips or a solid-core door may be needed. In addition, heavy-duty hinges may be needed to help support the weight of items hanging on the door.

Lighting

A closet will need to be well lighted with convenient switching. It is important that the light source give an excellent color rendition to facilitate coordinating of clothes. Some people like to have lighting in a closet area similar to their work place to assure color matches. Fixtures in the closet must be enclosed surface-mounted or recessed incandescent or surface-mounted fluorescent. Check local building codes and consult Chapter 7 for more information about lighting.

LINEN CLOSETS

Storage for household linens is often integrated into, or near, a bathroom. This can be as basic as storage for extra towels in the bathroom, or may include full storage for all household linens near the bathroom or bedroom area.

When designing a linen closet, start with an inventory of items to be stored. Will the closet be used for bath linens only? Will bedding be included? What about kitchen linens? Will additional space be needed for non-linen items such as soaps, grooming products, toilet paper or cleaning products?

Use *Form 16: Linen Closet Storage Inventory* to gather information about items stored in the linen closet. As with the other checklists, *Form 16*, found at the end of this chapter and on the CD accompanying this book, can be given to your client to complete, or you can use it at an interview. You may want to compare *Form 16* against *Form 4: Bathroom Storage Inventory*, discussed in Chapter 5, to see that there is no duplication.

As you plan the linen closet, review the storage principles presented in this chapter. Think about how your client will organize and group the items to be stored. The ones used most frequently should be easiest to see and reach. Heavy or bulky items may be stored on lower shelves for convenience.

Just as with the clothes closet, take advantage of storage accessories such as pullout shelves and bins, drawers and turntables. Perhaps your client will want to roll some items for storage, such as towels. Some household linens, such as table cloths or placemats, may be stored on hangers to minimize wrinkling.

Think about whether the linen storage is for short or long term storage. Some items like extra towels and bedding may only be used occasionally, such as for holiday guests. Enclosed, dust-proof, moisture-proof storage may be desirable. Other items such as everyday towels may be accessed regularly, and well-ventilated, easy-access storage may be the priority.

A lot of laundry is generated in the vicinity of the bathroom, from dirty clothes to towels and wash cloths. Plus, there is likely to be a bed near by, with sheets and pillowcases.

Planning a laundry area in or near the bathroom makes a lot of sense. It is a time- and work-saver as dirty clothes, towels and bed linens do not need to be carried to another part of the house for washing and drying, and then carried back to their area of use and/or storage. In addition, a laundry requires plumbing, which is already in the bathroom. For these reasons, your client may be considering incorporating a laundry in or near the bathroom.

What Type of Laundry?

Some people like the idea of having a complete laundry area centrally located near the bedrooms and bathrooms for convenience. Others may choose a "mini-laundry" area right in the bathroom for washing towels or doing quick loads of laundry while bathing, grooming or dressing. Still other people may want to use the bathroom to rinse out or hand wash single items, and then hang them up to drip-dry.

The client needs assessment (Chapter 5) should reveal what type of laundry area your client might like, in or near the bathroom. In addition, the checklists will help determine what type of laundry activities, equipment and supplies will need to be accommodated in the design. This section gives some specific information about planning a laundry area.

A laundry area in or near the bathroom can be convenient, but there are some factors to consider first.

- Who will use the laundry area?

  A laundry area used by different members of the household needs to be centrally located, for easy access. A personal or "mini-laundry" in the master suite might make sense for individual use, but not for the whole family. A laundry area near the bathroom might save hauling laundry to different parts of the house. However, a laundry area near the kitchen or family room might actually be more centrally located to family activities and thus more convenient to use.

- Is there adequate space for a laundry area?

  A laundry area is more than a washing machine. A well-designed complete laundry includes storage, hanging, and folding space, a sink, and adequate clearance to move and complete tasks. A mini-laundry may only be a combination or stacked washer and dryer. Will the laundry area interfere with other activities and space needs associated with the bathroom?

- What about access to the laundry?

  All users need access without invading private space. Another factor is door and hall width clearance for carrying laundry baskets and hanging clothes. If an outside clothesline is used, there needs to be a direct route to the outdoors.

- What about noise associated with laundry equipment?

  Many busy households put in loads of laundry late at night. This might be a problem when the laundry equipment is adjacent to the sleeping space.

- Is it feasible to provide the infrastructure for a laundry area in or near the bathroom?

  Water supply and drainage for the washing machine, and electrical or gas connections, as well as exhaust ventilation for the dryer, all need to be considered. The floor structure may need reinforcing for the weight or vibration of laundry equipment. A floor drain is good protection in event of a leak or other water problem. These features may be easy to provide in new construction, but more of a problem in a remodeling project.

- What about the mess of the laundry area?

  Laundry areas can be messy. Laundry areas seem to collect clothes, waiting for special treatment, or to be folded, ironed, or repaired. This is a utility area of the home, and many people prefer to close it off from other areas.

Laundry Equipment

A washing machine and automatic dryer anchor most laundry areas. A typical washer or dryer is 28 to 30 inches across the front and 25 to 30 inches deep. Most are about 36 inches high, although a back control panel will typically be 4 to 8 inches higher. Always check the exact size of the equipment in the manufacturer's specifications, or by measuring the actual equipment.

A washer can either be a top-loading or a front-loading model. Most dryers are front-loading, although there are top-loading models on the market. Washer doors can be hinged on either side, depending on the model. Some top-loading models may have door hinged at the back. Dryer doors can also be hinged on either side and some models are hinged on the bottom. Front-loading laundry appliances with front controls are desirable to improve access within the universal reach range.

Knowing the location and swing of the door is important to efficient placement of laundry equipment. It should be convenient to remove wet laundry from the washer and place it in the dryer without interference from the open door of either piece of equipment (Figure 8.16). This movement of laundry between appliances should determine how the appliances are placed in relationship to each other.

Front-loading washers and dryers may require the user to bend down to load and unload. An alternative is to install the equipment on a raised platform so that the door is easier to access (Figure 8.14). Planning the equipment at this height cuts down on bending and allows the door to swing open clear of the armrest or lap of a person using a wheelchair. If the equipment is raised, be sure that the user can still reach and read the controls.

Figure 8.14 Raising a front-loading washer or dryer, up to about 12 inches, reduces bending and makes access easier, but still allows most people to reach the controls. (Courtesy of GE)

Stacked Washer and Dryer

If space is limited, a stacked washer and dryer can be a good choice (Figure 8.15). A stacked washer and dryer can take up about the same floor space as a single washing machine (approximately 30 inches by 30 inches) yet provides the capacity for full loads of laundry. While stacked equipment saves floor space, the height of the equipment precludes locating any accessible storage above it.

If a stacked washer and dryer are selected, be sure that all controls and door openings can be accessed by the user. Some stackable units can be placed side by side under a 36 inch high counter. Careful planning of water connections, shut-offs, and dryer venting is required.

Smaller sized stacked washers and dryers are available, with reduced capacity. These smaller machines are good choices for a "mini-laundry" area or a smaller household.

Figure 8.15 A stacked washer and dryer can save floor space, and be a good choice for a laundry area in a bathroom. (Courtesy of GE)

Other Laundry Equipment

A laundry area may include other equipment for clothes maintenance, including irons, steamers, and specialty clothes care appliances. Your client may also want a sewing machine in the laundry area. Be sure to provide adequate space to use and store these additional appliances, as well as utility connections.

Utility Service

Utility service requirements for laundry equipment are specified by the manufacturer, and may be controlled by local building codes. Listed below are typical requirements.

- Washing Machine:

    $1/2$ inch hot and cold water supply

    2 inch vented drain

    120 volt, 20 ampere dedicated electrical circuit

- Electric Dryer:

    240 volt, 50 ampere dedicated electrical circuit

    Exterior ventilation within 20 to 25 feet of dryer exhaust outlet

- Gas Dryer

    $3/4$ inch natural or LP gas connection

    120 volt, 20 ampere dedicated electrical circuit (may be able to share electrical circuit with the washer if a 30 ampere circuit is used)

    Exterior ventilation within 20 to 25 feet of dryer exhaust outlet

One or more additional electrical circuits and receptacles are recommended in the laundry area, to use additional clothes care equipment, such as irons, sewing machines or clothes steamers. An electrical circuit for lighting is also needed. A sink in the laundry area is common, and water supply, drains, and vents are needed for this.

Exterior ventilation of the dryer is important, even though there is sometimes consideration of venting dryers to the inside. The thought behind venting a dryer to the inside is that heat is retained, which is seen as an advantage in cold climates in the winter. However, the problems with this practice far outweigh the energy savings. The excess moisture can lead to serious condensation and mold problems in the home (See Chapter 3, *Environmental Considerations*).

Odors from laundry products can be a problem. Lint in the exhaust air presents maintenance problems. Gadgets are available to add to the dryer exhaust vent to filter lint. However, these filters require regular maintenance, and failure to do so clogs the exhaust vent, leading to a fire hazard. If venting is a problem, condensing dryers that do not require an outside vent are available.

Building codes typically require vinyl, rubber, or other moisture-resistant flooring under laundry equipment. A floor drain near the washing machine is a desirable feature, to minimize the problems with water leaks. If this cannot be provided, the washer can be installed in a floor pan that would contain leaks and overflows.

Space Planning in the Laundry Area

Adequate space is needed in the laundry area to move, turn, bend and twist, while moving laundry in and out of the equipment. Space for a laundry basket or cart is also needed. A clearance of 42 inches in front of a washer, dryer, or stacked washer and dryer, is recommended (Figure 8.16A). This will give adequate space to access either front- or top-loading machines, allowing space for door swings and a person to kneel or bend (See also Figure 8.9).

When the washer and dryer are placed side by side, the 42-inch clearance space should be 66 inches wide (Figure 8.16B). If front-loading appliances are being used, check to see that this dimension allows adequate clearance for a door swing. If appliances are placed at right angles or across from each other, the clearance spaces for each machine overlap (Figure 8.16C and Figure 8.16D).

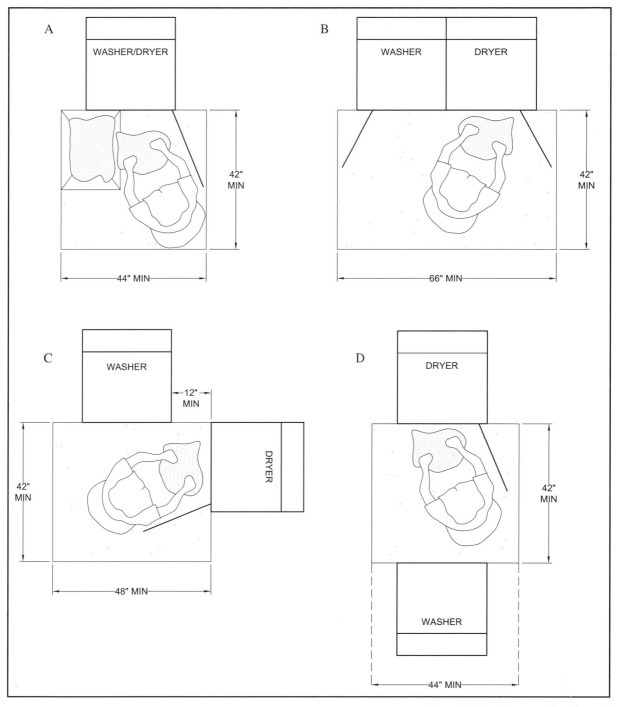

Figure 8.16 Clearance in front of laundry equipment provides space for bending and kneeling, as well as door swings and space for a laundry basket or cart.

If the person doing the laundry uses a mobility aid, such as a wheelchair or cane, these clearances will need to be increased. Refer back to *Form 1* in Chapter 5 for information on collecting clearances for mobility aids your client might use.

Laundry in Transition

Designing a laundry area is more than installing equipment with clearance space. The flow of laundry—mostly clothes—in and out of the space needs to be considered. Dirty laundry is brought into the area, clean laundry is moved out. During the transition, clothes, towels, bed linens, and other items may spend time "hanging out" in the laundry area. To help organize the laundry area, smooth the flow of laundry, and minimize clutter, consider the following ideas.

- Dirty laundry needs to be collected. Hampers, bins, or baskets in the laundry area can be used for short-term storage of dirty laundry (Figure 8.17). Good ventilation of the dirty laundry containers is necessary to dispel dampness and odors.

  Several containers might be used to pre-sort laundry. For example, white socks, t-shirts, and underwear might go into one container, jeans into another. (The effectiveness of this system depends on cooperation of everyone in the household!) Or, if several members of the household do laundry separately, each person can have their own container, using it to accumulate enough laundry for a washer load.

- Dirty laundry needs to be sorted before washing. Table or counter surface works well for this task, and then can later be used for folding and sorting clean laundry (Figure 8.17). A work surface 24 to 36 inches deep and 32 to 36 inches high would work for most people. The length of work surface depends on how much laundry is typically sorted and how much space is available.

  Several bins or baskets might be used to sort laundry. These items might rest on a work counter, or pull out from underneath a counter or from inside a cabinet.

- Hanging up items removed from the dryer minimizes wrinkles. Provide a space to hang shirts, blouses, skirts, dresses, and similar items. This hanging space should be convenient to the dryer. Garments on hangers should not block work areas or passages. Good ventilation is needed to allow garments to cool without wrinkling.

Refer to Figures 8.1, 8.2, 8.3 and 8.6, in the section on
"Clothes Storage" for information on planning space and
clearances for hanging clothes storage.

- Not everything goes into the dryer. Some items, like sweaters,
  need to be laid flat, on a clean, smooth surface, to dry. Other
  items are hung up to drip-dry—and they may drip while
  drying— so a waterproof area is needed. Delicate items, like
  lingerie, may be put over a drying rack. The amount of space
  devoted to these activities will depend on your client.

  If your client frequently air-dries laundry items, be sure that
  the area is adequately ventilated to prevent moisture problems.

- Clean laundry needs to be folded. A table or counter work
  surface, such as used for sorting dirty laundry, will provide
  a space to fold clean laundry, with a knee-space for seated
  work, when possible. If laundry is folded fresh from the dryer,
  wrinkles are minimized. Many people want space to sort clean
  laundry, by type of garment or item, or by its owner. Clean
  laundry may be stacked into a basket or cart for transport to
  storage areas in the home.

  Several bins or baskets might be used to sort laundry by its
  owner. Household members can then come claim their own
  laundry.

- A sink in the laundry area is a desirable feature (Figure 8.17).
  Some laundry products need to be diluted. Pre-rinsing may be
  helpful in removing stains. The sink can also be used for hand
  washing items or soaking soiled items.

  A laundry sink is typically placed next to or near the washer
  to facilitate plumbing connections, and for convenience of
  workflow. Unless your client does a lot of hand laundry, an
  extra deep utility or laundry type sink is not necessary. A small
  bar-type sink can work well. Select a gooseneck or pullout
  faucet for fitting bulky items under the water flow. Look for
  controls that are easy to operate with one hand.

- The laundry area needs adequate lighting that is conveniently
  switched. Good color rendition in the light sources is important
  for noting stains and other problems on fabrics. See Chapter 7
  for more information about lighting.

Figure 8.17 This laundry area includes many features, such as counter space for folding and sorting laundry, a bin for sorting laundry, a sink, sewing area and generous storage. (Courtesy of KraftMaid)

Storage

Easily accessible storage is needed for laundry supplies. Items such as detergent and fabric softener are used almost every time something is washed, and need to be easily reached when using the laundry equipment. Other laundry supplies, such as stain removers, special detergents, bleaches, wrinkle removers, and fabric fresheners, may be used less frequently, but still need to be convenient to the laundry equipment. Most of these items will fit on 8 to 10 inch deep shelves.

Storage in laundry areas is often placed over the laundry equipment. However, the depth of the washer or dryer reduces the height of the user's reach. Bringing a shelf forward can make items more accessible, as long as they will not get lost at the back of extra-deep shelves.

Keep in mind that some laundry products, such as detergent, come in large containers that are heavy and/or awkward to lift. These items should not be stored above shoulder height (typically 52 to 57 inches). Finally, shelves above laundry equipment should not interfere with door openings or access to controls. For all these reasons, storage areas adjacent to, rather than above, laundry equipment may be more desirable for the most frequently used items.

Other items may be stored in the laundry area, including hangers, clothespins, measuring cups for laundry products, stain removal guides, sponges, brushes, rags, and cleaning supplies. A divided drawer or small bins work well to collect items found in garment pockets or buttons that pop off. Some people keep basic sewing supplies in the laundry area so repairs can be made on the spot.

Open storage in the laundry area increases accessibility by making it easier to see stored items and eliminating cabinet doors that might not swing out of the way. However, the desirability of this depends on how open the laundry area is to view from other spaces in the home.

Laundry storage can be messy. Containers of detergents and other laundry products may drip when being used. Spills are inevitable. Storage areas, in fact all of the laundry area, should be made of durable, easily cleaned materials that are not damaged by exposure to water, detergents, and other laundry products. Vinyl, ceramic tiles, solid surface, and plastic laminates are popular materials used in laundry areas. For more about materials suitable to laundries, see the NKBA book *Kitchen & Bath Products*.

Ironing

Despite permanent-press fabrics and finishes, many people still want a place to iron clothes and household linens. The laundry area is a logical place to put an ironing area. Built-in ironing boards (refer to Figure 8.11) fold down from wall cupboards or pull out from underneath a countertop, yet are out of the way when not in use. Many of these include storage space for the iron as well. Racks are available to hang free-standing ironing boards, or ironing boards can fold up to store in utility closets.

Adequate space needs to be included in the laundry area for using the iron and ironing board (Figure 8.18). The amount of space may need to be increased if the user requires a mobility aid. Because an iron is very hot, the ironing area should not be in a passage or walk way. Most ironing boards adjust in height to allow a person to sit or stand to work and pull-out or drop-down versions create a full knee-space.

Figure 8.18 A typical ironing area would require a space that is 60 inches by 52 inches.

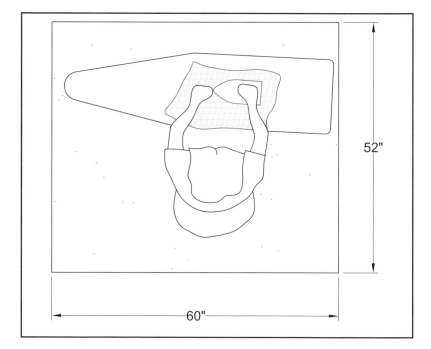

EXERCISE AREAS

An exercise space in or near the bathroom has many advantages and may be important to some clients.

Exercising at home can be more economical and more convenient than a membership to a health club. People are short on time, but can often spare 20 minutes for exercise if they can do it right there at home. The exercise area is accessible and does not require the motivation to drive to a health club. Home exercise equipment can be used in any weather, day or night. Some people will be more comfortable at home and prefer the privacy, rather than the more public health club or fitness center.

What Type of Exercise?

There are several things to be determined before planning an exercise space. Much of the information should be gathered during the client assessment discussed in Chapter 5. *Form 17: Assessment for Exercise Area,* at the end of this chapter, provides a checklist for recording information about exercise users, the type of exercise they participate in, and the type of equipment they may use. Find out about the client's fitness needs and exercise program. The client may have an established exercise program, but if they have not had the convenience of an exercise space at home, they need to think about how that space will impact their program. Here are some questions to consider.

- *Who will be participating in the exercise program and using the space?*

  Is this just for a single user or will a couple or other family members be participating? It is possible that guests (either overnight or visitors) may also participate in an exercise program. Will a personal trainer be involved in the exercise program?

- *How much time do the various users spend in their exercise program?*

  Do they spend 20 minutes on multiple exercise machines every evening or 30 minutes in an aerobics exercise program in the morning? Or do they just use the machine occasionally on a bad weather day when they cannot run or walk outside?

- *What exercise activities do they do?* This is critical in determining what equipment might be needed. Typical activities might be:

Flexibility exercise – stretches muscles. Includes yoga and warm-ups for other exercises.

Aerobic or cardio-vascular exercise – increases heart rate, stimulates circulation, strengthens heart and lungs, and induces weight loss through fat burning. Programs may include dancing, walking, jump-roping, running or swimming. Treadmills, bikes, stair climbers and elliptical runners support cardio-vascular exercise.

Strength training or weight conditioning programs – strengthens and tones muscles, burns fat and improves posture. Programs may include sit-ups and pushups, plyometrics or jump training, resistance training and weight lifting.

- *What are the resources available for designing the space?* Space will be needed for any equipment. Some programs can be completed in small areas, but some equipment requires a large amount of space.

- *Is new equipment needed?* If the client is selecting new equipment, they should try it out in a fitness center or equipment showroom.

- *Will a personal trainer be used?* A trainer may be an important partner in the selection of equipment and in planning the space.

LOCATION

A common location for an exercise or fitness area is off the master bathroom. This is ideal for adults looking for privacy or retreat. An exercise program that takes place as part of the morning preparations might be well suited in a master bathroom suite. Being close to showers, grooming space and clothing helps to make this a convenient activity that becomes readily incorporated into the daily routine.

If the exercise area is to be accessible to guests or other family members, then a space that is centrally located may be more suitable than the master bathroom. This common area could be next to a hall bath, in a loft or attic space, basement, or a room off a living area. Being close to a bathroom will still be important for many people wanting to refresh themselves after exercising. The space may also have to be flexible to meet multiple users' needs and exercise programs. The space could allow for more than one person at a station, such as partners doing the same exercise at the same time, or an instructor and student.

Exercise Equipment

Discussing the client's exercise program is critical in determining if the available space is adequate. The number and size of exercise equipment influence the space needed. To maximize the amount of exercise equipment in a limited space, fold-up models can be stored in a corner or closet.

- Some activities, such as aerobics, calisthenics, stretching and yoga, require no equipment other than a mat. Just allow the space needed to safely perform the activity.

- Stability balls are one of the most versatile pieces of exercise equipment. Sizes vary depending on the user. Common sizes are 18 inches, 22 inches and 26 inches.

- Sliders can be used for side-to-side or lateral exercises.

- Step benches are used for step-aerobic exercises.

- A punching or heavy bag is needed for kickboxing, boxing aerobics or karate.

- Cardio-vascular exercise equipment includes treadmills, bikes, rowing machines, stair climbers, elliptical runners and ski machines.

- Strength training equipment includes free-weight sets with weights, bars, clips and storage, as well as dumbbells and storage racks, single- and multi-station gyms, and elastic tubes and bands. Benches are often used, including slant boards for weight lifting or sit-ups. Reformers, including cables, pullers, springs, boxes and sliding boards, are used for Pilates.

Exercise equipment needs to be flexible if there will be multiple users of different heights, weights and fitness goals. For multiple users, the equipment and finishes also need to be especially durable.

Other Equipment

Often other activities are taking place at the same time as exercising. Some of these are essential to the exercise experience, i.e., watching an aerobics video. Sometimes an activity to engage the mind is needed, i.e., watching the morning news. Be sure to record this information on *Form 17*. Some non-exercise equipment to consider:

- Television and playback machines, such as VCR or DVD player, might be needed for instructional videos, popular with aerobics, Pilates and yoga.

Figure 8.19 The luxury shower is conveniently located adjacent to this exercise area with punching bag. (Courtesy of Kohler Company)

- Equipment may be needed to play music for aerobics, dancing or any exercise.

- A large easy-to-read clock, either analog or digital, may be needed for timing the exercise period or other activities. It should have a second hand, or count seconds.

- Mirrors on multiple walls can be used to ensure proper form.

- A juice bar, water cooler, beverage center or small refrigerator could add to the exercise experience by providing refreshment.

Mechanical and Structural Requirements

Some exercise equipment requires electrical connections. Most home equipment requires 110 volts and 20 amps, but some commercial equipment may require dedicated 220-volt receptacles. Floor receptacles may be desirable to reduce tripping hazards from cords.

Some exercise equipment is very heavy. Make sure the floor of the exercise area can handle the weight. In addition, the floor needs to be stiff enough to handle the stress of jumping and pounding from exercise activities.

Consider cushioning the entire floor with a dense mat to protect it and to help prevent transmission of sound to areas below, caused by jumping, loud music or dropped weights. In addition, wall construction and/or treatment should be planned to limit sound transmission to adjacent rooms. See Chapter 3 for more information on sound transmission through walls.

Use indirect lighting to avoid glare when the user is in a variety of positions. Fluorescent lamps do not put out as much heat as halogen or incandescent lamps. Avoid ceiling mounted or hanging light fixtures or pendants that could accidentally be damaged during exercises. See Chapter 7 for more information about lighting.

Plan for proper ventilation that will remove moisture and odor released into the air by exercising bodies. Information about ventilation is in Chapter 7.

Space Planning for Exercise

Use the anthropometric stature and body breadth measurements found in Chapter 4 as a guideline when figuring minimum floor space for exercises such as sit-ups and push ups. However, the client's side arm reach, forward thumb tip reach, vertical grip reach, and buttocks-leg length should also be considered when planning for stretching or calisthenics. These are a minimum.

When possible, use human body measurements from the largest percentile. If more than one person is using the space, plan for clearance between people. *Human Dimensions & Interior Space* recommends 3 inches to 6 inches between two persons' arms extended to the side. Keep in mind that exercise implies movement, and someone who is exercising may not remain centered in the space. Be generous with clearances.

Figure 8.20 Consider the space needed to stretch out on the floor and to conduct exercise while standing. The range of measurements given is for small women to tall men.

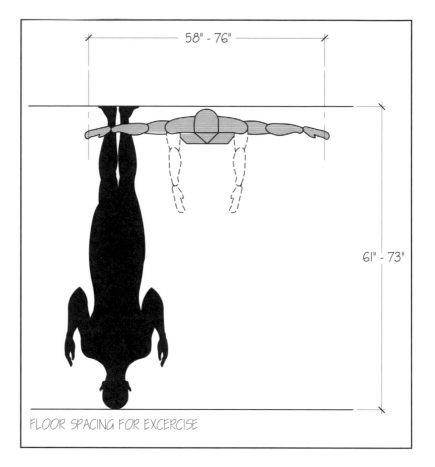

FLOOR SPACING FOR EXCERCISE

Ceiling Heights

In no other space in the home is ceiling height as critical as in the exercise area. This is especially true when an exercise program includes activities such as jumping jacks, jumping rope, or plyometrics, which may include jumping up and down on boxes or platforms. Dancing that includes lifts of another person requires a recommended ceiling height of 12 feet (144 inches).

Equipment

Sizes: To develop the space plan and to determine if the space is adequate, measure the existing equipment or obtain manufacturer's specifications on new equipment, just as you would for other fixtures and appliances in a bathroom.

The American Council on Exercise (ACE) has guidelines that can quickly help determine the space needed for common exercise equipment.

- Treadmills: 30 square feet

- Free weights: 20 to 50 square feet

- Bikes, recumbent and upright: 10 square feet

- Rowing machines: 20 square feet

- Stair climbers: 10 to 20 square feet

- Ski machines: 25 square feet

- Single-station gym: 35 square feet

- Multi-station gym: 50 to 200 square feet

Clearances: In addition to the dimension of the equipment, you must also provide a clear path of travel between each piece of equipment. There should be 30 inches minimum clearance or 36 inches if the client uses a mobility aid. Also consider how much additional space is needed for an exercise. For example, you may need to measure the length of the leg that extends past the bench during a leg extension strength exercise.

Storage

Like most activities, exercising requires "things" and they may need to be stored within, or close to, the exercise space. The section on closets provides some details for planning these spaces, but make sure you determine if the following are needed, and how they are being provided.

- Closets for equipment if it is stored after each use, or if an exercise area is to be used for a separate function.

- A locker area for clothes, shoes and accessories such as towels or water bottles.

- A bench or place to sit for putting on shoes and socks.

- A hamper for used clothes, socks and towels.

- Storage near exercise equipment for reading material such as books, magazines or newspapers.

- Storage for videos, CDs or DVDs.

THE HOME SPA

The luxury of the spa experience is being captured in the homes of many clients seeking relaxation and pampering. The popularity of day spas and resort spas has many consumers seeking their own space for caring for mind, body and soul. The home spa will be very individualized, depending on the client's desires. Different types of activities and equipment can be included, and the space can grow out of an existing bath or become a featured space in the home.

Some of the special features in a spa bath that provide hydrotherapy are a whirlpool tub, a soaking tub, a steam room, sauna, a massage table, and a chaise or sofa. Other spa activities could include chromatherapy and aromatherapy. Spaces for yoga and meditation might also be included in this space.

There are many considerations that must be addressed when designing a spa. Some of the information is gathered in the client assessment (Chapter 5), but there may be some special questions such as:

- *What type of spa activities would the client like to engage in?* Clients may request activities that they have experienced in a resort or day spa, such as steam baths, massages and saunas. Do they want to accommodate just one activity or multiple experiences?

- *Who will be using the home spa?* Will the spa be used by the adults or shared by family and guests? How many people will be using the spa at any one time? A soaking bath may be a private activity for one, while a spa tub might be used by a group. An assistant may come in to give a massage or pedicure.

Location

Often home spas are part of the master bathroom. It may already have a separate tub and shower, and upgrading or expanding the fixtures could create a spa space in the regularly used bathroom. Separating the spa area from the regularly used bath can create a space focused on the relaxing experience, not the day-to-day hassles of the morning rush to work.

Figure 8.21 This large master spa bathroom includes an elegant soaking tub. (Courtesy of Kohler Company)

315

Whirlpool baths are increasingly being requested for guest and secondary baths, and smaller fixtures can be fitted into trade-out installations. This allows all family and guests to have a pampering bath.

Figure 8.22 This 60-inch whirlpool tub will fit in many smaller bathrooms. Smaller sizes are also available. (Courtesy of Kohler Company)

A separate family spa close to the pool or outdoor hot tub might also be desirable in some homes. This location implies a social experience. Of course, a bathroom will be needed nearby for showers and dressing.

An outdoor component can add to the more traditional spa experience. An appropriate calming and beautiful view, or a privacy garden, can be important to meditation and relaxation. Sliding doors and windows can bring in fresh air and breezes. In addition, some spa activities can be conducted outside when the weather is appropriate.

Figure 8.23 A calming view and natural light add to the enjoyment of a whirlpool tub. (Courtesy of Lasco)

Home Spa Activities

There are many activities, procedures or therapies that a client may be interested in having in their home spa. Some require specialized equipment, discussed in the next section along with space planning requirements. However, some can be accomplished with spa products and very little extra space, still providing the client with a luxury experience. The following section explains some terms your clients might use in describing the activities they would like to have.

Hydrotherapy

This is the most basic treatment that can be offered in a home spa. Hydrotherapy uses water as the primary facilitator to treat muscles and reduce stress. Different forms of hydrotherapy include jetted or whirlpool baths, jetted showers, underwater massage, Vichy showers, Swiss showers, Scotch hose (to provide water pressure to certain areas), foot or hand baths, and combining hot/cold water treatments.

Figure 8.24 Hydrotherapy tubs can use jets, air or a combination. (Courtesy of Americh)

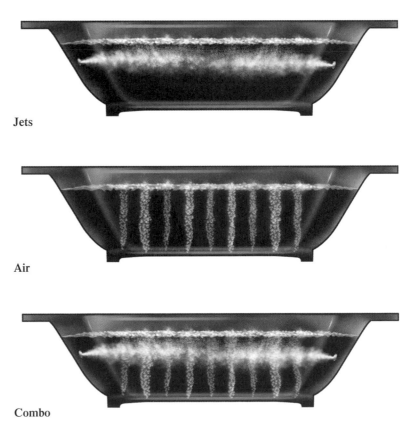

Jets

Air

Combo

Thalassotherapy

This is a long-term treatment of seawater in baths, showers and mud wraps. The premise is that the body absorbs the minerals from the seawater through osmosis. Thalassotherapy is supposed to help clear out the blood and keep the body in a balanced state. It might also be used as an inhalant to aid the upper respiratory tract. In a seawater bath (balenotherapy), the water is heated to 93°F for optimal skin treatment.

Cleansing Steam

Steam baths offer a way to cleanse and relax at the same time. In a steam bath, the humidity reaches 100 percent and cleans out the body's pores. A lukewarm shower follows the steam bath to add to the relaxing experience. Or a cold shower can be invigorating. Clients might want a steam bath or shower, or may plan to use a steam tent over a massage table.

Heat

The sauna uses dry heat and humidity at 15 percent to warm and relax the body. The low humidity is created by pouring water on hot rocks. Users go into the sauna for 5 to 15 minutes after a short shower. They sit or lay on wooden (cedar) benches in the insulated sauna room. They follow this with another shower, or visit the pool or plunge bath and then rest for a few minutes. Finally, they return to the sauna for about 20 minutes and then rest for 20 minutes before a final shower and light snack.

Heat therapy rooms use infrared heaters to radiate heat to the body. Infrared rooms operate at a lower temperature than saunas, maintain normal room humidity, and take less time to heat up. Pre-built units have some similar features to a sauna: cedar or alder lining, cedar benches with backrest, doors, controls and lighting. Infrared heat can be used for warm-ups for athletes, physical therapy or massages.

Aromatherapy

Aromas from essential oils are used to stimulate the nasal/olfactory senses. Essential oils are made from plant sources through a steam distillation process. Many commercial products are available for different applications including candles, oils, lotions and creams. Aromatherapy assumes that certain scents affect mood, emotions, mental responses, and circulatory and respiratory functions. For example, lavender might promote sleep, while peppermint might stimulate thinking (Figure 8.25).

Figure 8.25 Fragrances form the basis for aromatherapy approaches to dealing with numerous physical and mental conditions. (Printed with permission from Key Porter Books Ltd. Copyright © 1997, 2004 by Anne Harding and Janice Biehn)

Fragrance	Recommended Use
Cedarwood	Relieves colds and flu
Chamomile	Antidepressant; relieves insomnia, tension, headaches, arthritis, and PMS
Eucalyptus	Revitalizes sore muscles, headaches, colds, flu, arthritis
Geranium	Astringent, diuretic, antidepressant; relieves colds, arthritis, and PMS
Ginger	Relieves arthritis pain, nausea
Jasmine	Antidepressant, aphrodisiac
Lavender	Antiseptic, analgesic, relieves insomnia, tension, anxiety, and rashes
Orange blossom	Sedative, aphrodisiac; relieves insomnia
Peppermint	Soothes and aids digestion; relieves colds and flu
Rose	Relieves depression, insomnia, nausea, and PMS
Rosemary	Stimulant, memory-booster; relieves arthritis pain
Sandalwood	Treats depression, insomnia, nausea

Chromatherapy

This term is used to describe colored lights, usually in a tub, that are thought to influence the user's mood. The bather turns off all room lighting and focuses on the colored light from the tub, while practicing deep breathing and visualization techniques. Different colors have different effects (Figure 8.26). For instance, red is a stimulating color which is supposed to activate blood flow, while blue might be relaxing and help reduce all types of cramps.

Figure 8.26 Chromatherapy assumes colored lights can affect users' moods and health. (Courtesy of Ultra Baths)

Color	Some Effects
Red	Stimulant, energizing, clears congestion, relieves arthritis and muscle pain
Orange	Relieves arthritis and muscle pain, relieves stress on heart, aids respiratory functions
Yellow	Stimulates brain activity and digestive process
Green	Calming effect, revitalizes intellectual awareness, emotional balance
Blue	Antispasmodic properties, relaxing, relieves hypertension
Purple	Stimulates immune system, appetite regulator

Facials, Exfoliation, and Body Wraps

These are several beauty treatments that can be conducted at home. A facial involves steaming and deep cleaning the face, followed by a massage, a mask and moisturizer. Exfoliation is a way to remove dead skin from the entire body. It can be done simply by using a loofah with a graining paste in the shower. Body wraps might involve wrapping the body in a hot tea-soaked sheet. Another skin treatment is a body mask of mud.

Meditation and Yoga

Meditation has been suggested as a way to focus energy, reduce stress and gain calm. Yoga is a specific technique for combining body movements, breathing, and meditation. Quiet spaces are needed. Shrines may be requested to focus thoughts during meditation.

Massage

There are many types of massage treatments and body works that are used to help clients to relax, reduce pain and tone muscles. The specific type of massage will depend on the massage therapist and the needs of the client. Although the bath designer will not need to know all of the types of massage treatments, it might be helpful to be familiar with a few of the techniques.

- Cranio-Sacral massages focus on the head and neck area to loosen tight neck muscles.

- Deep tissue massage releases tension in deeper muscle layers by using slow strokes and finger pressure on contracted muscle areas.

- Feldenkrais massage is a clothes-on massage that helps with sports injuries and tension.

- Reflexology is a massage based on a system of points or meridians in the hands and feet that correspond to organs in the body.

- Reike is a body work technique using subtle stationary hand positions on points of tension or injury.

- Shiatsu is a body work technique of acupressure used on pressure points to improve energy flow.

- Swedish massage uses long strokes, kneading and friction techniques to relax muscles.

- Trager body work techniques help with joint movement.

Spa Supplies and Equipment

A home spa will need certain basic supplies and equipment, but it could be created in a bathroom with a bathtub and shower. The items depend on the treatments the client is using, but may well include candles, body brushes, loofahs, sponges, scrubbing mitts, oils, moisturizers, muds, towels, sheets, pillows, and a varied supply of nail care products. The more elaborate treatments require wet rooms and lounge chairs.

The specific fixtures and equipment that the client might request are:

Whirlpools. Whirlpools or jetted bathtubs are one of the most requested items in new and remodeled baths and provide the client with a form of hydrotherapy. Most new homebuyers expect a whirlpool tub in the master suite, and whirlpools are frequently placed in remodeled bathrooms that contain a tub and shower. Small 60 inch x 32 inch models are available, as are deep two-person models.

Consider who will be using the whirlpool and how much space they require. The shape of the seating, padding and angled support determine the user's comfort while in the tub. Ideally the client will be able to sit in a working tub before selecting it, to see if it is comfortable and if the water action meets their expectations.

Whirlpools are filled with heated water each time they are used. They have different jetted actions that move the water in the tub. This is an important variable in design and selection of the units. Some may have jets that force the water out at certain locations. Other jet actions may move the water in a rotating pattern.

The number of jets and their location in relation to the bather determine how effective they are as hydrotherapy. Air bubblers may line the bottom of the tub creating a soft massaging movement. The number of jets, and the integration of jets and air bubblers, will affect the quality of the whirlpool experience. The system should be integrated so that it works efficiently.

Figure 8.27 Whirlpool jets can be placed in different locations to create different patterns of water movement.

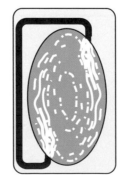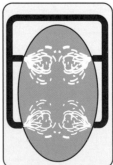

Whirlpool users will sit in the warm water (103/104°F for adults) for about 15–20 minutes. It is important to think about the user's view, which is why the tubs are often placed at a window. Some tubs come with DVD/CD/AM/FM stereo surround sound systems and plasma screen televisions, so the user can listen to relaxing music (or watch an action movie if desired). Tubs also may have different colored lights within the water to enhance chromatherapy.

Figure 8.28 Consider the user's view when planning a whirlpool. Some users may want a view out a window; others may prefer a TV. (Courtesy of Jacuzzi)

Other features to consider in selecting a whirlpool are electronic touch pads and remote controls. Extra water heaters may be needed to handle the demand of the larger tubs. The designer must plan for the location of the access panels, so that maintenance and repairs can be completed. Often a handheld shower is mounted on the whirlpool tub deck.

Spa tubs. Spa tubs are often referred to as hot tubs. They offer some of the same relaxing options as the whirlpool, but the water remains in the tub and is re-used. The water is thermostatically controlled and stays heated. Skimmers and filters are essential to maintain water quality. An insulated cover keeps the moisture and heat in the tub.

Spa tubs are not used for bathing. Users should shower before entering the hot tub. Some larger hot tubs are more suited for a social area since they can handle up to 10 people. Often these are placed outside and are accessible from the public parts of the house.

Soaking tubs. These tubs are also enjoying some popularity in the spa bathroom. They are deeper than standard tubs—25 inches instead of 15 inches—and they are often longer—as much as 78 inches. They relax the user by having them sink to their necks in warm water. Users should shower before entering, since soaps are not to be used in soaking.

Some of these tubs are free-standing and come in a variety of materials, such as copper, wood, acrylics and marble. The form of the tub can be designed to support the back or legs. A Japanese soaking tub is smaller and deeper, with a seat that the bather uses to submerge into the water.

Often soaking tubs are designed for a wall- or floor-mounted faucet. A larger hot water tank will be needed and extra reinforcement in the floor is necessary to support the weight of the filled tub.

Figure 8.29 Built-in or free standing soaking tubs are deep, allowing the user to submerge into deep warm water. (Courtesy of Ann Sacks)

Steam bathtubs or showers. These bathtubs or showers can be free-standing, or a system can be added to a standard shower or tub/shower design. The same considerations for designing a shower should be followed. However, the shower or bathtub must be sealed from the edge of the fixture to the ceiling to create the steam room. Seating is needed and the controls must be placed within the steam room.

Figure 8.30 A steam shower should have good shower design features, such as a seat, storage, and a grab bar. (Courtesy of Lasco)

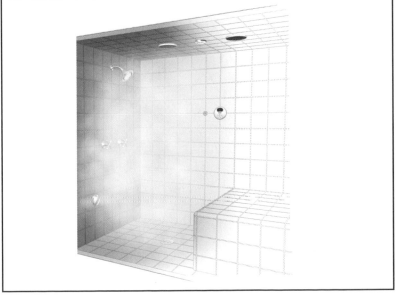

Figure 8.31 Controls are placed within the steam room. (Courtesy of Mr. Steam)

325

Saunas and infrared rooms. These are separate insulated rooms lined with cedar. In a sauna, a separate heater with rocks is placed in the room. Water can be sprinkled on the rocks occasionally to create steam at a low humidity to relieve the dryness in the sauna. In an infrared room, multiple infrared heaters are placed along the wall to provide direct heat on each user. The sauna or infrared room should allow at least 4 square feet (6 square feet is preferred) of space per person. The doors must swing out and should not lock. The sauna should be planned with the shower located nearby.

The bench in the sauna or infrared room should be 24 inches wide to allow for sitting and lying down. It should be about 18–20 inches high. A slanted back can also be provided to add a place to recline. Benches can be tiered to provide more seating, but a higher ceiling may be needed.

Figure 8.32 A sauna layout should consider bench height and depth, ceiling height, and floor clearance. (Redrawn from *Human Dimension & Interior Space* by Julius Panero and Martin Zelnik [1979, Watson-Guptill Publications] pg. 254)

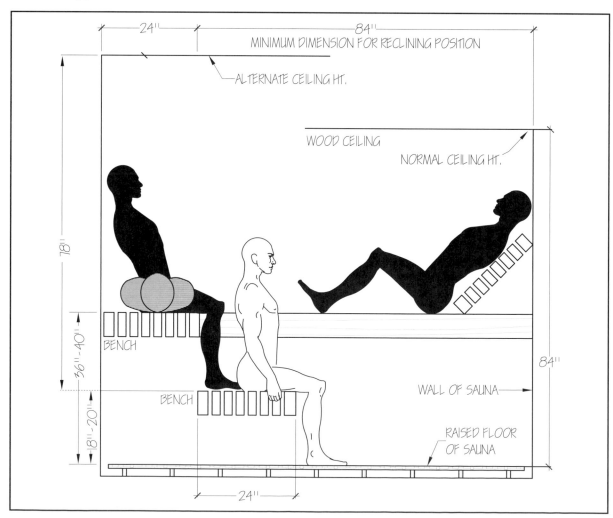

Vichy shower. This system provides hydrotherapy from an overhead shower rainbar with several shower heads. The user lies in a wet spa bed while a therapist administers the shower treatment. Handheld shower heads might also be used to pin-point water pressure on specific areas of the body. The wet spa bed may have a drain or be incorporated onto a wet room that will drain the water.

Massage tables. These tables can be portable or stationary, and electric lifts are available to adjust the height of the table. A standard size table ranges from 69 inches to 73 inches long and 26 inches to 37 inches wide, depending on manufacturer and model.

Figure 8.33 Prefabricated saunas can fit into the home spa area. (Courtesy of Helo)

UTILITIES AND INFRASTRUCTURE

Several pieces of hydrotherapy equipment will require extra water heaters, either larger tanks or on-demand heaters. Extra support in the floor may be needed to handle the weight of the equipment, especially when filled with water. Electrical service will need to be planned to accommodate the heaters and pumps. Extra plumbing and electrical requirements may call for extra wall and floor space. Access panels for maintenance and servicing of equipment should be planned. These and other considerations are discussed in Chapter 2.

Lighting

A variety of lighting will be needed in the spa area to support different activities. General indirect lighting should be provided for the safe use of equipment and for dressing. Many treatments are accomplished under low lights which are calming and relaxing. Some people use candles for lighting and for the aromatic effect during a relaxing soaking bath.

More focused task lighting may be needed for facials, manicures and pedicures. Other task lighting may be needed for preparing essential oils and other types of mixtures, reading and some food preparation. Lighting is discussed in more detail in Chapter 7.

Ventilation

Any hydrotherapy or steam treatment will put a great deal of moisture into the air, which must be removed with proper ventilation afterwards. Special care should be given to indoor spas or hot tubs, since warm water remains in the tub and chemicals are used to treat it. Strong odors and candle soot may need to be removed through ventilation. Refer to the ventilation information in Chapter 7 and the indoor air quality information in Chapter 3.

Floor Space

The design recommendations for special spa fixtures are the same as those for bathtubs and showers presented in Chapter 6. Check the measurements of the fixture or equipment specified and allow adequate clearance in front for access. Here are some key points:

- A recommended clear space of 30 inches is needed in front of any fixture.

- Space for larger dressing circles should be included (42 inches to 48 inches).

- 30 inches should be planned around massage tables or other equipment where an assistant or therapist might be applying treatment.

- Control valves should be reachable from both outside and within the fixture.

- Access panels should be easy to get to for repairs and maintenance.

Seating and Refreshments

A lounge area such as a chaise, or chair and ottoman, might provide another way to relax in the home spa along with storage for reading material.

Figure 8.34 A bench in front of a window can be a nice feature of a home spa. (Courtesy of Moen)

Many spa activities suggest that the client have refreshments, especially drinks, during or after, similar to exercise. A refreshment center may be needed in the spa area to store water, juice and healthy snacks, and a water cooler or a refrigerator would be a helpful feature.

The refreshment center might expand to a mini-kitchen if more extensive food preparation is desired. Some aromatherapy treatments require that mixtures be cooked or distilled. Although these treatments may be prepared in the kitchen, a small cooktop in a spa area may not be out of the question.

Storage

The home spa will need some of the same items and thus, some of the same storage, as found in the more typical bathroom. For example:

- Towels will need to be located near the various fixtures, and a place to store extra towels will be needed. Often larger bath sheets are used as wraps. These require more space to hang and store.

- Robes and soft soled shoes may be used and kept in this area. Plan hanging space or hooks for robes, and shelves for shoes.

- There may be several different types of bottles, jars, sponges, brushes, candles, foot massagers and other items used in some treatments. Consider shelves and drawer storage for them.

- Several treatments require mixing ingredients, so bowls, measuring cups and spoons may be needed.

Fireplace

A fireplace may be desired in a luxury bath or home spa. Although it might be considered a secondary heat source, it is more likely to be used for its ambiance, to set a relaxing and romantic mood. Several types could be included such as masonry fireplaces, vented gas fireplaces, or direct vent fireplaces. Unvented gas fireplaces are available, but are not approved for use in some states.

The masonry fireplace is the traditional wood-burning fireplace. It will require a hearth and a chimney with flue. It will need to be planned by a professional to assure that it is properly sized to draw correctly. Wood will be needed, and the fireplace will have to be cleaned regularly.

A fireplace that uses vented gas logs also relies on the hearth and chimney with a flue. A direct vent system does not require a chimney and can be placed in many different locations. Ductwork from the outside provides air for the system and removes waste to the outside. Check local building codes for installation requirements.

Installing a fireplace will add to the space requirements. Check the clearance required between the fireplace and any combustible materials. Include adequate circulation space around any hot surfaces.

Figure 8.35 A fireplace adds warmth and ambiance to a spa area. (Courtesy of Kohler Company)

SUMMARY

There is so much that can be added to the bathroom. Determining the lifestyle needs of your client is an important step in the interview and assessment process. Do they need their life enhanced by an organized and expansive closet? Or does the convenience of having the laundry near the dirty clothes appeal to their efficiency? Are they concerned about their health, wanting to stay active and in shape? Or does the pampering and relaxation of spa treatments represent their desire to take care of themselves? Whatever the client might want, you should be able to assess their space and budget and look for ways to enhance their lifestyle.

FORM 13: CLOTHES STORAGE INVENTORY FOR HANGING CLOTHES

Instructions: Use this inventory checklist to determine the number of items to be stored in the closet on hangers. Items are grouped by the typical rod height. You may not have each item listed, or you may not store it on hangers. There are blank lines to add clothing items that you have which are not listed.

✓	Clothing Item	Number of clothing items		
		Women	Men	Children
	Rod Height: 68" – 72"			
	Floor length gowns/evening dresses			
	Jumpsuits			
	Night gowns			
	Robes			
	Other:			
	Other:			
	Rod Height: 54" – 63"			
	Coats			
	Dresses			
	Night gowns			
	Slacks, pants, jeans			
	Other:			
	Other:			
	Rod Height: 45" – 48"			
	Jackets			
	Skirts			
	Slacks, pants, jeans (folded over)			
	Sweaters			
	Suits			
	Other:			
	Other:			
	Rod Height: 36" – 45"			
	Blouses or shirts			
	Jackets			
	Shorts			
	Sweaters			
	Other:			
	Other:			

Notes: Rod height is the length of the clothing item plus 10" (4" for the hanger and 6" floor clearance).

FORM 14: CLOTHES STORAGE INVENTORY FOR FOLDED, ROLLED, AND OTHER TYPES OF CLOTHES

Instructions: Use this inventory checklist to determine the number of items to be stored in the closet using built-in shelves, drawers, hooks, or other methods. Do not include items that will be stored on hangers, in furniture, such as dressers, or in other places besides the closet. You will probably not have each item listed. There are blank lines to add clothing items that you do have which are not listed. There are two lists, one for women and girls, and another for men and boys.

Women's and Girl's Clothing						
✓	**Clothing Item**	**Type of Storage**				
		Shelf	Drawer	Hook	Box	Other (describe)
	Belts					
	Boots					
	Bras					
	Blouses					
	Camisoles					
	Gloves, mittens					
	Handkerchiefs					
	Hats					
	Leggings, leotards					
	Jeans					
	Jewelry					
	Night gowns					
	Pajamas					
	Panty hose, stockings					
	Scarves					
	Shirts, dress					
	Shirts, knit (e.g. polo, rugby)					
	Shoes					
	Shorts					
	Slips, full, half					
	Socks					
	Sweaters					
	Sweatshirts					
	Swimsuits					
	Ties, ascots					
	T-shirts					
	Undershirts					
	Underwear					
	Additional items:					

FORM 14: CLOTHES STORAGE INVENTORY FOR FOLDED, ROLLED, AND OTHER TYPES OF CLOTHES (CONTINUED)

Men's and Boy's Clothing						
✓	**Clothing Item**	**Type of Storage**				
		Shelf	Drawer	Hook	Box	Other (describe)
	Belts					
	Boots					
	Gloves, mittens					
	Handkerchiefs					
	Hats					
	Jeans					
	Jewelry					
	Pajamas					
	Scarves					
	Shirts, dress					
	Shirts, knit (e.g. polo, rugby)					
	Shoes					
	Shorts					
	Socks					
	Sweaters					
	Sweatshirts					
	Swimsuits					
	Ties, ascots					
	T-shirts					
	Undershirts					
	Underwear					
	Additional items:					

FORM 15: WORKSHEET FOR FOLDED OR ROLLED CLOTHING

Use the information from FORM 14: Clothes Storage Inventory for Non-hanging Clothes to determine the number of garments. The number per stack is typically 2 to 6 items, depending on the number of garments and client preference. Determine the size of each stack. This information is then used to determine the total amount of shelf and/or drawer space that is needed.

Items Stored in Drawers					
✓	Garment	Number of garments	Number per stack	Dimensions in Inches, per Stack		
				Frontage	Depth	Stack Height
	Example:					
	T-shirts	18	12	12	16	5

FORM 15: WORKSHEET FOR FOLDED OR ROLLED CLOTHING (CONTINUED)

✓	Garment	Number of garments	Number per stack	Dimensions in Inches, per Stack		
Items Stored on Shelves						
				Frontage	Depth	Stack Height
	Example:					
	T-shirts	18	12	12	16	5

FORM 16: LINEN CLOSET STORAGE INVENTORY

Use this form to inventory how many items will be stored in the linen closet, and how much space will be needed.

The highlighted example shows an inventory where there are 18 wash cloths, which can be divided into stacks with a maximum of 6 per stack, for a total of 3 stacks. Each stack is 6" by 6" and 5" high. This information can then be used in planning the layout of the linen closet.

Linen		Number of items	Items per stack	Number of stacks	Dimensions in Inches, per Stack		
✓					Frontage	Depth	Stack Height
	Example:						
	Wash Cloths	18	6	3	6	6	5
	Bathroom Linens:						
	Bath mats						
	Towels, face or wash cloths						
	Towels, hand						
	Towels, bath						
	Towels, bath sheets						
	Towels, guest						
	Bedding:						
	Bed spreads						
	Blankets						
	Pillows						
	Pillowcases						
	Quilts						
	Sheets, twin						
	Sheets, double						
	Sheets, queen						
	Sheets, king						
	Kitchen Linens:						
	Coasters						
	Dish cloths						
	Dish towels						
	Hand towels						
	Hot mats						
	Napkins						
	Place mats						
	Table cloths						
	Table runners						
	Additional items to store in linen closet:						

FORM 17: ASSESSMENT FOR EXERCISE AREA

Record information about the users of the exercise area, the types of activities they prefer, equipment, and other requirements.

✓	Users	Exercise Users			Notes and Special Requirements
		Daily/weekly	Daily/weekly	Daily/weekly	
	Time Spent Exercising				
	Flexibility				
	Stretching				
	Yoga				
	Exercise Mat				
	Stability Balls				
	Other				
	Cardio-vascular/Aerobics				
	Dancing				
	Walking				
	Running				
	Martial Arts				
	Boxing/Kick boxing				
	Punching bags				
	Jump-roping				
	Mats				
	Swimming				
	Aerobic Equipment				
	Sliders				
	Step benches				
	Treadmills				
	Bikes				
	Rowing machines				
	Stair climbers				
	Elliptical				
	Ski machines				
	Others				

FORM 17: ASSESSMENT FOR EXERCISE AREA (CONTINUED)

✓	Users	Exercise Users						Notes and Special Requirements
		Daily/weekly		Daily/weekly		Daily/weekly		
	Strength-training							
	Sit-ups							
	Push-ups							
	Resistance training							
	Pilates							
	Reformer							
	Weight lifting							
	Free weights							
	Dumb bells							
	Weight bench							
	Single-station gym							
	Multi-station gym							
	Other							

What else would you like to have in the exercise area?

❏ Clock ❏ Mirrors

❏ Television ❏ Extra fan and/or ventilation

❏ DVD/VCR ❏ Refreshment center

❏ Stereo/Music ❏ Seating or Lounge area

CHAPTER 9: A Closer Look At Your Client

To the greatest extent possible, incorporate universal design into the bathroom in order to meet the needs of clients throughout their lifespan and the changes in their physical condition. In some cases, you may be asked to design a bathroom that functions for a client with a particular need or disability, and this chapter is an information source for those situations.

While universal design concepts have been included throughout the book, in this chapter, user characteristics and appropriate design concepts are grouped together to serve as an aid to the design process. Where appropriate, concepts will be explored in more depth to broaden your understanding, or additional resources may be mentioned to enable you to go further in solving client problems.

The tools presented in Chapter 5, *Assessing Needs*, give you a great way to gather information that can help you identify and plan for each client's needs. When a specific chronic condition or disability is involved, the client will often be your best source of information regarding unique needs and solutions.

In addition, health professionals involved with your client, such as occupational or physical therapists, make great team members. Their expertise is the human body and its workings, whereas yours is the space and its function and components. Keep in mind that when specific medical equipment is involved, your role as designer may be to provide appropriate space planning and to involve the equipment expert to execute the plan.

In short, if you are designing for a client whose needs are in common with any of the user groups identified here, check this chapter for ideas to help with the design of their bathroom.

ACCESS CONSIDERATIONS

Bathroom space planning considers the given parameters of the job, the NKBA Bathroom Planning Guidelines and Access Standards found in Chapter 11, and a client's preferences and budget. In addition, space planning must consider clear floor space and support requirements based on the client's specific needs and abilities. The following information should help you to accomplish this.

The user groups and design concepts listed here are not in any way complete, but they will provide a good start in your effort. There is much overlap because, for example, the knee space that allows access at a vanity for a person using a wheelchair also provides for seated use by a pregnant woman experiencing fatigue. It can also function as a storage place for a step stool for a child. In some cases, information is repeated and in others, different sections of the chapter and book are referenced.

Across the Lifespan

From childhood to old age, we are growing and changing. While many of our needs as young children are similar to our needs as aging adults, there are also differences.

CHILDREN

A child's body is constantly changing and growing, their senses finding new discoveries everyday. Their language and reasoning skills are only just beginning to develop. Children see the world differently than adults and often do not understand danger or the consequences of their actions. They are small in stature, have limited reach, stamina, balance, strength, and dexterity, coupled with huge spurts of energy. In addition, they have a short attention span and, occasionally, a lack of body function or control. In designing spaces they will inhabit, it is critical to acknowledge their limited awareness of risk/safety factors and lack of understanding.

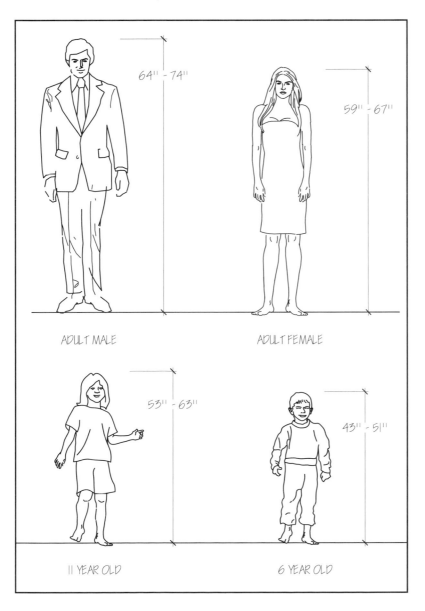

ADULT MALE   ADULT FEMALE

11 YEAR OLD   6 YEAR OLD

Figure 9.1 Differences between a child and even the smallest of adult females (5th percentile) require adjustments to the location of the adjustable showerhead, storage, controls, support, and more.

343

Typical design considerations include:

- Lower or adjustable heights for fixtures, fittings, storage, and controls, or other accommodation to smaller stature.

- Assistance in accessing fixtures, fittings, storage, and controls, including support.

- Safety measures regarding water, medicines and slippery surfaces.

- Lower sight lines.

- Storage for bath and toileting equipment and toys.

- Supplemental heat.

- Doors without locks.

- Flexible equipment and assistive devices that can change as a child grows.

Bathroom Design Implications. While low child-height fixtures are ideal for small children in a daycare or learning environment, in a home these fixtures will need to be replaced with standard ones as the child grows. Often standard-sized fixtures are used and adjustments are made to support children using the bathroom independently. Until children can use the bathroom by themselves, they will probably need assistance. Clear floor space should allow for a parent or caregiver to assist in completing bathroom activities.

Grooming Center. Children will be completing the same activities at the lavatory as adults. Small children will be learning to brush teeth, and wash hands and face, so it is important that the grooming center be planned to help them learn these basic hygienic activities. The following are some ways to make this area convenient:

- A step stool at the vanity eliminates the need to climb on the counter to use the sink or access storage.

- An open knee space provides storage for the stepstool, or an inverted vanity cabinet can be built so the drawer at the bottom can be converted to a step.

Figure 9.2 A pull-out step at the vanity provides flexibility in access as a child grows. The lights placed on the side of the mirror assure that children can see themselves clearly. (Courtesy of Kohler Company)

- A full-length mirror or mirrors that can be tilted will be within a child's sight line.

- Lamps along the height/length of the mirror provide a light source at eye level, regardless of a child's height. Use cool lights with the lamp out of direct reach and sight.

- Ease counter edges to avoid potential hazards for an unstable toddler's head or busy child's shoulder or hip.

- Place a maximum amount of storage at the lower end of the reach range and plan the location of a child's "stuff" well within easy reach.

- Plan storage for medications that is out of the children's reach.

Bathing and Shower Center. While a high percentage of adults prefer to shower, a bathtub should be planned to bathe small children. For young children, bathing can be a fun experience, but often adult supervision is needed. Showering may be desired by older children. Other considerations include the following.

- Plan grab bars to assist the child getting in and out of the tub and to help the parent or caregiver bathing the child.

- Consider a bathtub design that allows the parent or caregiver to comfortably sit while bathing the child, and also allows the child to sit to enter and exit the tub.

- Place controls that the child is to use within their sight and reach range.

- Use anti-scald, temperature limiting devices to prevent scalding or burning.

- Specify an adjustable-height spray with a generous length of hose (60 inches minimum) that can be lowered for use by children who shower and for use in the tub by a parent or caregiver.

Toileting Center. Learning to use the toilet is a major development in early childhood. Often temporary solutions are found to make a standard toilet the appropriate size for young children. Step stools, seats, and potty chairs can be helpful during the progression of toilet training.

MIDDLE YEARS

From childhood to advancing elder status, the middle years cover a broad range of change that affects our abilities. To name a few, this is a time of growth spurts, broken bones and activity-related injuries, pregnancy, parenthood, increased responsibilities and related stresses, and caring for parents and children. During this time, many people experience increased strength, stamina, balance and dexterity, with decreased time and conflicting demands for their attention span.

According to some sources, people reach their physical prime at around age 16 and then have a long period of gradual changes in their bodies and abilities. Changes in vision, hearing, and memory subsequently become common to the aging process. NKBA's Bathroom Planning Guidelines are useful in designing a bathroom for this age group.

AGING

People then reach a point in the growth process where a number of their abilities begin to change again. They adapt themselves to the changes as they age and may not notice any difference until the environment is not supporting them. Being able to use the bathroom is critical for the independence of an older person, and the design of the space can make a difference. Just a few of the changes common as we age are included here.

Mental Changes. Some memory loss or occasional forgetfulness, as opposed to overall mental decline, is very common. The ability to learn does not decrease with age, but stereotypes cause many to fear the loss of mental ability as they age. Reaction time generally is longer. Reduced physical and reaction abilities cause many to prefer home where things are familiar, allowing for a sense of security.

Vision Changes. Physical changes in the eyes increase with age and can lead to vision impairment, such as difficulty seeing in dim light, increased light sensitivity, difficulty focusing on moving objects, and a decrease in peripheral vision. More time is needed for the eyes to adjust when transitioning between light and dark areas. Reading glasses become a common need beginning in the 40s, and lenses begin to yellow, causing difficulty in distinguishing some colors. The section on "Vision Impairments or Loss" in this chapter has additional information.

Hearing Changes. Another common occurrence is some level of hearing loss, usually beginning with difficulties with high frequencies and progressing to lower frequencies. Ringing in the ears is also common. Hearing loss and the inability to communicate can cause significant emotional stress, and potential negative effects can be reduced through design. The section on "Auditory Impairments or Loss" in this chapter has additional information.

Other Sensory Changes. People may experience a general and gradual decline in other senses. They may have a change in their ability to taste, including a decline in the recognition of sweet, sour, and salty foods, and often complain about a bitter taste in the mouth or food tasting bland. Some experience a decline in ability to smell such odors as smoke and leaking gas. Sensitivity to touch may decline as well. Some people have increased thresholds of pain, and a decreased sensitivity to internal body temperature.

Bone and Muscle Changes. People experience a decrease in strength due to bone and muscle loss, causing an increase in accidents and fractures. Decreased mobility can be caused by changes in joints, stooped posture, and/or decrease in height, and common disorders such as arthritis, osteoarthritis and osteoporosis. As people "shrink" in height, reach ranges are shorter than those of middle aged people, moving closer to the range of children. See this chapter's "Mobility" section for additional information.

Internal Functions. Changes in internal functions cause increased incidence of high blood sugar, gallstones, diverticulitis, constipation, and loss of bowel control. Changes in kidney and bladder function can inhibit urinary control and cause dehydration. Changes in the nervous system result in slower movements, and decreased balance and coordination due to inefficiency of the nervous system and central brain processes. Many people experience a sleeping pattern change, requiring less sleep or experiencing less sound sleep.

Typical design considerations include:

- Adjusted heights of fixtures, fittings, storage and controls, for an accommodation to shortened stature and reduced balance.

- Intuitive controls and organization to compensate for memory losses.

- Increased support throughout the space.

- Optional seating at the major bathroom centers.

- Dual cueing on safety devices, such as a smoke alarm that flashes and sounds its warning.

- Increased and adjustable lighting.

- Reduced risk of glare and increased intentional contrast used for way-finding.

- Quick and easy access to the toilet, including in the middle of the night.

- Protection from scalding.

- Eased edges to reduce the risk of injury.

- Insulation to reduce excess noise.

- Raised heights in seating at the toilet, tub or shower.

- Increased and even heating.

Bathroom Design Implications. Sufficient clear floor space for functional passage is a design challenge for this age group. As strength, stamina and balance decrease, minimal passage clearances give people support as they move through a space. But with a mobility aid, more generous spaces are mandatory. Generous passage with integral options for support is one possible solution.

Plan reinforcement in the walls throughout the space for additional support as user needs change. A good way to provide flexibility for additional grab bar installations is to install a layer of 3/4 inch plywood before the cement board or sheetrock (refer to Figure 6.38 for technique). Increase use of support rails should compliment the aesthetics of the bath, as with a chair rail moulding designed to double as a support.

Install single-lever, easy-to-operate controls at faucets and doors. Use controls for windows, lighting and fixtures that are easy to reach, read, and operate.

Figure 9.3 Controls should be easy to read, easy to operate and within reach but not in the way. (Courtesy of Kohler Company)

Grooming. Beside single-lever faucet controls, some ideas specific to the vanity and lavatory include:

- Plan multiple-height vanities with opportunities for flexible knee spaces below. Remember to incorporate support for the lavatory and counter at a knee space, and to cover the plumbing for protection. (See the "Mobility" section in this chapter for more information.)

- Storage should be placed at the point of use and within easy reach. See Chapter 6 for information on planning storage.

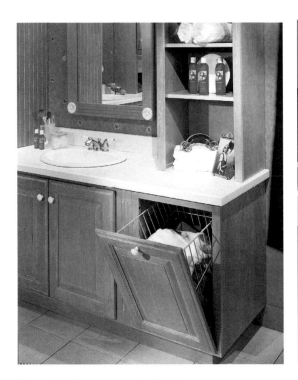 

Figure 9.4 Because much of what we store in the bathroom is small, thoughtful design can often result in storage right where it is needed. (Courtesy of Decora)

- Increased lighting should be from varied sources, natural and artificial, with adjustable controls.

- Provide for minimal glare through careful selection of materials and attention to light sources, including windows.

Bathing and Showering. Beside consideration for grab bars and single-lever handles, the following ideas should be considered:

- Specify a hand-held spray with 60 inch long hose for flexibility in use.

- Plan adjustable-height, multiple-head showers for flexibility in the numbers and needs of users.

Figure 9.5 This shower exudes luxury and the flexibility of multiple, adjustable height showerheads. (Courtesy of John A. Petrie, CMKBD – Mechanicsburg, Pennsylvania)

- Locate the tub/shower controls offset towards the room.

- Plan for the option of sitting in the shower and to enter the tub.

- Plan tub deck and shower benches at 17 inches to 18 inches above the finished floor maximum for a comfortable height.

- Plan shower and other seats to allow a user to put their feet under the seat for leverage.

- Install slip resistant floors.

- Plan a no-threshold shower when possible (see mobility section).

Toileting. Grab bars should be planned at the toilet area. Also plan toilet seat heights to be supportive to the users, usually 17 inches to 18 inches optimum, an increase in height from the traditional 15 inches, plus or minus. Because we shrink in height as we age, be sure to consider your client's specific needs when determining toilet seat heights. When doing more than one bathroom, consider specifying variable heights.

- Plan a bidet or select a toilet with a washlet system for personal hygiene and to cut down on constipation, a condition that can become more common with age.

- As a minimum, plan a GFCI receptacle in the toileting area for possible addition of a washlet system.

- Consider features available as technology changes, including heated seats, self-closing covers, and health monitoring systems.

Other Areas. Some extras to enhance safety and security:

- Install a phone and/or an intercom in the bathroom for added security.

- Space in the bathroom for other creature comforts, such as exercise, reading, or massage, creates a sanctuary and private retreat away from the rest of the home. See Chapter 8 for ideas.

- Space for physical therapy and storage of associated equipment/supplies may be needed.

- A "morning kitchen" or a kitchen in or near the bedroom suite provides a place for coffee, vitamins, and breakfast, or a late night snack close at hand. It usually includes under-counter refrigeration, a compact microwave, a coffee maker and a small sink. Not only is a morning kitchen convenient, in households where more than two generations live or visit, it can also provide privacy and some independence. It can also serve as a station for a caregiver, keeping medication close to the bedroom.

MOBILITY

Have you ever tried to walk a straight line on a moving airplane or train, or use steps that are slippery with water or ice? Have you ever tried to pass through a space not big enough to accommodate you? Do you remember, as a child, trying to reach the faucet at the lavatory?

Changes in mobility include body stiffness and rigidity, as well as diminished strength, stamina, balance and range of motion, usually in the spine, legs and/or lower body. This includes those who use a wheelchair, scooter, walker, crutches, braces or other mobility aids. Less obvious, this group also includes those whose mobility is challenged, sometimes temporarily, by pregnancy, excess weight, cardio-vascular or respiratory problems, injury or fatigue. It also includes people who have difficulty bending or stooping.

Measurements used to plan the bathroom should include any assistive device the client uses. The wheelchair or mobility aid should be measured, just as you would document a client's height or body breadth. Standard dimensions for a person using a mobility aid are listed in Chapter 4, but in fact, each client and each mobility aid is unique. In the assessment tools in Chapter 5, you will find several diagrams to use when measuring people and their mobility aids.

Typical design considerations include:

- Increased clear floor space to maneuver, with particular attention to the door.

- Space to store and recharge mobility aid, with consideration to the associated noise.

- Attention to the client's transfer methods, particularly at the toilet and tub/shower.

- Space and support for approach and use of a vanity with a knee space.

- Organized storage and function with minimal movement.

- Private storage of medical/hygiene equipment and products.

- Consideration of the client's methods of personal hygiene.

- Attention to sight lines, especially if the client is seated.

- Attention to adjustments in functional reach range.

- Method of getting into and out of the space, especially if there is an emergency.

- Safety.

Bathroom Design Implications

Doorways. Although a 32-inch clear door opening is allowed in access standards, entry doors into the bath should maintain a clearance of 34 inches, which is the typical clearance of a 36 inch door minus the thickness of the door and doorstop. When you consider the standard clear floor space for a person in a wheelchair is 30 inches wide, this seems a bare minimum.

Swing-away hinges allow the door to swing out of the door opening and increase the clear space by 1 inch to $1^{1}/_{2}$ inches, the thickness of the door.

A clear floor space 18 inches to 24 inches wide on the pull side of a standard door is necessary to permit a person using a mobility aid to position themselves next to the door, beside the handle/lever, and out of the way of the door swing, in order to pull it open. This clear space is detailed in Chapter 6 (Figure 6.8) and Chapter 11. This dimension varies based on the type of door and the approach.

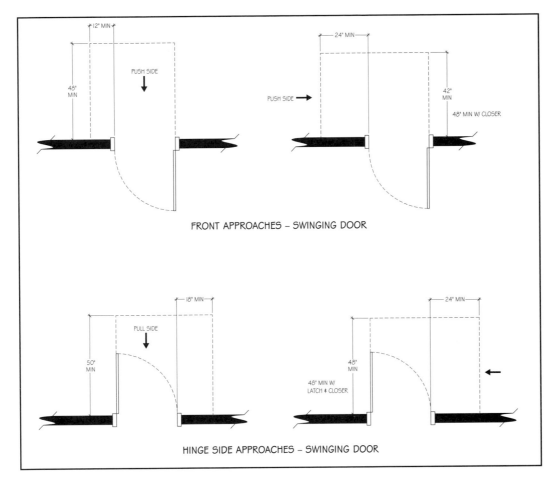

FRONT APPROACHES – SWINGING DOOR

HINGE SIDE APPROACHES – SWINGING DOOR

Figure 9.6 Beyond the basic clearances listed in the Access Standards, these recommendations help clarify space needed, based on door style and approach.

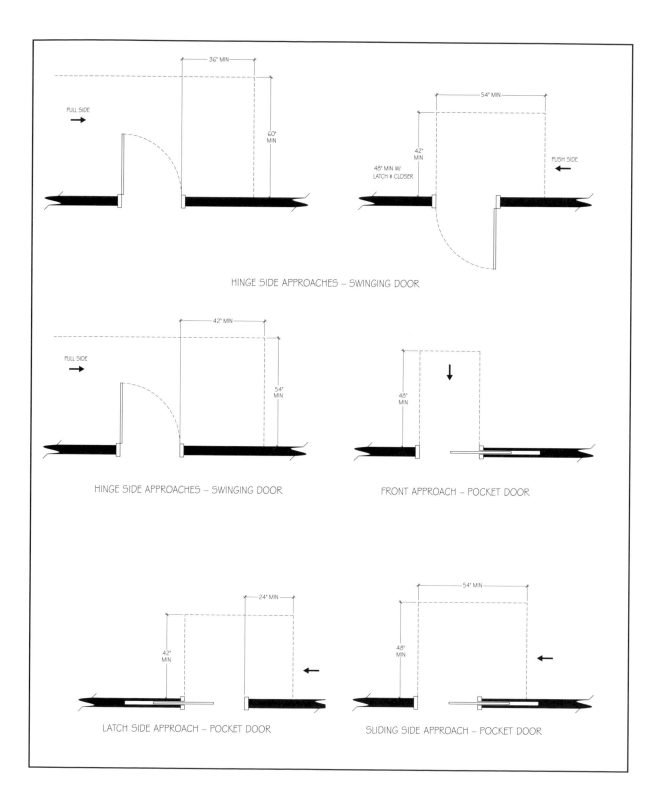

HINGE SIDE APPROACHES – SWINGING DOOR

HINGE SIDE APPROACHES – SWINGING DOOR

FRONT APPROACH – POCKET DOOR

LATCH SIDE APPROACH – POCKET DOOR

SLIDING SIDE APPROACH – POCKET DOOR

In older homes, hallways will sometimes be less than the 42 inches desired. When the width of the hallway can not be changed, sometimes a creative solution can come from alternative door designs.

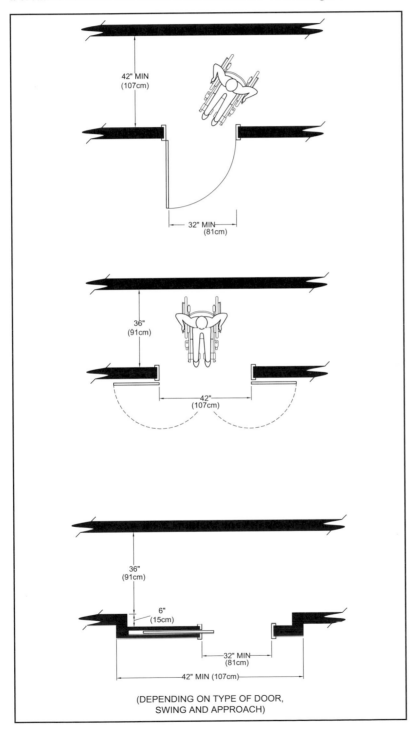

Figure 9.7 To accommodate a 90° turn by a person using a wheelchair, widening the space outside the door (hallway) or the door opening is a good idea.

Clear Floor Space. A 48-inch x 30-inch clear floor space at each fixture is a minimum for people who use mobility aids (based on the wheelchair), and can be planned for a parallel or perpendicular approach. Remember that wheelchairs are unique. Scooters and other individual aids may be larger, so whenever possible measure your client with the device.

A space that requires as few turns as necessary provides easier maneuvering for a person using a wheelchair or other mobility aid.

A 60-inch turning space is the diameter needed for a 360-degree circular turn in a wheelchair.

A T-turn, 36 inches x 36 inches x 60 inches, is not as flexible, but it does work well and it is sometimes easier to plan into a space, particularly with a knee space under the lavatory (See Figure 6.14 in Chapter 6).

Grooming. The recommended distance from the centerline of the lavatory to the side wall or obstruction is 20 inches, which allows more than enough space for a front approach (30 inches x 48 inches). However, if you wish to allow for a parallel approach as well (48 inches x 30 inches), you will need to increase the distance from the centerline to the side wall to 24 inches. Keep in mind that clear floor spaces can overlap, so for example, when two lavatories are side by side, the original guideline might be enough.

- **Knee space**. When planning a knee space at the vanity, the minimum dimensions are 30 inches wide by 27 inches high by 19 inches deep under the counter, as mentioned in Chapter 6 (Figure 6.26). The exact counter height for a specific client will be determined by the height of their wheelchair arm, or their knees if the wheelchair arms are not an issue.

- A preferred knee space width is a minimum 36 inches, as this allows the knee space to function as one leg of a T-turn, and for ease of movement in general.

- Remember to include sufficient support for the sink and counter at a knee space, as the front edge of that counter will become a significant support as one approaches the vanity.

- A maximum sink depth of 6 1/2 inches is recommended in order to keep the work surface no higher than 34 inches (28 inches to 34 inches preferred).

- Also remember to cover the plumbing or otherwise prevent contact between it and the user. Protective coverings include material to match surrounding cabinetry or the lavatory, or they may be designed from custom railing systems to coordinate with the accessories. These coverings protect both the plumbing and the user and will need to be durable.

- **Storage**. Plan the maximum amount of storage within the 15 inch to 48 inch universal reach range.

  Shallow storage will accommodate most bath supplies and will minimize obstruction of clear floor space while providing storage at the point of use.

  Raising toe kicks on vanity and storage cabinets 9 inches to 12 inches provides clearance for wheelchair footrests and other mobility aids, increasing clear floor space. Whenever possible, measure your client's foot in the footrest for specific clearance requirements.

  Rolling storage carts can be moved out of an area to increase clear floor space.

- **Lighting**. Lighting should be placed to avoid glare and shadows.

  Consider halogen or fluorescent tube lamps along the sides of the mirror so the light source is at eye level, regardless of a person's standing or sitting eye height.

  A full-length mirror or mirrors can be tilted into a position for accommodating people of any height.

  Controls must be within the comfortable reach range of your client, with the universal range as a guide (15–48" AFF above finished floor).

359

Bathing and Showering. In front of the tub or shower, an additional 12 inches to 18 inches on either side of the fixture improves access to the controls and to the transfer surface (Figure 9.8). The Access Standard indicates that a minimum of 12 inches is needed at the head of the tub.

Shower clear floor spaces are impacted by the shower design. Further detail on the clear space needed at these showers is available in Chapter 6 (Figure 6.44) and Chapter 11.

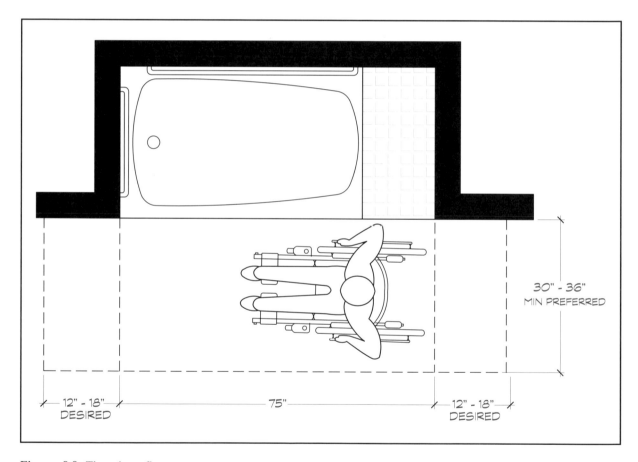

Figure 9.8 The clear floor space should extend at least 12 inches to 18 inches beyond the walls of the tub to allow for positioning of the wheelchair to access controls and transfer.

- **Roll-in Shower**. A roll-in shower is a large waterproof area with no threshold so a person in a wheelchair can roll in and remain in the chair while showering. 60 inches wide by 48 inches or 60 inches deep is ideal (Figure 9.9). Most access standards suggest a minimum 60 inches wide by 30 inches deep, which allows for conversion from a traditional bathtub to a shower in the existing space. But to help with water containment, a minimum depth of 36 inches to 42 inches is preferred for a roll-in shower.

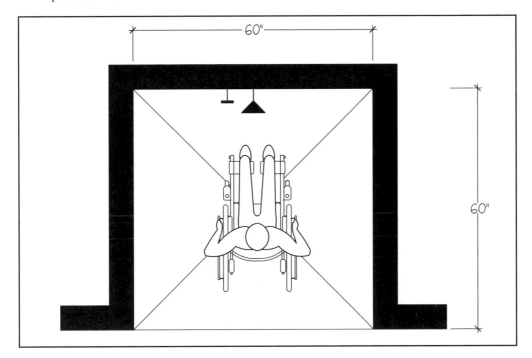

The threshold at the shower should not be greater than $1/4$ inch if square or $1/2$ inch if beveled.

When the size and direction of flow of the water are sufficient, doors and thresholds can be omitted, with functional and aesthetic appeal.

Figure 9.9 While 30 inches x 60 inches is the stated minimum in access standards and guidelines, a more generous size, like 60 inches x 60 inches, improves water containment and maneuverability.

Figure 9.10 In example A, the thresholds have been eliminated in this shower with a double entry. In example B, doors and threshold have been eliminated in this serpentine shower with a trough drain at the entry.

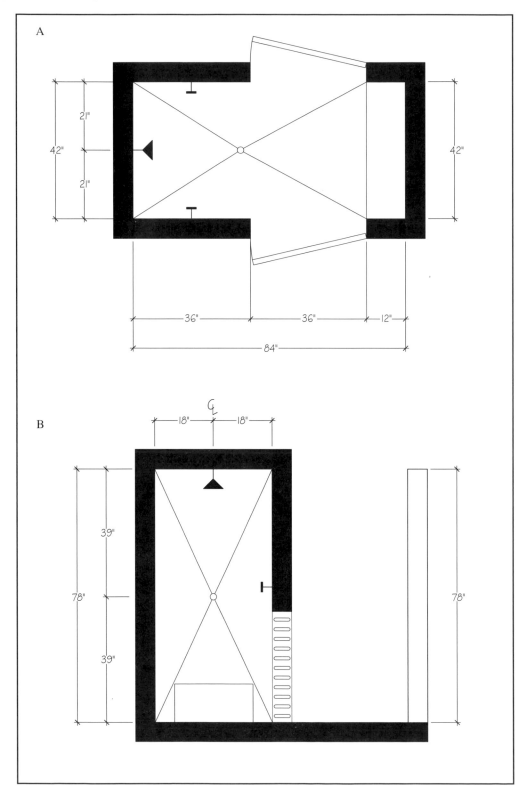

When planning a no-threshold shower, a pitch in the level of the floor of $^1/4$ inch per foot will aid in water containment. This pitch will decrease when the entire bath is built as a wet area. A trough drain placed where water is to be collected can further improve the design as it provides greater area and a smoother floor surface. Examples and further discussion of this are found in Chapter 6 and the NKBA book *Kitchen & Bath Systems*.

A "wet room", made of waterproof materials and constructed with the waterproof membrane extended under the floor beyond the shower area, can be part of a no threshold shower.

- **Transfer Shower**. A transfer shower is designated at an optimum 36 inches wide by 36 inches deep. This size of shower is precise to provide safe transfer, and create a space in which a person has both support and fixture controls within reach at all times. It is important to note that, based on a client's needs, the transfer shower, although smaller, can be the better choice.

Figure 9.11 With the appropriate clear space beyond the control wall and the seat wall of the shower, some wheelchair users can more directly and independently transfer and use the space.

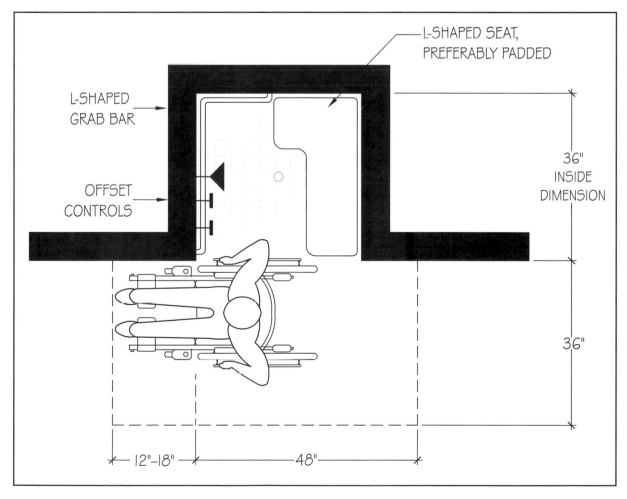

- **Controls**. Offset shower and bathtub controls reduce reaching. If the tub or shower surround is to be replaced, the existing controls and diverters can be offset 6 inches towards the outside of the tub or shower. The offset reduces bending and will allow the user to turn on the water before entering the tub or shower.

  In a tub, the controls should be placed between the top of the tub and the grab bar, (typically at 33 inches to 36 inches above the floor). In the shower, the controls are usually placed above the 33-inch to 36-inch high grab bars, and no higher than the 48-inch upper reach range limit.

  In a custom walk-in or roll-in shower, the controls should be placed at the point of entry.

  In place of, or in addition to, a fixed wall-mounted showerhead, an adjustable-height hand spray that can be lowered for seated users, with a minimum 60 inch long hose, is a good addition. The added length on the hose simply increases the distance it can be moved, making it more flexible in use.

  Attention must be given to the position of the control or diverter for use by the seated user.

Figure 9.12 This adjustable handheld shower is placed on a suspended column which leaves clear floor space for maneuvering. (Courtesy of Kohler Company)

- **Flooring**. Use slip resistant flooring inside and outside a bathing area to reduce falls.

  A combination of different flooring materials may have differing thicknesses, and installation should eliminate any uneven surfaces between materials.

  Use easy-to-maneuver flooring, such as slip-resistant tile or vinyl. Commercial quality resilient flooring resists wear, is easy to maintain and clean, and in some cases, has raised dots or granular materials to improve slip-resistance. Slip-resistant coatings can be applied to the floors.

- **Grab Bars.** Throughout the bathroom, reinforce the walls and enlist client input for actual locations of grab bars. When this is not possible or practical, there are a number of access code referenced locations for grab bar placement in the tub/shower and toileting area. A recommended height for grab bars is usually 33 inches to 36 inches off the floor; however each client is unique, so adjust the height to fit the user. Further details of reinforcement and basic grab bar locations are found in Chapter 6.

  While most access standards or guidelines specify horizontal grab bars, arguments can be made for vertical and angled support as well. While these installations allow a user support at a variety of heights as they stand or sit while transferring, there is increased risk of slipping. With the slip resistant surfaces available on grab bars today, and considering our natural inclination to grasp on an angle, they deserve consideration.

  Alternative grab bar designs, like a fold-down bar, can provide more flexible solutions, particularly when there is not sufficient side wall support.

A

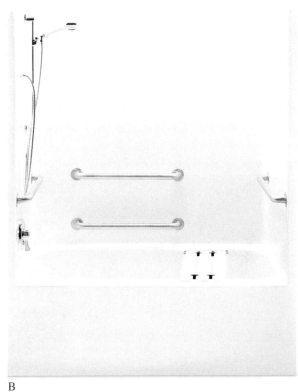

B

C

Figure 9.13 These examples illustrate the variety of grab bar applications, including attaching a showerhead to a bar. (Courtesy of **(A)** Moen, **(B)** Lasco and **(C)** Hewi)

- **Seats and Transfer Areas**

Fold-up shower seats do not interfere with the clear space of the shower when they are closed, and are desirable for those who wish to sit for part or all of a shower

A built-in surface at the head of the bathtub improves transfer and increases the clear floor space in front of the bathtub.

Whether in a shower or tub, the recommended depth of the built-in seat is a minimum of 15 inches, with a preferred height of 17 inches to 19 inches, and it should gently slope towards the tub or shower base at $1/4$ inch per 12 inches to avoid standing water.

The deck of a drop-in or undermount tub can serve as a transfer seat. The deck may include supplementary drainage, so that water does not stand. The deck surface needs to withstand a minimum load of 250 pounds. If the tub is under-mounted, the surface deck should overlap the tub flange to eliminate a permeable seam.

When there is no room for a built-in transfer surface at the tub or shower, a removable seat can be used. Separate bathtub and shower seats provide flexibility, but require storage space when not in use. Care must be given to ensure the stability of the seat.

Figure 9.14 This seat is both flexible and solid in that it folds up out of the way when not in use, but is attached securely to wall support. (Courtesy of Lasco)

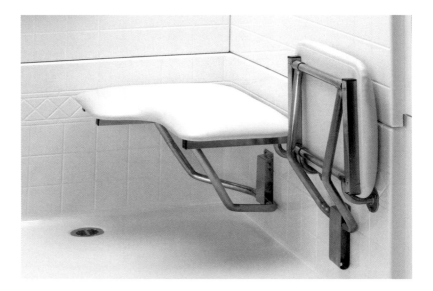

If using a shower curtain, the rod must extend over the seat, and a custom curtain (extra wide) or double curtains may be required.

Lifting devices specified and installed by medical equipment professionals can be used to lower and lift a person in and out of the bathtub. The space plan will need to accommodate the function of the lift and its storage when not in use. Structural adaptation for the lift may be required.

Toileting. The complexities of transfer onto and off of the toilet make this a space where each situation may have a different "best practice".

The raised height toilet that was first created to facilitate transfer from a wheelchair has become popular as "comfort height" or "right height" because it is often more comfortable for a person with arthritis or other conditions that make sitting and standing more difficult. In reality, transfer from a chair sometimes requires varied heights.

Transfer also impacts the amount of clear floor space at the toilet, depending on how a person transfers onto the fixture and whether or not an aide is involved. Two common approaches are illustrated, but transfer is unique to each user and should be discussed with your client.

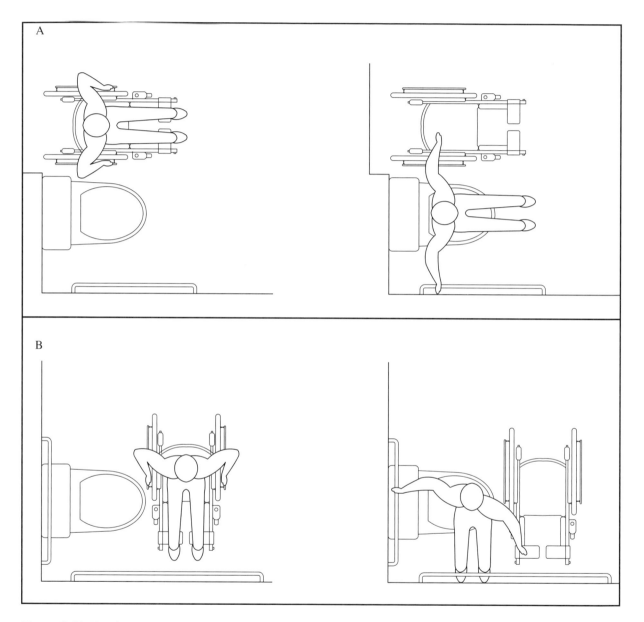

Figure 9.15 Planning space at the toilet (or tub/shower) becomes more complex because a person needs space not just to approach, but to transfer. **(A)** Parallel approach requires more space to the side of the toilet. **(B)** A perpendicular approach requires clearance in front of the toilet.

Transfer from a wheelchair to a toilet seat relies on the height of both seats being equal. Traditional toilet heights have been as low as 15 inches, and a standard chair height is 17 inches to 19 inches. Because the chair height can change over a person's lifetime, it is sometimes best to plan flexibility in the height of the toilet.

DEXTERITY, STRENGTH, BALANCE, AND STAMINA

Have you ever tried to lift a 20-pound box of laundry detergent and place it on a shelf above your head using only one arm? Or struggled to lift a wriggling and wet 25-pound child out of a bathtub?

Included in this user group are those who are fatigued or frail from illness or age, and the multitudes of people with limited upper body strength. Also included are individuals with pain, or limited joint or muscle motion, due to temporary or minor injuries and illness. Specific conditions include arthritis, carpel tunnel syndrome, asthma, allergies, chemical sensitivities, post-polio syndrome, stroke, Parkinson's disease, multiple sclerosis, ALS, cerebral palsy and numerous additional unique physical conditions.

Typical design considerations include:

- Placement of storage, controls, and work spaces within a limited reach range.

- Organization of space for limited movement and reduced strength and bending.

- Use of lighter weight objects that are easier to move, lift, use and store.

- Opportunity to sit while grooming, bathing, and dressing.

- Easy to use controls and fixtures.

Bathroom Design Implications

- Controls, handles, and door/drawer pulls (not knobs) should be operable with one hand, require only a minimal amount of strength for operation, and not require tight grasping, pinching or twisting of the wrist. They should also be placed at heights within a reach range that is comfortable to the client.

- Motion-sensor light switches eliminate the use of hands for operation.

- Opportunities to operate from a seated position preserve strength.

- Support for passing through a space relieves demands on balance, stamina, and strength.

- Lever or loop handles on faucets are the easiest to use. Smooth round handles should be avoided.

371

Figure 9.16 Decorative motion sensor faucets are available for the home. (Courtesy of Toto)

- An electronic or battery-operated motion-sensor faucet eliminates the use of hands for operation.

- Install wall-mounted hair dryers that require one or no hands.

- Drawers on full-extension slides, open shelves or extra countertop surface improve access to stored items.

- Rolling storage is flexible, allowing stored items to be moved into place easily when in use.

- Storage should be placed at the point of use and within easy reach, and organized for minimum required movement, including storage of heaviest items at no-bend and minimal lifting heights.

- Design the option of sitting to use the space.

- Grab bars can be used to assist with balance, especially in a slippery area, and should be placed to best fit the client. For clients with limited strength, grab bars serve as an aid to transfer into the tub/shower and toilet, as well as a place to rest an arm for balance, while bending or reaching controls. See Chapter 6 for information on installation of grab bars.

- Shampoo and soap dispensers, installed in the bathtub/shower within reach of the user, reduce strength and dexterity needed to squeeze shampoo out of the bottle.

- The inclusion of a bidet, or a washing system that is incorporated into the toilet, can be a solution to personal hygiene challenges when reaching and bending are difficult. An electrical connection is required for some of the systems that are integrated into the toilet, so a GFCI receptacle should be planned near the toilet. If the system is not installed, an receptacle near the toilet will allow for the easy addition of such a system at a later date.

VISION

Have you ever driven west into a setting sun, or struggled to focus when entering a dark theater from a bright lobby?

Because vision changes are a natural part of the aging process, many people would not consider themselves disabled, but would benefit from responsive design. This user group also includes anyone who is blind or who has partial vision loss due to cataracts, glaucoma, retinitis, macular degeneration, or eye injuries, as well as anyone with congenital vision impairments or those caused by other conditions. Depending on their condition, user needs will be different.

Typical design considerations include:

- Increased lighting.

- Ability to adjust lighting levels (ambient down and task up).

- Increased tactile and audio cueing for way-finding, function, and warnings.

- Passage or maneuvering space clear of clutter and obstructions.

- Allowance for a dog trained to assist the client.

- Careful use of color and contrast.

- Selection of materials and lighting to reduce glare.

Bathroom Design Implications

- Reduce the risk of glare from lighting by minimizing the direct sight line to the light source.

- Rather than, or in addition to, overhead ambient lighting, use side lighting at the mirror placed at eye level to best illuminate the face and cut down on shadows.

- Include a lighted, magnifying mirror.

- Plan responsive lighting concepts for nocturnal visits to the bathroom, such as motion sensor lighting, night lighting that fades on/off, or glow-in-the-dark grout.

- Use switches that are lighted in the off position so that controls can be seen in the dark.

- As eyes age, it becomes difficult to differentiate colors with minimal contrast, such as navy, black, brown or pastels. The contrast created by placing light objects against darker backgrounds, or vice versa, can be useful on controls, work surfaces and storage.

373

- Color contrast can be used to highlight edges or borders, as in the edge of a counter or a border around the floor.

- Eased counter edges and rounded corners are helpful, and they may be used as a tactile guide.

- Colors and patterns should be chosen with consideration of the total room in terms of contrast and light.

- Use tactile cueing to identify hot or cold water, and to aid in way-finding such as on the edge of a counter.

- Use matte or low-sheen surfaces that reduce glare.

- Reduce the number and depth of obstructions by planning shallow storage areas with open shelves, and tambour, sliding, up-lifting or other doors that will not protrude into the passage space.

- Lighting storage interiors will improve visibility.

- A shampoo and soap dispenser installed in the bathtub/shower will help eliminate items falling or being rearranged in an unknown order.

HEARING AND SPEECH

Have you ever tried to have a conversation on a cell phone with background noise? Or tried to have a conversation in a noisy bar or restaurant?

Many people experience some loss of hearing as they age, often beginning with high frequencies or ringing in the ears.

Also in this user group are people who are deaf or who have a loss of hearing as a result of illness, disease, blockages in the inner ear, damage from prolonged exposure to excessive noise, head injuries, stroke, or other causes. Again, people may not identify a change in hearing as a disability, but a space can be designed to be more accommodating, if you examine common needs and possible responses.

Typical design considerations include:

- Reduced ambient noise.

- Avoidance of any extremely high or low pitched sounds.

- Visual cueing in function and warnings.

- Clear sight lines.

- Safety.

Bathroom Design Implications

- Choose quiet ventilation to minimize background noise distortion for someone with partial hearing.

- Reverberation of noise off hard surfaces makes it more difficult for a person with limited hearing to perceive sound, so incorporate sound-absorbing materials in the bathroom to improve acoustics.

- Include wall and window treatments that absorb some of the room's noise, such as cork, carpet and fabrics, with appropriate consideration to the moisture exposure.

- Choose appliances and controls that incorporate indicator lights as an additional way to determine on/off or hot/cold.

- Include a smoke detector with both an audible and a visual or flashing alarm.

- Design good lighting.

- Provide clear sight lines throughout the space so a person who cannot hear will be able to see throughout the space.

COGNITION

Have you ever been in a country where a language foreign to you is spoken and tried to use the phone, or driven through the day and night and tried to follow oral directions to the nearest motel or gas station?

This user group includes anyone with limited comprehension or memory, some confusion or reduced reasoning. A few of the contributing factors include injury, illness, learning disability, stroke, general aging, using a foreign language, or youth/limited vocabulary and reasoning skills. The primary driver with a client who has cognitive impairments is safety, and involving caregivers in the design process is critical.

Typical design considerations include:
- Safety and security concerns.
- Organization and patterning to help interpret function.
- Repetition and reminders for completing tasks.
- Simple one-step operations.
- Creating familiar spaces.
- Visual cueing.

Figure 9.17 Controls that use light to indicate hot/cold, such as on this faucet, provide good visual cueing. (Courtesy of KWC)

Bathroom Design Implications

- Overuse of contrast, particularly on walls and floor borders, can block a person from maneuvering and must be carefully planned.

- Plan a door that swings out of the room with no lock.

- Electronic sensor controls on faucets, lighting and ventilation help ensure that things are shut off when the user is finished.

- Intuitive cueing, such as using a blue color for cold and a red color for hot, is easy to recognize.

- Specify an anti-scald faucet device.

- Open storage and generous counters allow for easy view and ordering of stored items, which may be helpful when memory fails.

- A shower can be easier and safer to use than a tub.

- Planning the entire bathroom as a wet area with a supplemental or second drain in the room will make maintenance easier.

- Toilets with an automatic flush will increase sanitation and odor control.

SUMMARY

In this chapter, you have been presented with groups of physical characteristics and related design concepts to help stimulate and streamline your process when working on a space that is to accommodate a client with a specific disability. It is worth repeating that just as there is no average person, no two people with disabilities are alike. These general groups have been formed simply to help pull together and further explore the design concepts discussed throughout the book and particularly in Chapter 6. Hopefully, you will continue to build on the lists and grow your library of access-related design. As you do, you'll discover that most of the access "solutions" are better for everyone and you'll be experiencing that "Aha" of universal design.

CHAPTER 10: Putting It All Together

Design is a process—but not a neat, tidy, linear process. Moving from the idea, or the wish, for a new bathroom to the finished product involves a lot of going back and forth, checking and rechecking. A bathroom design involves a dose of inspiration, a spark of creativity, but mostly a lot of hard work.

This book has presented a lot of information about bathrooms, what to include and how to arrange the space. It has emphasized how to gather information about your clients to help focus your design to meet their needs and desires. This chapter will help you figure out how to organize this wealth of information and translate it into an actual bathroom design.

The first part of this chapter discusses the overall design process, how to move from an idea to a complete design. The second part focuses on the design program, the part of the design process where you organize all your information and ideas into a plan for the bathroom design. The third part, the design drawing, presents a method to move from a conceptual design to an actual design layout. Throughout are examples of a simple bathroom design moving from program to drawing.

While the focus here is on developing a single design drawing through use of the design process, in reality, you will probably use this process to develop several alternative designs to present to your client. These alternatives will then be evaluated by you and your client in making the final selections for the bathroom design.

THE DESIGN PROCESS

There are many different ways to approach design, probably as many as there are designers. As you gain more experience, you will develop a method and unique style that is personally successful.

If you are a new designer, you can benefit by following a formal structure for the design process. This will help you become adept at sequencing the steps in developing a design and assure that no parts of the process are forgotten. If you are an experienced designer, by reviewing a formal design process, you may get a fresh approach and spark new creativity. What follows is a brief discussion of one approach to the design process.

SUMMARY OF THE DESIGN PROCESS

- Identify the client.
- Organize the information.
- Identify the activity spaces.
- Visualize the activity spaces.
- Develop the visual diagram.
- Refine the visual diagram.
- Think in three dimensions.
- Evaluate the plan.
- Think about details, details, details.

- **Identify the client.** Gather information about the client. This is both the tangible—such as anthropometric information and a list of items for storage—and intangible, such as ambience desired in the space or style preferences. Chapter 5 of this book provides a detailed guide to gathering information and assessing client needs. You may also want additional research at this stage, learning about things such as products or materials that the client wants.

- **Organize the information.** Develop the first part of your design program by determining the goals and objectives for the design. Prioritize the needs and wants of the client and identify the limitations of the project. (Design programming will be discussed in more detail later in this chapter.)

- **Identify the activity spaces.** Develop the second part of the design program by preparing the User Analysis, which groups design requirements by the major activities that will take place in the bathroom space. (See Figure 10.2 for an example of a User Analysis.) In most cases, this will mean that you are organizing information by the centers described in Chapter 6.

  Check your User Analysis against the client needs assessment information (Chapter 5) to make sure that you have accommodated the client's priority needs. You may even want to share the User Analysis with the client as a double check.

- **Visualize the activity spaces**. This is the stage when you are moving from verbal and quantitative information to visual ideas. Many designers use bubble diagrams to represent activity spaces or various centers, and to explore the relationships of the different spaces. For example, you may have a bubble for the bathtub, another for the toilet area, and so on. (See Figure 10.1 for an example of a bubble diagram.)

- **Develop the visual diagram**. Select the best two or three bubble diagrams for refinement. Prepare a room outline, to scale ($^1/_2$ inch equals 1 foot), and note project parameters, such as windows or doors that are fixed in location.

  Start using templates for each center or activity space, and place them on your room outline, using the bubble diagrams as your guide. A template is a scale drawing representing the fixtures, cabinetry and clearances for a center or activity space. (See Figures 10.4 for examples of design templates.) Templates allow you to see how spaces fit together and how your design ideas will work in the actual bathroom space.

  Check your visual diagram against the User Analysis.

- **Refine the visual diagram**. You will be moving from the bubble diagram to the arrangement of templates to a sketch of a floor plan. Work in scale. Evaluate your visual diagram against the project parameters.

- **Think in three dimensions**. Use elevation or perspective sketches to develop the vertical elements for your design. Changes in the floor plan may be required.

- **Evaluate the plan**. Check the preliminary design against the design program. Review the relationship of the centers. Evaluate zoning and circulation within the bathroom as well as in relationship to adjacent rooms. Evaluate your plan against the Bathroom Planning Guidelines (Figure 10.13) and, if appropriate, the Bathroom Access Standards (Figure 10.14).

- **Think about details, details, details**. Lay out the design of the bathroom in dimensioned drawings. Specify the actual fixtures, cabinetry, materials and other items in the space, so that you can verify sizes, installation requirements, clearances and other details. Check dimensions to make sure that everything will fit as you envision.

Figure 10.1 A bubble diagram is a simple sketch to show how different activity areas can be arranged in the bathroom space. Each "bubble" is an activity area. This bubble diagram is an example of one bathroom arrangement, and will be the same bathroom design that is carried through in Figures 10.5 to 10.12.

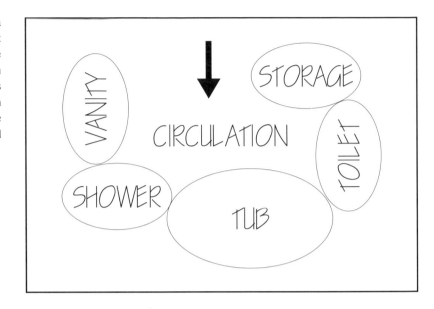

THE DESIGN PROGRAM

Let's imagine that you have just completed an exciting meeting with your client. Lots of ideas were shared back and forth. Enticing possibilities for a grand bathroom design were explored. You are eager to sketch, pull out material samples, and develop your thoughts into a new design. Ready to go? What? Write a design program? No, you say, let's just go straight to the design. You can incorporate the client's needs as you go along.

If you skip the design program, how will you know what to design?

Design programming is an important and necessary part of successful designing. When we discussed the design process, did you note how often we recommended you check your developing design against the design program? Think of the design program as the contract between you and your client. It is an organized directory of all the client's needs, wants and wishes for the bathroom design, plus the important parameters of the total design.

Chapter 5 talked about the design program as the next step in the needs assessment process. Developing the design program allows you to make sure you have—and understand—all the information necessary for the bathroom design. A typical design program is in three parts:

- Goals and purpose

- Objectives and priorities

- Activities and relationships

Goals and Purpose

Can you briefly describe the goals of the design project? Think of this part of the design program as the overview. It should include a specific description of the client(s), the type and scope of the project, the budget, and your role and responsibilities in the project. Include the major criteria for the bathroom design and any unique aspects of the project. Most of the information you need will come from *Form 1: Getting to Know Your Client* and *Form 5: Your Client's Bathroom Preferences*.

You might want to share your goal statements with your client to determine that you have interpreted the project correctly. The statements could also be included in your contract.

Objectives

Objectives are used to operationalize your goals. If goals tell what you want to do, objectives tell how you are going to do it. Objectives are written with active verbs and the outcomes can be measured.

- **Goal:** The bathroom will have a relaxing atmosphere.

- **Objectives:** Install a soaking tub. Put lights in tub area on a dimmer switch. Specify a cabinet for a CD player.

Write objectives to identify the client's major wants and needs. Use the development of the objectives to sort out priorities—must have, should or want to have, and desire or would like to have.

To write objectives for the design program, you will want to focus on the information in *Form 5: Your Client's Bathroom Preferences*. It will also be important to review *Form 3: Checklist for Bathroom Activities* and *Form 4: Bathroom Storage Inventory* as these checklists may reveal priorities. For example, a frequent activity or a need for specialized storage should be reflected in the objectives for the design.

Activities and Relationships

This section is the crux of the design program. Focus on the various activities that will take place in the bathroom and what is needed in the design to support them. You may want to group activities together into centers. For example, teeth brushing, hair combing and face washing all have similar requirements and could be grouped together as part of the grooming center. *Form 3: Checklist for Bathroom Activities* and *Form 4: Bathroom Storage Inventory* are designed in sections by centers so that you can collect activity and storage information in an organized fashion.

Since the focus is on the activities taking place in the space, the emphasis is on who is doing what. Organize the activity information into a User Analysis chart (See Figure 10.2 for a sample User Analysis chart). You might want to prepare a User Analysis for each center in the bathroom or group of related activities. The User Analysis includes the following information:

- Activities that take place in the space

- Who will be doing the activities; the users

- Frequency of activities

- Fixtures, fittings, furnishings, accessories, and any other physical items needed to support the activities, including special sizes or characteristics

- Storage to support the activities

- Amount of space for the activities including clearances, and relationships to other spaces

- Ambience requirements

- Special requirements, such as safety features

- Future changes to be accommodated

- Summary of Planning Guidelines or Access Standards relevant to the activities and requirements of the client and their bathroom

Preparing the User Analysis as a chart or table helps to organize the information into an easily referenced format to which you can refer during the development of your design. Using a spreadsheet program or the table function in a word-processing program on your computer makes it easy to prepare a User Analysis. However, it is a good idea to leave some open space for extra notes if changes are needed.

Activity Space	Users	Frequency	Fixtures, Fittings, Furniture, Etc.	Storage	Space and Relationships	Ambience	Special Needs	Future Needs	Guidelines
Shower area – full body shower, wash hair, shave legs	Anne, Sam	daily	Tile shower, 48" by 48" preferred, 42" by 42" minimum: adjustable height shower head; interior seat	Interior shelf for toiletries towel rack adjacent	30" clear space for access and door swing: 6" wet wall; Adjacent to bathtub to share wet wall	Adjustable light level ventilation fan	Non-slip floor	None noted	Planning Guidelines 4, 9, 10, 11 12, 13, 14, 15, 16, 18, 26

Figure 10.2 This is an example of a User Analysis chart, showing information for a shower area. This could be used in the design shown in Figure 10.6.

As you develop your User Analysis, you will be relying on the client interview and needs assessment to determine what activities will take place in the bathroom. Using the prepared assessment forms can help assure that all activities are considered. However, you will want to review your User Analysis to make sure that it is inclusive.

Some activities are so common and routine that we might not think about them. For example, your clients might tell you that they brush their teeth at the lavatory (affecting height of lavatory, and storage for toothbrush and toothpaste), but assume you know that means they also rinse their mouth with water, and then use mouthwash (requiring storage for a drinking glass and the mouthwash).

As you develop the User Analysis, it is a good time to review the Bathroom Planning Guidelines and Access Standards that apply to the space you are designing. You can note the number of the Guidelines, as in our example, or note detail, such as "pressure balanced shower control."

RELATIONSHIP MATRIX

The detail you include in your User Analysis will depend on the complexity of the project. For a larger project, especially if it involves multiple spaces, you may want to use a matrix to graph the relationship among the activity areas. The matrix can help you more easily see the relationships among activity spaces, and assist in determining how you will group and separate activities into different centers and spaces.

Figure 10.3 This is an example of a matrix showing visual access. Similar matrices could be developed for physical access or auditory access. This matrix was used in developing the visual diagram shown in Figure 10.6.

Toilet				
3	Shower			
3	1	Bathtub		
3	2	2	Lavatory	
3	3	3	2	Bedroom

1. Direct visual access acceptable
2. Partial or indirect visual access acceptable
3. No visual access

To read the matrix: you read down a column and across a row from the right to the cell where the column and row meet. For example, the yellow highlighted cell is in the shower column and the lavatory row. There is a number 2 in the cell. That tells us that partial or indirect visual access is acceptable. However, if we look at the pink highlighted cell, in the shower column and the bedroom row, we see that there is a 3, which means that there should be no visual access.

THE DESIGN DRAWING

Moving from the design program to the completed design solution is an exciting and creative process. It is also a process that requires accuracy and verification. In this section, we will discuss a process for moving from the design program to a dimensioned design drawing of your design solution. We will emphasize the importance of checking and rechecking dimensions to verify that your design solution will work in "real space". This section tells you how to manage the technical details—you supply the creativity!

The emphasis in this chapter (and this book) is developing your bathroom design and recording your ideas. If you need more information about the specifics of drafting, refer to the NKBA book *Kitchen & Bath Drawing*.

Templates

We discussed moving in the design process from the design program, to visualizing the activity spaces with a bubble diagram, to developing a visual diagram. As you take your conceptual ideas, the bubble diagrams, and begin refining them, it is important to begin working to scale. First, this gives you a realistic picture of space relationships and possibilities—very important in the often-limited spaces of a bathroom. Second, it helps prevent you from making mistakes. If you work with the right proportions and sizes from the beginning, you tend to "see" the space relationships more clearly and are less likely to misjudge clearances and space needs.

A helpful way to develop your visual diagram is to use design templates. A design template is used to represent an activity space or a center, and includes any fixtures or equipment, plus the clearances needed.

For example, you can have a toilet center template, which would show the toilet, plus the recommended clearances in front and to the sides. A shower space template would include the shower, the thickness needed for the plumbing wall, the shower door swing, and clearance for access to the shower.

It is a good idea to prepare design templates in both plan and elevation view. This can be very useful as you evaluate your design in three dimensions.

Figure 10.4 (A) shows a design template for a plan view of a standard size toilet, using recommended side (Planning Guideline 20) and front (Planning Guideline 4) clearances. Note that a 6 inch wet wall for plumbing is included in the template. (B) shows a design template for a front elevation of a standard toilet with grab bars on the back and right side. (C) shows a simplified design template in plan view, with clearance areas marked.

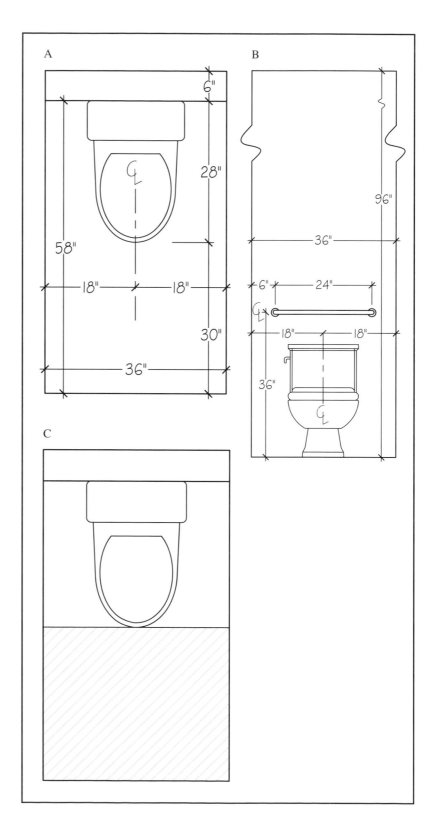

Draw your design templates in a scale of $^1/_2$ inch equals 1 foot. Since this is the recommended scale for bathrooms drawings, starting in this scale will be a time saver.

Based on your design program, you will need to develop a number of design templates for a particular bathroom design. Consider special needs and requests of your client. You may develop alternative templates for the same activity space. For example, you may develop two design templates for different sized showers and then determine which will work best in the final design.

Label your design templates. This will facilitate using them to lay out the bathroom plan. It will also help you develop a timesaving file of design templates for future use. For example, if you have design templates for 36 inch, 42 inch, and 48 inch showers with clearances from one project, you can likely use them on many other bathroom designs. Depending on your preferred style of working, design templates can be saved in computer files or on sturdy paper.

ROOM OUTLINE

An important foundation for producing your visual diagram, and eventually your design drawing, is the room outline. The room outline is a scaled drawing of the perimeter of the bathroom space. Prepare a drawing of all walls and fixed structural or architectural features, such as windows and doors.

The information you need to complete the room outline should be found on the following needs assessment forms from Chapter 5: *Form 7: Dimensions of the Bathroom—Floor Plan*; *Form 9: Dimensions of Mechanical Devices*; *Form 10: Window Measurements*; *Form 11: Door Measurements*; and *Form 12: Fixture Measurements*.

In some bathroom design projects, walls, windows, doors, and other structural features are fixed, and cannot be moved or altered. For example, moving windows affects the exterior design of the home, and the client may not want to change this. In other projects, you may have some options to relocate some features or even expand the space. Perhaps a doorway can be moved or an interior wall removed. This is the type of information recorded on *Form 6: Jobsite Inspection*, and perhaps, *Form 5: Your Client's Bathroom Preferences*.

You may find it useful to prepare two room outlines. One shows the existing room space as it is. The second removes features that can be changed but retains the fixed features. The second drawing will help you see the possibilities of the space (Figure 10.5).

You may have other limitations on your design that should be noted on your room outline. All structural, mechanical, electrical and plumbing parameters need to be noted. For example, the location of one or more plumbing fixtures may be predetermined. Or, the location of heating and cooling vents may be fixed.

Add any additional information to your drawing that will help in design decisions. Note what types of spaces surround the bathroom. Note interior and exterior walls. The height of windows or any fixed structural features will be useful to know. The location of existing walls (that can be changed) could be noted, if preferred, to allow economical planning of the design.

It is important to note all restraints and options on your room outline. Noting these features helps assure that your design will remain within the parameters of your project.

Verify all room measurements and check your room drawing. The room outline must accurately represent the space of the bathroom.

Figure 10.5 (A) Shows the existing bathroom space with project parameters. **(B)** Shows the room outline as altered. Non-fixed features are removed, the exterior wall is bumped out, fixed features are included, and dimensions are shown. This room outline will be used to develop the visual diagram shown in Figure 10.6.

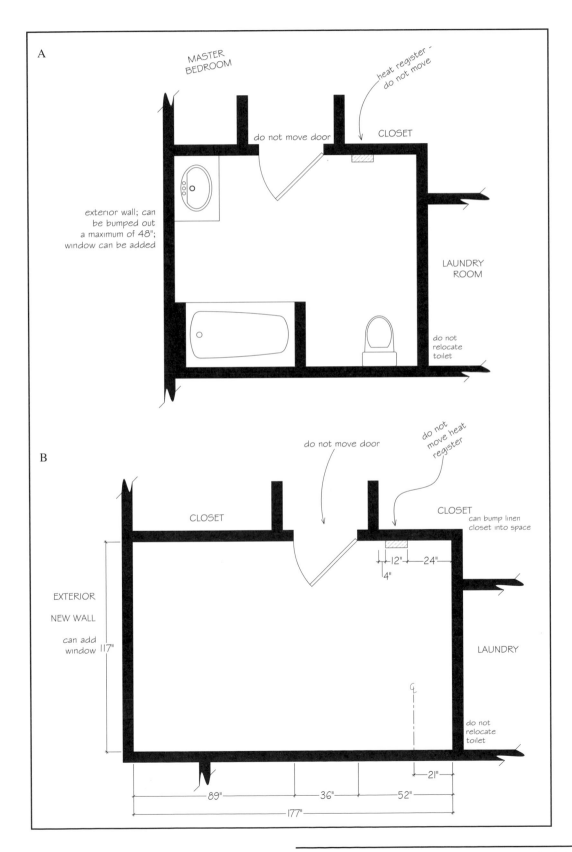

VISUAL DIAGRAMS

Your bubble diagrams suggested ways to arrange the spaces in the bathroom. Now it is time to see if these ideas can be translated into a design that will work in the actual space. This is the development of the visual diagram.

Using the design templates that you developed, begin placing them in the room outline. Use the ideas generated by the bubble diagrams to guide your work. Refer to the information on the room outline to see if your design ideas are possible within the existing space.

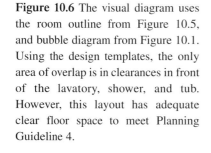

Figure 10.6 The visual diagram uses the room outline from Figure 10.5, and bubble diagram from Figure 10.1. Using the design templates, the only area of overlap is in clearances in front of the lavatory, shower, and tub. However, this layout has adequate clear floor space to meet Planning Guideline 4.

You will want to try a number of different layouts before you achieve the best solution. As you consider a possible layout, review the information on your room outline that details project parameters. Refer back to the design program, especially the User Analysis, to remind yourself what the design layout needs to accomplish.

If you are having trouble getting everything into the space, reconsider the templates you are using. Could space clearances overlap without compromising function or safety? Could a smaller fixture be used and still meet client needs?

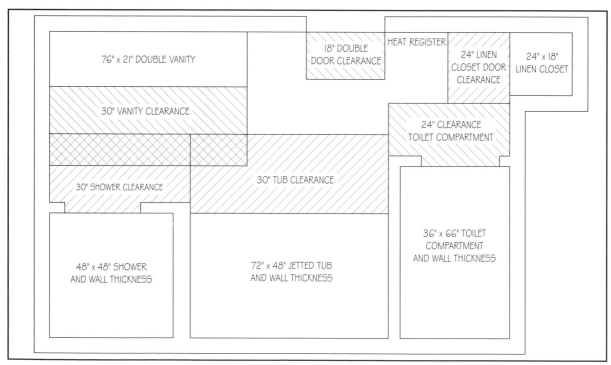

Three Dimensions and Vertical Diagrams

Very early in the design process, think in three dimensions. For example, placing the toilet next to the vanity may work fine in plan, but how will it look vertically? We experience space in multiple dimensions, so we must design for all perspectives.

After you have developed one or more visual diagrams that appear to work in plan, develop some three-dimensional sketches. Elevation sketches of a wall, to scale, are useful to evaluate spatial relationships of fixtures, cabinetry and structural features. Design templates of elevation views can speed the process.

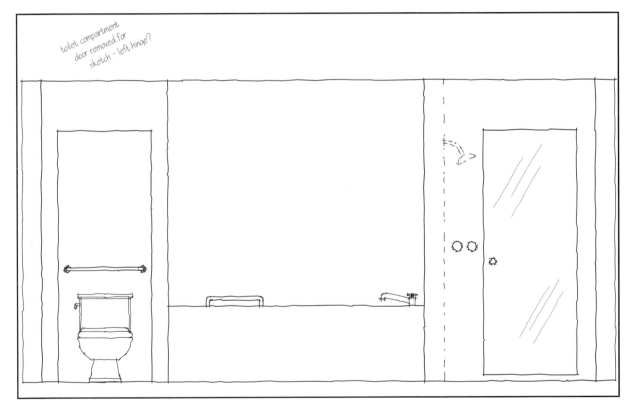

toilet compartment
door removed for
sketch – left hinge?

Figure 10.7 A rough elevation sketch, taken from the visual diagram in Figure 10.6, begins to show vertical relationships and encourages you to begin thinking about details such as the placement of plumbing fittings and door swings.

Many computer programs used in developing designs will generate perspective views. This technology is an excellent way to view your design from different angles and evaluate its effectiveness. Keep in mind, however, that these perspectives are interpretive—they give you a sense of the space but do not show all details.

After reviewing your visual diagrams, in plan and vertical views, select the best design layout. Review your design program to determine that the layout meets the goals and objectives. Verify that the design layout is appropriate to the structural and mechanical parameters of the project. Refer back to *Form 8: Dimensions of the Bathroom – Elevations* for details of the existing space. If you are working on new construction, consult project documents.

Now you are ready to detail your design solution in a complete dimensioned drawing.

PRIORITY AREAS

Start your dimensioned design drawing with the priority areas of the plan. These are the elements that are not moveable, demand the most space, or are most important to the client. For example, you might start your dimensioned drawing with the toilet area because plumbing connections dictate the location. Or you might start with a shower, because that is going to be the focal element.

Let's say you are going to start with the toilet area. Place the toilet, draw the centerline, and dimension the needed clearances on either side of the toilet. Planning Guideline 20 recommends 18 inches of clearance on either side of the toilet, so place the toilet so that there is 18 inches of clearance from the centerline to the wall (Figure 10.8). An additional 18 inches of clearance is needed on the other side of the toilet.

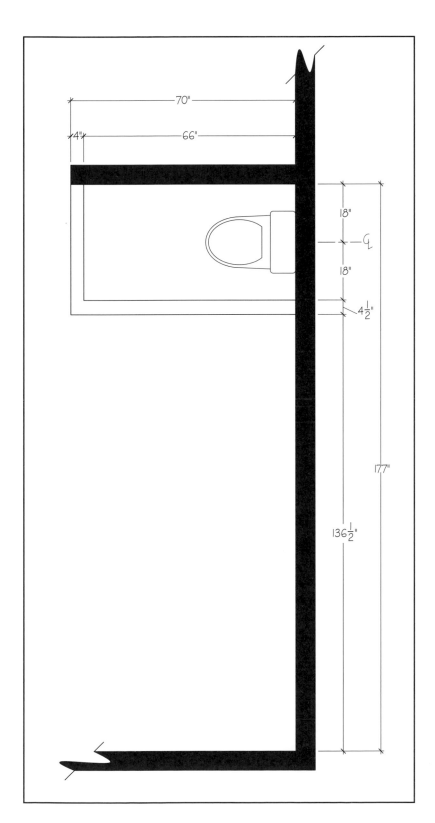

Figure 10.8 In this example, based on the visual diagram in Figure 10.6, the toilet compartment is placed first as this location is preferred by the client.

In our example, the toilet and clearances take 36 inches (18 inches + 18 inches). Because the toilet will be in a compartment, an additional $4\frac{1}{2}$ inches of wall thickness must be included in our calculations (Only one wall thickness is needed as the toilet compartment is against the room wall). Therefore, the toilet compartment uses $40\frac{1}{2}$ inches. The total dimension of the wall where the toilet is placed is 177 inches. So we can determine how much space is remaining for the placement of the jetted tub and custom shower, as is shown here and illustrated in Figure 10.8.

177	inches	total wall length
- 18	inches	clearance from centerline of toilet to wall
159	inches	
- 18	inches	needed clearance from centerline of toilet, on opposite side
141	inches	
- 4 $\frac{1}{2}$	inches	wall thickness for toilet compartment
136 $\frac{1}{2}$	inches	available wall length for placement of jetted tub and custom shower

If there is a second priority area in your plan, follow the same procedure for placing the fixture, cabinetry, or other elements. Determine the needed clearances, and subtract from the overall wall dimension. For example, Figure 10.9 shows the placement of the custom shower in the bathroom, after the toilet has been located. In our example, we have allowed $6\frac{1}{2}$ inches for the wall between the shower and the bathtub, so that there is room for plumbing in the wall (wet wall) as well as the installation of ceramic tile—while maintaining a minimum clear dimension of 48 inches in the shower interior.

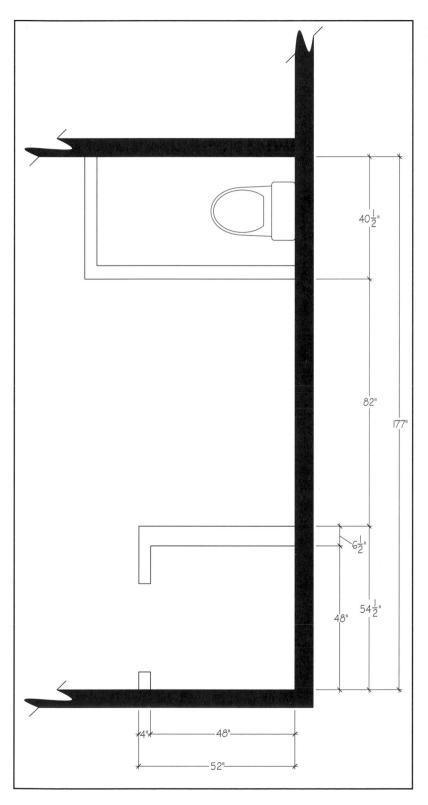

Figure 10.9 Continuing the drawing begun in Figure 10.8, a 48 inch custom shower is placed on the same wall as the toilet.

After placing the custom shower, verify the remaining wall length, as follows:

$$
\begin{array}{rl}
136\,{}^{1}\!/_{2}\ \text{inches} & \text{wall length remaining} \\
-\ 48\quad\ \text{inches} & \text{shower interior dimension} \\
\hline
88\,{}^{1}\!/_{2}\ \text{inches} & \\
-\ 6\,{}^{1}\!/_{2}\ \text{inches} & \text{wall thickness for shower} \\
\hline
82\quad\ \text{inches} & \text{available wall length for placement of jetted tub}
\end{array}
$$

Finishing the Floor Plan

After the priority areas are placed and dimensioned, add the other fixtures and features in the plan. Continue checking dimensions by subtracting the amount of clearances for each fixture from the remaining wall space. Be sure to verify dimensions in each direction, such as each side and in front of the fixture. Allow for door swings.

Sometimes, at this point, the dimensions do not work out. You may find that your total space, for fixtures, cabinetry, and clearances comes to more or less than the length of a wall. If this is the case, you may need to consider different alternatives.

If you have extra space, you may decide to increase the clearances around the fixtures. This is a good solution if you do not have a lot of extra space. For example, instead of the recommended 20 inches of clearance from the centerline of the lavatory to a wall, you could increase the clearance to 22 inches.

Another alternative is to increase the size of a fixture, such as selecting a 42-inch shower instead of a 36 inch. The same idea could be implemented by selecting a 36-inch vanity cabinet instead of a 30 inch. However, if you have a large amount of additional space, you might want to reconsider your design to determine if you have chosen the best solution.

In our example (Figures 10.8 through 10.9), we have 82 inches remaining after the toilet and shower are placed. The jetted tub needs 72 inches. No additional wall thickness is needed as we are placing the tub between two full height walls. Therefore, we have 10 inches (82 inches – 72 inches = 10 inches) extra space. We can solve this by adding 6 inches clearance to the toilet compartment (3 inches on each side), and lengthening the deck of the jetted rub by 4 inches (2 inches on each side) (Figure 10.10).

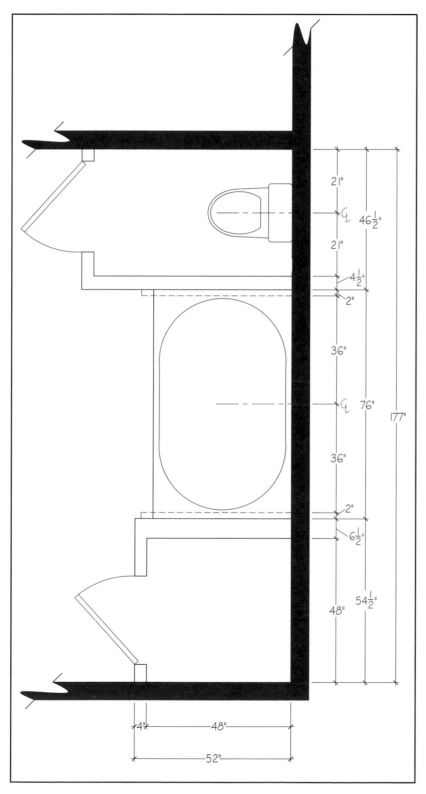

Figure 10.10 After adjustments, the drawing of the wall begun in Figure 10.8 is complete.

If you are short on space, the solution can be more challenging. As you consider each alternative, review your design program to make sure that changes do not compromise important needs of the design. Think about design solutions that work best for your client. Some ideas for alternatives:

- Reduce the clearances around a fixture. If you have allowed generous clearances, you might reduce one or more of them. In the toilet area for example, instead of the recommended 18 inches of clearance on either side of the centerline, you might use 17 inches or 16 inches. Do not reduce clearances to less than the minimums identified in the Bathroom Planning Guidelines as code-based requirements.

- Use smaller fixtures or cabinetry. For example, instead of a 42 inch square shower, consider a 42 inch by 36 inch, or 36 inch square shower. Again, make sure that you meet code-based minimums.

- Choose alternative fixtures or design elements. For example, instead of two, side-by-side vanities, each with a lavatory, choose one larger vanity cabinet with a single lavatory, which takes less total space. Or, choose a full-height, pantry style cabinet to provide the same amount of storage as two vanity cabinets, but in less floor space.

- Choose cabinetry with smaller doors, to reduce door swings. This might be a smaller cabinet, such as going from a 24-inch cabinet to a 21-inch cabinet, or going from a single-door 24-inch cabinet to a two-door cabinet. However, consider the functionality of the size of the door opening and the continuity of cabinet spacing when making size alterations.

You may need to try several alternatives to make sure your layout fits the actual space. As you are exploring alternatives, be sure that you are working with the actual dimensions of the various fixtures, cabinets and other items to be placed in the bathroom. Do not depend on the size shown on a drawing template or a generic example in a computer program.

After you have placed each item on the dimensioned drawing, verify all your dimensions. Start at one corner and check your dimensions across the wall. In our example (Figures 10.8 through 10.10), we can verify our dimensions as follows:

177	inches	total wall length
- 21	inches	clearance from wall to centerline of toilet
156	inches	
- 21	inches	clearance from centerline of toilet to wall
135	inches	
- 4 1/2	inches	wall thickness for toilet compartment
130 1/2	inches	
- 2	inches	extended tub deck
128 1/2	inches	
- 72	inches	jetted tub
56 1/2	inches	
- 2	inches	extended tub deck
54 1/2	inches	
- 6 1/2	inches	wall thickness for shower
48	inches	
- 48	inches	shower interior dimension
0	inches	

Check your math. You can double-check your calculations by adding dimensions, working from the opposite corner from which you did the subtraction.

Vertical Relationships

Dimensioned elevation drawings of each wall of the bathroom are needed to determine the vertical relationships of the bathroom design. You may choose to place all items on the floor plan and verify the dimensions before drawing the elevations, and verifying vertical placement and dimensions. Or, you may choose to work with one wall at a time—place the fixtures, cabinets, clearances, and other elements on the floor plan, and then draw the elevation. If you are developing your design using computer software, you will likely find it easy to develop elevations as you go along.

Begin drawing the elevation of a wall by drawing an outline of the wall, showing the length and height of the wall. Include any architectural and structural features. Dimension these basic elements of the elevation.

Just as you did with the dimensioned drawing of the floor plan, start with the priority areas. For example, if you started with the toilet area, project the centerline and side clearances of the toilet onto the elevation. Sketch the toilet to show the approximate width of the fixture. Mark the height of the fixture—as determined from actual measurements or product specifications, and dimension this on the elevation (Figure 10.11). Show other details, such as grab bars.

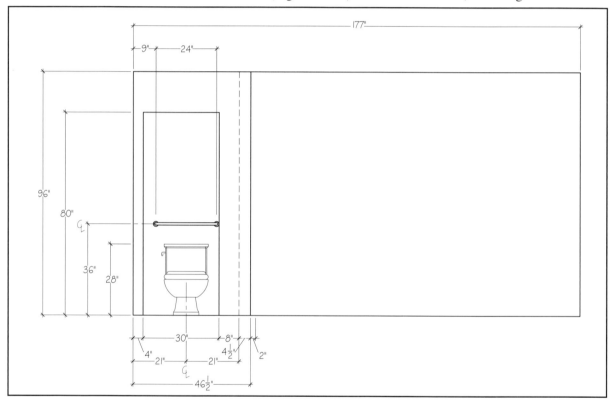

Figure 10.11 Using the wall drawn in Figure 10.10, the elevation is started with the priority area of the toilet compartment.

Continue drawing the elevation by adding items from the floor plan for which the height is known, such as cabinets and fixtures. Dimension the heights of each item. Detail items that are important to the design and the visual continuity of the elevation design, such as cabinet doors and hardware placement.

Now, place items that were not identified in your dimensioned drawing of the floor plan, such as mirrors, towel racks, toilet paper holders, light fixtures and mouldings. Review the elevation for both the vertical and horizontal relationships of line and shape.

Consider the functional placement of items, such as the relationship of a mirror to the user's eye height, and clearances below towel racks for hanging towels. You may need to do a detail drawing, such as an inside elevation of a shower.

Check all dimensions on the elevation drawing. Verify that individual items are dimensioned correctly and that all vertical dimensions are correctly added.

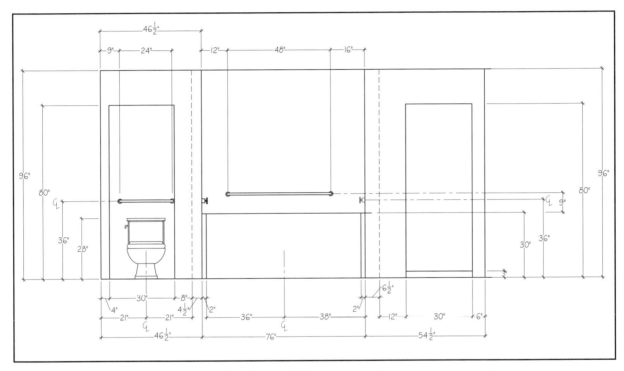

It is useful to develop all the wall elevations and then compare them together. Consider how your eye will be drawn across the room, and the horizontal relationships from one wall to the next. Is there a unity to your design? What type of rhythm is established by the vertical and horizontal elements in the space? Are all the functional requirements of the design program being met?

Figure 10.12 The custom shower and jetted tub are added to the elevation drawing started in Figure 10.11. Additional details, such as towel bars and fittings, can now be added to this drawing.

Evaluating and Checking

Begin the evaluation of your plan by scoring your design against the Bathroom Planning Guidelines. This is an important step to make sure your have developed a design that is functional as well as safe. Figure 10.13 is a checklist that you can use to score your plan against the Bathroom Planning Guidelines.

Review your plan against each guideline on the checklist. Your design must meet or exceed all the code requirements and should meet the "Recommended" Planning Guidelines, unless there are extenuating circumstances that prevent this from happening.

Depending on your client and their needs, you will also want to review your plan against the Access Standards. In your User Analysis, you will have noted the relevant Access Standards. Figure 10.14 is a checklist to evaluate your plan, using the Access Standards.

The final step in developing the design drawing is to check all dimensions. Double-checking for accuracy is critical.

- Verify all jobsite or construction dimensions. If necessary, return to the jobsite and re-measure. The success of your final design is dependent on working from accurate information.

- Verify the construction constraints. Review all mechanical, electrical and plumbing information for accuracy. Consult the plumber, electrician, or contractor, if needed.

- Verify that the actual dimensions of the space were transferred to the room outline that was the starting point of your dimensioned drawing.

- Verify the placement of all centerlines of fixtures. First, verify the sizes of all fixtures from actual measurements or product specifications, and determine that there is adequate space for all fixtures. Review the clearances for centerlines that are recommended and/or required in the Bathroom Planning Guidelines, and verify that you have met these.

- Verify the size of the cabinets, both vertically and horizontally. Check the dimensioned sizes on your drawing against the product literature or actual measurements.

- Verify the centerline placement for all accessories, such as towel bars, just as you did for the fixture centerlines.

- Verify all vertical relationships. Double-check the heights of fixtures and fittings, and review that there will be adequate clearance, as needed above or below items.

Figure 10.13 The Bathroom Planning Checklist provides an easy way to score your plan against the Bathroom Planning Guidelines.

BATHROOM PLANNING CHECKLIST – GUIDELINES

Use this check sheet to determine that a bathroom design meets all code requirements and incorporates the Recommended Planning Guidelines.

Guideline	Code Requirements	Planning Guidelines
1. Door entry is 32" clear opening	▒	
2. Door does not interfere with fixture		
Door does not interfere with cabinet		
3. Ceiling height over fixtures is 80"		
4. 30" clear space at lavatory	▒	
21" clear space at lavatory		
30" clear space at tub	▒	
21" clear space at bathtub		
30" clear space at shower	▒	
24" clear space at shower		
30" clear space at toilet/bidet	▒	
21" clear space at toilet		
5. Single lavatory centered at 20"	▒	
Single lavatory centered on 15" or 4" from wall		
6. Double lavatory centered on 36"	▒	
Double lavatory centered on 30", or 4" a part		
7. Lavatory between 32" and 43" high	▒	
8. Counter edges clipped or rounded		
9. Shower size at least 36" x 36"	▒	
Shower size is 30" x 30" to 36" x 36"		
10. Shower controls 38" – 48", useable inside and outside the spray	▒	
Bathtub controls between tub rim and 33"	▒	
11. Tub/shower controls pressure balanced and/or thermostatic mixing		
12. Shower includes seat 17" – 19" above shower floor, 15" deep,	▒	
Shower seat does not infringe on shower size		
13. Waterproof material in shower 3" above showerhead rough-in		
Waterproof material extends to 72" from finished floor		
14. Grab bars at tub/shower areas 33" – 36" from floor	▒	
Walls reinforced for grab bars at tub/shower	▒	
15. Tempered glass used at tub/shower door, enclosure less than 60" and at window and doors below 18" from floor		
16. Shower door opens out or no shower door		
17. No steps at tub	▒	
18. Slip resistant flooring	▒	
19. Access panels installed per manufacturers' instructions		
20. Toilet/bidet placed 18" on center	▒	
Toilet/bidet placed 15" – 18" on center		
21. Toilet compartment is 36" x 66"	▒	
Toilet compartment is between 30" x 60" and 36" x 66"		

BATHROOM PLANNING CHECKLIST – GUIDELINES – CONTINUED –

Guideline	Code Requirements	Planning Guidelines
22. Adequate storage is provided		
23. Mirror placed at user height		
Toilet paper 8" – 12" to front of toilet, centered 26" above the floor		
Other accessories located where needed		
24. GFCI receptacles located where needed		
At least one GFCI receptacle within 36" of outside edge of lavatory		
No switches or receptacles within or accessible from tub/shower		
25. General and task lighting provided, at least one switch at entry		
Light in tub/shower "suitable for damp location"		
No hanging fixture over tub zone of 3' x 8'		
26. Mechanical exhaust vented to the outside		
3 sq. ft window 50% operable or mechanical system of 50 cfm		
27. Supplemental heat source		
Room can be heated to 68 degrees F		

Figure 10.14 This Bathroom Planning Checklist provides an easy way to score your plan against the Bathroom Planning Access Standards.

BATHROOM PLANNING CHECKLIST – ACCESS STANDARDS

Use this check sheet to determine that a bathroom design meets all Code Requirements and incorporates the Access Standard appropriate to meet the client's needs.

Guideline and Access Standards	Code Requirements	Access Standards
1. Door entry is 34" clear opening (36" wide door)		
2. Door does not interfere with fixture, cabinet		
18" clear space on pull side or door		
3. Ceiling height over fixtures is 80"		
4. Minimum 30" x 48" clear space at lavatory, tub, shower, toilet/bidet		
Minimum 36" wide knee space (at least 27" high)		
Transfer space at toilet		
5. Single lavatory centered at 20"		
6. Double lavatory centered on 36"		
7. Lavatory no higher than 34"		
Lavatory controls within user's reach, easy to operate		
8. Counter edges clipped or rounded		
9. Transfer shower (36" x 36") or		
Roll-in shower (36" – 42" x 60")		
10. Shower controls 38" – 48" AFF, offset toward the room, with minimal effort, identified with red and blue indicators		
Include handheld spray unit with minimum 60" hose		
11. Tub/shower controls pressure balanced and/or thermostatic mixing		
12. Shower includes seat 17" – 19" above shower floor, 15" deep		
13. Waterproof material in shower 3" above showerhead rough-in		
Waterproof material in shower extends to 72" above the floor		
14. Grab bars at tub/shower and toilet areas 33" – 36" from floor		
Prefer walls reinforced for grab bars throughout bathroom		
15. Tempered glass used at tub/shower door, enclosure less than 60" and at windows and doors below 18" from floor		
16. Thresholds should be no more than 1/2" high		
17. No steps at tub		
18. Slip resistant flooring		
19. Access panels installed per manufacturers' instructions		
20. Toilet/bidet placed 18" on center		
Toilet/bidet seat between 15" and 19" AFF		
21. Privacy created at toilet without needing compartment		
22. Storage 15" to 48" above the floor		
23. Full height mirrors or placed at user height, maximum 40" above the floor		
Toilet paper 7" – 9" to front of toilet, centered 15" – 48" above the floor		
Accessories should be 15" to 48" above the floor		
24. GFCI receptacles located where needed, 15" to 48" above the floor.		

BATHROOM PLANNING CHECKLIST – ACCESS STANDARDS – CONTINUED

Guideline and Access Standards	Code Requirements	Access Standards
25. General and task lighting provided, at least one switch at entry		
Switches 15" – 48" above the floor and operable with minimal effort		
Task lighting beside vanity mirror		
26. Mechanical exhaust vented to the outside, with control 15" – 48" above the floor, operable with minimal effort, easy to read, and with minimal noise pollution.		
27. Supplemental heat source, with thermostats at 15" – 48" above the floor and operable with minimal effort.		

Meet Rose and Vincent. Their bathroom remodeling project is an example of how to prepare a design program. We interviewed Rose and Vincent at their home. We used the various forms and checklists from Chapter 5 to collect information for their design project. Then, we developed this design program.

After you read the design program, look at one of the designs that was prepared for Rose and Vincent. Do you think the design meets their needs? Is the design solution functional, safe and convenient? Use the Bathroom Planning Checklists (Figure 10.13 and Figure 10.14) to evaluate the plan.

This sample design program focuses on space planning, the emphasis in this book. If you were developing a design program, you might want to give more attention to color, style and visual impact. This information is covered in the NKBA book *Kitchen & Bath Design Principles*.

A Sample Design Program

GOALS AND PURPOSE

Client description: Rose and Vincent are a couple in their early 50s. They are both employed full time as professionals. Vincent has Parkinson's disease, which may lead to mobility problems in the future.

Project description and goals: Rose and Vincent have a spacious bathroom off their bedroom, which they would like to remodel to be more accessible in the event Vincent needs to use mobility aids in the future (Figure 10.15). In the existing bathroom, the toilet compartment may be limiting to accessibility. The door to the toilet compartment, and access to the closet, create a bottleneck in front of the vanity, especially in the morning. The jetted tub is seldom used, and can be removed to provide space for a larger shower. Only one vanity is needed in the bathroom, as a second vanity is going to be put into the adjoining bedroom. Storage is limited in the bathroom.

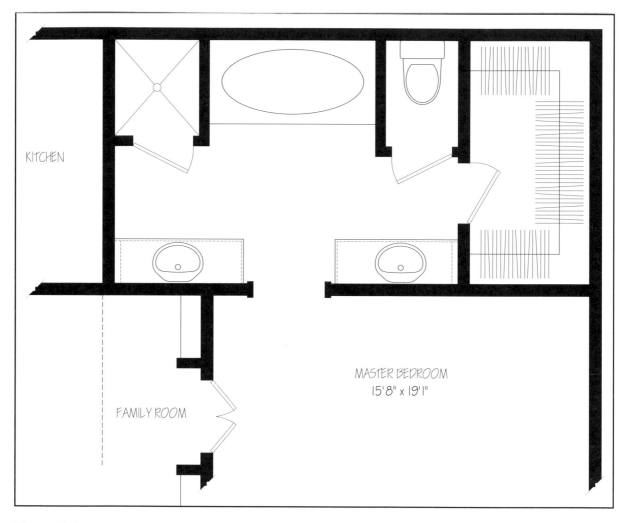

Figure 10.15 Rose and Vincent's bathroom is spacious but not planned to meet their current and future needs.

KITCHEN

FAMILY ROOM

MASTER BEDROOM
15'8" x 19'1"

In their remodeled bathroom, Rose and Vincent would like a large, accessible shower, more space around the toilet, a single vanity, improved traffic flow, generous storage, natural light, easy maintenance, and traditional, but simple styling.

SCOPE OF THE PROJECT

The designer will:

- Develop a design that meets the client needs.

- Select all fixtures, fittings and finish materials.

- Prepare drawings and specifications for completion of the project.

- Supervise construction and installation of the project.

OBJECTIVES AND PRIORITIES

- Design a shower that is large enough to use with a mobility aid.

- Design an open toilet area that would meet accessibility for a mobility aid if needed in the future.

- Provide at least one tall cabinet with generous storage for towels, grooming products and medicines.

- Improve traffic flow to the closet by moving the adjacent vanity and enlarging the door.

- Allow a turning circle of 60 inches in the bathroom.

- Design a vanity area with open access space below the lavatory for seated use.

- Specify a window in the exterior wall.

- Select easy maintenance materials that resist moisture and are simple to clean.

- Specify materials and products with traditional, but simple styling.

ACTIVITIES AND RELATIONSHIPS

A User Analysis was prepared for Rose and Vincent's remodeling project, and is presented in Figure 10.16.

Activity Space	Users	Frequency	Fixtures, Fittings, Furniture, Etc.	Storage
Shower area – full body shower, wash hair, shave legs, relaxation	Rose, Vincent	daily	Tile shower, 60" x 60"; no threshold; interior seat (flip-up); pressure balance control with one-hand operation & accessible from outside the shower, grab bars	Interior shelf for toiletries; 2 towel racks adjacent
Vanity area – teeth brushing, face washing & shaving, hair combing; hand washing	Vincent will be primary user	daily	Vanity counter at least 48" x 21"; lavatory, 34" AFF integral to counter; fittings operate with one hand; large mirror, maximum 40" AFF; 4 receptacles	Drawer storage – minimum 2 15" drawers; more desirable
Toilet area – elimination; reading	Rose, Vincent	daily	Standard size toilet; low-profile; grab bars	Toilet paper holder, magazine basket
Storage area – towels, grooming supplies, cleaning products, personal hygiene, medicines	Rose will be primary user	daily	Tall cabinet, minimum 18" deep and 48" frontage 50% pullout shelves	

Figure 10.16 *User Analysis for Rose and Vincent's Bathroom Design*
Information for preparing the User Analysis would come from the needs assessment forms. More information about materials, color and style could be added.

Space and Relationships	Ambience	Special Needs	Future	Guidelines
60" x 30" clear space for access	Adjustable light level; ventilation fan	Non-slip floor	Replace shower door with curtain for easier access	Planning Guidelines: 4, 9, 10, 11, 12, 13, 14, 15, 16, 18, 26 Access Standards: 4, 9, 10, 12, 14, 16
30" clear space in front; knee space under lavatory; out of path to closet	Adjustable light level; side placement preferred		Ability to sit at lavatory	Planning Guidelines: 2, 4, 7, 8, 23, 15 Access Standards; 7, 14, 23
Clear space 56" from back wall and 60" from side wall; 18" clearance on centerline for fixture placement	Adjustable light level		Ability to transfer from front or right side	Planning Guidelines: 4, 14, 20, 24 Access Standards: 14, 24
Clear space to include door swing		Hardware operable with one hand; mirror on inside of one door	Adjustable height shelves	Planning Guidelines: 1, 22 Access Standards:

THE DESIGN SOLUTION

From Rose and Vincent's design program, we developed several bubble diagrams, all of which could be developed into designs. For our example, we drew design templates and laid out the templates within the room outline for one design. After choosing the best layout, we tried some elevation sketches and then refined the floor plan drawing. Finally, we carefully checked all our dimensions and clearances. Now it's time for you to evaluate our work.

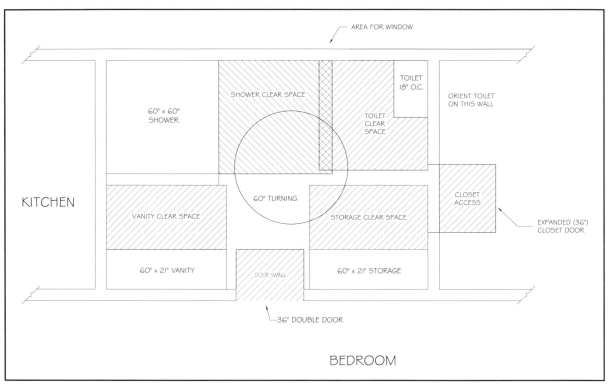

Figure 10.17 This visual diagram proposes a design solution for Rose and Vincent that will meet their needs.

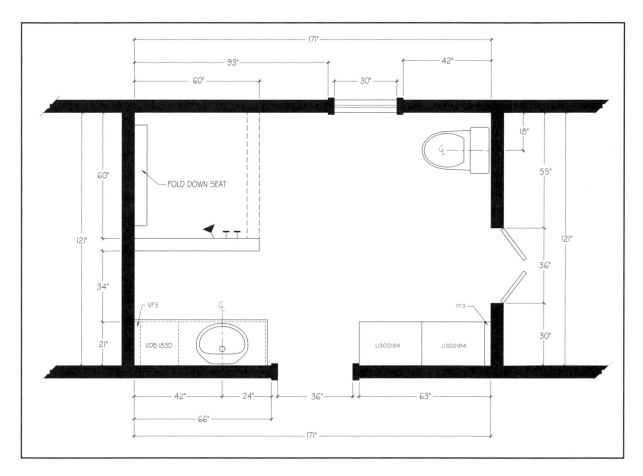

Figure 10.18 A large shower, adequate clear space in front of all fixtures, generous storage, a turning circle, and convenient traffic flow are included in the final design.

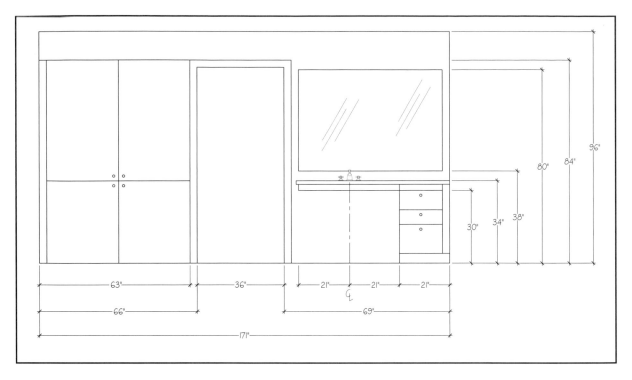

Figure 10.19 This elevation shows the vanity wall. Additional elevations should be developed to finalize the design.

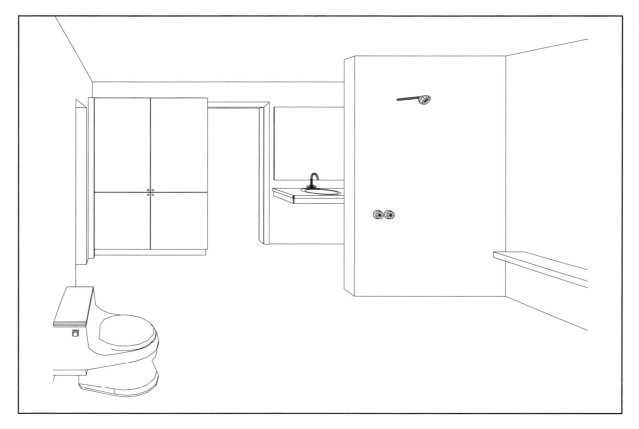

Figure 10.20 A perspective drawing gives the viewer a nice sense of the space.

BATHROOM PLANNING GUIDELINE 1
DOOR/ENTRY

Recommended:

The clear opening of a doorway should be at least 32". This would require a minimum 2'-10" door.

If the existing structure precludes changing the opening then a minimum 2'-0" door is allowable.

Code Requirement:

State or local codes may apply.

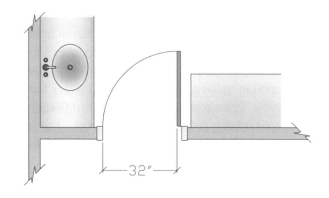

ACCESS STANDARD

Recommended:

The clear opening of a doorway should be at least 34". This would require a minimum 3'-0" door.

Code Reference:

• Clear openings of doorways with swinging doors shall be measured between the face of door and stop, with the door open 90 degrees.

• When a passage exceeds 24" in depth, the minimum width clearance increases to 36".

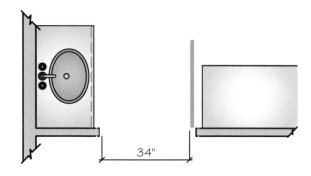

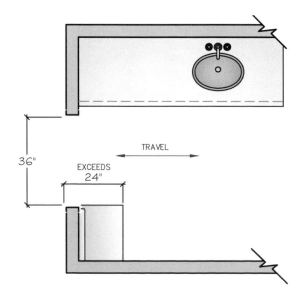

BATHROOM PLANNING GUIDELINE 2
DOOR INTERFERENCE

Recommended:

See Code Reference.

Code Requirement:

- No entry or fixture doors should interfere with one another and/or the safe use of the fixtures or cabinets. (IRC P 2705.1.6)

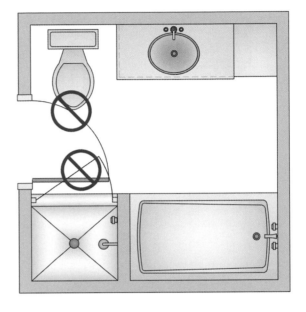

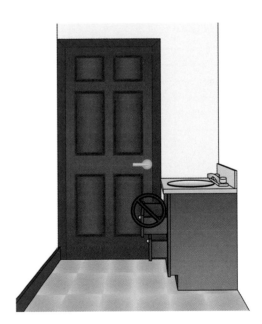

BATHROOM PLANNING GUIDELINE 2
DOOR INTERFERENCE *CONTINUED*

ACCESS STANDARD

Recommended:

The door area should include clear floor space for maneuvering which varies according to the type of door and the direction of approach.

Code Reference:

- For a standard hinged door or a swinging door, the minimum clearance on the pull side of the door should be the width of the door plus 18" by 60".

- The minimum clearance on the push side of the door should be the width of the door by 48".

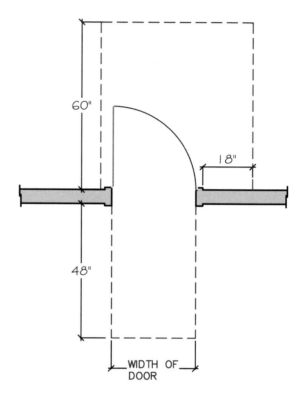

BATHROOM PLANNING GUIDELINE 3
CEILING HEIGHT

Recommended:

See Code Requirement

Code Requirement:

- Bathrooms shall have a minimum floor to ceiling height of 80" over the fixture and at the front clearance area for fixtures.

- A shower or tub equipped with a shower head shall have a minimum floor to ceiling height of 80" above a minimum area 30" x 30" at the shower head.

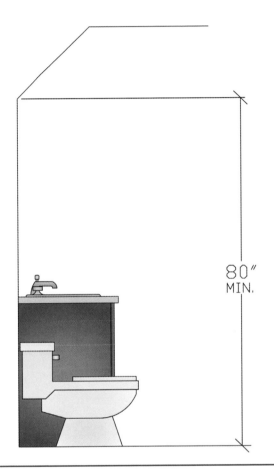

80"
MIN.

ACCESS STANDARD

Recommended:

Bathroom guideline code requirement meets access standard.

BATHROOM PLANNING GUIDELINE 4
CLEAR SPACE

Recommended:

Plan a clear floor space of at least 30" from the front edge of all fixtures (i.e., lavatory, toilet, bidet, tub and shower) to any opposite bath fixture, wall or obstacle.

Code Requirement:

- A minimum space of at least 21" must be planned in front of lavatory, toilet, bidet and tub. (IRC P 2705.1.5)

- A minimum space of at least 24" must be planned in front of a shower entry. (IRC R 307.1)

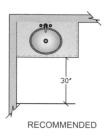
RECOMMENDED

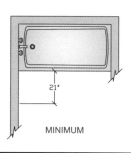
RECOMMENDED

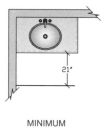
MINIMUM

MINIMUM

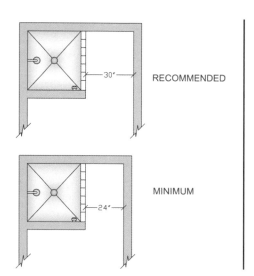
RECOMMENDED

MINIMUM

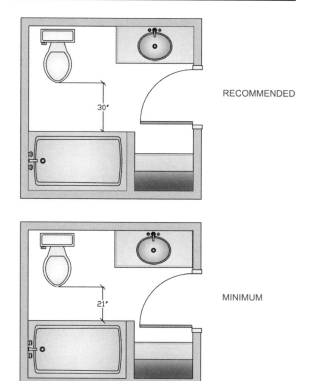
RECOMMENDED

MINIMUM

BATHROOM PLANNING GUIDELINE 4
CLEAR SPACE *CONTINUED*

ACCESS STANDARD

Recommended:

Plan a minimum clear floor space of 30" x 48" at each fixture, plus space for maneuvering including approach and turning for a person using a wheelchair.

Plan a knee space at the lavatory or work space to allow for a seated user. Recommended minimum size of a knee space is 36" wide x 27" high x 8" deep, increasing to 17" deep in the toe space, which extends 9" from the floor. Insulation for exposed pipes should be provided.

Consider the user's method of transfer to the toilet to plan a clear space to fit the user's needs.

Code Reference:

- A clear floor space of at least 30" (762 mm) by 48" (1219 mm) should be provided at each fixture. (ANSI 305.3). Clear spaces can overlap. (ANSI 1002.11.2)

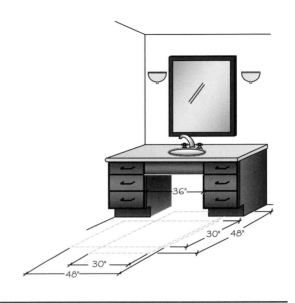

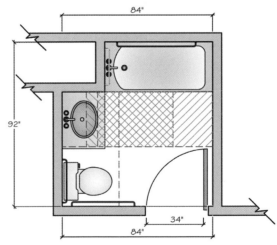

FIXTURE CLEAR FLOOR SPACE

- Include a wheelchair turning space with a diameter of at least 60" (1524 mm), which can include knee* and toe* clearances. (ANSI 304.3.1).

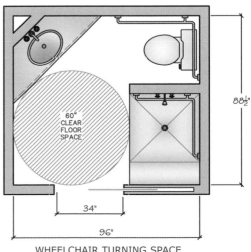

WHEELCHAIR TURNING SPACE

BATHROOM PLANNING GUIDELINE 4
CLEAR SPACE *CONTINUED*

ACCESS STANDARD *CONTINUED*

Code Reference:

- A wheelchair turning space could utilize a T-shaped space, which is a 60" square with two 12" wide x 24" deep areas removed from two corners of the square. This leaves a minimum 36" wide base and two 36" wide arms. T-shaped wheelchair turning-spaces can include knee* and toe* clearances. (ANSI 304.3.2)

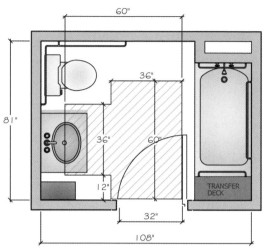

MINIMUM 36" x 36" x 60"
SPACE FOR T-TURNS

Knee clearance must be a minimum 30" wide (36" to use as part of the T-turn) and maintain a 27" clear space under the cabinet, counter or sink for a depth of 8". The next 11" of depth may slope down to a height of 9", with a clear space of at least 17" extending beneath the element. (ANSI 306.3)

Toe clearance space under a cabinet or fixture is between the floor and 9" (229 mm) above the floor. Where toe clearance is required as part of a clear floor space, the toe clearance should extend 17" minimum beneath the element. (ANSI 306.2)

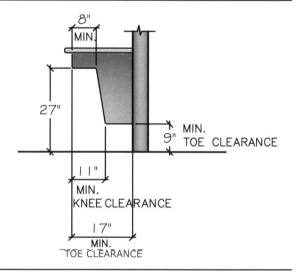

Grooming

- The clear floor space should be centered on the lavatory. (ANSI 1002.10.1)

Bathing and Showering

- Clearance in front of bathtubs should extend the length of the bathtub and be at least 30" (762 mm) wide. (ANSI 607.2)

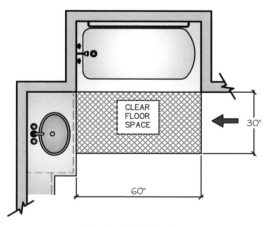

PARALLEL APPROACH

BATHROOM PLANNING GUIDELINE 4
CLEAR SPACE *CONTINUED*

ACCESS STANDARD *CONTINUED*

Code Reference:

Bathing and Showering

- When a permanent seat is provided at the head of the bathtub, the clearance should extend a minimum of 12" (305 mm) beyond the wall at the head end of the bathtub. (ANSI 607.2)

- The clearance in front of the transfer-type shower compartment should be at least 48" (1219 mm) long measured from the control wall and 36" (914 mm) wide. (ANSI 608.2)

- The clearance in front of a roll-in-type shower compartment should be at least 60" (1524 mm) long next to the open face of the shower compartment and 30" (762 mm) wide. (ANSI 608.2)

Toileting

- When both a parallel and a forward approach to the toilet are provided, the clearance should be at least 56" (1422 mm) measured perpendicular from the rear wall, and 60" (1524 mm) measured perpendicular from the sidewall. No other fixture or obstruction should be within the clearance area. (ANSI 604.3.1, 1002.11.5.2.3)

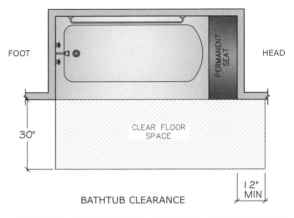

BATHTUB CLEARANCE

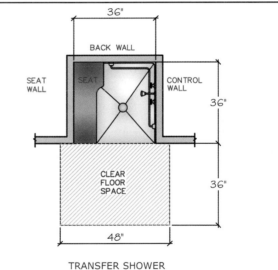

TRANSFER SHOWER

TOILET APPROACH

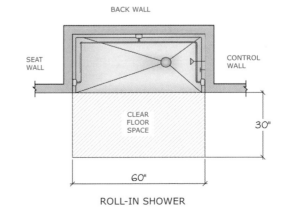

ROLL-IN SHOWER

BATHROOM PLANNING GUIDELINE 5
SINGLE LAVATORY PLACEMENT

Recommended:

The distance from the centerline of the lavatory to the sidewall/tall obstacle should be at least 20".

Code Requirement:

- The minimum distance from the centerline of the lavatory to a wall is 15". (IPC 405.3.1)

- The minimum distance between a wall and the edge of a freestanding or wall-hung lavatory is 4". (IRC R 307.1)

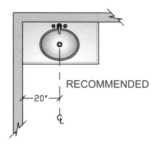

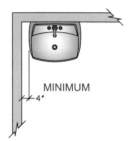

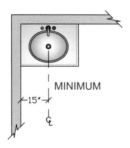

ACCESS STANDARD

Recommended:

Bathroom guideline recommendation meets access standard.

BATHROOM PLANNING GUIDELINE 6
DOUBLE LAVATORY PLACEMENT

Recommended:

The distance between the centerlines of two lavatories should be at least 36".

Code Requirement:

- The minimum distance between the centerlines of two lavatories should be at least 30". (IPC 405.3.1)

- The minimum distance between the edges of two freestanding or wall-hung lavatories is 4". (IRC R 307.1)

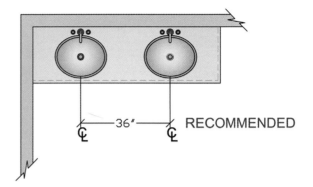

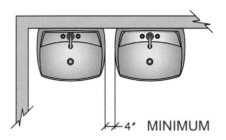

ACCESS STANDARD

Recommended:

Bathroom guideline recommendation meets access standard.

BATHROOM PLANNING GUIDELINE 7
LAVATORY/VANITY HEIGHT

Recommended:

The height for a lavatory varies between 32" – 43" to fit the user.

Code Requirement:

State or local codes may apply.

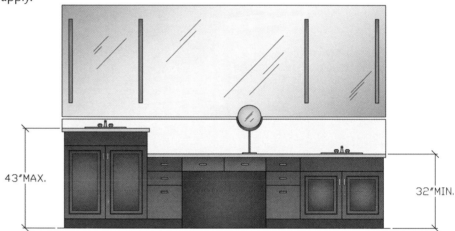

ACCESS STANDARD

Recommended:

Lavatory controls should be within the user's reach and operable with minimal effort.

Code Reference:

• The front of the lavatory sink should be no more than 34" (864 mm) above the floor, measured to the higher of the fixture or counter surface. (ANSI 606.3)

• Lavatory controls should be operable with one hand and not require tight grasping, pinching, or twisting of the wrist. (ANSI 309.4)

BATHROOM PLANNING GUIDELINE 8
COUNTER

Recommended:

Specify clipped or round corners rather than sharp edges on all counters.

Code Requirements:

State or local codes may apply.

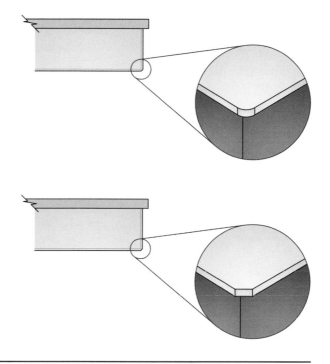

ACCESS STANDARD

Recommended:

Bathroom guideline recommendation meets access standard.

BATHROOM PLANNING GUIDELINE 9
SHOWER SIZE

Recommended:

The interior shower size is at least 36" x 36".

Code Requirement:

- The minimum interior shower size is 30" x 30" or 900 square inches, in which a disc of 30" in diameter must fit. (IRC P 2708.1, IPC 417.4)

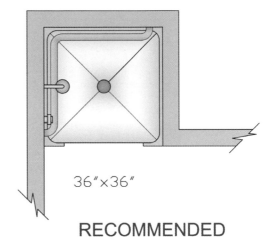

36"x36"

RECOMMENDED

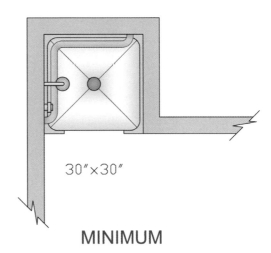

30"x30"

MINIMUM

BATHROOM PLANNING GUIDELINE 9
SHOWER SIZE *CONTINUED*

ACCESS STANDARD

Recommended:

Plan either a transfer* or a roll-in** shower.

A transfer shower, (36" x 36") provides support to a standing person or one who can stand to transfer.

***A roll-in shower is a waterproof area large enough for a person in a wheelchair to remain in the chair to shower. A preferred minimum size for roll-in shower is 36" – 42" x 60".*

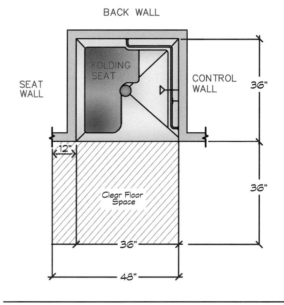

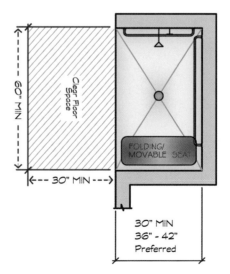

BATHROOM PLANNING GUIDELINE 9
SHOWER SIZE *CONTINUED*

ACCESS STANDARD *CONTINUED*

Recommended:

Roll-in shower entries: For a 60" deep shower, a 32" wide entry is adequate. For a 42" deep shower, the entry must be at least 36" wide to allow for turning space.

Code Reference:

- Transfer-type shower compartments should have an inside finished dimension of 36" (914 mm) x 36" (914 mm), and have a minimum of 36" (914 mm) wide entry on the face of the shower compartment. A seat must be provided within the 36" x 36" area. (ANSI 608)

- Roll-in-type shower compartments should have a minimum inside finished dimension of at least 30" (762 mm) wide by 60" (1524 mm) deep, and have a minimum of a 60" (1524 mm) wide entry on the face of the shower compartment. (ANSI 608.2.2)

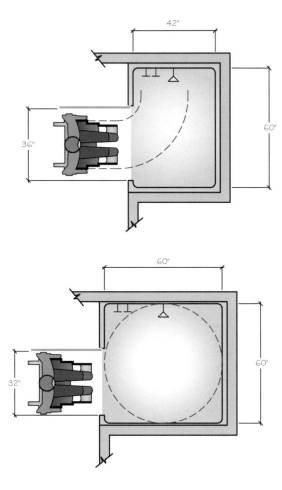

BATHROOM PLANNING GUIDELINE 10
TUB/SHOWER CONTROLS

Recommended:

a. The shower controls should be accessible from both inside and outside the shower spray and be located between 38" – 48" above the floor depending on user's height.

b. The tub controls should be accessible from both inside and outside the tub and be located between the rim of the bathtub and 33" above the floor.

Code Requirement:

State or local codes may apply.

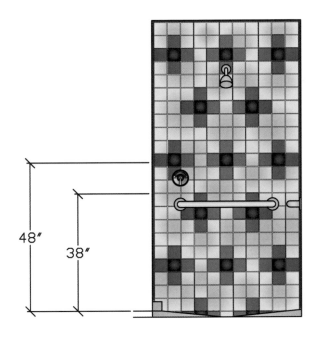

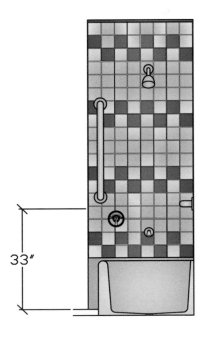

BATHROOM PLANNING GUIDELINE 10
TUB/SHOWER CONTROLS *CONTINUED*

ACCESS STANDARD

Recommended:

Controls should be offset towards the room and easy to grasp, as with lever or loop handles **(a and b)**.

Hot and cold should be identified with red and blue indicators.

Provide a handheld spray at a height accessible to the user **(b)**.

Code Reference:

- Tub/shower controls should be operable with one hand and not require tight grasping. (ANSI 309.4)

- Controls should be on an end wall of the bathtub, between the rim and grab bar, and between the open side of the bathtub and the mid-point of the width of the tub. (ANSI 607.5) **(a)**

- Controls in roll-in showers should be above the grab bar, but no higher than 48" (1219 mm) above the shower floor. In transfer type shower compartments, controls, faucets, and the shower unit should be on the sidewall opposite the seat, between 38" (965 mm) and 48" (1219 mm) above the shower floor. (ANSI 608.5) **(b)**

- A handheld spray unit should be provided with a hose at least 59" (1499 mm) long that can be used as a fixed showerhead and as a handheld shower. In transfer type showers, the controls and shower unit should be on the control wall within 15" (381 mm) of the centerline of the seat **(c)**. In roll-in type showers, shower spray units mounted on the back wall should be no more than 27" from the sidewall. If an adjustable height showerhead mounted on a vertical bar is used, the bar should not obstruct the use of the grab bars. (ANSI 608.6)

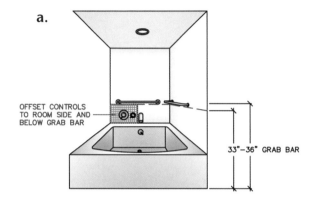

a.

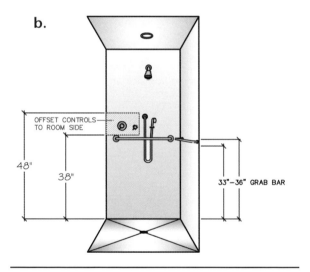

b.

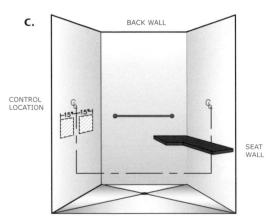

c.

BATHROOM PLANNING GUIDELINE 11
SHOWER/TUB CONTROL VALVES

Recommended:

See below

Code Requirement:

Shower and tub/shower control valves must be one of the following:

- pressure balanced

- thermostatic mixing

- combination pressure balance/thermostatic mixing valve types (IRC P2708.3)

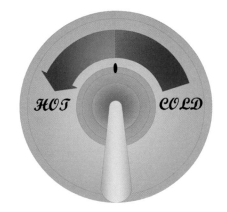

ACCESS STANDARD

Recommended:

Bathroom guideline code requirement meets access standard.

BATHROOM PLANNING GUIDELINE 12
SHOWER/TUB SEAT

Recommended:

Plan a seat within the shower that is 17" – 19" above the shower floor and 15" deep.

Code Requirement:

• Shower seat must not infringe on the minimum interior size of the shower (900 square inches). (IRC P 2708.1)

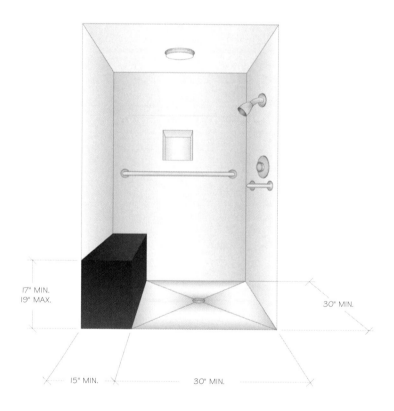

17" MIN.
19" MAX.

30" MIN.

15" MIN.   30" MIN.

BATHROOM PLANNING GUIDELINE 12
SHOWER/TUB SEAT *CONTINUED*

ACCESS STANDARD

Recommended:

Plan a seat in the shower and/or bathtub to fit the parameters of the space and the needs of the user.

Code Reference:

* A removable in-tub seat should be at least 15" (381 mm) – 16" (406 mm) deep and capable of secure placement. (ANSI 610.2)

* A permanent tub seat should be at least 15" (381 mm) deep and positioned at the head end of the bathtub. The top of the seat should be between 17" (432 mm) and 19" (483 mm) above the bathroom floor. (ANSI 610.2)

* Where a seat is provided in a roll-in shower, it should be a folding type and on the wall adjacent to the controls. The top of the seat should be between 17" (432 mm) and 19" (483 mm) above the bathroom floor.

* In a transfer-type shower, the seat should be a folding type and extend from the back wall to a point within 3" (76 mm) of the shower entry. (ANSI 610.3)

* The materials and installation of the shower and/or bathtub seat must support a minimum of 250 pounds of pressure. (ANSI 610.4)

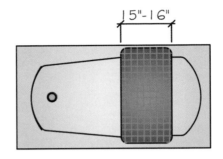

REMOVEABLE IN—TUB SEAT

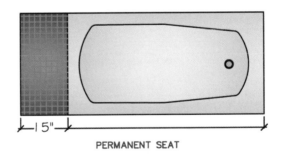

PERMANENT SEAT

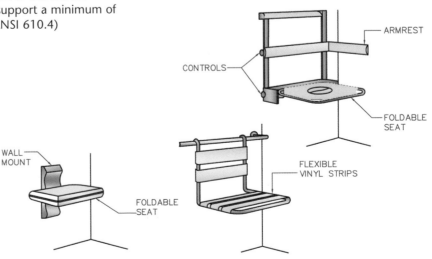

BATHROOM PLANNING GUIDELINE 13
TUB/SHOWER SURROUND

Recommended:

The wall area above a tub or shower pan should be covered in a waterproof material extending at least 3" above the showerhead rough in.

Code Requirement:

- The wall area above a tub or shower pan must be covered in a waterproof material to a height of not less than 72" above the finished floor. (IPC 417.4.1, IRC R 307.2)

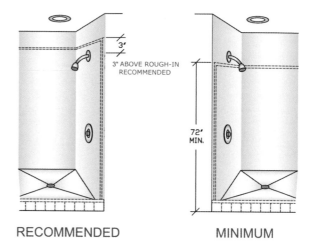

RECOMMENDED   MINIMUM

ACCESS STANDARD

Recommended:

Bathroom guideline recommendation meets access standard.

BATHROOM PLANNING GUIDELINE 14
GRAB BARS

Recommended:

Plan grab bars to facilitate access to and maneuvering within the tub and shower areas.

Tub and shower walls should be prepared (reinforced) at time of construction to allow for installation of grab bars to support a static load of 250 lbs.

Grab bars should be placed at least 33" – 36" above the floor.

Grab bars must be 1¼" to 2" in diameter and extend 1½" from the wall.

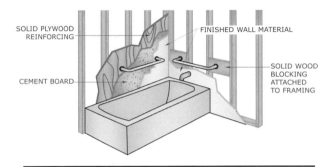

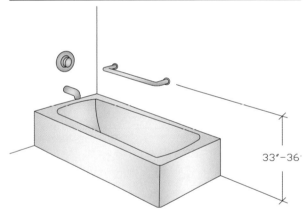

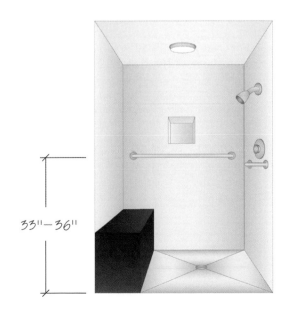

BATHROOM PLANNING GUIDELINE 14
GRAB BARS *CONTINUED*

ACCESS STANDARD

Recommended:

Walls throughout the bathroom should be prepared (reinforced) at time of construction to allow for installation of grab bars to support a minimum of 250 lbs. of pressure.

Grab bars should be placed according to the needs and height of the user, particularly near the tub/shower and the toilet.

Code Reference:

Grab bars should be installed at the tub, shower, and toilet according to the following:

- *Bathtubs with permanent seats:* Two horizontal grab bars **(a1)** should be provided on the back wall, one between 33" (838 mm) and 36" (914 mm) above the floor and the other 9" above the rim of the bathtub **(a2)**. Each grab bar should be no more than 15" (381 mm) from the head end wall or 12" (305 mm) from the foot end wall. A grab bar 24" (610 mm) long should be provided on the foot end wall at the front edge of the bathtub. (ANSI 607.4.1)

- *Bathtubs without permanent seats:* Two horizontal grab bars should be provided on the back wall, one between 33" (838 mm) and 36" (914 mm) above the floor and the other 9" above the rim of the bathtub **(a3)**. Each grab bar should be at least 24" (610 mm) long and no more than 24" (610 mm) from the head end wall or 12" (305 mm) from the foot end wall. A grab bar 24" (610 mm) long should be provided on the foot end wall at the front edge of the bathtub. A grab bar 12" (305 mm) long should be provided on the head end wall at the front edge of the bathtub **(a4)**. (ANSI 607.4.2)

a1.

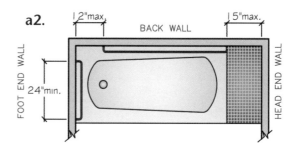

a2.

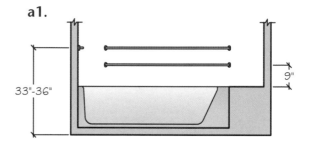

a3.

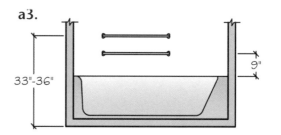

a4.

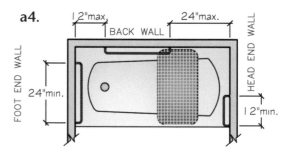

BATHROOM PLANNING GUIDELINE 14
GRAB BARS *CONTINUED*

Code Reference *Continued*:

- *Transfer-type showers:* Grab bars should be mounted in a horizontal position, between 33" and 36" above the floor, across the control wall and across the back wall to a point 18" from the control wall. (ANSI 608.3.1) **(b)**

- *Roll-in type shower:* Grab bars should be mounted in a horizontal position, between 33" and 36" above the floor, on all three walls of the shower, but not behind a seat. Grab bars should be no more than 6" from each adjacent wall. (ANSI 608.3.2) **(c1, c2 and c3)**

- *Toilet:* Grab bars should be provided on the rear wall and on the sidewall closest to the toilet. Sidewall grab bar should be at least 42" (1067 mm) long and located between 12" (305 mm) and 54" (1372 mm) from the rear wall. The rear grab bar should be at least 24" (610 mm) long, centered on the toilet. Where space permits, the bar should be at least 36" (914 mm) long, with the additional length provided on the transfer side of the toilet. (ANSI 604.5) **(d1 and d2)**

b.

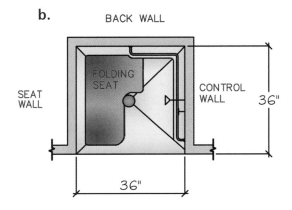

BATHROOM PLANNING GUIDELINE 14
GRAB BARS *CONTINUED*

c1.

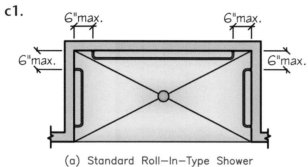

(a) Standard Roll–In–Type Shower

c2.

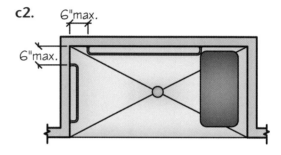

(b) Roll–In–Type Shower with Seat

c3.

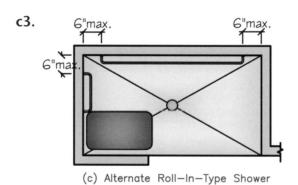

(c) Alternate Roll–In–Type Shower

d1.

d2.

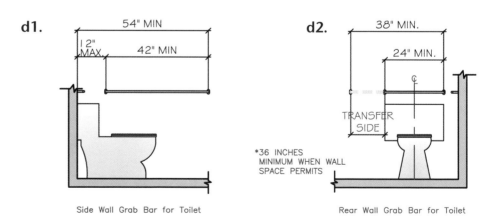

Side Wall Grab Bar for Toilet

Rear Wall Grab Bar for Toilet

BATHROOM PLANNING GUIDELINE 15
GLAZING

Recommended:

See Code Requirement

Code Requirement:

- Glass used in tub or shower enclosures (i.e. tub or shower door) or partitions must be tempered or an approved equal and must be permanently marked as such. (IRC R 308.1)

- If the tub or shower surround has glass windows or walls, the glazing must be tempered glass or approved equal when the bottom edge of glazing is less than 60" above any standing or walking surface. (IRC R 308.4.5)

- Any glazing (i.e. windows or doors) whose bottom edge is less than 18" above the floor must be tempered glass or approved equal. (IRC R 308.4.7.2)

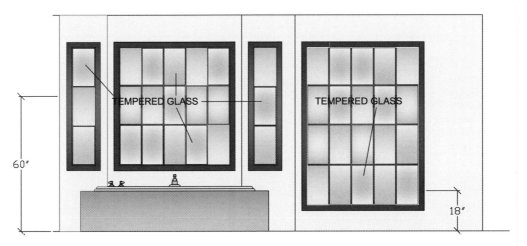

ACCESS STANDARD

Recommended:

Bathroom guideline code requirements meet access standard.

443

BATHROOM PLANNING GUIDELINE 16
TUB/SHOWER DOOR

Recommended:

See Code Requirement

Code Requirement:

- Hinged shower doors shall open outward.
  (IRC P 2708.1)

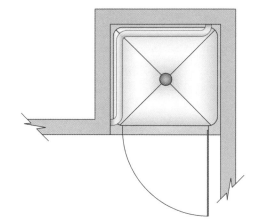

ACCESS STANDARD

Recommended:

Minimize thresholds at the shower entry to no more that ½".

Code Requirement:

- Shower compartment thresholds should be no more than ½" (13 mm) high. Changes in level of no more than ¼" (6 mm) high are permitted, but changes in level between ¼" (6 mm) high and ½" (13 mm) high should be beveled with a slope not steeper than 1:2. (ANSI 608.7.303)

BATHROOM PLANNING GUIDELINE 17
STEPS

Recommended:

Steps should not be placed outside a tub.

If steps are used a grab bar/handrail is mandatory.

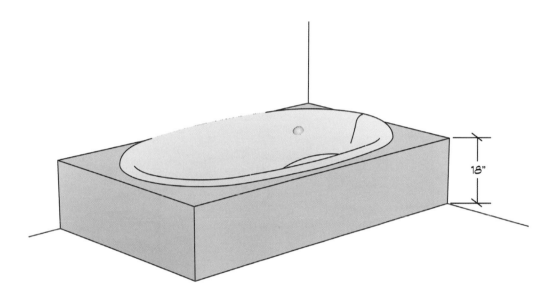

ACCESS STANDARD

Recommended:

Bathroom guideline recommendation meets access standard.

BATHROOM PLANNING GUIDELINE 18
FLOORING

Recommended:

Slip-resistant surfaces should be specified for the
general bath flooring, shower floors, and tub/shower
bottoms.

Code Requirement:

State or local codes may apply.

ACCESS STANDARD

Recommended:

Bathroom guideline recommendation meets access
standard.

Code Reference:

- Plan a slope for the bathtub or shower drain with
  a maximum slope of 1:48 pitch ¼ inch per foot
  (ratio 1:48). (ANSI 403.3)

BATHROOM PLANNING GUIDELINE 19
EQUIPMENT ACCESS

Recommended:

See below

Code Requirement:

- All equipment, including access panels, must be installed as per manufacturers' specifications. (IRC M 1307.1)

- All manufacturers' instructions must be available for installers and inspectors and left for homeowners. (IRC P 2720.1)

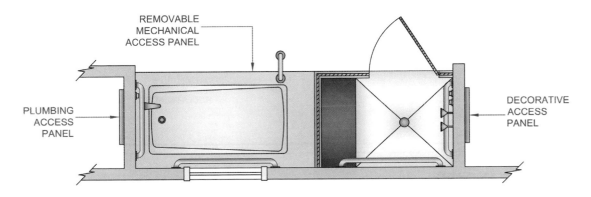

ACCESS STANDARD

Recommended:

Bathroom guideline code requirement meets access standard.

BATHROOM PLANNING GUIDELINE 22
STORAGE

Recommended:

Provide adequate, accessible storage for toiletries, bath linens, grooming and general bathroom supplies at point of use.

Code Requirement:

State or local codes may apply.

ACCESS STANDARD

Recommended:

Plan storage of frequently used items 15" to 48" above the floor.

Code Reference:

- Where a forward or side reach is unobstructed, the high reach should be 48" maximum and the low reach should be 15" minimum above the floor. (ANSI 308.2.1, 308.3.1)

- Where a forward or side reach is obstructed by a 20" – 25" deep counter, the high reach should be 44" maximum. (ANSI 308.2.2, 308.3.2)

- Door/drawer pulls should be operable with one hand, require only a minimal amount of strength for operation, and should not require tight grasping. (ANSI 309.4)

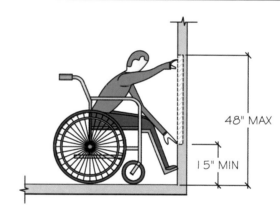

UNOBSTRUCTED FORWARD REACH

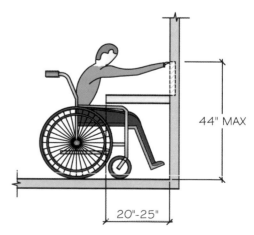

OBSTRUCTED HIGH FORWARD REACH

BATHROOM PLANNING GUIDELINE 23
ACCESSORIES

Recommended:

a   Place a mirror above or near the lavatory at a height that takes the user's eye height into consideration.

b   The toilet paper holder should be located 8" – 12" in front of the edge of the toilet bowl, centered at 26" above the floor.

c   Additional accessories, such as towel holders, soap dishes, etc., should be conveniently located near all bath fixtures.

Code Requirement:

State or local codes may apply.

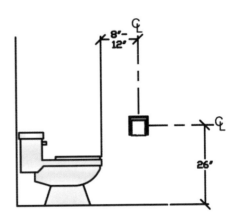

BATHROOM PLANNING GUIDELINE 25
LIGHTING

Recommended:

In addition to general lighting, task lighting should be provided for each functional area in the bathroom (i.e. grooming, showering).

Code Requirement:

- At least one wall-switch controlled light must be provided. Switch must be placed at the entrance of the bathroom. (IRC E 3901.6, IRC E 3803.2)

- All light fixtures installed within tub and shower spaces should be marked "suitable for damp/wet locations". (IRC E 3903.8)

- Hanging fixtures cannot be located within a zone of 3' feet horizontally and 8' vertically from the top of the bathtub rim or shower stall threshold. (IRC E 3903.10)

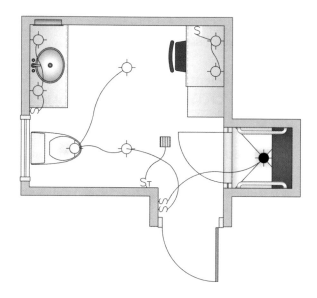

ACCESS STANDARD

Recommended:

Task lighting at the vanity should be beside the mirror and at eye level and with the lamp not visible to the eye.

Lighting controls should be between 15" and 48" above the floor and operable with a closed fist and with minimal effort.

Code Reference:

- Operable parts should be operable with one hand and not require tight grasping, pitching, or twisting of the wrist. The force required to activate operable parts should be 5 pounds maximum. (ANSI A117.1 309.4)

- See Access Standard 22 for specifications for reach range for controls.

BATHROOM PLANNING GUIDELINE 26
VENTILATION

Recommended:

Plan a mechanical exhaust system, vented to the outside, for each enclosed area.

Code Requirement:

- Minimum ventilation for the bathroom is to be a window of at least 3 sq. ft. of which 50% is operable, or a mechanical ventilation system of at least 50 cubic feet per minute (cfm) ducted to the outside. (IRC R 303.3, IRC M 1506.3)

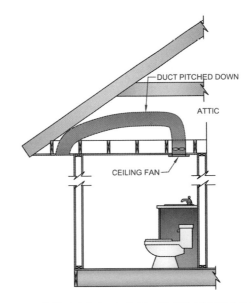

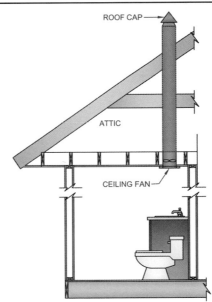

ACCESS STANDARD

Recommended:

Ventilation controls should be placed 15" – 48" above the floor, operable with minimal effort, easy to read, and with minimal noise pollution.

Code Reference:

- See Access Standard 25 for operable controls.

- See Access Standard 22 for reach range for controls.

BATHROOM PLANNING GUIDELINE 27
HEAT

Recommended:

A supplemental heat source, i.e., heat lamp, toe kick heater, or floor heat should be considered.

Code Requirement:

- All bathrooms should have an appropriate heat source to maintain a minimum room temperature of 68 degrees Fahrenheit (20 Celsius). (IRC R 303.8)

TOEKICK HEATER

WALL HEATER

HEAT LAMP   HEAT / FAN / LIGHT

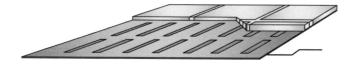

RADIANT FLOOR SYSTEM

ACCESS STANDARD

Recommended:

See Code Reference.

Code Reference:

- See Access Standard 25 for operable controls.

- Access Standard 22 for reach range for controls.

GLOSSARY

A

Absolute humidity: The actual amount of water vapor in the air.

Accessibility or accessible design: Characteristics of spaces or products that meet prescribed requirements for particular variations in ability, i.e. "wheelchair accessible."

Americans with Disabilities Act Accessibility Guidelines (ADAAG): Guidelines for compliance with the accessibility requirements of the Americans with Disabilities Act (ADA) (1991).

Adaptable design: Features that are either adjustable or capable of being easily added or removed to "adapt" the unit to individual needs or preferences.

ACH (Air changes per hour): Used to measure the ventilation rate of a room or building; 1 ACH means that, in one hour, a volume of air equal to the volume of the room has been exhausted and replaced with outside air.

Aerobic exercise: Exercise to increase heart rate; cardiovascular exercise.

Ambient noise: The level of acoustic noise at a given location, such as in a room.

ANSI A117.1 – Accessible and Useable Buildings and Facilities: Original American National Standards Institute (ANSI) guidelines for accessible design in commercial and residential spaces. Now the International Code Council (ICC)/ANSI A117.1 the referenced technical standard for compliance with the accessibility requirements of International Building Code and many other state and local codes. Used as reference for NKBA Access Standards.

Anthropometry: The study of human measurements, such as size and proportion, and parameters, such as reach range and visual range.

Anti-microbial finish: A material that has an applied finish, or ingredient in the product, that inhibits the growth of microorganisms, such as bacteria or fungi.

Aromatherapy: Using the scent from the essential oils of plants to affect mood and sense of well-being.

B

Back drafting: Used to describe a situation where combustion by-products, from furnaces, water heaters, fireplaces, stoves, and other fuel-burning appliances, are pulled back into the house instead of exhausting through the flue or chimney; the situation can occur when the air pressure inside the home is less than outside, and is usually the result of running exhaust fans and appliances without providing adequate make-up air.

Barrier-free design: An older term for universal design, based on the concept of solutions that removed barriers in the environment.

Bidet: A personal hygiene fixture with a hot and cold water supply that is designed for personal cleanliness; used to wash the perinea and genital area.

Biological pollutants: Indoor air pollutants that come from living sources, including molds, insects, and animals; more likely to be found in moist places.

C

CADR (Clean Air Delivery Rate): A measure of the efficiency of a portable air cleaner, based on the percentage of particles removed from the air and the speed at which the particles are removed.

Canadian Electric Code (CEC): A code for electrical safety in Canada. It is almost identical to the National Electric Code (NEC) used in the United States.

Cardiovascular exercise: Exercise to increase heart rate; aerobic exercise.

Center: Area where a task occurs, including the fixture, clear space, storage and other components that support the function of the task. In the bathroom the centers are: grooming, bathing/showering, and toileting.

Certified Bath Designer (CBD): NKBA designation for a bathroom designer who has passed the certification examination.

CFM: Cubic feet per minute; used as a measure of the amount of air a fan can move.

Chamber pot: A small ceramic or metal pot, stored under the bed, in a cabinet or stool (often called a commode or closestool), or it would sit out in the room if highly decorated. The pot was used until the 19th Century as an indoor toilet when the weather was bad or during the night.

Chromatherapy: Using color to affect mood and sense of well-being, using colored lights in a bathtub.

Circuit breaker: A device that is designed to protect electrical equipment and people from damage caused by overload or short circuit. It can be reset to resume operation.

Claw foot tub: A tub mounted off of the floor on four legs; the base of each leg is shaped like a claw foot.

Clear floor space: Area which is free of obstruction within an overall space, typically used in reference to the recommendations for clearances at a center (i.e. the lavatory or the shower) or for a particular activity (i.e. bathing or exercising).

Comfort zone: A body buffer zone that we maintain between others and ourselves.

Compartmentalized bathroom: A bathroom where individual activities, like toileting or showering, are separated by walls into individual compartments.

Composting toilet: A fully self-contained toilet that requires no water inlet, or sewer connection, and uses chemicals in order to operate. It works like a septic tank with bacterial action breaking down the solid waste into a soil-type residue.

Condensation: The process where water changes from a gaseous stage to a liquid stage; heat is released by condensation.

Console sink: A sink basin supported by legs. The legs can be metal or wooden.

Covenant: Sometimes called a restrictive covenant, this is a legally binding clause in a property deed that imposes a limitation or requirement on the use of the property.

D

Dental lavatory: A small sink used for brushing teeth that was typically located at a lower height for children to reach; promoted by the plumbing industry as a way to open the bathroom to multiple users.

Dew point: The temperature at which water vapor condenses; the dew point temperature is a function of humidity: when the relative humidity is 100%, the air is saturated and can hold no more water vapor, therefore, if there is more water vapor, or the temperature drops below the dew point, condensation occurs.

Dressing circle: Space needed to put clothes on and off, 42 to 48 inches in diameter.

Dual cueing: Also called redundant cueing, refers to the use of different modes (pictorial, verbal, tactile) to communicate necessary information effectively to the user, regardless of ambient conditions or the user's sensory abilities.

E

Earth closet: An indoor privy where dry soil was added to a reservoir below the seat after each use to absorb moisture and retain offensive odors; periodically the soil contents were removed and used as compost.

Egress: A path or opening for exiting a room or building.

Ergonomic design: The application of human factor data to the design of products and spaces to improve function and efficiency.

Exfoliation: Removing layers of dry, flaking skin.

F

Fair Housing Accessibility Guidelines (FHAG): Accessibility regulations affecting the design of multi-family housing built since 1991. FHAG make up the technical guidance for compliance with the accessibility requirements of the Fair Housing Amendments Act of 1988.

Fenestration: The arrangement of windows in a building.

Fitting: A term used for a device that controls water entering or leaving a fixture. Faucets, spouts, drain, controls, water supply lines and diverter valves are all considered fittings.

Fixture: Any fixed part of the structural design, such as tubs, bidets, toilets, and lavatories.

Functional anthropometry: The measurements of the body in motion.

Fuse: A device that can interrupt the flow of electrical current when a circuit is overloaded.

G

GFCI: Ground fault circuit interrupter is a device that monitors the electric current on a circuit to make sure the amount of current going out is the same as that returning to the electric receptacle. Serving as a safety device, the slightest difference in current will shut off the current.

Grab bars: Safety bars installed in bathtubs and showers to prevent falls. A device, usually installed on a wall, that provide support while rising from, sitting in, entering, or exiting a bathtub or shower.

H

"Hard" water: Water with a high content of minerals, usually calcium and magnesium; often leads to plumbing problems from mineral deposits.

Homeowner's association: An organization of the property owners in a specific housing development or neighborhood. Responsibilities of the association will vary, but often include management of commons area and oversight of requirements affecting the community as a whole; requirements for membership and dues may be a condition of property ownership.

Hot tub: A large container of heated water used for soaking. The original hot tub resembled a barrel. They usually did not have moving water. Currently used similarly to a spa tub – large tub holding warm water, having whirlpool action, and seating for multiple users.

Humidity: The amount of water vapor in the air.

Hydronic systems: A heating system that uses circulating hot water as the heat source; the water is distributed through tubes in the floor or free-standing radiators.

Hydrotherapy: Refers to a variety of bathing options that use hot water, water movement, and/or pressure to stimulate or relax the body.

I

International Residential Code (IRC): Building code developed by the International Code Council for single-family housing. Used as reference for NKBA Kitchen and Bathroom Planning Guidelines.

J

Jetted bathtub: A large basin of hot water with air jets around the perimeter to create a pulsing action on the bather; whirlpool tub.

Joists: A level or nearly level member used in a series to frame a floor or ceiling structure.

L

Latrine: A pit dug in the ground used for disposing of and decomposing human waste. Also a communal toilet, often used in camps and military barracks.

Lavatory: A fixture with running water and drainpipe, for washing hands and face, shaving, etc.

Lifespan design: The aspect of universal design that provides for changes that occur in the lifespan of the home and its owners.

Load-bearing wall: Exterior and interior walls of the home that support the structure vertically. Openings in any load-bearing wall must be reinforced to carry the live and dead weight of the structural load.

M

Massage: A rubbing or kneading of the body to stimulate circulation and make muscles or joints supple. Several techniques focus on various parts of the body.

N

National Electric Code: A code for electrical safety adopted by states and local jurisdictions.

O

Off-gas: A term used to describe the release or evaporation of chemicals into the air from building materials as they dry, cure, or age; the process can be more rapid if temperature and/or humidity is increased.

P

Pedestal lavatory: A free-standing fixture with a wide top and narrow base that conceals the plumbing.

Peripheral vision: Scope of vision on both sides of the eyes. Range often diminishes with age.

pH: A scale used to measure the acidity or alkalinity of water, with values from 1 to 14; neutral is 7; decreasing numbers below 7 mean greater acidity and increasing numbers above 7 mean greater alkalinity.

Pocket door: A door that slides horizontally on a track and is typically moved inside a wall for storage.

Popliteal: A human body measurement relating to the back part of the leg behind the knee.

Powder room: A small bathroom for guests near the public areas of the home. Consists of a sink and toilet.

Primary Drinking Water Standards: Federally mandated standards for acceptable levels of certain pollutants in water; used to assure that water is safe to drink or ingest.

Privates: A Latin word meaning secret, not publicly known; used to form the word privy.

Privy: An English word used during the 17th and 18th Centuries to describe what is commonly known as the outhouse, a toileting facility located outside the house and consisting of a seat over an opening placed in a small building.

R

Radon: A naturally occurring radioactive gas found in soil and ground water; tasteless, odorless, and colorless and detectable only through testing equipment; can seep into homes and build to levels that can be a health threat; long-term exposure can lead to lung cancer.

Relative humidity: A ratio, usually expressed as a percent, of the actual amount of water vapor in the air to the maximum amount (saturation) of water vapor the air could hold at the current temperature.

Roll-in shower: Shower without a threshold that is large enough for a wheelchair to enter.

Rough-in: Where the shower head or other plumbing fitting will be placed in the wall or floor.

S

Safe harbors: Standards that are legally recognized as compliance with the requirements of a code or guideline.

Sauna: A Finnish steam bath. A room that uses dry heat and steam to cleanse and relax the user Steam is produced by pouring water over heated rocks.

Sconce: A light fixture that is fixed to a wall.

Secondary Drinking Water Standards: Voluntary standards for acceptable levels of certain pollutants in water; used to assure that water is functional and aesthetic for typical household uses, such as bathing and laundry.

Septic tank: A large tank where solid matter or sewage from a home is disintegrated by bacteria.

Shut-off valve: A valve control that allows the user to shut off the water entering a fixture. These valves are usually located close to the fixture.

Sight lines: The range or visual field in direct line with a person's eyes, impacted by the position a person will be in when the space or product is being used. This is useful in planning heights of fixtures, fittings, lighting, windows, and more.

Siphon action water closet: A vacuum action creates pressure to more efficiently flush away the waste and use less water in the process; this action is used in most modern toilets today.

Soaking tub: Extra deep tub that allows the user to submerge to their neck.

Sone: A unit of loudness, which is a subjective characteristic of a sound; the sone scale is based on data from people judging the loudness of pure tones; as an example, a noise at four sones is perceived to be four times as loud as a noise of one sone.

Spa tub: A large tub holding warm water having whirlpool action and seating for multiple users; hot tub.

Static anthropometry: The study of the measurements of the body at rest.

Storage Principles: A series of recommendations, developed through research, to increase both the efficiency of storage space and the ease of use. The most common principles are:

Store items at the first or last place of use.

Items used together should be stored together.

Like articles should be stored or grouped together.

Stored items should be easy to locate at a glance.

Frequently used items should be within easy reach.

Strength training exercise: Exercise using weights to develop strength and muscle tone.

Sub-flooring: The flooring applied directly to the floor joists on top of which the finished floor rests.

T

Tactile cueing: Using textural elements to communicate necessary information through touch to the user.

Task lighting: Added lighting for specific tasks, like grooming, dressing, reading, etc.

Thalassotherapy: A form of hydrotherapy that uses seawater in baths, showers, or mud baths.

Toe kick: An indented space in cabinetry near the floor to accommodate the feet while standing next to a cabinetry.

Transfer Shower: A shower open on one side with a seat adjacent to the opening, and grab bars on all three sides, that allows for a person to transfer from a wheelchair to the seat.

Transformer: An electrical device by which alternating current of one voltage is changed to another voltage.

Trans-generational design: Another term for universal design, referring to design that acknowledges and supports the multiple generations more commonly living in a home.

Truss: A framework of beams forming a rigid structure such as a roof truss.

Turkish bath: A steam bath that is followed by a shower and massage; developed when Roman bathing customs were combined with those of the nomadic people, such as the Byzantines.

U

Uniform Federal Accessibility Standards (UFAS): The technical standard referenced by two federal mandates for accessibility for federal buildings; the Architectural Barriers Act (ABA) and Section 504 of the Rehabilitation Act of 1973 (Section 504).

Universal design: The design of products and environments to be useable by all people to the greatest extent possible.

V

Vanity: Bathroom cabinet with the lavatory on the top.

Vernacular housing: Housing styles that are typical or common to a region and have developed over time in response to factors such as available building materials, climate, and cultural heritage.

Vessel lavatory: A lavatory bowl or basin that sits on top of the counter or ledge.

Vichy shower: A seven headed rain bar with pressure spray treatment used to apply water and warmed essential oils to relax and stimulate the mind and body.

Visit-ability: The condition of a home that has been planned to allow for a guest with accessibility needs. Includes a level entry, wide doorways, and an accessible bathroom on the first floor.

Vitreous china: A ceramic material fired at high temperatures to form a nonporous, glass-like material.

Volatile organic compounds (VOCs): A class of organic compounds that are easily evaporated into the air and used in the manufacturing, installation, and maintenance of many building products; many VOCs are toxic, and may contribute to urban smog, the greenhouse effect, and global warming.

W

Waste pipe: The pipe that carries water and waste away from a water using fixture.

Water closet: A term for an indoor privy where water was used to wash down human waste.

Water vapor: Water in a gaseous form.

Wet spa bed: A massage table with a shallow pool that holds water and drains.

Wet wall: A wall containing supply lines and soil and waste lines.

Whirlpool: A bath with jets that move warm water into a swirling motion; jetted bathtub.

Following is a completed sample of the NKBA's Bath Design Survey Form. Familiarity with this form is a requirement for certification.

Superior Bath Design
1700 West 27th Street

Designer: Dee Jacobs, CBD

Bath Design Survey Form

Date: 25 August
Name: Beth and Josh Cooper
Residence: 5612 Eagle Ridge Drive
Jobsite Address: Same

Client 1: Beth	Client 2: Josh
Home Phone: 612-555-6700	Home Phone: 612-555-6700
Work Phone: Same	Work Phone: 621-555-4349
Cell Phone: 612-555-9822	Cell Phone: 612-555-9823
Email: b_cooper@cooper.net	Email: jcooper@primetime.net

Appointment	Allied Professional
Schedule: Fridays after noon best for Josh	Name: Francis Kirkpatrick, AIA
Call When Ready: Contact Beth as needed.	Firm: Kirkpatrick, steen and Shipman
Times Available: After noon Fridays	Address: United Bank Towers, Suite 3106
Directions: Copper Ridge Estates off of West Ridge Parkway	Office Phone: 1-800-555-2111
Bear to right, third street on left. 8th house on left. White house with green shutters.	Cell Phone: 612-555-7611
	Email: Francis@kirksteenship.com

Notes: We were recommended by Larry Westberry. Larry and Josh work together. We did a project for Larry about 3 years ago. Garry was the designer.

©2006 NKBA BMF9   Page 1 of 19

Copyright 2006 by NKBA. All rights reserved. No part of this document may be reproduced in any form by photostat, microfilm, xerography, or any other means, or incorporated into any informational retrieval system, electronic or mechanical, or transmitted, in any form or by any means, without the prior consent of the copyright owner.

General Client Information

1.   *What type of project is this?* ☒Renovation ☐New Construction

2.   *Have you ever purchased a bathroom before?* ☐Yes ☒No

3.   *When would you like to start the project?* As soon after October 15 as possible. _____ Complete the Project? By march 1st. _____

4.   *How much time do you / will you spend at the jobsite residence?* Primary residence _____

5.   *How did you learn about our firm?* Recommended by Larry Westburry. _____

6.   *Has anyone else assisted you in preparing a design for the bath?* No. _____

7.   *Do you plan on retaining an interior designer or architect to assist in the bath planning?*
     If so, Name: Francis Kirkpatrick, AIA _____ Phone: See above. _____

8.   *Do you have a specific builder / contractor or other subcontractor / specialist with whom you would like to work?*
     If so, Name: N/A _____ Phone: _____

9.   *What portion of the project, if any, will be your responsibility?* Faux painting by Beth in tub surround area. _____

10. *What budget range have you established for your bath project?*
     ☐$5,000–$10,000 ☐$10,000–$20,000 ☐$20,000–$30,000 ☐$30,000–$50,000 ☒$50,000–$60,000 ☐$60,000–$75,000 ☐$75,000+

11. *How long do you intend to own the jobsite residence?* No plans at this time to move. _____

     a.   Is return on investment a primary concern? They would like to build value in their home. _____

     b.   Do you plan on renting the jobsite residence? No _____

12. *What family members will share in the final decision-making process?* Joint, Beth and Josh _____

13. *Would you like our firm to assist you in securing project financing?* ☐Yes ☒No

14. *What do you dislike most about your present bath?* Poor use of space, color of existing tile, small shower. _____
     _____

15. *What do you like most about your present bath?* Large window on west wall. _____
     _____

16. *Sustainable design ideas important to your family:*

☒Use of "Green" Products	General products made from recycled materials: ☐Cabinets ☐Counters ☐Floors ☐Walls ☐Building Materials	
	☒ Wood products supplied by environmentally responsible manufacturers _____	
☒Water usage:	☐Sustainable design details incorporated into the plan	
☒Water efficient fixtures: ☒Toilet ☐Bathtub ☒Shower		
☒Energy efficient lighting systems:		

17. *If you are remodeling:* Is there a room addition planned? ☐Yes ☒No

     a.   When was the house built? 1982 _____ How old is the present bath? 1982 _____

     b.   Are you considering relocating ☐windows ☒doors ☒walls in your new plan?

18. *If you are building a new home:*

     a.   Are you able to relocate ☐windows ☐doors ☐walls at this stage of construction? ☐Yes ☐No

     b.   Are you able to relocate walls at this stages of construction ☐Yes ☐No

19. *Is there a view from the bathroom to be considered:* ☒Yes ☐No

     a.   Sun exposure _____

     b.   From where in the bathroom should the view be visible? ☒Bathtub ☐Vanity ☐Shower ☐Other _____

     c.   What about privacy? Backs up to National Forest, not an issue. _____

Copyright 2006 by NKBA. All rights reserved. No part of this document may be reproduced in any form by photostat, microfilm, xerography, or any other means, or incorporated into any informational retrieval system, electronic or mechanical, or transmitted, in any form or by any means, without the prior consent of the copyright owner.

Specific Bath Questions

1. *Is this a* ☒Master ☐Children ☐Other Family Member ☐Guest ☐Special Area:_____ *bathroom?*
2. *How many bathrooms are in the home?* 2 1/2
3. *Who will use the bathroom?* Beth and Josh
4. *Characteristics of family members who use the bathroom*: Are you planning on enlarging your family while living here? ☐Yes ☐No

Name	Age	Handed	Height	Physical Limitations/Mobility Aids
1. Beth	48	☒R ☐L	5' 6"	
2. Josh	50	☒R ☐L	5' 10"	
3.		☐R ☐L		
4.		☐R ☐L		
5.		☐R ☐L		

5. *Personal Information about the bathroom*:
   a. Will more than one person be using the bathroom at the same time? Yes   How often? Daily
   b. What types of bathroom activities can be done in a shared bathroom space? Grooming, shower, bathing.
   c. What types of bathroom activities need to be done in private? toilet compartment
   d. How important is auditory privacy? Low   Are bathroom noises a problem? No
6. *Visitability*:
   a. Will this bathroom be used by visitors to the home? ☐Yes ☒No   How often?
   b. Will the visitors be children or adults? N/A
   c. Do any regular or frequent visitors have any physical limitation? No
7. *Do you prefer separate showering and bathing areas?* Not required
8. *Would you like to consider a tub that will accommodate more than one person?* yes
9. *Would you like to consider a shower that will accommodate more than one person?* yes
10. *Do you prefer the water closet and/or bidet be separate from the other fixtures, and placed in its own compartment?* Yes
11. *Checklist for Bathroom activities*:

Grooming Activities		Location					Person		
		Vanity / Lavatory	Dressing Table	Bathtub	Shower	Other Room	Person #1	Person #2	Person #3
Body:	Washing	☐	☐	☐	☒	☐	☒	☒	☐
	Shave - Face	☒	☐	☐	☐	☐	☐	☒	☐
	Shave - Body	☐	☐	☐	☒	☐	☒	☐	☐
	Apply Lotion	☐	☒	☐	☐	☐	☒	☐	☐
	Hair washing	☐	☐	☐	☒	☐	☒	☒	☐
Teeth:	Brush	☒	☐	☐	☐	☐	☒	☒	☐
	Floss	☒	☐	☐	☐	☐	☒	☒	☐
Nails:	Finger	☐	☒	☐	☐	☐	☒	☒	☐
	Toe	☐	☐	☐	☐	☒	☒	☒	☐
Cosmetics:	Apply	☐	☒	☐	☐	☐	☒	☐	☐
	Remove	☐	☒	☐	☐	☐	☒	☐	☐
Face:	Skin Care	☐	☒	☐	☐	☐	☒	☐	☐
Hair:	Blow Dry	☒	☐	☐	☐	☐	☒	☒	☐
	Brush / Style	☒	☐	☐	☐	☐	☒	☒	☐
	Color	☒	☐	☐	☐	☐	☒	☐	☐
	Cut / Trim	☐	☐	☐	☐	☐	☐	☐	☐
First Aid:	Treating cuts and burns	☒	☐	☐	☐	☐	☒	☒	☐
Hands:	Apply Lotion	☐	☒	☐	☐	☐	☒	☐	☐
	Wash	☒	☐	☐	☐	☐	☒	☒	☐
Medicines / Vitamins:		☐	☐	☐	☐	☒	☒	☒	☐

©2006 NKBA BMF9

Copyright 2006 by NKBA. All rights reserved. No part of this document may be reproduced in any form by photostat, microfilm, xerography, or any other means, or incorporated into any informational retrieval system, electronic or mechanical, or transmitted, in any form or by any means, without the prior consent of the copyright owner.

Bathing / Showering Activities		Location			Person		
		Bathtub	Shower	Other Room	Person #1	Person #2	Person #3
Bathing:	With Someone	☐	☐	☐	☐	☐	☐
	Assisting an Adult	☐	☐	☐	☐	☐	☐
	Bathing Pets	☐	☐	☐	☐	☐	☐
	Soaking / Relaxing	☒	☐	☐	☒	☐	☐
Showering:	With Someone	☐	☒	☐	☒	☒	☐
	Assisting an Adult	☐	☐	☐	☐	☐	☐
	Steam Showering	☐	☐	☐	☐	☐	☐
Sauna:	Relaxing	☐	☐	☒	☒	☒	☐
Other:		☐	☐	☐	☐	☐	☐
		☐	☐	☐	☐	☐	☐
		☐	☐	☐	☐	☐	☐

Toileting Activities	Person		
	Person #1	Person #2	Person #3
Assisting an Adult:	☐	☐	☐
Toileting:	☒	☒	☐
Personal Cleansing:	☐	☐	☐
Diaper Changing:	☐	☐	☐
Reading:	☐	☐	☐

Other Bathroom Activities	Location					Person		
	Vanity / Lavatory	Dressing Table	Bathtub	Shower	Other Room	Person #1	Person #2	Person #3
Display Collections	☐	☐	☒	☐	☐	☐	☐	☐
Undressing / Hamper	☒	☐	☐	☐	☐	☒	☒	☐
Dressing: Underwear / Sleep clothes	☐	☐	☐	☐	☒	☒	☒	☐
Dressing: "Street" Clothes:	☐	☐	☐	☐	☒	☒	☒	☐
Drink Beverages	☐	☐	☐	☐	☒	☒	☒	☐
Eat Snacks	☐	☐	☐	☐	☒	☒	☒	☐
Exercise w/o equipment	☐	☐	☐	☐	☒	☒	☒	☐
Exercise using equipment	☐	☐	☐	☐	☒	☒	☒	☐
Grow Plants	☐	☐	☒	☐	☐	☒	☐	☐
Laundry: Air Dry	☐	☐	☐	☐	☒	☐	☐	☐
Laundry: Hand-wash	☐	☐	☐	☐	☒	☐	☐	☐
Laundry: Machine Wash	☐	☐	☐	☐	☒	☐	☐	☐
Laundry: Sort / Fold	☐	☐	☐	☐	☒	☐	☐	☐
Listen to Music	☒	☐	☐	☐	☐	☒	☒	☐
Massage	☐	☐	☐	☐	☐	☐	☐	☐
Meditation	☐	☐	☐	☐	☐	☐	☐	☐
Personal Pampering	☒	☒	☐	☐	☐	☒	☒	☐
Exercise Equipment	☐	☐	☐	☐	☒	☐	☒	☐
Polish Shoes	☐	☐	☐	☐	☒	☐	☒	☐
Read: Books / Newspapers	☐	☐	☐	☐	☒	☒	☒	☐
Supervise Children	☐	☐	☐	☐	☐	☐	☐	☐
Talk on Telephone	☒	☒	☐	☐	☐	☐	☒	☒
Talking with People	☐	☐	☐	☐	☐	☐	☐	☐
Tanning / Sunning	☐	☐	☐	☐	☐	☐	☐	☐
Watch Television	☒	☒	☐	☐	☐	☒	☒	☐
Other:	☐	☐	☐	☐	☐	☐	☐	☐
	☐	☐	☐	☐	☐	☐	☐	☐

12. *What appliances do you plan on using in the bathroom:*

☒ Blowdryer ☒ Handheld ☐ Wall Mounted	☒ Electrical Toothbrush	☒ Radio/DVD/VCR	☐ Valet
	☒ Electrical Razor	☒ Television	☐ Washer & Dryer
	☒ Fireplace ☐ Wood Burning ☒ Gas	☒ Towel Warmer ☐ Hydronic (hot water) ☒ Electric	☐ Other:
☒ Curling Iron	☒ Hot Rollers	☒ Scale	☐ Other:

©2006 NKBA BMF9

Copyright 2006 by NKBA. All rights reserved. No part of this document may be reproduced in any form by photostat, microfilm, xerography, or any other means, or incorporated into any informational retrieval system, electronic or mechanical, or transmitted, in any form or by any means, without the prior consent of the copyright owner.

Storage Checklist

Item	User		Type of Equipment	Shelf / Drawer Space Required
Make-up Storage	(person #1)	☒Yes ☐No	Misc containers	Drawers at least 24"
	(person #2)	☐Yes ☒No		
Shaving Storage	(person #1)	☐Yes ☒No		
	(person #2)	☒Yes ☐No	Electric Shaver and misc containers	3 Shelves at least 8" deep
Hair Grooming Equipment	(person #1)	☒Yes ☐No	Rollers, brushes, ect.	18" to 24' Drawer Storage
	(person #2)	☒Yes ☐No	Brush and hair spray	12" to 18" Shelf Space
Hand and Foot Grooming Equip	(person #1)	☒Yes ☐No	Drawer	Small Drawer
	(person #2)	☐Yes ☒No		
Personal Hygiene Equipment	(person #1)	☒Yes ☐No	Basic Supplies	Drawers at least 24"
	(person #2)	☐Yes ☒No		
Medicine / First Aid		☒Yes ☐No	Basic small packages and liquid containers	18" to 24' Shelf Storage
Bathroom Paper Product Storage		☒Yes ☐No	Toilet paper and tissue	48" to 72' Shelf Storage
Bath Towel Storage		☒Yes ☐No	Include bath sheets	72' to 96" Shelf Storage
Household Bedroom Linen		☐Yes ☒No		
Personal Pampering Equip	(person #1)	☒Yes ☐No	At Vanity/Dressing Area	Drawers at least 36"
	(person #2)	☐Yes ☒No		
	(person #3)	☐Yes ☒No		
	(person #4)	☐Yes ☐No		
Exercise Equipment	(person #1)	☐Yes ☒No		
	(person #2)	☐Yes ☒No		
	(person #3)	☐Yes ☒No		
	(person #4)	☐Yes ☒No		
Pet Grooming / Bathing Area		☐Yes ☒No		
Cleaning Supply Storage		☒Yes ☐No	Under vanity sink	Bottom of vanity
Shoe Polishing Paraphemalia		☐Yes ☒No		

Item	User				
Other _____	Hanging	☐Yes ☒No	Shelf Lengh:	Double Pole: ☐	Single Pole: ☐
_____	Shoes	# of Pairs _____	Boxed: ☐Yes ☐No	Shelf Length:_____	
_____	Folded Clothing	# of Drawers / Pull-outs_____			
_____	Accessories	☐Yes ☐No	Types:_____	Wall Space for Racks:_____	
_____	Hats	Rack: ☐Yes ☐No	Boxes: ☐Yes ☐No	Shelf Space:_____	
_____	Full Length Mirror	☒Yes ☐No			
Other _____	Hanging	☐Yes ☐No	Shelf Length:	Double Pole: ☐	Single Pole: ☐
_____	Shoes	# of Pairs_____	Boxed: ☐Yes ☐No	Shelf Length:_____	
_____	Folded Clothing	# of Drawers:_____			
_____	Accessories	☐Yes ☐No	Types:		
_____	Hats	Rack: ☐Yes ☐No	Boxes: ☐Yes ☐No		
_____	Full Length Mirror	☒Yes ☐No			

©2006 NKBA BMF9

Copyright 2006 by NKBA. All rights reserved. No part of this document may be reproduced in any form by photostat, microfilm, xerography, or any other means, or incorporated into any informational hygrieval retrieval system, electronic or mechanical, or transmitted, in any form or by any means, without the prior consent of the copyright owner.

Storage Checklist (Continued)

Laundry Facilities	☐Yes ☒No	Equipment Size:
Mini Kitchen	☒Yes ☐No	What Type of Equipment? ☒Bar Sink ☒Coffeemaker ☐Cooktop ☒Microwave ☒Refrigerator ☐ Other:_____ ☐Other:_____
Other:		

Design Information

1. *What type of feeling would you like your new bathroom space to have? Have you created a scrapbook of notes, photos and ideas of bathrooms that you like?*

   ☐American Country ☐Asian / Warm Contemporary ☒Old World European ☐Sleek Contemporary

   ☐American Formal ☐Craftsman / Arts and Crafts ☐Personal Design Statement (Eclectic) ☐Traditional

   They have pictures from bed and breakfast locations in Europe the they would like to duplicate._____
   _____
   _____
   _____
   _____

2. *What colors do you like?* Blue and cream colors_____
   And dislike? Red and orange_____
   What colors are you considering for you new bathroom? Blue and cream colors_____
   What are the color preferences of other family members? Green_____

3. *Are there specific materials, fixtures, cabinetry or other features that you have pre-selected and want included in the project?*_____
   Walls with texture, bidet, old world look in vanities_____

4. *Design Notes*: The large bath space is not planned very well. Large vanitys but without drawers or shelving. Large toilet compartmet but poor use of space. Use the window as a focal point. so thought about ageing in place._____
   _____
   _____
   _____

Special Details:

©2006 NKBA BMF9

Copyright 2006 by NKBA. All rights reserved. No part of this document may be reproduced in any form by photostat, microfilm, xerography, or any other means, or incorporated into any informational retrieval system, electronic or mechanical, or transmitted, in any form or by any means, without the prior consent of the copyright owner.

Cabinetry

Key: BS= Bath Specialist
O= Owner OA= Owners Agent

Style	Base	Wall	Tall
Furniture (Unfitted)	☒	☒	☒
Built-In (Fitted)	☐	☐	☐
Construction			
Framed	☒	☒	☒
Frameless	☐	☐	☐
Door Type			
Full Overlay	☐	☐	☐
Partial Overlay	☐	☐	☐
Lip	☐	☐	☐
Inset	☒	☒	☒
Hardware			
Knob	☐	☒	☒
Pull	☒	☐	☒
Finger Pull	☐	☐	☐
Material	☐	☐	☐

Source

Use Existing: ☐Yes ☒No
Furnished by: BS ☒ O/OA ☐
Installed by: BS ☒ O/OA ☐

Face Material	Base	Wall	Tall
Wood-Species	☒	☒	☒
Laminate	☐	☐	☐
Paint	☐	☐	☐
Acrylic	☐	☐	☐
Metal	☐	☐	☐
Other: Walnut	☐	☐	☐
Door Style			
Wellsley	☒	☒	☒
	☐	☐	☐
	☐	☐	☐
Color and Finish			
Medium Walnut Stain	☒	☐	☒
Med. Walnut Stain w/glaze	☐	☒	☐
	☐	☐	☐
	☐	☐	☐

Soffit / Fascia

Use Existing: ☐Yes ☒No
Furnished by: BS ☒ O/OA ☐
Installed by: BS ☒ O/OA ☐

Fascia / Soffit Construction

☐Open ☒Extended ☐Flush ☐Recessed ☐Remove

☐Other: Soffit only over vanities

Fascia / Soffit Materials

☐Wallpaper ☐Wood ☐Display Rail ☒Paint ☐Lighted

☐Cornice ☐Other:

Surfaces

Key: BS= Bath Specialist
O= Owner OA= Owners Agent

Material	Vanity	Shower Walls	Tub Platform	Other
Concrete	☐	☐	☐	
Cultured Marble	☐	☐	☐	
Decorative Laminate	☐	☐	☐	
Engineered Stone (Quartz)	☐	☐	☐	
Granite	☐	☐	☐	
Marble	☒	☒	☒	
Solid Surface	☐	☐	☐	
Tile	☐	☐	☐	
Size				
Grout				
Wood	☐	☐	☐	
Other Stone:				
Special Notes				

Source

Use Existing: ☐Yes ☒No
Furnished by: BS ☒ O/OA ☐
Installed by: BS ☒ O/OA ☐

Edge Treatment	Vanity	Shower Walls	Tub Platform	Other
Thickness	3/4"	1/2"	1/2"	
Shape:				
Bevel	☐	☐	☐	
Ogee	☐	☐	☐	
Bull Nose Full	☒	☐	☐	
½ Full	☐	☐	☐	
Square	☐	☐	☐	
Other:				
Backsplash				
Height	Full			
End Splash Sides				
Countertop ext. over Water Closet	N/A			
Special Notes				

©2006 NKBA BMF9

Copyright 2006 by NKBA. All rights reserved. No part of this document may be reproduced in any form by photostat, microfilm, xerography, or any other means, or incorporated into any informational retrieval system, electronic or mechanical, or transmitted, in any form or by any means, without the prior consent of the copyright owner.

Bath Fixtures & Fittings - Water Closet

Use Existing	Furnished by		Installed by	
☐Yes ☒No	BS ☒	O/OA ☐	BS ☒	O/OA ☐

☐ 1 Piece Low Profile		☒ 2 Piece Standard Height	Color: Cream	
☐ Wall Hung		☒ Elongated Seat	Seat: Cream	
☐ Round Seat		☐ Other_____	Trip Lever Finish: Brass	
☐ Comfort Height		☐ Other_____	Stop & Supply Finish: Brass	

Bath Fixtures & Fittings - Bidet / Bidet Seat

Use Existing	Furnished by		Installed by	
☐Yes ☒No	BS ☒	O/OA ☐	BS ☒	O/OA ☐

☐ Vertical Spray Vacuum Breaker	Color: Cream	Other:_____	
☒ Horizontal Spray	Faucet Finish: Brass	Other:_____	

Bath Fixtures & Fittings - Bathtub

Use Existing	Furnished by		Installed by	
☐Yes ☒No	BS ☒	O/OA ☐	BS ☒	O/OA ☐

Material				Placement		
☒Cast Iron	☐Fiberglass	☐Ceramic Tile	☐Cult Marble	☒Left Drain		☐Right Drain
☐Steel	☐Acrylic	☐__	☐_____	**Fitting #1**		
Configuration				Type: #7334	Finish: Brass	Location: L/ front
☒Platform	☐Skirted	☐Platform w/ Steps	☐Free Standing	**Fitting #2**		
				Type: #7644	Finish: Brass	Location: R/Front

Bath Fixtures & Fittings - Shower

Use Existing	Furnished by		Installed by	
☐Yes ☒No	BS ☒	O/OA ☐	BS ☒	O/OA ☐

Fabricated			Fittings			
☐1 Piece		☐Multiple Piece	Shower #1	Valve Type: #6641	Head Type: Rain	Finish: Brass
Custom			Shower #2	Valve Type: #6670	Head Type: Rain	Finish: Brass
Shower Wall Material: Marble Walls	Shower Floor/ Pan Material: Tile	Bench Seat Material: Teak	Shower #3	Valve Type:	Head Type:	Finish:
Height: 84"			Shower #4- Body Sprays	Finish: Brass		
			Shower #5- Hand-Held	Finish: Brass		
			Diverter	Finish: Brass		
Configuration						
Drain	Finish: Brass		Grooming	Recess:	Size:	
Bench	Size: 15' Min		Other			

Copyright 2006 by NKBA. All rights reserved. No part of this document may be reproduced in any form by photostat, microfilm, xerography, or any other means, or incorporated into any informational retrieval system, electronic or mechanical, or transmitted, in any form or by any means, without the prior consent of the copyright owner.

471

Bath Fixtures & Fittings - Lavatory

Use Existing	Furnished by		Installed by	
☐Yes ☒No	BS ☒	O/OA ☐	BS ☒	O/OA ☐

Material				Fittings	
☒Porcelain	☐Glass	☐Cast Iron	☐__	☐4" Centers	☐8" Centers
☐Stainless Steel	☐Decorative Metal	☐Composition	☐__	☐Single Hole	☒Wall Mounted

Configuration				Finish
☐Pedestal/Trap Cover	☐Rimmed	☒Under-Counter	☐Wall Hung	☒Cream
☐Vessel	☐Self-Rimmed	☐Integral	☐Other:_____	☐

Ventilation

Use Existing	Furnished by		Installed by	
☐Yes ☒No	BS ☒	O/OA ☐	BS ☒	O/OA ☐
☐Fan	☒Fan, Light (Combo)	☐Fan, Light, Heat (Combo)	☐Switch	☒Timer

CFM Capacity: 80-100 | Duct Work Space: Through ceiling

Heating

Use Existing	Furnished by		Installed by	
☐Yes ☒No	BS ☒	O/OA ☐	BS ☐	O/OA ☐
☒Auxiliary	☒Timer	Placement: Mid room		
☐Switch				

Enclosures (Steam Door/s, Shower, Doors, Drapes, Etc.)

Use Existing	Furnished by		Installed by	
☐Yes ☒No	BS ☒	O/OA ☐	BS ☒	O/OA ☐

Tub	Finish:	Size:	Type:	Material:
Shower	Finish: Frosted	Size: TBD	Type: Beveled	Material: Glass
Steam	Finish:	Size:	Type:	Material:
Sauna	Finish:	Size:	Type:	Material:

Curtain Rod Finish: | Size: | Curtains (Color) | Size:

Light Fixtures

Use Existing	Furnished by		Installed by	
☐Yes ☒No	BS ☒	O/OA ☐	BS ☒	O/OA ☐

General				Ambient			
☐Incandescent	☐Halogen	☒Fluorescent	☐Xenon	☒Cove	☐Recessed	☐Pendant	☐Surface Mounted
Decorative				☐Track	☐Incandescent	☐Halogen	☒Fluorescent
☐Incandescent	☐Halogen	☐Fluorescent	☐Xenon	**Special Details**			
Task Lighting							
☐Incandescent	☐Halogen	☒Fluorescent	☐Xenon				

©2006 NKBA BMF9   Page 9 of 19

Copyright 2006 by NKBA. All rights reserved. No part of this document may be reproduced in any form by photostat, microfilm, xerography, or any other means, or incorporated into any informational retrieval system, electronic or mechanical, or transmitted, in any form or by any means, without the prior consent of the copyright owner.

Accessories

Use Existing	Furnished by		Installed by	
☐Yes ☒No	BS ☒	O/OA ☐	BS ☒	O/OA ☐

Glass Shelves	Qty: 4		Support: Brass	Size: 30"	
	Finish: Srd		Edge Treatment: Rounded		
Medicine Cabinet	Qty: 1	☐Surface Mount	☒Recessed	Size: ☐	
	Finish: Std	Mirror Size: ☐	Mirror 30"x36"		
Mirror	Qty: 2	☒Surface Mount	☐Frame	Full width over vanity	
Towel Bars	Qty: 3	Finish: Brass	Size: 24"	No: JB24700	
Towel Rings	Qty: 2	Finish: Brass	Size: 6"	No: JB06700	
Robe Hooks	Qty: 4	Finish: Brass	Size: #RH8700	No: JBRH8700	
Tub Soap Dish	Qty: 1	☐Surface Mount	☒Recessed	Finish: Brass	Placement: Center Back Deck
Shower Soap Dish	Qty: 1	☐Surface Mount	☒Recessed	Finish: Brass	Placement: Center Rear
Bidet Soap Dish	Qty: 1	☒Surface Mount	☐Recessed	Finish: Brass	Placement: Rt of center
Lavatory Soap Dish	Qty: N/A	☐Surface Mount	☐Recessed	Finish:	Placement:
Tub Grab Bars	Qty: 1	Finish: Brass		Placement: Rt front Deck	
Toilet Grab Bars	Qty: N/A	Finish:		Placement:	
Paper Holder	Qty: 1	☐Surface Mount	☒Recessed	Finish: Brass	Placement: Right side
Magazine Rack	Qty: N/A	☐Surface Mount	☐Recessed	Finish:	Placement:
Soap/Lotion Dispenser	Qty: N/A	Finish:		Placement:	
Tumbler Holder	Qty: N/A	Finish:		Placement:	
Toothbrush Holder	Qty: N/A	Finish:		Placement:	
TV	Qty: 1	Finish: N/A		Placement: Behind Mirroe in closet on shelf	

Sauna

Use Existing	Furnished by		Installed by	
☐Yes ☒No	BS ☐	O/OA ☐	BS ☐	O/OA ☐
Capacity:	Interior:	Style:	Heater:	
Timer Location:	Wall Material:	Floor Material:	Other: Not part of project	

Steam Bath

Use Existing	Furnished by		Installed by	
☐Yes ☒No	BS ☐	O/OA ☐	BS ☐	O/OA ☐
☐Tub ☐Shower	Steam Generator Location:	Timer Location:	Wall Material:	Floor Material:

Copyright 2006 by NKBA. All rights reserved. No part of this document may be reproduced in any form by photostat, microfilm, xerography, or any other means, or incorporated into any informational retrieval system, electronic or mechanical, or transmitted, in any form or by any means, without the prior consent of the copyright owner.

Exercise Equipment

Treadmill	Size:	Clearance Required: 30 sq. ft
Free Weights	Size:	Clearance Required: 20-30 sq. ft.
Bikes, Recumbent & Upright	Size:	Clearance Required: 10 sq. ft.
Rowing Machines	Size:	Clearance Required: 20 sq. ft.
Stair Climbers	Size:	Clearance Required: 10 to 20 sq. ft.
Ski Machines	Size:	Clearance Required: 25 sq. ft.
Single-Station Gym	Size:	Clearance Required: 35 sq. ft.
Multi-Station Gym	Size:	Clearance Required: 50 to 200 sq. ft.
Yoga Matte	Size:	Clearance Required:

Flooring

Use Existing	Furnished by		Installed by	
☐Yes ☒No	BS ☒	O/OA ☐	BS ☒	O/OA ☐

Floor Preparation

☒Removal:
☒Leveling:
☒Shim:
☐Subfloor Material:
☒Underlayment:
☒Baseboard:
☒Transition Treatment

Floor Covering

Material

☐	Bamboo	☐	Carpet	☒	Ceramic Tile	☐	Cork
☐	Laminate	☐	Linoleum	☐	Vinyl-Sheet	☐	Vinyl-Tile
☐	Wood	☐	Wood-Engineered	☐	Stone	☐	Other

Color or Pattern:

Describe: Xville Patter # 564008

Windows

Check all that apply.
Slider = S   Casement = C   Double-Hung = DH   Skylight = SL   Bow = BO   Bay = BA
Vinyl = V   Aluminum = A   Aluminum Clad = AC   Wood = W   Glass Block = GB

Use Existing	Furnished by		Installed by	
☒Yes ☐No	KS ☐	O/OA ☐	KS ☐	O/OA ☐

Interior Wall Patch:	Exterior Wall Patch:	Sink Vent Relocation: As required

Window #	Configuration	New Windows Sizes	
1	Wood /Picture window	No changes to window	Screen: ☐Yes ☒No
			Screen: ☐Yes ☐No
			Screen: ☐Yes ☐No
			Screen: ☐Yes ☐No
			Screen: ☐Yes ☐No
			Screen: ☐Yes ☐No

Copyright 2006 by NKBA. All rights reserved. No part of this document may be reproduced in any form by photostat, microfilm, xerography, or any other means, or incorporated into any informational retrieval system, electronic or mechanical, or transmitted, in any form or by any means, without the prior consent of the copyright owner.

Doors

Check all that apply.
Bi-Fold = BF   Slider = S   Pocket = P   French = F   Swing = SW
Solid Core = SC   Steel = ST   Hollow Core = HC

☒Yes ☐No

	Furnished by		Installed by	
	KS ☒	O/OA ☐	KS ☒	O/OA ☐

Door #	Configuration	Hinge	Size	Screen
1	SW	☒Yes ☐No	3068 New door	Screen: ☐Yes ☒No
2	S	☐Yes ☒No	6068 New door	Screen: ☒Yes ☐No
3	S	☒Yes ☐No	3068 To toilet and Bidet area	Screen: ☐Yes ☐No
		☐Yes ☐No		Screen: ☐Yes ☐No
		☐Yes ☐No		Screen: ☐Yes ☐No
		☐Yes ☐No		Screen: ☐Yes ☐No
		☐Yes ☐No		Screen: ☐Yes ☐No
		☐Yes ☐No		Screen: ☐Yes ☐No

Hardware Finish: Brass   ☐Passage ☒Privacy ☐Knob ☒Lever

Decorative Surfaces

Use Existing	Furnished by		Installed by	
☐Yes ☒No	BS ☒	O/OA ☐	BS ☒	O/OA ☐

Wall Preparation	☒New Plaster/Drywall	☐Clean	☐Patch Exist	☒Remove Exist. Covering:	
Wall Finish	☒New Plaster/Drywall	☐Clean	☐Patch Exist	☒Remove Exist. Covering:	
Ceiling Finish	☒Paint	☐Wallpaper	☐Suspended	☐Vaulted	☐Other:_____
Ceiling Preparation	☒New Plaster / Drywall	☐Clean	☒Patch Exist	☐Remove Existing Covering	
	Other:_____		Repairs:_____		
Window Treatment	☐Blinds	☐Fabric	☒Shutters	Other:_____	

©2006 NKBA BMF9

Copyright 2006 by NKBA. All rights reserved. No part of this document may be reproduced in any form by photostat, microfilm, xerography, or any other means, or incorporated into any informational retrieval system, electronic or mechanical, or transmitted, in any form or by any means, without the prior consent of the copyright owner.

Construction	Source			Category
	Use	Responsibility		
	Existing	BS	O / OA	
HVAC Details: Reroute ductwork to new location	☒	☒	☐	Air Conditioning System Age: _6 Years_ Planned Improvements: _None at this time_ Heating System Age: _Same as above_ Planned Improvements: _Same_ Bathroom Exhaust Fan Age: _Replace existing_ Planned Improvements:_____
Electrical Work: Update to code and new circuits as required. Owners firm to do all electrical. BS to supply plan.	☐	☐	☒	New Service Panel: _As neededAs needed_ Code Updates: _As nded_ Modifications to Exist. Service: _As nded_ Heated Floor: ☒Yes ☐No Heated Towel Bar: ☐Yes ☒No
Plumbing: **As per plan**	☐	☒	☐	New Rough-In Requirements: _As needed_ New Drainage Requirements: _As per plan_ New Vent Stack Requirements: _As needed_ Modifications to Exist. Lines: _As needed_
General Carpentry: By BS	☐	☒	☐	**Demolition Work** Exist. Fixture and Equip. Removal: _Save old cabinetry_ Trash Removal: _To trash container at rt of driveway_ **Reconstruction Work (Except as previously noted.)** Widows: _N/A_ Doors: _As noted_ Interior Walls: _As noted_ Exterior Walls: _At sliding door opening_ Insulated: _N/A_ Cabinet Install. / Trim-Out: _As required_
Miscellaneous Work: As needed	☐	☒	☐	Jobsite / Room Clean-up: _Broom clean each day_ Building Permits: _All required except electrical_ Structural Engineering / Architectural Fees: _If required_ Inspection Fees: _As required_ Jobsite Delivery: _To rt side of garage_ Other: _Remove construction trailer each weekend._ _Neighborhood requirement. By 7:00PM Friday to 6:00AM_ _Monday_

Copyright 2006 by NKBA. All rights reserved. No part of this document may be reproduced in any form by photostat, microfilm, xerography, or any other means, or incorporated into any informational retrieval system, electronic or mechanical, or transmitted, in any form or by any means, without the prior consent of the copyright owner.

Existing Construction Details

1. *Age of Home*: Build in 1982   *Access Roads to Home:* All min two lane paved
   Delivery Truck Clearances: Lowest underpass 15'6"   *Elevator Size Limitations:* N/A
   Access to Bath: ☒Through House ☐Exterior Access

2. *Type of Neighborhood:*
   ☐Rural ☐Suburban ☐Urban ☐Historic ☐Mixed Use ☐Multi-Family ☒Gated Community ☐Planned Development

3. *Type of Home:*
   ☒Single Family ☐Duplex ☐Townhouse ☐Condominium ☐Apartment / Flat ☐Other:_____

4. *Structure of Home:*
   ☒One Story ☐Two-Story ☐Three-Story ☐Ranch ☐Split-Level ☐Split-Foyer/Raised Ranch ☐Other:_____

5. *Approximate Size of Home:* 2,3000 sq. ft.

6. *Style of Home (Exterior):* Colonial

7. *Is the home historic?* ☐Yes ☒No   What time period?_____
   Are there historic covenants or restrictions affecting the home? No, only development restrictions concerning parking of construction vehicals.
   _____

8. *Is the home part of a Homeowner's Association?* ☒Yes ☐No
   Are there Homeowner's Association covenants or restrictions affecting the home? ☒Yes ☐No   See above.
   _____

9. *Style of Home (Interior)*
   Colors: White, off white to soft grays and power blues.
   Materials: Paint and some wall paper
   Furniture: Mixed
   Accessories: Mixed
   Other:_____
   _____
   _____

10. *Room Below Bathroom* Unfinished basement   *Room Above Bathroom* Unfinished attic

Copyright 2006 by NKBA. All rights reserved. No part of this document may be reproduced in any form by photostat, microfilm, xerography, or any other means, or incorporated into any informational retrieval system, electronic or mechanical, or transmitted, in any form or by any means, without the prior consent of the copyright owner.

Existing Construction Details- continued

11. *Condition of* –

Surface Walls Good

Floors: Good

Ceilings: Good

Soffit/Fascia: N/A

Squareness of Corners: Good   Parallel Wall to Within ¾) Yes

Is there any hazardous material to be removed? None noted

12. *Construction of Floor:* ☐Slab ☒Frame

13. *Direction of Floor Joists:* ☐Parallel to Longest Bathroom Wall ☒Perpendicular to Bathroom Longest Wall   Joist Height: 2 x 10

14. *Exterior:* ☒Brick ☐Aluminum ☐Stucco ☐Wood ☐Other:

15. *Interior:* ☒Drywall ☐Lath & Plaster ☐Wood ☐Other:

16. *Windows Can Be Changed:* ☐Yes ☒No   Doors Can Be Relocated: ☒Yes ☐No   Walls Can Be Relocated: ☒Yes ☐No

17. *Windows:* ☐Sliders ☐Double-Hung ☐Skylights ☐Casement ☐Greenhouse ☐Bow/Bay ☒ Other: Picture

18. *Sewage System:* ☒City Service ☐Septic System ☐Other:

19. *Type of Roof Material:* Tile   *Age of Roof* Existing

Access:

Can Equipment Fit Into The Room? Large items after opening for exterior sliding glass door.

Basement: Some storage OK   Attic: No storage at all   Crawl Space: N/A

Material Storage: In Basement   Trash Collection Area: Right of driveway BS to provide container.

HVAC: Describe Existing System: Heating: Central H/A   Ventilation: Through roof   Air Conditioning: Central H/A

Plumbing:

Location of Existing Vent Stack: Main stack behind toilet will be difficult to relocate.   Type of Trap: P

Add Additional Line: As needed. OK to drop below joists in basement.

Electrical

GFCI Existing: ☒Yes ☐No

New Wiring Access: ☐Hard ☒Average ☐Easy   Number of Open Circuits for Expansion: 6

Existing Electrical Service Capacity: 200 amp   Number of 120V Circuits: 4 open   Number of 240V Circuits: 1 open

Copyright 2006 by NKBA. All rights reserved. No part of this document may be reproduced in any form by photostat, microfilm, xerography, or any other means, or incorporated into any informational retrieval system, electronic or mechanical, or transmitted, in any form or by any means, without the prior consent of the copyright owner.

Existing Plumbing Center Lines

21 ¹/₂"   21 ¹/₂"

12"

21"   47 ¹/₂"   21"

Using new
fixtures

Water Closet   Bidet
   Width: <u>N/A</u>   <u>N/A</u>
   Height: <u>N/A</u>   <u>N/A</u>
   Depth: <u>N/A</u>   <u>N/A</u>
Type of W.C.: Wall Hung☐ 2 Piece☐ 1 Piece☐
   Wall Hung: Width: <u>N/A</u> Height: <u>N/A</u>
Distance Tank for Walls: <u>N/A</u>
Soil Stack Location: <u>Behind existing toilet</u>
Water Supply Height: <u>9"AFF</u> Of Floor: _____

Lavatory
   Water Supply: Floor☒ Wall☐
   Drain out of: Floor☐ Wall☒
   Bottom of Trap to Floor: <u>12"</u>
Type of Lavatory: Wall Hung☐ In Vanity☐ Pedestal☐
   Wall Mount: Width: <u>N/A</u> Height: _____
Vanity: Width: <u>N/A</u> Height: _____ Depth: _____
   Vent Pipe Location: <u>Behind existing lavs</u>

Tub   Shower
   Width: <u>N/A</u>   <u>N/A</u>
   Height: <u>N/A</u>   <u>N/A</u>
   Depth: <u>N/A</u>   <u>N/A</u>
Tub/Shower Material: Cast Iron☐   Steel☐   Fiberglass☐   Other☐
Tub/Shower Surround: Yes☐   No☐
   Surround Material: Tub_____   Shower_____
   Surround With: _____ Height: _____ Width: _____
Shower Stub Out Height: _____
Plumbing Access Below: Yes☒   No☐
Type of Drain: Cast Iron☐   Copper☐   Plastic☒
Type of Trap: Drum☐   P☒
Bathroom on: First Floor☒   Second Floor☐   Other☐ _____

©2006 NKBA BMF9

Copyright 2006 by NKBA. All rights reserved. No part of this document may be reproduced in any form by photostat, microfilm, xerography, or any other means, or incorporated into any informational retrieval system, electronic or mechanical, or transmitted, in any form or by any means, without the prior consent of the copyright owner.

Existing Construction Details

Doors							
No.	A	B	C	D	E	F	G
1	96"	81"	32"	2 1/4"	49 3/4"	36 1/4"	77 3/4"
2	N/A						

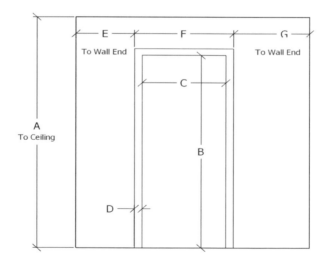

Copyright 2006 by NKBA. All rights reserved. No part of this document may be reproduced in any form by photostat, microfilm, xerography, or any other means, or incorporated into any informational retrieval system, electronic or mechanical, or transmitted, in any form or by any means, without the prior consent of the copyright owner.

Bath Planning

Existing Construction Details (continued)

				Windows					
No.	A	B	C	D	E	F	G	H	I
1	96"	42 1/2"	41 1/4"	2 1/4"	51 1/4"	44 3/4"	45"	45 3/4"	32 3/4"

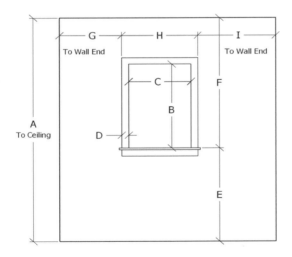

©2006 NKBA BMF9

Copyright 2006 by NKBA. All rights reserved. No part of this document may be reproduced in any form by photostat, microfilm, xerography, or any other means, or incorporated into any informational retrieval system, electronic or mechanical, or transmitted, in any form or by any means, without the prior consent of the copyright owner.

Existing Mechanical Details

Register or Fan							
No.	A	B	C	D	E	F	G
1	96"	153"	5¹/₄"	5"	49¹/₂"	5¹/₄"	62³/₄"

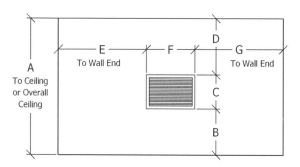

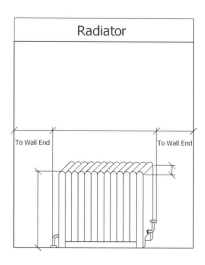

Radiator

Baseboard Heat

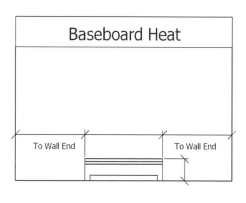

Copyright 2006 by NKBA. All rights reserved. No part of this document may be reproduced in any form by photostat, microfilm, xerography, or any other means, or incorporated into any informational retrieval system, electronic or mechanical, or transmitted, in any form or by any means, without the prior consent of the copyright owner.

LIST OF PHOTOS

LIST OF DRAWINGS, FORMS, ILLUSTRATIONS AND TABLES

Chapter 6

Chapter 3

American Lung Association
61 Broadway, 6th Floor
NY, NY 10006
www.lungusa.org

Canada Mortgage and Housing Corp.
Housing Information Center
700 Montreal Road
Ottawa, ON, Canada K1A 0P7
www.cmhc-schl.gc.ca

Children's Environmental Health Network
110 Maryland Avenue NE, Suite 505
Washington, DC 20002
www.cehn.org

Environmental Health Center, National Safety
Council
1121 Spring Lake Drive
Itasca, IL 60143-3201
www.nsc.org/ehc.htm

Health Environments and Consumer Safety,
Health Canada
Brooke Claxton Building
Ottawa, ON, Canada K1A 0K9
www.hc-sc.gc.ca/

Healthy Indoor Air for America's Homes
Montana State University Extension Service, Taylor Hall
Bozeman, MT 59717
www.heathyindoorair.org

Help Yourself to a Healthy Home
(An Environmental Risk-Assessment Guide
for the Home)
303 Hiram Smith Hall
1545 Observatory Drive
Madison, WI 53706
www.uwex.edu/homeasyst/

National Center for Environmental Health
Centers for Disease Control
1600 Clifton Rd.
Atlanta, GA 30333
www.cdc.gov/nceh

National Center for Lead-Safe Housing
www.leadsafehousing.org

National Institute of Environmental Health
Sciences
111 T.W. Alexander Drive
Research Triangle Park, NC 27709
www.niehs.nih.gov

U.S. Environmental Protection Agency
Ariel Rios Building
1200 Pennsylvania Avenue, N.W.
Washington, DC 20460
www.epa.gov

U.S. Green Building Council
1015 18th Street, NW, Suite 508
Washington, DC 20036
www.usgbc.org

Water Quality Association
International Headquarters & Laboratory
4151 Naperville Road
Lisle, IL 60532-3696
www.wqa.org

Chapter 4

Barrier Free Architecturals, Inc.
2700 Dufferin St., Unit 24
Toronto, ON, Canada M6B 4J3
www.barrierfree.org

U.S. Access Board
1331 F. Street, NW
Suite 1000
Washington, DC 20004-1111
www.access-board.gov

U.S. Department of Housing and Urban Development
Tech. assistance on Section 504
& Fair Housing: 800-827-5005
Publications Center: 800-767-7468
www.hud.gov/

Chapter 9

AARP American Association of Retired Persons
601 E Street NW
Washington, DC 20049
www.aarp.org

Abledata
8630 Fenton Street, Suite 930
Silver Spring, MD 20910
www.abledata.com

Access One
25679 Gramford Avenue
Wyoming, MN 55092
www.beyondbarriers.com

ADA & IT Technical Assistant Centers
www.adata.org

Adaptive Environments
374 Congress Street, Suite 301
Boston, MA 02210
www.adaptiveenvironments.org

Alzheimer's Association
225 North Michigan Avenue, Suite 1700
Chicago, IL 60601-7633
http://www.alz.org

Alzheimer's Disease Education & Referral Center
ADEAR Center
P.O. Box 8250
Silver Spring, MD 20907-8250
www.alzheimers.org

American Foundation for the Blind
11 Penn Plaza, Suite 300
New York, NY 10001
www.afb.org

American Heart Association National Center
7272 Greenville Avenue
Dallas, TX 75231
http://www.americanheart.org

American National Standards Institute
1819 L Street, NW, 6th floor
Washington, D.C., 20036
www.ansi.org

American Occupational Therapy Association
4720 Montgomery Lane
P.O. Box 31220
Bethesda, MD 20850
www.aota.org

American Stroke Association
National Center
7272 Greenville Avenue
Dallas, TX 75231
http://www.strokeassociation.org

Amputee Coalition of America
900 East Hill Avenue, Suite 285
Knoxville, TN 37915-2568
www.amputee-coalition.org

Area Agencies on Aging
www.aoa.dhhs.gov/agingsites/state.html

Arthritis Foundation
1330 West Peachtree Street
P.O. Box 7669
Atlanta, GA 30309
www.arthritis.org

Center for Inclusive Design and Environmental Access (IDEA Center)
School of Architecture and Planning
University of Buffalo
378 Hayes Hall
3435 Main Street
Buffalo, NY 14214-3087
www.ap.buffalo.edu/idea/

The Center for Universal Design
North Carolina State University
50 Pullen Road
Brooks Hall, Room 104
Campus Box 8613
Raleigh, NC 27695
www.design.ncsu.edu:8120/cud

Council for Exceptional Children
1110 North Glebe Road, Suite 300
Arlington, VA 22201
www.cec.sped.org

Cystic Fibrosis Foundation
6931 Arlington Road
Bethesda, MD 20814
www.cff.org

Disability Rights Education Defense Fund
1730 M Street N.W. Suite 801
Washington, DC 20036
http://www.dredf.org

Disabled American Veterans
807 Maine Ave., S.W.
Washington, D.C. 20024
http://www.dav.org

Easter Seal Society
230 West Monroe Street, Suite 1800
Chicago, IL 60606
http://www.easter-seals.org

Eldercare Locator
c/o Administration on Aging
220 Independence Avenue SW
Washington, DC 20201
www.eldercare.gov

Harris Communications, Inc.
15155 Technology Drive
Eden Prairie, MN 55344-2277
www.harriscomm.com

Home Modification List Serve
Homemodification-list@listserv.acsu.buffalo.edu

Independent Living Research Utilization Project
2323 South Shepard Street, Suite 1000
Houston, TX 77019
http://www.ilru.org

Lifease Inc.
2451 15th St N.W., Suite D
New Brighton, MN 55112
http://www.lifease.com

Lighthouse International
111 East 59th Street
New York, N.Y. 10022-1202
www.lighthouse.org

Muscular Dystrophy Association
3300 East Sunrise Drive
Tucson, AZ 85718
http://www.mdausa.org

National Association of the Deaf
814 Thayer Avenue
Silver Spring, MD 20910-4500
http://www.nad.org

National Council on Independent Living
1916 Wilson Boulevard, Suite 209
Arlington, VA 22201
http://www.ncil.org

National Institute on Aging
Building 31, Room 5C27
31 Center Drive, MSC 2292
Bethesda, MD 20892
http://www.nia.nih.gov/

National Institute on Deafness and Other
Communication Disorders
National Institutes of Health
31 Center Drive, MSC 2320
Bethesda, MD USA 20892-2320
http://www.nidcd.nih.gov

National Institute on Disability and Rehabilitation Research
US Department of Education
400 Maryland Avenue, S.W.
Washington, DC 20202-2572
www.ed.gov/about/offices/list/osers/nidrr/index.html?
src=mr

National Kitchen & Bath Association
687 Willow Grove Street
Hackettstown, NJ 07840
www.nkba.org

National Rehabilitation Information Center
4200 Forbes Boulevard, Suite 202,
Lanham, MD 20706
http://www.naric.com

National Resource Center on Supportive Housing and Home Modifications,
Andrus Gerontology Center,
University of Southern California
3715 McClintock Avenue
Los Angeles, CA 90089-0191
www.homemods.org

Paralyzed Veterans of America
801 Eighteenth Street, NW
Washington, DC 20006-3517
www.pva.org

ProMatura Group, LLC
142 Hwy 30 E
Oxford, MS 38655
http://www.promatura.com

Rehabilitation Engineering and Assistive Technology Society of North America (RESNA)
1700 North Moore Street
Suite 1540
Arlington, VA 22209-1903
www.resna.org

Trace Research and Development Center
University of Wisconsin
2107 Engineering Centers Bldg.
1500 Highland Avenue
Madison, WI 53706
www.trace.wisc.edu

U.S. Dept. of Justice
Tech. Assist. on ADA
950 Pennsylvania Avenue, NW
Civil Rights Division
Disability Rights Section - NYAV
Washington, D.C. 20530
www.usdoj.gov/crt/ada/adahom1.htm

Visitability List Serve
visitability-list@ACSU.buffalo.edu

Volunteers for Medical Engineering
2301 Argonne Drive
Baltimore, MD 21218
www.toad.net/~vme

INDEX